Kulturstiftung Sibirien

Studies in Social and Cultural Anthropology

Series Editors:
Erich Kasten and David Koester

Editorial Board:
Dittmar Dahlmann, Michael Dürr, Gail Fondahl, Tjeerd de Graaf,
Roberte Hamayon, Marjorie Mandelstam-Balzer, Anna Sirina and Hiroki Takakura

Tatiana Bulgakova

Nanai Shamanic Culture in Indigenous Discourse

Verlag der Kulturstiftung Sibirien
SEC Publications

Bibliografische Informationen der Deutschen Nationalbibliothek:
Die Deutsche Nationalbibliothek verzeichnet diese Publikation in der Deutschen
Nationalbibliografie: detaillierte bibliografische Daten sind im Internet über
<http://dnb.d-nb.de> abrufbar.

Cover illustration:
Yurgi Mergen, painting by 10 years old Sonia Demina, Troitskoe, Khabarovskii Krai

Typesetting:
Kulturstiftung Sibirien gGmbH, Fürstenberg/Havel

Printer:
Books on Demand GmbH, Norderstedt

Electronic edition: www.siberian-studies.org/publications/nanaishaman.html

ISBN: 978-3-942883-14-6

CONTENTS

Preface

Part 1
Research into shamanic culture's mysteries

Recording secret shamanic experience in the field 11
Contradictory data 13
Informational lacunas 15
Concealed information 16
Shamans' self-advertisement 17
Overcoming barriers to comprehension 18

Hermeneutic temptation

Collision of interpretations 20
The interpretations of shamanic 'self-wounding' 24
'Self-wounding' as a demonstration of shamanic abilities 26
'Self-wounding' as a means of fighting against an enemy 27
'Self-wounding' as self-sacrifice to spirits 28

Part 2
Rivalry in shamanic healing

Collective clan disease

Inherited spirituality 35
Acute condition of clan collective disease 37
Chronic condition of clan collective disease 41
Clan collective disease caused by a clan member's death 45
Clan collective disease caused by its members excessively approaching the spirits 50
Social and spiritual aspects of collective clan disease 54

How to 'open' more souls

Spiritual reasons for diseases 59
Recovery in exchange for a contract about the long-term worship 63
Souls given up for temporary use 64
Hired body 69
When the steps towards opening to the spirits are exhausted 73
Disease as a coercion to converge to spirits 76
Multiplicity of initiations 77

Which shaman is better

Rumors which form shamanic hierarchy 82
Shamans talking about themselves to non-shamans 87
Non-shamans about shamans 90
Shamans talking about themselves to other shamans 92
Shamans about other shamans 94
Shamans talking to each other 97

Part 3
Shamanising by arts

Why tales have happy endings

Tale as a road 103
Encoding and hiding information by means of telling tales 105
Tales as meeting places for enemies 108

Violence in tale marriage

The spirit-cohabitant as bait 111
Beating the shamanic spirit-cohabitant 113
Threat of violence from the non-shamanic spirit-cohabitant 118

Cruel bride from a tale

'Amotivational' cruelty 121
Hard tasks for the bridegroom 123
Shooting as a defence against the bride's spirits 125
The bridegroom able to survive takes a gratuitous bride 127
Marriage as a truce in shamanic war 129
Unreliability of the marriage truce 132

Spirits as dancing masters

Seven obedient to shaman 137
Shaman subordinated to *seven* 139
Seven's demands in offering 140
Seven's activivation during sacrifice 142
Seven's activation after sacrifice 146
Dance as a kind of *seven's* behavior 147

Shaman on the stage

Shaman as an actor 152
An actor performed the role of a shaman 161
Ethnic mixing in the image of a staged shaman 162

Part 4
Political and legal labours ruled by shamanic spirits

Spiritual nature of judicial authority

Coexistence of potestative and political systems 166
The traditional conception of authority 167
The judge's spirit-helpers 168
The invisible roads where people are murdered 170
Election of a judge 172
The traditional court as a clan institution 174
Trial as replacement for blood revenge 175
Approval of impunity and neutralisation of complainant's aspirations 177
Democracy or 'spiritocracy'? 180

Sacrifice interpreted as a robbery

Shamanic congregation compelled to sacrifice 184
Shamans compelled to sacrifice 187
Shamanic measures of self-defense in case the sacrifice failed 189
Robbing as a display of mercy 190

Spirits against Soviet rule: anti-shamanic persecutions

Beginning of persecutions 193
Arresting of shamans 198
Official permission to shamanise 202
Anti-shamanic propaganda 204
Shamans' persecutors 207
The spiritual dimension of Soviet Rule 210
Shamanic spirits against Soviet Rule 211
Conspiratorial shamanic practice 216
Some consequences of the cultural transformation 217

Epilogue 220

Appendix to "Shaman on the stage" 224

Nanai words and shamanic terms 235

Shamans and informants 239

References 245

Index 254

PREFACE

The information presented in this book is mostly based on field materials collected among the Nanai (Manchu-Tungus group, which belongs to the smallest of three subfamilies of the Altaic language family).[1] The lengthy fieldwork (almost yearly field seasons from 1980 to 2012) fell during the period of rapid socio-cultural change, which gave me the possibility to watch rapid socio-cultural transformations and changes in my informants' world view. During the first half of this period, there still existed a small group of elders who preserved shamanic praxis in its traditional classical form.[2] The culture of precisely this group of shamanists is the basic topic of this book. In 1980–1990 most of the shamanists either hardly spoke Russian or did not speak it at all. Even if the informants spoke both Russian and Nanai, when they discussed shamanic issues, their speech in Nanai was much clearer and richer. Specific shamanic vocabulary contains many words with no equivalent word in Russian because of the lack of basic Russian words for the denomination of some shamanic concepts. That was the reason why the material was recorded mostly in Nanai. Further processing consisted of two stages. First, audio recordings were transcribed and translated with the help of my friends and informants Raisa Alekseevna Bel'dy, Lydiia Timofeevna Kile, Nikolai Petrovich Bel'dy, Mariia Vasil'evna Bel'dy and Raisa Aleksandrovna Samar. In some cases, because of the huge amount of the material recorded, Raisa Alekseevna Bel'dy dictated the translation to me from a soundtrack. This second stage was necessary because the texts were usually full of incomprehensible expressions, which non-shamans, though they spoke Nanai fluently, were not able to understand. This stage consisted of the most important and decisive help of the informant-shamans, who were only able to translate and explain the complexities. Each new field season I returned to the same informants to share my ideas with them, which generalise the previous field data and to get their more precise definitions and refinements. Thus the present paper turned out to be in fact a collective work accomplished together with my informants and assistants, whose help I greatly appreciate.[3]

---

1   The Nanai (Russian: *nanaitsy*) inhabit the banks of the river Amur (Khabarovskii Krai, Russia) and subsidiaries of the Ussuri river (Primorskii Krai, Russia). A small group of Nanai lives in China, between the rivers of Sungari and Ussuri. There are about 12,000 Nanai living in Russia. The Nanai language is part of the southern group of Manchu-Tungus languages. In Nanai religious beliefs shamanism was important. Their main activity was fishing and fish was also their main diet. Fish was caught mainly in summer and autumn, after that it was dried for people and dogs. Nanai were also engaged in hunting, however, hunting was for them a secondary source of food. The villages of Khabarovsk region, where the field material was collected, are Troitskoe, Dzari, Naichin, Daerga, Dada, Lidoga, Sinda, Upper Nergen, Achan, Dzhuen, and Belgo.

2   I succeeded in working with 16 shamans and a number of their relatives and patients.

3   Some parts of this book were published earlier as separate articles: Nanai fairy tales about the

I am very much indebted to Chris Hann, Günther Schlee and Joachim Otto Habeck for having given me the possibility to work on this text at the Max Planck Institute for Social Anthropology (Halle, Germany) and to Professor Alain Supiot for allowing me the intellectually stimulating and inspirational setting of the Nantes Institute for Advanced Study (France) for completing this book. I thank Michály Hoppál for his idea of publishing this book and I also acknowledge the help and advice of my friends and colleagues Olle Sundström, Barbara Duden, Roberte Hamayon, Alexandra Lavrillier, Virginie Vaté, Piers Vitebsky, Marjorie Mandelstam Balzer, Anna-Leena Siikala, Patricia Gray, David Koester, Patrick Plattet, Art Leete, Eva Toulouze, Laur Vallikivi, Aimar Ventsel and Valentina Kharitonova. I also thank the language editors of earlier versions: Heidi Hansson, Maureen Penelope Howard, Patricia Gray, Tiina Mallo, Kealani Smith and Kathryn Harriman.

I am particularly grateful to the Foundation for Siberian Cultures that invited me for a research stay in January 2012 (http://www.kulturstiftung-sibirien.de/pro_1272_E.html), during which I was able to discuss and design with Erich Kasten the publication of the given volume. Most of the texts on which this work is based will be published in Nanai and Russian in the series *Languages and Cultures of the Russian Far East* at the Kulturstiftung Sibirien. (For the first volume of this edition see: http://www.siberian-studies.org/publications/nanaiskazki_E.html). I would like to express warm thanks especially to Roberte Hamayon and to Marjorie Mandelstam Balzer for their most valuable advice during the final stages of this project. My thanks go also to Beverley Stewart for her careful and thoughtful copy-editing of the English text. The most cordial gratitude is to my informants,[4] who during many years were my close friends and whose support cannot be overemphasised.

Cruel Bride, in *Religion and the Re-identification of Ethnic Groups*, 5 (1), 2011: 5–21; Shamans' Qualities in Emic Discourse, in *Sibirica* 9 (2), 2010: 48–72; Collective Clan Disease, in *Journal of Northern Studies* (2) 2009: 51–81; Das schamanische Heilungsritual der Nanai – eine Art 'kleine Initiation', in *Schamanen Sibiriens. Magier, Mittler, Heiler*, E. Kasten (Hg.), 2009: 96–111, Berlin: Dietrich Reimer Verlag; Dancing *sevens* – Shamanic Spirits Participation in Sacrifice, in *Shamanhood and Endangered Languages*, J. Pentikäinen and P. Simoncsics (eds.), 2005: 237–251; Tale as a Road, Where Shaman Must Win. In *Shamanism in the Interdisciplinary Context*, A. Leete and R. P. Firnhaber (eds.) 2004: 215–226. Boca Raton/Florida: Brown Walker Press; Nanai Shamans under Double Oppression – Was the Persecution by Soviet Power Stronger than the Power of Shamanistic Spirits, in *Pro Ethnologia 15*, 2003: 131–157; Sacrifice or Robbery? One Event in the Light of Different Worldviews, in *Pro Ethnologia 17*, 2005: 115–126. Most of those articles were noticeably revised in the course of the preparation of this book.

4 See the appendix for the list of the informants.

1 RESEARCH INTO SHAMANIC CULTURE'S MYSTERIES

RECORDING SECRET SHAMANIC EXPERIENCES IN THE FIELD

> You, I know, but no one else knows. They must not know.
> Everyone cannot (know); such things never happen. No one should know.
> It is not necessary for them to know.
> Certainly! Only to those, who are marked (by spirits),
> do (the spirits) give the possibility to see!
> *(Conversation of two shamans)*

The romantic mysteriousness of shamanic praxis is caused not only by its impenetrable spiritual profoundness, which lies beyond one's comprehension, but mostly by its principal discretion and closeness. Secrecy is based on the principle of shamans' rivalry and 'deliberate isolationism' (Kenin-Lopsan):[5] on competition for possession of the spirit-helpers (none of them can belong at the same time to two or more persons), on interpersonal antagonism (shamans keep their secrets not only from non-initiated ones, but mostly from each other), and on inter-clan discord caused by that rivalry.[6] Despite the fact that 'inter-shaman enmity does not become openly apparent' (it itself is a secret), shamans 'are not able to unite into the cooperative communities' (Hamayon 2009: 7), 'they were always unsocial persons and did not tolerate team spirit' (Kharitonova 2006: 161).[7]

Shamans' inclination to hide from their rivals information about their personal experiences is balanced by their high degree of adaptability to the constantly changing outward circumstances. Both the need to shut themselves off and the necessity to adapt make each shaman's inner life unique and exceptional. This combination of the uniqueness of the individual strategy and of the open dynamic type of ideas and technical methods was noticed by Roberte Hamayon, who confirms that the 'necessity to adapt to the concrete object of the ritual and to the conditions of the certain moment results in the fact that it (shamanic praxis – T. B.) is inevitably open to im-

---

5   This and all further citations from the Russian language sources are translated into English by the author.

6   'Shamans were always self-employed persons; they could not tolerate any solidarity, either in their progress or in their activity' (Kharitonova 2006: 161).

7   'Shamans are single-handed by nature' (Kenin-Lopsan), they fight against each other (Shirokogoroff 1919: 55). K. V. Pimenova refers to the widespread opinion, which is proved by the folklore material, that 'shamans could not bear each other and that their chance meetings unavoidably ended in one of them magically "eating" the weaker one, who perished because of that' (Pimenova 2006: 199).

provisation', that 'it depends on the personality of the one who performs it', and that the dynamic nature of shamanic praxis 'excludes any dogmatism' (Hamayon 2009: 7). According to Galina N. Gracheva's observation, shamans 'very quickly and productively absorb any strange influences; they incorporate them into their established worldview and into their field of activity. By this means they empower themselves and widen their possibilities' (Gracheva 1983: 129). Evgenii A. Khelimskii (2000: 159) also noted flexibility of shamanic praxis as of 'an essentially open system, which can absorb personal experience and worldview of any certain shaman'.[8]

Fixing such dynamic and esoteric material in the field presents a specific complexity for the researcher. Thus it seemed that reservedness must manifest itself in shamans' unwillingness to communicate. But on the contrary, the scholars usually noticed shamans' talkativeness and communicativeness. From the 1950s until the mid-1980s, the famous ethnographer Anna V. Smoliak (1991: 8) explored shamanism in the same Nanai villages, where later I worked. According to her words, her informants 'displayed great interest in her research and strove to fix their knowledge and beliefs precisely'. As far as willingness to communicate is concerned, Sergei M. Shirokogoroff (field research in 1912–1918) wrote of his Evenk informants that if the shamans felt from the researcher at least some consideration, they explained to him or her more and more. Shirokogoroff (2004: 118) noticed that it was much easier to communicate with the shamans than, for example, with some European professionals who are preoccupied with the desire to demonstrate their authority and hide their vocational secrets. In my field I faced the phenomenon, mentioned by Galina Lindquist (2006: 68), not only do shamans not mind being interviewed, on the contrary, they even compete to be chosen for scientific research.

Despite the fact that the Nanai have not lost shamanism as such, it has been transformed to such a degree that it has turned into a considerably dissimilar phenomenon that must be called neo-shamanism, and the ethnographic material concerning its classical variant, which was available until the late 1990s, has become absolutely inaccessible now. Being aware of socio-religious change and of the vanishing of shamanism, the last classical Nanai shamans themselves expressed the wish to preserve in books at least some information about themselves[9] and willingly encouraged researchers to record it. My informant-shamans eagerly helped me to

8   'Worldview and even pantheonism (not to mention the team of the spirit-helpers) can be modified under the influence of impressions which are received by a shaman in the course of his or her ecstatic travels into the worlds of supernatural powers. The important factors in this modification are the outward contacts. Changing outward life circumstances, the appearance of some new realities, push a shaman to enter into contact with those supernatural powers, which according to his or her ideas, are connected with those innovations and are able to exert influence upon them in that way' (Khelimskii 2000: 159).

9   In the 1980s, the young Nanai were no longer interested in their native language, culture and shamanism. Now, after time passed, one can ascertain that my informants' apprehension was not unfounded.

transcribe and translate audio records of the long-lasting ceremonies performed by them. They enthusiastically commented on the content of some abstruse fragments, dictated for recording the specific ritual words, which no one dictionary contains, and also verbalised the phrases which were deafened in audio-recording by loud drum beating. In addition, they found me competent informant-assistants, who could explain to me the most difficult patches of ceremonies, not only in Nanai, but also in Russian. Informants' commutability and long duration of field work gave me the possibility to base the research on emic approach. Nevertheless, shamans' communicativeness does not always mean openness. Signs of reticence and suppression were contradictoriness and incompleteness of data, which can be discovered only by analysing a large amount of information.

Contradictory data

Even the data collected by the most professional scholars can be contradictory. For example, it would seem that mythological ideas should be common for the shamanic community, but in reality different authors present them differently. According to Yurii A. Sem, the Nanai consider that the Upper World is 'a complicated construction consisting of several tiers with stars, constellations and planets. The inner arch is covered with the layers of many-coloured clouds which hide from people the sky's stony gravity. The outer arch of the Upper World is the world, where any vital forces originate' (Sem 1990: 128). According to N. Karger and I. Koz'minskii (1929: 10), the Nanai consider that the sky consists of three layers, copper, silver and golden ones. Anna V. Smoliak affirms that the Nanai's way is to think that the sky is divided into nine layers. The first and the second ones are the spheres of constellations. On the third layer there is a city with people, hills, rivers and taiga. From the fourth to the ninth layer there are trees, and on the fifth one there is a deity, Laoia. From the sixth to the ninth layers are the places where dragons dwell (Smoliak 1991: 13–14). Having perused those data, I tried to specify from my informants what Nanai mythological ideas about the Upper World actually are. Their answers not only did not help me to clarify the contradictory information, but confused it even more. The shaman Ol'ga Egorovna[10] assured me that there is nothing but clouds in the Upper World. 'White clouds are on the first layer. On the second one there are pink clouds. Farther one can find black clouds. The black clouds are the worst ones. There are also yellow clouds, and are golden-like ones. Clouds' colour is golden-like, but they are actually like dust. Nasty is that yellow dust!' Another informant, Galina Ulgovna, said that 'in the Upper World there are transparent crystal houses which are shot with blue.

---

10   My informants strongly objected to my giving their pseudonyms and asked me to mention only their real names. Besides, using the real names corresponds with the traditions of Soviet ethnography.

Near those houses there are people in many-coloured dresses and lots of flowers'.
The shaman Mingo told me that in the Upper World there is a Manchurian city. All
the houses and the streets in that city are full of shining red, pink, yellow and blue
fluttering flags. In that city, Manchurian shamans keep the souls of their patients.
Thereby, there are not any mythological ideas of the Upper World common to all
the Nanai. We deal not with (or not only with) generally accepted ideas, but with a
multiplicity of subjective conceptions which originate not from collective referring
to the same folklore plot, but from multifarious individual spiritual experiences.
When I asked shaman Lingdze about a road to *buni* (the world of the departed), that
was supposed to be a well-known and wide-spread Nanai mythological idea, she did
not refer to some generally known folklore plots, but instead answered me thus:

> If I had dreamt this road, I would have known what it was like. But now I can-
> not say anything about it because I have never gone there in my dreams. What
> that place is like, what is situated there, I will not tell you any lies. I could have
> invented something and lied. But I have not actually been there. I have never
> gone there in my dreams. (Lingdze)

For shamans, penetration into the world (or the land) of dreams (in Nanai *'tolkin'*)
is one of the main ways of communication with the spirits and the primary, and the
only reliable source of spiritual information.[11] When I asked the same question not
of shamans, but of the ordinary shamanists, who did not consult the primary sources,
they would repeat some well-known mythological idea common to their community.
Shamanic knowledge is obtained experimentally, and different informants, who
have diverse experiences of communication with spirits and of staying in the spiritual world, have different ideas. Only part of the information, which is obtained by
the initiated ones (sometimes after being re-interpreted and misrepresented), is later
passed to non-shamans, and it leads to formation of the common mythological conception. Therefore the reason for emic data discrepancy is the fact that those data are
given by different persons at different stages of initiation. When a researcher accepts
the informants' statements which concern their exclusively personal experience, for
description of the ideas common to the entire group and tries to generalise them, it
could lead to contradictory and erroneous conclusions.

To consider that the common ideas are attached to the entire community was
typical for Soviet ethnography. In that ethnography, it was accepted to focus atten-

---

11   It is believed that not only shamans, but ordinary persons can also have informative dreams,
     but only the shaman, with help of his or her spirits, can interpret them. Nevertheless there are
     religious specialists, *komoko nai*, who are in closer contact with spirits than ordinary people
     and at the same time in less intimate contact with spirits if to compare them with shamans.
     Despite the fact that the dreams of *komoko nai* are informative, unlike shamans they do not
     have any spirit-helpers, and only the shaman can find out the degree of a person's contact with
     the spiritual world and define the spiritual status of that person.

tion not on certain persons as bearers of the ideas and on the individual change-ability of those ideas, but on the ideas that were stable and isolated from the bearers, which were presented in that ethnographic literature as an abstract collective subject. In connection with this there were such typical expressions as 'traditional consciousness considered that [...] the folklore tradition describes [...], attention of the traditional society was compelled by [...], public conscience proceeded from [...]' etc. Within such discourse the personal difference of independent shamans' experiences was not taken into consideration.

In spite of the predominant Soviet ethnographical paradigm, the best Soviet ethnographers though recognised the difference of informants' interpretations conditioned by individual distinctions of shamanic practice. Thus, Anna V. Smoliak wrote that dissimilarities of interpretations among the Nanai 'seem to be completely natural. They did not have any shamanic school; they did not visit shamanic ceremonies with each other. There was a peculiar competition among them and that is why they did not communicate much to each other. Each of them comprehended and explained their shamanic qualities in their own way' (Smoliak 1991: 144). That is one of the typical traps for a researcher of shamanism: the information about the chance individual experiment can be taken as the information in general use.

Informational lacunas

Besides contradiction of data, there are also some informational lacunas, which can remain unfilled, despite prolonged investigations. For example, neither such outstanding researchers as Leo Ya. Shternberg or Ivan A. Lopatin nor anyone else who wrote about Nanai shamanism, mentioned existence of *dëkaso* (spiritual depository of shamans patients' souls) or shamanic spiritual territories *gora* and *dërgil*, where shamans move around during their ceremonies. Anna V. Smoliak was the first one who in 1991 published the Nanai terms *dëkaso*, *gora* and *dërgil* and described the phenomena which they indicate. It is important to draw attention to the fact that ordinary Nanai, who are the bearers of shamanic tradition (e.g., shamans' clients), but not shamans, do not know anything about those phenomena. As Anna V. Smoliak (1991: 139–140) writes, 'no dictionary contains the words similar to *gora* and *dërgil*. When Molo Onenko (shaman, Smoliak's informant – T. B.) told me about those territories, his fellow villagers refused to believe in them. He himself confessed that talking about it he had broken the taboo'.

I can give one more example. In 1927 Leo Ya. Shternberg (1927) published the information collected from a Nanai shaman, which made him the author of the theory of sexual electiveness in shamanism. In 1970–1973, Anna V. Smoliak conducted her fieldwork in the same villages as Shternberg, but did not find anything in support of Shternberg's theory. As a result, referring to the ethnographic literature about shamanism of the other indigenous peoples of the North, she completely denied that theory (Smoliak 1991: 86). In 1980–2012, when I worked in the same Nanai villages, my extensive field material nevertheless corroborated Shternberg's data. Probably for some reasons, Smoliak's informants did not dare to talk to her about such intimate topics, which they discussed with Shternberg. Deficiency of information about a phenomenon does not always point to absence of that phenomenon itself.

Concealed information

One of the reasons why our knowledge about shamanism unevenly concerns its different domains is the presence of certain topics intentionally concealed by shamans. Thus, while investigating the phenomenon of shamanic warfare among Evenks, Sergei Shirokogoroff stated that shamans usually do not confess that they participate in inter-shamanic struggle, and that made serious difficulties for his research. Some informants affirmed that warfare was widespread among shamans, but others totally denied its existence. Only by means of watching them and finding the consequences of enmity could one come to a conclusion that inter-shamanic struggle nevertheless occurred (Shirokogoroff 1999: 371). Due to the fact that discourse about shamanic warfare is hidden, despite its being a prevalent phenomenon, one can find only extremely limited information about it in the literature. Hiding information can be the result of informants' intentions to report about what shows them to the best advantage and to hold back the facts which could show them in a bad light.

Neo-shaman Boris D. Bazarov, in the preface to his book, promised his readers to open all the shamanic secrets at last, but in the conclusion he nevertheless confessed that it was impossible, that shamans not only hide the information, but are able 'to reveal neither their trance condition, nor how they communicate with the spirits in their altered states of consciousness, nor why they behave this or that way'. All the topics he lists concern the hidden spheres of shamanic experience. He also acknowledges that shamans are not able to realise everything that they are doing in trance, because after getting out of a trance they do not remember many details of their experience (Bazarov 2000: 266).

Nevertheless the trend to hiding the information is not implicit, and in some situations informant-shamans themselves willingly (even with no request from the scholar) talk about their secret experience. One of the last classical Nanai shamans, Lingdze Bel'dy, told me: 'For me it is all the same, I will tell about everything, I will relate it all to people, because after I die, there will not be anyone who would be able to talk about it'.

Shamans' self-advertisement

Intentional concealment becomes apparent in the selectivity of that information which has been chosen to be given to the non-initiated people. The message that forms favourable public opinion about the speaker and misleads the shaman-rivals corresponds not to opening the data, but rather to its disguise.[12] To define what kind of information is hidden is easy if we appeal to the literature about shamanism. Discussion in the literature about the essence of shamanism deals firstly with its outward features such as the shaman's costume, drum, description of ceremonies and ecstasies, description of the beyond, etc. At the same time its internal manifestations often remain far above scholars' interests. There is, for example, the issue of the question of social connection between groups and shamans who guard them (Kortt 1992: 15).

I can add that in the field information about the success of shamanic treatment and divination as well as the demonstration of shamanic miracles, which can show people their shamanic power is publicly open and widely discussed. The list of taboos with descriptions of their breaking is also easily accessible. But the hidden information concerns shamans' relations with spirits and shamanic territories of the beyond. It is also data about manipulations with patients' souls who are kept in the special depositories, conflicts with the alien shamans, etc. The open information creates a positive public opinion and a favourable shaman's image, but the negative data, the data which can be used against the concrete shaman's purposes, are concealed. For example, information about some concrete circumstances of the shamanic inter-clan conflict can either harm one of the shaman's fight or frighten off a shaman's potential clients who would not like a shaman to use their souls as a resource in his or her fight (lack of clients can considerably limit a shaman's powers).

Shamanic secrets are firstly hidden from the shamanic community, and they can be more easily opened to scholars than to ordinary shamanists. My Nanai friends, who helped me in the field, repeatedly noticed that the elders are more frank and outspoken with me and with the other researchers than with them. Despite the fact that they live close to shamans and participate in their rituals, they do not know some shamans' secrets. The reason is that local people can be once involved in shamanic business as shamans' potential clients, but a researcher stands above the potentially conflicting interests of a local shamanic community. That distinction becomes especially obvious in cases when a researcher is local. The supervisor of postgraduate students from among indigenous Siberian peoples, Nadezhda V. Lukina (2002: 73–74), wrote that because of her students' relationship to some spirits, certain research topics were prohibited to them. 'I have such a patron spirit that I must not study that', said one of her students. A moment came, when in answer to my question I heard: 'I do not know it and I am not supposed to know it'. That is why some aspects

---

12   The trend towards concealment of the information excludes written recording of the texts.

important for scientific investigations were left behind the actual research by the indigenous students' (ibid.).

Overcoming barriers to comprehension

Despite the fact that some domains of shamanic knowledge are hidden, in the works of Vladimir G. Bogoraz, Ivan Lopatin, Andrei A. Popov, Anna V. Smoliak, Roberte Hamayon, Sergei M. Shirokogoroff, Leo Ya. Shternberg and other outstanding scholars, one can nevertheless find lots of data which concern shamanic secrets. One of the means, which ensures the possibility to penetrate into the deep layers of shamanic culture, is long duration of field research. What also helped me was that I periodically visited the same informants during the course of several years. Such recurring visits gave me the opportunity to check with the informants my explanations and interpretations of the data which had been received from them in previous trips.

For example, I recorded shaman Kada Kile's story about her aunt shaman four times (four trips to Lidoga village during three field seasons in 1992–1994). The first time she told me that once her aunt shaman fell asleep for seven days without waking up, and then all the members of her family died. I decided that that information had nothing to do with shamanism; it concerned some health problems in that family and probably partly referred to the demographic situation in the region.

During the next field season Kada added to her story that before her aunt awoke, a huge tree that was growing by their house was suddenly cleaved in two and fell down. She also said that soon after it happened, all her aunt's children died, and then she died herself. I interpreted it as an occasional coincidence, which was explained by means of the popular symbol of a tree as an expression of vital force. A tree falling could be interpreted as a bad sign and frighten the members of the family. Later they began explaining it as a fact, which predicted the misfortune. It was information to reason about symbolic and pre-logical thinking.

A year later I learned that the reason for the long sleep was that Kada's aunt went in her dream with the purpose of having revenge on another shaman, and that the falling of the tree was the action of that alien enemy, whom Kada's aunt met in her dreams. A tree falling meant that she suffered a defeat in the fight with him.

During the next field season, one year later, Kada revealed to me that the reason for this entire event was that aunt's husband, shaman, had an enemy, another shaman who lived in another area and whom he had never met, but just dreamt of. Besides, suddenly I found out the connection of this story to another one. That was a story about the shaman who died while another shaman was performing a ceremony to heal him. It was found out that the shaman who died during the ceremony was none other than Kada's aunt's husband. And that unsuccessful shamanic ceremony was performed because he tried to release his spirits locked up somewhere by the alien shaman, his enemy. It also explained why the aunt was sleeping for so long. Being sure of her shamanic ability, the aunt decided to have revenge upon the alien shaman who killed her husband. That is why she intentionally went to sleep for a week. In her dreams, she was looking for the adversary shaman and then dreaming that she battled against him. The fall of the tree, the death of her children and then her own death were considered nothing other than the result of her defeat in that invisible inter-shamanic warfare in the beyond. Thus, only in this fourth time were all the texts, which had been recorded before, elucidated with a different light and revealed such meaning that I did not even suspect to find in them when I first heard that story. The previous imperfect and therefore inadequate understanding of the material is probably just an unavoidable stage of the research. But when one realises it, he or she would be better not to hurry to draw conclusions and build uncertain interpretations and theories based on incomplete data.

The relative informational isolation of the shamanists makes shamanic culture twofold. On one hand, it is emic culture aimed at internal use and hidden from the uninitiated bearers of shamanic tradition and, on the other hand, it is etic culture revealed to the rest of the people. The reason for such a distinction is hidden conflict between initiated and uninitiated actors within shamanic practice. It is exactly this distinction in shamans' interests which makes shamans conceal their real purposes and use twofold identity, the nominal and the actual one (etic and emic). Not only can the interests of a shaman and his group be in conflict, but also in conflict is intergroup communication and colliding (disagreeing) that concerns the separate actors within each of the groups. That is why we deal with a multiplicity of inter-personal and inter-group conceptual structures (Girts 1997: 178), which complicates the research considerably.

If the interests of an active actor contradict the interests of the rest of society, the active actor (shaman) hides his intentions behind a fictitious interpretation. In turn, the community, which in the first place is focussed on advantageous outcomes, receives its communication with the initiated actors and accepts that interpretation. As a result, the distorted interpretations cover the deeply hidden conflict situations with the outwardly peaceful consensus. That way the superficial and even false interpretation promotes peacekeeping and forces uninitiated people to act in accordance with the wishes of initiated ones. In the final analysis, it is one of the most important means which promotes the preservation of shamanic practice. Manipulation with information is an inalienable part of shamanic activity; it results from shamans' fight for reputation and trends like a distinctive art of 'shamanic public relations'.

Manipulated and extremely changeable shamanic praxis, which varies 'not only from one shaman to another within the certain community, but also from one to another ritual performed by the same shaman', (Hamayon 2009: 7) escapes researchers' attention, which makes Hamayon even consider that 'it renders impossible disclosure of its conceptual framework and strengthens the tendency of reduction of shamanic activity to merely the individual psychology of shamans' (ibid.). Nevertheless, the discovery of a conceptual framework would be impossible only in the case where the shamanic praxis was completely chaotic and was not ruled by any objective regulations. However, those regularities certainly exist and that can be proved by the fact that, despite all the diversity of shamanic experience, practice and shamanic definition, language excels in showing the perceptible striking resemblance and in the 'similarity in the different traditions all around the world' (Torchinov 1998).

In spite of the difference between the certain ideas and the concrete methods used by the different shamans, and despite the fact that the shamanic worldview is not recorded in any universally recognised dogmatic texts, shamanic activity is not absolutely spontaneous and irregular. There are similar purposes, common value guidelines, general regulations, and leading ideas which are exposed by specific personal experiences and which determine the strategy of shamans' actions in the different regions in similar ways. Undoubtedly shamans themselves are fully aware of their purposes, values and ideas, so the researcher's task can consist in revealing the general principles and basic regulations, according to which shamanists construct their praxis. To reveal them it would not be sufficient to record a limited number of random informants' narratives; it would rather be necessary to rely on possibly a maximal amount of utterances of different shamanists during different periods of their activity. Numerous utterances in the context of discourse formed in the course of shamanic practice can become a useful tool for learning the general regulations which control people's views and ways of interacting. No utterance occurs in isolation, but in dialogue, contrast or opposition to other utterances or discourses, and by means of discourse analysis one can explore how space is being socially and/or religiously constructed and contested and 'how texts work in socio-cultural practice' (Fairclough 1995: 7). In our case, we hope to get information about some essential social relations of shamanists and basic regulations of their praxis by revealing the repeated dominating models detected in changeable discourses.

HERMENEUTIC TEMPTATION

> It's just an idle fuss to talk about it!
> Who will believe in it?
> *(Shaman Lingdze Bel'dy)*

Collision of interpretations

One of the factors which soundly complicates the investigation of shamanism is the researcher's own world view, which makes him or her interpret the material according to his or her own convictions. Beliefs and ideological factors adversely affect research, and even when trying to avoid making value judgments, the researcher cannot adequately understand the informants' explanations and cannot stop thinking. Morton Klass (1995: 4) stated that really now, what sort of people continue – generation after generation! – to believe in, and to devote their lives to, beliefs and practices that we know to be false and preposterous and absurd? [...] Surely, if they had even a bit of the sense and discrimination that *we* have, they would perceive the total wrongness of what they have been doing and believing and would turn away from it. The researcher's own attitude toward the material being studied is a serious obstacle that often prevents the adequate understanding of it.

The bearers of the Nanai tradition, with whom I have worked, usually realise this problem and when answering my questions suspect that I would never be able to understand their answers. Not only have we hardly understood the tradition bearers, also they do not always understand us. We perceive their culture in our own way, and they also reinterpret our culture in their own, and often unexpected way. It becomes most vividly apparent in the cases when a person involved in the process of cultural exchange still continues to be a tradition bearer and sees the innovative culture through the prism of his own, essential, mother culture. Such is the example of Nikolai Petrovich Bel'dy who experienced the process of becoming a shaman while at the same time becoming a staunch supporter of communism. 'I entered the Communist Party sincerely!' He said:

> In 1945 I entered the party and began to dream not just shamanic stuff. I dreamed that I was on a platform, speaking to the meeting, and calling on everyone to go and fight for the ideals of communism. Asia Grigorievna stayed with us that night. Later on she told us: 'At night I heard someone speaking. I put my ear closer. It was our Kolia who was oratorically platformed in his sleep. It was so powerful and fine! He did it so well! He was sleeping and talking. I looked at him, his face was contorted, and he was just firing off his speech. Then he woke up, got up, went to the bathroom, lay down again, turned on his side, and began to sing in a shamanic way. He sang also fine and well!' (Nikolai Petrovich)

One can appreciate this method of mastering the ideas of communism, if one is familiar with the tradition of shamanic singing while asleep. Such singing is usually explained by the fact that persons (usually neophytes) start to sing in their sleep after meeting shamanic spirits in their dreams, and communists, as the shamanists state, would not be able to fulfil their activity without the help of some special communist spirits.

There is no way to remove the contradiction between the researcher's opinion and the informant's view. The most forthcoming informant's explanations do not usually suit and satisfy the investigator. The researcher does not completely believe in what the informant says, and explains the informant's words as being a different (and because of such difference, a doubtful) interpretation. Turner (2000: 261) wrote that mainline anthropologists have studiously ignored the central matter of [...] the information – central in the people's own view – and only used the material as if it were metaphor or symbol, not reality, commenting that such and such 'metaphor' is congruent with the function, structure, or psychological mindset of the society. [...] What are the ethics of this kind of analysis, this dissection? May we continue in this age of multi-power as well as multi-cultures to enter a foreign society, however politely, measure it up according to our own standards, then come back home and dissertated upon it in a way entirely estranged from the ethos of the people concerned?

In the process of interpretation, the data is estranged from the context. But as generalisation and summarisation are nevertheless necessary, one must invent an artificial wholeness which replaces the lost natural one. It is achieved through a simulated combination of both the studied facts and the researcher's own ideas concerning these facts. Thus, our personal thoughts regarding the ideas of other people unwittingly become the object of research. V. N. Rokitianskii refers to this unintentional substitution of the research object as the hermeneutic temptation. 'There are four sections of hermeneutics: pre-comprehension, comprehension, interpretation, and explanation.

In their fieldwork, ethnographers usually concentrate only on pre-comprehension. There is an opinion that this is the right way to fix the facts 'objectively'. Using such a positivist way of thinking, comprehension is simply missed. As a rule, when

FIGURE 1: Fieldwork situation, during which we discuss information with somebody from another village. Vera Chubovna Geiker and Raisa Alekseevna Bel'dy.

starting from a position of pre-comprehension, the researchers 'jump' right to inter-pretation (they insert the fact into the certain context of knowledge) or even to ex-planation (they point at the certain, conforming it to laws). Both these operations are accompanied by references to some scholars of authority' (Rokitianskii 1994: 83). In this process, comprehension without interpretation is in principle, impossible. The active reciprocal position towards the perceived material is appropriated. Despite his intentions, the researcher brings his private attitude into the material. A human be-ing has a Midas's curse: everything he touches becomes his 'own stuff', everywhere the imprints of his life and spiritual experience are left behind; everything is under-stood according to his own measure. The initiative of cognition-penetration is taken, as Mikhail Bakhtin (2000: 227) stated, during the process of dialogue: the activity of the cognate person corresponds to the activity of the facts which are open to him. Such an activity is inherent within any holistic comprehension. 'Whoever hears and understands the meaning of the speech takes an active reciprocal position towards it. He agrees or does not agree with it (completely or partly), he supplements it, ap-plies it, prepares to accomplish it, etc. while the reciprocal position of the hearer is formed from the very beginning, sometimes from the very first word of the speaker' (Bakhtin 1979: 246). The percipient is the part of the statement that is heard. If such a 'dialogic clash of two minds' becomes inevitable in any humanitarian science, it manifests itself much more strongly in cases when the subject under discussion is religion, or more specifically, when the subject under discussion is something that directly concerns every participant taking part in the dialogue, even if one of those participants is a researcher.

The ethnographical description of an alien culture cannot be unprejudiced (trustworthy). Most certainly, it depends upon the context, which is stipulated by the ethnographer's social surroundings and his own beliefs.

Nevertheless, is it possible to overcome such hermeneutic temptation? If it is pos-sible, how can we rearrange the emphasis of the process of our cognation, neutralise our own pre-comprehension and then achieve the comprehension of the subject we research? I suppose that the easiest way is to ask all the interpretations and expla-nations of the facts that we record from the bearers of tradition themselves, to give them the floor. In this chapter, we compare the different ways in which a single fact of shamanic practice – 'self-wounding' – is interpreted both by the scholars and by the bearers of shamanic tradition. This well-known fact is one of the most un-believable shamanic phenomena and usually provokes misunderstanding between the researcher and the shaman, thereby becoming the source of a researchers' un-intentional reinterpretation.

The interpretations of shamanic 'self-wounding' [13]

Performing a ritual, a shaman sometimes thrusts a knife or some other sharp instrument into his own flesh and then removes it, not being harmed. This trick either leaves no wound on his body at all, or the wound is healed extremely quickly. It is known among different Northern peoples including the Nanai.

> It was in Naikhin. The shaman did *meuri* (danced in a shamanic way) on the waterfront and asked someone to run a lance through his chest. It must not be done gently! It must be done hard and quickly! After they pierced his chest, the end of the lance jutted out of his back, but he continued to dance in this way. Then he pulled the lance out, blew his nose, spat onto his palm and covered his wound with mucus and spit. Only a red spot was left after that. (Kseniia Ivanovna)

Similar stories are told about walking on burning coals.

> I was already grown by that time, before going to the Army, when I saw how my aunt Tungus's mother danced. The people sacrificed a pig. [...] They heated the fireplace. My aunt began to shamanise. She brought her spirits in, fed them (sacrificed to them) and the ritual was about to finish. We were playing with bones. The old men told us: 'Rake the burning coals out of the ash!' We began to rake them right on the clay floor. We raked quite a lot. The coals were hot; they clicked, crackled. The people began to talk about something, but I don't remember what exactly they said. They said that she had brought in another spirit. Then my aunt took off her socks, rolled up her pants and began to dance right on these burning coals. She was dancing until these coals got dark and soft. Then she finished. She wiped off her feet with her socks, put them on and put on her shoes. Nothing bad had happened to her, her feet were not burnt. (Nikolai Petrovich)

Shamans can not only walk on burning coals, but swallow them as well. People told me that it was an impressive sight to see a shaman holding burning coals in his mouth. In the darkness you could see, as they said, light from his mouth right through his teeth.

Researcher-materialists contend that shamans who performed such tricks were only conjurers and charlatans who deliberately deceived their trusting onlookers. That interpretation with exposure of shamanic 'cool deceptions' and 'conjurer's tricks' was strongly encouraged by the Soviet atheistic ideology. According to

---

13   According to the emic perspective, 'self-wounding' represents performing tricks (in Nanai *'erde'*) with the purpose of intentionally demonstrating a shaman's personal power.

Vladimir Bogoraz, the shamans sometimes used wooden knives instead of real ones in order to deceive people. But even if a knife was real, not wooden, Bogoraz suspected deception, as it was in the case when shaman Upunge demonstrated to Bogoraz her abilities and cut with a real knife the stomach of her son.

> Willing to show me her art, Upunge ordered her son, a 14-year old boy, to take off all his clothes and to lie on his back. [...] She seemingly opened his abdominal cavity with an adroit movement by holding the knife handle in her right hand and then directing its tip with the fingers of her left hand. It actually looked like a cut. Small streams spurted out from under both sides of her fingers; they rose up and dropped to the floor. Finally Upunge took her hand away, and we saw a fresh wound full of blood on the boy's body. Upunge then pressed her face to the wound and began to quickly lick the blood and mumble some incantations. [...] When she raised her head, we saw that the boy's body was absolutely unharmed; there was not even a trace of a wound. (Bogoraz 1939: 127–128)

Vladimir Bogoraz's debunking of this trick is not very convincing when compared with the description of it given before. The deception was, as Vladimir Bogoraz considers, that 'at some point, Upunge's daughter had given her lumps of snow from the big copper. [...] There was probably some frozen blood from a seal in the snow. [...] The snow and the blood melted in the shaman's mouth and she let the blood out of her mouth onto the boy's body unnoticed. [...] The folds on his stomach were so full of blood, it looked as if it were a fresh wound' (Bogoraz 1939: 127–128). Lev Belikov, the researcher of Chukchi folklore and language, who worked in Chukotka as a teacher in 1930s, also worked on such exposures and performed conjuring tricks similar to those done by the shamans. Once he secretly tied a bladder full of blood to his body beneath his clothes, and then stabbed himself right before the Chukchi's eyes, pretending that he had thrust a knife into his flesh. After that he 'came to life again'. Such methods of atheistic propaganda in exposing shamanic tricks helped him gain authority among the Chukchi (Polomoshinov 1987: 221).

A different interpretation of shamanic self-wounding is given by Mihály Hoppál. Hoppál (1992: 156) argues that the shaman does not deceive people at all, but actually does wound himself. In explaining this, he uses the idea of suffering derived from Christianity and writes that the individual, the shaman, suffers alone for the community. Hoppál considers that when shaman wounds himself, he experiences pain and willingly bears it because it gives him the capacity to heal people and to save them from their own suffering. By means of that, he 'takes upon himself the illness and the pains' of community, receives into himself the cause of the illness, and thereby relieves his patients of pain (Hoppál 1992: 151–152). Hoppál's assumption regarding the shamanic ability to cure people, gained after his sacrifice, coincides with authentic ideas, but the difference is in the way of understanding its essence: as it will be shown later, for a shaman self-wounding has nothing to do with suffering. Matthias Alexander Castrén's explanation is to a greater extent closer to the authentic understanding. According to him, the Nenets shamans pierce themselves in cases when they are possessed and 'transported' because of a 'miraculous spirits' presence. A Nenets shaman 'must beat and cut himself with a knife and other sharp instruments when obeying the will of his spirits' (Castrén 1858: 288). Indeed shamans consider that they must do such tricks because only then will some special spirit-helpers come to them.

'Self-wounding' as a demonstration of shamanic abilities

From the emic perspective, the shaman cuts himself only because of the spirits present, but the reasons for such a deed can vary depending on the situation. One such situation relates to the necessity to demonstrate unusual shamanic abilities (in Nanai *'yamali'*), which is a part of a shaman's power strategy. To strike onlookers, shaman Nikolai Tumali 'thrust a lance right through his body. One end of the lance jutted out of his chest, while the other end would stick out of his back' (Ol'ga Egorovna). By means of self-wounding, shamans also demonstrated their power before local authorities in order to get some support (e.g., to receive official permission to shamanise). In pre-Soviet times, shamans would probably wound themselves in answer to the authorities' demand to demonstrate their shamanic power.

> Officials took the shaman to the meeting house and sat down before him. The old man put on his belt with metal hangings and then began to dance. He was dancing, and dancing and then he took his shirt off, thrust three knives into his chest and went on with dancing. Then he yelled, and all three knives dropped off to the ground. The wounds were red, but there was no blood. He was dancing, and while he was dancing he grabbed a lance and pushed it into his stomach! He was dancing and the lance jutted out one end. He was dancing and dancing, and then he pulled it out. And there was just a red spot. [...] Then he said to the official: 'Now let me take your eyes out!' (The official) became alarmed. He did not want anything to happen. 'If you don't believe in shamans, bring a dog here!' the shaman said. They found a small dog from somewhere. The shaman pointed his stick at it and then shouted. The dog's eyes fell out of the eye-sockets. 'Now let's try it with you!' Now the official was frightened. 'No, don't!' he said. (Ol'ga Egorovna)

Here is another variant of the same story.

A lot of people gathered together on the waterfront. The shaman Chongida Onenko came and invited his spirit-helpers. At that time the governor was still coming, but Chongida had already started shamanising. He sang in a shamanic way and told people what places (of the invisible world) he was visiting. It was as if he saw these places. He danced in a shamanic way and narrated everything to people. Then (when the governor came) Chongida asked Ebuke to run his chest through with a lance. Ebuke was a *tudin*.[14] He took the lance, stabbed the shaman with it, and continued to hold the end of the lance. If he was not a *tudin*, he would not have been able to hold the end of the lance. There were a lot of old men but only Ebuke could hold the lance. They began to dance together. Ebuke tired of holding the end of the lance. He went where the shaman pushed him. Even if he dug his heels into the ground, he still could not hold his ground. When Chongida finished, the lance dropped of his wound by itself. The governor asked him: 'What else can you do?' – 'I can', he answered, 'take out a human's or animal's eyes'. – 'No, that's all, that's all!' the governor said. They finished, and the governor gave Chongida a paper with permission to shamanise. (Toë Petrovna)

'Self-wounding' as a means of fighting against an enemy

Another reason why shamans run sharp objects through their bodies, according to the shamans' explanations, is that they have a need to fight enemies. If a shaman struggles in his dreams against a shaman of an alien clan (the shaman-enemies usually do not meet each other physically), he may attack his or her soul by means of striking not his enemy's but his own flesh. As shamanists believe, that self-wounding results in that shaman's wound quickly disappearing and his flesh remaining unharmed, whereas the hostile shaman, who is far away at the moment, dies of the wound which suddenly appears on his body.

A shaman (from Kondon village) was fighting against his enemy. He asked for nine needles. Then he lay down on his back and stuck all those needles into his chest. When he got up, all the needles were left on the bed.
Were they long needles?
No, they were regular needles. He was not hurt. The needles went through his body and dropped out of his back. (Kseniia Ivanovna)

The shaman used that method of fighting because an alien shaman, who was far from that place, as Kseniia Ivanovna explained, wanted to kill him.

---

14 The *tudin* is a person like a shaman, who possesses the spirit-helpers and has unusual abilities.

But the shaman learned about it from his spirits, so he stuck the needles into his own body. That's why he recovered. They quarrelled with each other. (Kseniia Ivanovna)

However, in the next invisible attack of the same unknown opponent was for him fatal and ended with his death, because he could not perform self-wounding.

It (happened to the same shaman) in 1943 or 1944. He and his wife went to the taiga to go fishing. They set up a tent. He was there with his wife, but we were here (in the village). He was fishing, when he suddenly fell ill. He fell badly ill. He told his wife: 'Give me a knife!' But his wife was frightened and did not give it to him. That is why he died.
What would have happened if she had given it to him?
If she had given it to him, he would have done it! But he died. Then his wife dreamt an old woman, who told her not to cry and not to fear. They were only two hunting there, in taiga. Where would she go for the night (after her husband's death)? The village was far away. She could not go there. The current in the Gorin River was so rapid (impossible for her to row a boat)! But he (her husband) would have stayed alive and would have continued to fish if he had had the opportunity to thrust the knife (into his body)! It was his wife, who did not give him a knife, and his enemy killed him. Who had seen such an enemy? It is like a dream. Such an accident occurred there. (If she had given him a knife), he would have probably done something with his enemy, he would probably have killed him. His enemy was an enemy of his home (of his clan). The shaman goes everywhere *kherimi* (hovering, being invisible). He goes *kherimi* everywhere and that is why he certainly gains enemies. (Kseniia Ivanovna)

'Self-wounding' as self-sacrifice to spirits

The most common traditional interpretation of the 'trick' examined is that it is a type of offering to the shamanic spirits. The shaman increases his ability to heal because by stabbing himself, he sacrifices to his spirits, some of whom require exactly such 'nourishment'.

The Zaksor clan was the root of shamanism of Kiakta. She was a strong shaman. When she did *meuri* (danced in a shamanic way), she took a knife and thrust it deep into her chest. Then she pulled it out, but there was nothing! No trace! She nourished her spirit this way. It was her spirit that forced her to do it when she was dancing in a shamanic way. (Toë Petrovna)

In this case, shamanic dance is a means of bringing a spirit into a shaman's body, and when the spirit arrives, the shaman's self-wounding is believed to be a means of offering to it.

For a sacrifice, the shaman sticks a lance into his body and then pulls it out. It is a long lance, and he dances around two or three rounds with it in his body. Then it goes away by itself. And there is not even a wound left. (Aleksei Kisovich)

According to Aleksei Kisovich's version, a spirit-helper, which is placed inside the shaman's body, catches the lance's point with its mouth. Ol'ga Egorovna explains it in this way:

When a shaman prepares for this trick, he calls his special spirit, the three-headed serpent *gasiko*[15] to come. *Gasiko* is believed to be a huge black serpent. This invisible creature comes into the shaman's body and opens its three mouths. The shaman knows exactly where each of the serpent's mouths is placed in his body, so he inserts the knife into each of those mouths. The serpent has three heads; that is why the shaman has to stab his body in three places. If someone were to say something at that moment, the shaman would die. So at the beginning of this rite the shaman asks people not to make any noise. 'Be quiet!' he commands. 'Don't say anything!' [...] When he thrusts the knife into his chest, they must not utter a sound. Otherwise he would die. No one else could stick the knife into his body; he must do it himself. Everybody must keep silent. If someone cried out 'ai-ai-ai!' he would die. It's a very, very dangerous thing! (Ol'ga Egorovna)

Shaman Toë Petrovna affirms Ol'ga Egorovna's explanation:

---

15   Only those Nanai shamans, who possess the spirit-helper *gasiko*, can cut themselves. Not every shaman possesses *gasiko* so not every shaman is able to cut himself. Mariia Petrovna Bel'dy was one such possessor. Her friend Dusiia affirms that she saw those spirits with her own eyes. 'They were such big snakes', she said. 'When Mariia Petrovna danced in a shamanic way, they came out of her mouth. When she danced, there was a voice in her ears saying: 'Let's go play! Let's go play!' Someone whispered to her like this. And she went shamanising to the people; they made her shamanise. (As it was learned later, those people had wanted her to shamanise). She began to dance and two snakes appeared out of the corners of her lips. Their heads rose up, but their bodies hung down, they went down, and reached to her waist. Only from the two corners of her lips! They were actual snakes with red mouths. It was them, *gasiko*'. *Gasiko* is a name of a *seven* (shamanic spirit-helper). Shaman Ol'ga Egorovna adds to it that '*gasiko* is one of the most dangerous of the shamanic spirits. If its owner does something the wrong way, it can kill him'.

In general it is really deadly to shamanise. A shaman thrusts a knife (in his body), and his or her spirit-helper seizes this knife and swallows its tip. When she pulls the knife out, the spirit releases it. That's why there is no wound left on shaman's body. (Toë Petrovna)

As there is not much data about such interpretations in the literature, one can suppose that it is not widespread among the Northern peoples. However, it is possible also to suppose that this way of interpretation of shaman's self-wounding might be widespread, and yet being hidden from uninitiated persons, it remains unfamiliar to us. Some similar indigenous ideas recorded far from the Nanai region can probably partly prove it. Here is A.M. Sengepov's explanation of a shaman's self-wounding among Khanty:

I saw it with my own eyes. He stabbed his chest. I told him: 'What a miracle!' 'There are such miracles', he answered, 'and shamanic abilities are not given to anyone. The Russians would say that he used hypnosis. But among Khanty, the explanation would be that the shaman had a serpent mouth in his body. He did not simply stick a knife into his flesh; he rather inserted the knife into the serpent's mouth. He did not hide anything from me, and told me all the details. All this is the truth. Not much blood flows out. Just a little! To mark the action he intentionally runs (his knife) over his skin. [...] We say: 'The serpent's mouth shows its poison'.That's all. He takes the knife out of himself, and his flesh is intact. He does not die. Such miracles! (in: Moldanova 1999: 91).

Thrusting sharp items into body is not considered to be the only form of unusual sacrificial 'feeding spirits'.Dancing on burning coals is explained in a similar way to thrusting knives into the body. Walking on burning coals and swallowing them is also perceived as a sacrifice to a special spirit, which needs fire. Shamanists believe that different spirits require different means of sacrifice (a pheasant's heart, metal sawdust, dust, a cobweb etc.). Special 'dish' intended for a certain spirit is called *kala*. Burning by fire and cutting by knives are examples of such *kala*, which are suggested to spirits within sacrifice ritual.

Fire and burning coals are *kala* for a spirit. Sometimes he (the shaman) swallows burning coals. Sometimes he lies on burning coals without being burnt. Why is not he burnt? Because his spirit which needs fire eats it! It is that spirit, which helped this shaman before, when he was sick, and now it must be fed with coals, with hot fire. And how glad (that spirit) is! 'Ha-ha-ha!' (it shouts)! (Ivan Torokovich)

Shaman Lingdze observed sacrifice by means of burning coals, which was considered to be equal to vodka, another popular *kala*:

> There was an old woman who lived here. She was seriously ill and was looking for medicine from the sky. She lit a fire and put the burning coals on the floor. She also put out three empty glasses. They were old Manchurian glasses! Then she covered them (the glasses) with paper. She danced barefooted on the burning coals and sang. We could not understand what she was singing about and she danced for a long, long time. She stepped barefooted onto the coals. No socks, no shoes! Nobody was allowed to say: 'It's hot! It hurts!' Before she was satisfied by stepping on the fire, a long time passed and it was forbidden to say anything like that. She herself would stop dancing when she wanted. She would make a round and finish. When she had finally stopped, she turned on the light and checked those three glasses. There was already medicine (vodka) in them! Who had poured the medicine into those empty glasses? A night! A late night! (Lingdze)

By inflicting wounds upon his own body, the shaman offers the spirits his own blood and that means that he suggests himself as sacrificial food to his spirits. The method by which the injury is caused is sometimes strikingly similar to the technique of sacrificing an animal within the certain shamanic cultures. Thus if in some cultures people suffocate a sacrificial animal, shamans also suffocate themselves while demonstrating miracles during their rituals. One of Nenets' shamanic self-sacrificing rituals performed by means of suffocation was described by A.M. Castrén (1858: 123): 'A fortune-teller tied a rope round his neck, and two men firmly grabbed the ends of this rope. The fortune-teller was covered with a big cloth, and two men pulled both ends of the rope'. The similar example performed among the Chukchi was described by Bogoraz (1936: 130), who perceived the incident directly as an imitation of suicide: 'The belt is tied round the shaman's neck. Two people tighten the belt, holding its ends, but the shaman remains, of course, safe and sound'. The fact that the shaman sacrifices himself to the spirits, but at the same time remains alive and unharmed is also in accordance with certain traditions of the peoples of the North: they sometimes sacrifice even an animal (a reindeer), leaving it alive (Dolgikh 1960: 79).[16]

---

16 Sometimes a shaman inflicts a wound (sacrifices) not to him/herself, but his/her child (because the child is of the same blood). Andrei Golovnev speaks about such children's sacrifices to the fire among the Selkups. 'The fire demands an offering. Such an offering sometimes must be what is the most dear for a woman (it is the author's interpretation!), her child. Several times I have seen children in the tundra with recent burn marks' (Golovnev 1995: 484). The same is seen in the example from Vladimir Bogoraz given before.

The idea that shamanic self-wounding has sacrificial intention is indirectly evidenced by the fact that sometimes all the people present at the ceremony are obliged to taste their shaman's blood.

> Ganka went behind the curtain. His helper was holding his drum and uninterruptedly beating on it in the silence. [...] When he (Ganka) came out from behind the curtain, there were three vessels in his hands. He let his own blood trickle down into these vessels and everyone who was there had to taste it or at least be annointed with it. There was not much blood. [...] He drank it himself and then put seven blood spots on his own face, on the face of his helper, on his small son and on me. (Lehtisalo 1998: 121)

Andrei Golovnev mentions the same ritual with the shaman's blood, performed in another region: 'A Yamal shaman stabbed herself with the sharp handle of her drum, then gathered her blood into a cup and gave it to a person to drink'. But Golovnev interpreted that ritual as a means to make that person lucky and rich. The same custom is frequently practiced also during other sacrifices. Each person who is present at the place where the sacrifice was offered, should either try the sacrifice food (especially sacrifice vodka) or be annointed with it (Golovnev 1995: 484). Accustoming people to shaman's blood can be considered to be a logical deed, if we remember Marcel Mauss's (2000) idea that sacrifice is a means of setting blood kindred among the clan and the deity.

Self-wounding is considered to be dangerous for shamans. If a shaman does something wrong during the ritual, he could die. But he does not suffer in the process of doing it. The shamans are convinced that the knife is thrust not into their own flesh but into their spirits' mouths; and when dancing on the fire they also feed their spirits; that is why, as the informants argue, they do not feel any pain at all. 'When you insert a knife into the serpent's mouth it does not hurt!' Ol'ga Egorovna explains:

> Does it hurt, when a shaman puts a burning coal into his mouth?
> Does it hurt? No, it does not hurt! It is a spirit that eats fire. Another person eats it! When a spirit eats it, you never feel pain! When she walks on burning coals, it does not hurt either. It is a spirit that does it, it is a spirit that walks. By doing this, a shaman gets medicine for himself. But are we able to do something like that? No, we are not! [...] Because we've never seen that being (that spirit), which eats fire.[17] (Ol'ga Egorovna)

---

17 Despite the fact that Lingdze is a shamaness, according to her explanation, she does not have a *seven* which needs fire as nourishment.

In the light of these explanations, Mihály Hoppál's assumption concerning the essence of self-wounding can be called into question. A shaman is not an individual who bears pain and suffers alone for his community. First, performing the ritual, the shaman does not bear any pain and does not suffer. Second, the shaman performs self-wounding not for the community, but for himself. If he did not do it, he would be sick and suffer himself. 'People say that a shaman would die if he did not walk on burning coals' (Nesulta Borisovna). A shaman must also do it when he is in danger and urgently needs a sacrifice for his spirits.

The shamans, who have told us about shamanic 'self-wounding', accepted as natural the researchers' disbelief and distrust. That is why they tried to help us by offering a 'scientific' explanation of that phenomenon, which would correspond, they think, with the contemporary scientific viewpoint. Thus the shaman Gara Kisovna explained that everything concerning shamanic 'self-wounding' was nothing else but simply 'hypnosis' (she used the Russian word there). It was a shaman's attempt to adapt to our scholars' misinterpretations and incredulity.

2 RIVALRY IN SHAMANIC HEALING

COLLECTIVE CLAN DISEASE

> *Ochiki* (spirits of violence) are like a disease, like an infection.
> They go on from one to another along the clan line.
> If a shaman has healed you (freed you from those spirits)
> they would pass to your clansman.
> *(Ivan Torokovich)*

> When a shaman heals his own clansman, his spirit-helpers do not obey,
> because they themselves belong to the same clan.
> (The patient) is of their own smell, of their own blood, of their own clan,
> and they are not able to find his (soul's) traces.
> *(Nikolai Petrovich)*

Inherited spirituality

According to Nanai emic ideas, shamanic disease, which affects a shaman in the period of his or her formation, also affects his or her agnates, who begin to suffer from nervous disorders and other problems but recover at their new shaman's incarnation. A similar spiritual correlation within the group of agnates becomes apparent also when a shaman is involved in a situation which connects him or her with the spiritual world (murder, death, incest, etc.), so that the consequences of such events influence not only the shaman, but also his or her kin.

From the emic perspective, relations with the spirits have not only spiritual, but also somatic components (emerging for instance, in the idea about human-spiritual cohabitation), which opens up possibilities for spirituality to be inherited by descendants. These circumstances suggest that the social factors that unite the clan (exogamy etc.), are secondary to the religious factors, and are probably used as a means to adapt to the spiritual problems that shamanists face. It is social adaptation to the religious practice that calls into being the certain social units, rather than religion as an expression of society itself. Running the danger of collective clan disease, people have to remember their clan peculiarity and exclusiveness and undertake common efforts for its avoidance. Being aware of their patrilineal descent and of their own place in it, people can define the circle of possible persons who are subject to similar mental and other troubles and who should look together for the means to a cure. The wish to ensure spiritual safety results in the social prescriptions and taboos that form the patrilineal clan.

Clan relationships and clan beliefs are still topical for the Nanai elders who have been my informants for a long time. They have lost most of their traditional culture. Their clans have neither territorial nor economic unity any more, but they remember their clan descent, in some cases in connection with shamanic or non-shamanic spiritual practice, which helps them to explain much of human contacts with the world of spirits. The native understanding of the social and religious aspects of clan relationships differs considerably from accepted scholarly ideas in Russian ethnology. Following some of their foreign colleagues, Russian researchers[18] consider the social basis of clanship to be primary and clan religious ideas are needed only to mark and emphasise this basis. To explain, e.g., the prevalence of unilineal descent and the division of relatives into agnates and cognates, researchers call attention to some social advantages of this classification of relatives.[19] From their viewpoint, the advantages consist of the fact that because of unilineal descent, each member of the group gets a clear idea of who of his or her relatives belong to his group, and to whom he or she is connected with mutual aid duty. From this perspective, ideas about common spirits belonging to a certain lineage (totemic name and so on), are only needed to identify the members of the group and to consolidate those agnates who live far apart from each other. In other words, from this perspective, religious principles are secondary and derive from social principles.

The bearers of Nanai tradition perceive the correlation of those two principles differently. They believe that it is the religious needs and problems which are primary and most important. From their viewpoint, social clan rules of behaviour do not originate from the necessity to distribute rights and duties among the relatives, but are merely a means to adapt to the fact that clan spirits (*seven, amban*[20] and

---

18 S. A. Tokarev, I. S. Vdovin, D. K. Zelenin, and others.
19 This is, for instance, the position of George Murdoch.
20 The spirits known to the Nanai cannot be counted and described within an integral system. V. Diószegi (1949) tried to figure out the system of Nanai spirits. He made a big job, classifying many images, but he constantly revealed contradictions in his system. He explained it by the insufficiency of his materials, but as Anna Smoliak notices, he was wrong with that explanation. The contradictions refer to the very essence of Nanai faith (Smoliak 1991: 73). The Nanai pantheon is not stable and its personages cannot be listed in principle. There are numerous concrete spirits, which can be gained and then lost at any time. At the same time we can talk about the functional and changeable peculiarities of the concrete spirits. Some of those peculiarities are fixed in the Nanai terms *seven* (benevolent spirits) and *amban* (evil spirits). *Seven* and *amban* are not special categories of spirits but qualifications of their temporary usability. Depending on the changeable situations, the same spirits can be named differently. For the talk about clan collective spirituality it is important to refer to those spirits, which could be (but not all of them are) attached to the clan system, since they could be inherited: benevolent *seven* and evil *amban*. The entire clan was collectively under the influence of those spirits, but at the same time some of them were able to establish closer relationships with individual clansmen (not only with shamans). A spirit is considered to be benevolent *seven* as long as it can be traded for a good purpose, but the evil is that one, which either temporarily or never

others) influence the group of agnates in the same way. It is mainly common spiritual problems that force them to unite into lineages and clans to be able to resist the negative spiritual influence (or to use the benefits of dependence on their clan spirits) together.

This perspective, which so far has been very much neglected in the research, can be revealed as a result of an emic approach. The emic approach here is based on research into material recorded from the informants in their native language and on the ideas elaborated by the bearers of the tradition themselves. This helps us to see the phenomena studied in the light of the native people's understanding. But the advantages of an emic approach are nevertheless limited. The Nanai way of describing the phenomenon is not the same thing as the phenomenon itself, it is just their interpretation of it.

It is this interpretation that I try to describe, however not the fact itself, but how the natives understand it is my object here. Even so, the Nanai mostly relate concrete facts and situations and do not summarise the abstract concepts that correspond to them. They do not have, for example, a word for 'clan disease', which I introduce here, or even for such a well-known phenomenon as 'shamanic disease'. Formulating abstract concepts, I have had to step back from the emic approach, and my concern was only that any abstract idea should be derived from and based on my informants' ideas and as often as possible specified with them in additional field work.

Acute condition of clan collective disease

Collective shamanic disease, which affects a group of clansmen among the Evenks, was first described by the Russian scholar Sergei M. Shirokogoroff.[21] According to

---

can be dictated to by a human. In certain circumstances *seven* can unexpectedly change its mind from help to harm, and be named as *amban*, or symmetrically, *amban*, on the contrary, can suddenly start helping and be called *seven*. Someone's *seven* is usually harmful for the other people (especially for people from alien clans) and from the point of those other people the same spirit is evil; for them it is not a *seven*, but an *amban*. Thus, those two qualifications *seven* and *amban* are interchangeable. *Seven* is an *amban*, which is temporarily (for example, during the life-time of a certain shaman) tamed or such a harmful spirit that potentially can be 'domesticated'.Nanai also believe that there are such *amban* that never submit to human will and therefore can never turn into *seven*. The significance of *amban* in this system is emphasised by the fact that this is a Manchu term *amban*, and was typical of the Qing Dynasty, with the meaning of 'important or high official'. It 'was used unofficially for the imperial residents supervising Inner Asia (including Mongolia)' (Atwood 2004: 11). The *amban* were 'career officials specializing in military-police functions or border affairs' (Ibid: 12). Thus, the term *amban* (in Nanai evil or harmful spirit) originally has an administrative character.

21 The Evenks belong to the northern branch of the Manchu-Tungusic group of people. They live in the Evenk autonomous district and some other districts of Eastern Siberia. There are 29,900 Evenks in the Russian Federation (information from 1992) and 35,000 in China. In addition

his description, the symptoms of the disease are the following: Some of the young men would lose normal sleep, would sit on their beds, speak and sing in a half-sleeping state. [...] They would be distracted, and absent-minded; they would neglect or miss their work duties and would gradually be completely disabled. Some other clanspeople might run to the rocks or into the forests where they would remain for days without food and some of them would even perish. Others, who are inclined to 'olonism' ('Arctic hysteria' or so-called 'imitative mania'), might become dangerous during momentary uncontrolled states; they might throw various utensils, burning wood or hot water. [...] Other clanspeople would have 'nervous attacks' at moments of great responsibility, e.g. during the crossing of rivers, holding children, handling hot water and fire. Accident after accident would follow and several people might perish. This would be a case of a real mass psychosis which might put the clan into a state of complete social and economic paralysis threatening the very existence of the clan (Shirokogoroff 1999: 264).

In another book he describes the symptoms of collective disease in this way: 'People might become nervous, commit acts of inexplicable rudeness and even crimes. Common irritation and inclination to hysterical fits spreads and the death-rate increases' (Shirokogoroff 1919: 44). According to Shirokogoroff (1919: 61), when the disease attacks the entire clan, the normal life of that clan ends which has fatal consequences for the very existence of the clan. The consequences of clan disease consist of malnourishment, a decrease in the birth rate, and an increase in the death rate. The collective disease can develop to such an extent that the entire clan, as Shirokogoroff writes, may risk death. All the proceedings of normal clan life are interrupted, sometimes for a long time, and this condition may last for several years (Shirokogoroff 1919: 44).

Siberian people's susceptibility to different mental and nervous illnesses, to periodical mass hysteria, to mass visual and acoustic hallucinations and to depression had repeatedly been noticed by other scholars.[22] What was new in Shirokogoroff's writings was that he was the first to notice that the mass disease embraces not any one group of people, but the kinship group of the patrilineal clan. It confirms that the collective disease usually attacks a consanguineous patrilineal group, including all the men sharing a common male ancestor, as well as the women born within that patrilineal group, i. e. the men's sisters and daughters married to members of other clans. The group subject to collective disease usually excludes women taken as wives

---

to Evenks, Evens live near the coast of the Sea of Okhotsk and in Northern Yakutiia. They belong to the northern branch of the Manchu-Tungusic group of people. Here I use material on the culture of the southern branch of the Manchu-Tungusic group of people. These are the Nanai (12,000), the Ul'chi (3,173), the Udege (1,902), the Negidals (587), the Orok (200), and the Orochi (883), who live in the Far-East of Russia in the basin of the Amur river, in the Khabarovsk region, and the Primor'e region and on Sakhalin Island (Russia).

22   The phenomenon of mass hysteria is mentioned, for example, in Mitskevich (1929) and Vita-shevskii (1911).

from the other clans. But in some cases, the married women, especially those who have some shamanic-like abilities, may also suffer from collective disease in their husbands' clans in addition to being affected by spiritual troubles in their fathers' clan. As a result, they remain in an in-between position between the two clans, although women's dependence on their fathers' clans' spirituality is considered to be stronger.[23] My informants told me that as a rule a woman-shaman travels in her shamanic trips along her father's clan's invisible spiritual 'roads'. She has access to her husband's shamanic spirits only in some specific situations, e. g., if she secretly steals them from her husband or if her husband lends them to her of his own accord.

Shirokogoroff was not only the first to show that the Evenks who suffer from collective hysteria belong to the same kinship group. He was also the first to point out the connection between the mass mental diseases and the formation of a new clan shaman. He drew attention to the connection between the individual call for shamanic practice and the mass mental diseases and even mass failures of business, which strike the whole group of the neophyte-shaman's relatives (Shirokogoroff 1919: 48). The collective disease symptoms cited from Shirokogoroff above are the typical symptoms of shamanic initiation disease. The only specificity is that not only a neophyte has them, but also several of his or her clanspeople. Not only are these symptoms typical of shamanic disease, but the situation when they appear also reveals their shamanic nature. The collective clan disease emerges when the clan is without a shaman, and continues during the entire initiation period of a new shaman. 'Terrible inexplicable disease appears when the clan is without a shaman, that is, after the previous shaman's death and before the initiation of the next shaman' (Shirokogoroff 1919: 43). Shirokogoroff describes a case where there were two candidates for shamanship within a clan, and only one of them could eventually become the clan shaman. Both candidates suffered from shamanic disease, but, as Shirokogoroff writes:

> At the same time there were also fits among the other members of the clan, and misfortune, in business and in private life, struck the members of the entire clan. The common opinion of the clanspeople inclined to the idea that a shaman was really needed. (Shirokogoroff 1919: 45)

If none of the sufferers became a shaman, the disease among the clan intensified, exhibited new modifications and spread, embracing more and more clanspeople (Shirokogoroff 1919: 61). Another argument supporting the idea that collective clan

---

23 Using obsolete terminology, it would be possible to say that the group predisposed to collective disease should be more precisely determined as 'sib'. But because of the ambiguity of women's position, on the one hand, and trying to follow both the contemporary terminology and that of the tradition to which Shirokogoroff belongs, on the other hand, I refer to the kinship group attacked by the collective disease as 'clan'.

disease may be of a shamanic nature is that, understood from the emic perspective, it is caused by spirits which, having been released after the clan shaman's death, try to find a new 'master':

> Looking for a new 'master' among the clanspeople, urging them to sacrifices or trying merely to draw the clanspeople's attention to themselves, maybe even avenging themselves, the clan spirits prevent the clanspeople from earning their living in the hunt; as a result, mass failures of business threaten the clan with starvation and mortal danger. (Shirokogoroff 1919: 48)

The collective disease should also be called *shamanic* since it can only be cured by setting up a new shaman. The fact that not only a man, but also a woman can become a shaman and can pass her father clan's spirits to, for instance, her son complicates the spiritual situation of the clan since not only paternal but also maternal clan spirits can influence the clanspeople. It does not abolish the domination of paternal clan spirits and of patrilineal descent, however (Smoliak 1991: 35). Firstly, patrilineal descent prevails; secondly, matrilineal descent often joins the main patrilineal one. However, women's participation in shamanising breaks the spiritual homogeneity of the clan and complicates the measures of spiritual security against collective clan disease. Different Siberian indigenous peoples guarded against this in different ways. Thus, in the past, Buriat parents, as Matvei Khangalov (2004: 126) wrote, killed their daughters, and brothers killed their sisters in order to retain shamanic inheritance within the paternal line. Manchu-Tungus and other indigenous peoples permitted female shamanism, but to secure against its possible negative consequences they used the double or threefold clan exogamic system, which is based on the mutual exchange of women between two or three clans. I suppose that such a system helped them to limit the number of spirits that may influence people of the clans involved and make it easier to manage them.

It is important to highlight the fact that not only the disease itself, but also recovery from it are collective in nature. The group hysteria can only be cured if the spirits choose one of the affected people and make him or her a shaman (Shirokogoroff 1919: 43). As soon as one of the afflicted becomes a shaman, she or he recovers, together with all the rest of the clanspeople. In the clan, as Shirokogoroff writes, the disease ceases simultaneously at the moment when the spirits enter one of the clan members. Thus the shaman is, one might say, a safety valve which alleviates the mental disease of the whole clan (Shirokogoroff 1919: 61). Seen from the emic perspective, this synchronous convalescence of all the sick clanspeople is the result of the spirits having achieved their object by moving into one of them.

Chronic condition of clan collective disease

Shamanic disease precedes shamanic initiation and is considered to leave the neo-phyte right after he or she has been initiated as a shaman. My field material however shows that the state of being a full-fledged shaman can hardly be determined as a state of enjoying full health as well. It would be more correct to assert that sha-manic disease as such remains, only changed from an acute condition into a chronic one and with exacerbation transformed to remission. The dependence on the spir-its continues to keep the shaman in the peculiar world of night- and day-dreams and visions. It makes him or her especially vulnerable and predisposed to a relapse, which can be caused by some mistakes in ritual practice, some careless words or the spirits' own groundless temporary disinclination towards their master.

'If a shaman was to say something wrong in his ritual or if his patient would not keep the promise to sacrifice, (the shamanic spirit) would send disease back to him', says my informant, Nikolai Petrovich. 'If you mistakenly said even one or two wrong words', the shaman Lingdze says, 'you will die. I am not able to talk a lot. I can let any number of words go out of my mouth, but if some of them are wrong, I will die'. She confesses that sometimes it is not easy to please the spirits in order to remain safe from the shamanic disease. 'However hard a shaman might try, whatever he might do, if he will say something or sit silently; in any case he will fall ill'. People become shamans to get a release from the torture of shamanic disease. Shamanic initiation indeed relieves the shaman's suffering, but it is not necessarily a case of complete recovery.

'When people become shamans, do they really want to die?' the shaman Lingdze asks. 'On the contrary, they hope to live for a long time, but sometimes it does not turn out like that. Someone has become a shaman, but in spite of that (in spite of recovery) he may not even be able to live'. She gives as an example women belonging to the Soian lineage of the Bel'dy clan and asserts that not one of them survived after they had become shamans.

'All of them died. They died young because they became shamans. They died despite the fact that they were young. What is that? What a *seven* is that? It is a *seven* which crushes people! It is a *seven* which murders people! Such a being! I do not know how to live!'

Lingdze is not of the Soian lineage, and became a shaman long ago, so according to widespread opinion she must be healthy and completely free of shamanic disease, but actually this is not the case. Telling me about one of her spirit-helpers, she says: 'It (the *seven*) torments me. They are such creatures on my shamanic road, which constantly torment me. I must overcome its (the *seven's*) obstinacy and drown out its voice. All the time she begs for food and torments me. I cannot find the proper food to feed it. They (the *seven*) cannot find any food at my place and leave me. I feel as if someone has been hitting me with a stick, I am not able to do anything. I am like a piece of wood with a hammer beating against me. Such a person I became. I am not capable of anything'.

Some of the full-fledged shamans have plenty of problems with their *seven*, while others encounter fewer troubles. Their dependence on the spirits and the possible recurrence of shamanic disease does not completely leave them after the initiation, although the disease is transformed into a remission state. The dependence on spirits lasts, however, and produces special dreams and abilities and sometimes (especially in a shaman's old age) it may exacerbate the disease in new ways. The same changes may affect the entire clan. A time of crisis, when the clan does not have a shaman, leads to an acute condition of the collective disease. But even at a more peaceful time, when the clan has received its shaman, the clan's condition can hardly be described as one of perfect health and well-being. It is rather a regressive, remissive stage of the same chronic ailment with temporarily slowed-down symptoms. The collective convalescence is only the lull. The clan remains dependent on its clan spirits and exists as if within a common spiritual 'electric field'. The clan spirits influence both the clan shaman and the ordinary clansmen, although in different ways. The entire totality of clan spirits influences to a different degree all the clansmen, but there is a selection among the possible *seven* for all shamans within a clan (usually there is more than one clan shaman at the same time) because, as it was said earlier, shamans of a same clan cannot have the same *seven*.[24] Besides, the relationship between a sha-man and his spirits is active and in certain periods of his life the shaman is able to possess and rule his spirits. The ordinary clansmen, on the other hand, are passive and submissive in relation to the same spirits. They experience their pressure, but have only limited influence on them.

This passive nature of their dependence on the spirits becomes apparent in dreams and visions. It is considered that through their dreams and visions clans-people can visit the same space of the invisible spiritual world, they can watch the same phenomena there and even meet each other. Evdokiia Chubovna, for example, told me about a dream she had that was also shared by some of her relatives on her husband's side. The day before the dream Evdokiia Chubovna visited the funeral of her aunt on her mother's side who was a shaman. From the funeral she brought home a photograph and some rags. That very night, after she returned home, she dreamt that she was searching for something in a box of photos. There was also an old man, her husband's paternal grandfather, who she regularly has been dreaming

---

24 As getting those spirits is random, as it is not inherited according any certain rules (for some reasons *seven* can suddenly leave one clan shaman and pass to another one within the same clan), one could not say that this would mean that the social unit that matters for ruling re-lationships between shamans is smaller than the clan (lineage?). At the same time I have to remind the reader that (as I have already said) I do not have enough field material to define with confidence all the characteristics of the social unit (clan or merely lineage) I am talking about and the word 'clan' is used here as a merely conventional term.

about since she was married. Her husband's grandfather was standing near her in her dream, watching all her movements. Evdokiia Chubovna also dreamt about her husband who was also there looking at her angrily. 'I was wondering', says Evdokiia Chubovna, 'why he was looking so angrily at me and what I was doing wrong'. Then in her dream, Evdokiia Chubovna found the photograph that she had brought home from the funeral. The moment when she finally found the photo, the departed shaman-woman (who had been interred at the funeral) came into the room singing and dancing in a shamanic way. 'She passed by me over there', said Evdokiia Chubovna and pointed at the corner of her room where, as she said, the shaman-woman was dancing in her dream. 'She passed by me and stayed over there as if she was begging for something'. At the end of her vision, Evdokiia Chubovna dreamt that Mariia (her husband's aunt, who was staying in another room) also came into her room, stood motionless and watched the shaman. As soon as the shaman left her room, Evdokiia Chubovna woke up and turned on the light. That very moment Mariia indeed came into her room with the words: 'What have you brought here from the funeral? What did you pick up there? The (departed) woman is shamanising round the house. She is begging for something!' – 'Ouch! I answered, (said Evdokiia Chubovna), I have picked up a photograph and some rags there!' Evdokiia Chubovna believes that the departed shaman came to her home looking for the photograph she took away from her place. 'She was probably searching for the photograph', says Evdokiia Chubovna. 'Then I told her: "A-a!" I said, I said it aloud: "Aunt, I said, in the morning I will get up and give it back to you!" In the morning I got up and threw everything away. "Have your possession!" I called to her. "Have it!" And I threw away (the photograph and the rags). I threw them over there, into the ravine! That was all! Since then nothing happened any more! Nobody came to me again to beg for that photograph'. Evdokiia Chubovna affirms that both her husband, who slept in the same room, and Mariia, her husband's aunt (his father's sister), who spent the night in another room, watched the same dream as she did. 'An outsider would not be able to see it', Evdokiia Chubovna says. 'Mariia does not live in our house, but she is my husband's relative'. That is why, as Evdokiia Chubovna interprets it, she was among those who shared the same night vision.

Evdokiia Chubovna is not a shaman and she has no shamanic spirits, but she is subject to her father's and her husband's clan spiritual 'field', and passively sensitive to those two clans' spirituality. In some dreams she penetrates the spiritual space of her original clan. For instance, before marriage, she and two of her sisters dreamt about a tiger that was believed to be their fourth unmarried sister Varvara's spirit-lover and some tiger cubs that were supposed to be Varvara's spirit-children.[25] 'All of us dreamt about them', Evdokiia Chubovna says. 'We watched them! The tiger was mostly sitting and lying outside, under the window. All of us dreamt that it was outside'.

---

25 Varvara died young on the eve of her wedding. Her sisters believe that the tiger, her spirit husband, was jealous and killed Varvara to prevent her wedding.

Query: 'It was not only Varvara who saw it, but all of you?'
Evdokiia Chubovna: 'Yes, all of us saw, that they (her "cohabitant" the tiger and her "children" the tiger cubs) approached us and watched us. They were probably interested in how we lived. Maybe they thought we were sick or something! That's most likely why they visited us!'

Varvara seemed to be becoming a shaman and in her dreams a tiger appeared as a potential spirit-helper, but all her three sisters belonging to the same spiritual reality, which was common for their father's clan, were able in their dreams to watch passively the spiritual events happening between their neophyte-shaman sister and her spirit-cohabitant. Later, in their declining years all the sisters suffered from shamanic-like diseases caused by their father's clan spirits, which pushed the sisters to become shamans.[26] Though they nevertheless never actually became shamans, under the influence of their common clans' spirituality they were able to act in their dreamlands and to meet each other there. When Chiku Chubovna, one of the sisters, fell ill, the shaman woman Kada healed her. After the ritual, the patient's sister Evdokiia Chubovna dreamt that she was looking for Chiku Chubovna and at last she found the place where her sick sister was. At the same time Chiku Chubovna had a night vision that their sister Vera Chubovna, whose shamanic-like abilities were stronger than hers, came to them and led them out. Vera Chubovna, for her part, affirmed that she also dreamt about the same event.[27]

The space of dreams (the same spiritual space the shaman is believed to penetrate in his or her ceremonies) is believed to be collective and to belong to the clan, or rather to a certain lineage. Ordinary people enter this space as passive observers (mostly in their night dreams) and have no ability to change anything there. It is only the shaman (or rather his or her spirits) that can operate and act within the spiritual zone.

The clan roads, where people 'travel' in their dreams, are also called the roads of words and tunes. It is believed that the spirits give the people who belong to the same lineage the ability not only to dream similar dreams but also to improvise songs using similar clan melodies. The content of the night visions, on the one hand, and the melodic type of the song improvisations, on the other, can sometimes give people information enough to define exactly to which clan a person belongs. For example, when the future shaman Kada, as a little girl, began to sing in a shamanic-like way

---

26 Each sister went under the influence of different clan spirits, which were trying to become their personal spirit-helpers. I remind the reader that the shamans of a same clan are not able to have the same spirits.

27 Healing a person, the shaman travels within the spiritual world looking for his or her soul, finds it and returns to the patient. In their dreams two of Chiku Chubovna's sisters performed the shamanic healing ceremony. They confessed that they did not actually trust the shaman Kada's ability.

and tell people about her night dreams, her father began to suspect that she did not belong to his clan and was not his real daughter. Then he made his wife confess that he indeed was not Kada's biological father, because Kada was born as a consequence of incest and her biological father was her mother's brother.

Clan collective disease caused by a clan member's death

The spiritual unity of the clan manifests itself, as we saw, even in the regular quiet time, when nothing special happens. When some events draw the clanspeople closer to the clan spirits it becomes much more obvious. Such events affecting one of the clanspeople open her or him to the clan's spiritual world, and may harmfully affect the rest of the clan.

One of the obvious situations that bring people closer to the spiritual world is death. The Nanai consider that every person dies because the spirits, which accompanied a person during his or her entire life, finally possess his or her soul. After death the soul of the departed one goes away to *buni* (the world beyond), but the spirit, the former companion of the departed one, becomes a harmful spirit danger- ous especially to the clanspeople of a departed person.[28] (In everyday communica- tion that spirit is usually identified with the deceased person). Irrespective of their deeds during their lives, all of them are believed to become destructive *amban*.[29] The departed ones are supposed to come to their living relatives in dreams and visions to frighten them, to be in the way of their business in order to force them to sacrifice. 'After a person dies, he becomes an *amban* (evil spirit). It is certainly bad! *Amban* will come to frighten somebody' (Mariia Vasil'evna). The death of each member of

---

28 The idea of danger caused by the departed ones is also known to other Siberian peoples. Thus Anokhin wrote: 'The departed people become evil spirits. They are divided into the clans (*seok*)' (1924: 6). 'Being artful and troublesome, they squeeze through the doors and chinks into the living quarters and attack people trying to eat them' (1924: 6–7). 'The relatives of the departed one at first, when the soul of the dead person still remains on the earth, live with a heavy heart and in fear for their well-being. The accidents which can happen during that time force the relatives to move to another place in order to be saved from the importunate activity of the departed one' (1924: 22). Anokhin also mentions the case when a relative of a departed person had to move to another place because his young wife also died and his two best horses perished after they fell from the bridge into the water (ibid).

29 Nanai did not borrow from Christian missionaries the idea of postmortem reward. According to their worldview, after death everyone's soul departs to his or her clan zone of the world beyond, but the spirit, which was attached to that person during his or her life, starts harm- ing clanspeople, that is, it turns into *amban*. Only later some of those harmful spirits can be successfully worshipped (they can start helping as a result of that worship) and because of that come to be considered as beneficial spirits *seven*. Thus, not the souls of the dead of a given clan become *seven*, but the spirits which were attached to the people and which accompanied them during their lives.

the clan is like an additional 'window' to the spiritual world which connects the whole clan to it. The living feel it to a greater or lesser extent, but all are connected to their departed clanspeople. Some of the departed clanspeople can be tamed and used for worship; in this case they become benevolent spirits. Most of them are considered to be dangerous and must be driven away with the help of special rituals. Mariia Vasil'evna describes one such ritual conducted in order to heal a woman from an illness which was believed to be caused by a departed clansman. 'I came when they tried to frighten an *amban*', Mariia Vasil'evna remembers. 'Now it seems funny, of course. But then I was scared to hear it. They frightened the *amban*! They were the deceased people who were hanging around! One (of the dead persons) even looked in through the window!'

> *Query*: 'Were they departed relatives?'
> *Mariia Vasil'evna*: 'Right! They (people who were in the room) shouted that such and such (a deceased woman) is looking in (from the street) through the window! It was really horrible! They shouted this way! Did they actually see (the deceased woman) or what? But why would they have shouted in vain? Why would they have shouted in vain, that such a woman was looking in through the window? She has become an *amban*. Well, the deceased woman! She has already become an *amban* (an evil spirit)! Her *panian* (soul) (has turned into *amban*)! It is scared! I covered myself with the blanket. I even sweated! I did not shout myself! Why would I shout? I only listened. They even said the name of the woman (who looked through the window). She was their relative'.
> *Query*: 'Do only departed relatives come?'
> *Mariia Vasil'evna*: 'Yes. They also come to be in the way of their business. They come to their clanspeople. [...] Strangers would certainly not come!'
> *Query*: 'So, they come to their own?'
> *Mariia Vasil'evna*: 'Right, sure! Their own people are familiar to them'.

The maximum closeness to the spiritual world is believed to occur between someone's death and funeral. These days are the most dangerous, especially for the closest clanspeople. The shaman, Ol'ga Egorovna, says that departed people are unsafe for their grandchildren and children. The dead people would not be able to harm strangers or unrelated people; they only crush some of their relatives and take them (their souls) along with them into their graves. The person whose soul is taken away by a dead one is supposed to fall ill and will also die soon. 'The departed woman embraces her living husband. The dead man gives a hug to his living wife, to his daughters and sons', Ol'ga Egorovna explains. According to the informants' opinion, men are threatened by the dead of his patriclan, but for women, the dead people of both her husband's and her father's clans' may be dangerous. 'Both my husband's

FIGURE 2: Kada Kile is demonstrating her funeral dress, which she has prepared herself and which she stores in a chest for the time of her death.

and my father's dead relatives become *kochali* and *amban* (evil spirits) for me', Mariia Vasil'evna explains. 'But unrelated deceased people surely won't come to me'. The shaman, Ol'ga Egorovna, says that she has first-hand knowledge, having chanced to watch how her departed neighbour tried to take a daughter together with her to the grave. Coming to the funeral, Ol'ga Egorovna sat on the sofa in the corridor and looked through the open door into the room where the coffin was.

Lariska was her (the departed woman's) youngest daughter. She (the deceased woman) loved that daughter Lariska. [...] I looked and watched. [...] I saw it with my own eyes! The (dead) mother rose up (from her coffin) and was about to catch (Lariska). I shouted once and (the deceased) fell down back into the coffin. I was sitting in the corridor, when she (the deceased) got up. I uttered a scream, and everybody (those who were present at the funeral) leaped to their feet. I saw it with my open eyes! Well, now it is okay, (Larisa) is still alive. She works in Komsomolsk. (Ol'ga Egorovna)

Ol'ga Egorovna considers that in her time her own deceased mother also tried to take her away into her grave.

My (deceased) mother embraced me. I watched it in a night dream. [...] After that on the third day, when we went to bury her, they had already hammered the coffin shut and begun to lower it into the grave. I felt that they buried me together with my mother. I once uttered a scream. I screamed! It was unbearable! Then my brother Semën told me: 'What? Should I open the coffin?' Semën said. 'Open it!' I answered. They opened it slightly with the axe. Only for such space (about 30 cm)! That is from there [...]! I twice uttered a scream and I (my soul) climbed out (of the coffin). I said: 'Hammer it shut again, I have already gotten out of it!' And they hammered it shut. If I had been an ordinary person (not a shaman) they would have buried me together (with my mother). [...] We have a lot of cases like that. (The deceased one) embraces the living ones. (Ol'ga Egorovna)

The deceased or dying people do not only approach the spiritual world themselves, but also draw their clansmen closer to it and thereby put them in danger. According to Vladimir K. Arsen'ev's field data, collected among the Udege, another Manchu-Tungusic people, shortly before someone's death not only the strangers, but even the closest relatives went out of the room and left the dying person alone in order to prevent her or him from looking at the relatives. If they nevertheless stayed in the room, they covered the face of the dying person, who was still alive, with a towel.

The reason was that the dying one should not be able to draw the other people into the beyond by means of his or her gaze (Startsev 2005). The Nanai tried to save living people from their deceased relatives by means of a similar ritual. They tied one end of a thread to the dead person's hand and another end to the hand of one of his or her relatives. Then the shaman uttered a scream and tore the thread. At that very moment the relative would move away without glancing back at the coffin. Then the same action was repeated with each of the relatives present at the funeral. In this way, the living tried to separate themselves from the dead relative. It was not possible to determine exactly what relatives would be endangered in the case of an ordinary death. It probably does not endanger the whole clan, but only the closest relatives who live in the same home as the departed person. But in the case of an extraordinary death (violent death, attacks by tiger or bear, drowning or death by fire), the entire clan of the dead person was undoubtedly believed to be endangered. Tiger or bear attack was considered to be not just an accident; the spirits are thought to enter these animals and when the spirit-animals attack someone, they mark not only their victim, but the entire clan. If people are drowned *galigda* or torn by a tiger or a bear, they are believed to be marked by a taiga or water spirit, and fate hangs over their entire clan. People from the other clans cannot borrow hunting and fishing-tackle from this clan (*galigdako gurun* – people with a drowned one) because misfortune will be passed on with these things (Gaer 1991: 109). If they nevertheless took something from the clan where somebody had drowned or been torn by a tiger or a bear, they would perform a special ritual.

To prevent the negative impact of it they made a toy bow and a small arrow. The person who had borrowed something from the forbidden people should break off, pinch off or cut off a small piece of the borrowed thing and tie it to an arrow. Then he was to shoot the arrow from the bow toward the place where the forbidden people live with the words: 'Go to your owner! Take your entire bad fate away with you!' (Gaer 1991: 109).

Clan blood revenge may probably also be explained by means of the unit of living and dead clansmen, forming a collective by sharing the same spiritual invisible space. Evidently blood revenge is needed not to 'pacify the soul of the murdered person' and not to 'defend the safety of the living people', as scholars sometimes affirm. It is surely not the manifestation of 'a healthy highly developed person of integrity with a whole-hearted religious-social world view, which creates the harmony of personal and public benefit', as Leo Ya. Shternberg writes (1933: 113). It is rather, as the same author asserts in another place, 'a burden, weighing upon the clan' (Shternberg 1904: 38). The 'window' to the spiritual world is opened each time even in connection with a clan member's ordinary death, but the spiritual world becomes particularly close and dangerous for the clan when somebody is murdered. One clan member's misfortune can spread to the other clanspeople. Clan spirits become especially close and harmful and misfortune increases. So after somebody has been murdered, some of his or her clanspeople must also suffer and shed their blood. E. A. Kreinovich, who collected his materials among the Nivkhs, witnessed the following case. Red blood was squirting from Kurchuk's mouth. The Nivkhs were staying around him as powerless as he was, and kept silent. It was pulmonary bleeding. In the intervals between the coughing fits, Kurchuk repeated: 'It is *takht* (spirit-bird) that is doing it! The people who were standing around confirmed: 'That is true! *Takht* is doing that! It is drinking his blood' (Kreinovich 1973: 389).

The Nivkhs explained to Kreinovich that in Kurchuk's clan somebody had been murdered, but his clansmen did not exact any revenge. The spiritual regulation was, however, that 'for the murdered victim, the victim's kin should give more blood, because *takht* needs blood'. If the victim's clan did not shed the blood of someone from the murderer's clan, the spirits themselves would shed the blood of someone from the victim's clan instead. In other words, some of the victim's clanspeople would begin to suffer from throat bleeding or from bronchial haemorrhage, etc. Kreinovich writes: 'Never and nowhere else among the other Nivkhs did I see so many people seriously ill with tuberculosis as in this clan in the village Chaivo. They explain the disease as a result of their failure to revenge their murdered clansman' (Kreinovich 1973: 389). Kreinovich considers that blood is needed for the 'unavenged soul of the victim', but he does not explain why this 'unavenged soul' avenges itself not upon its offender and his clan, but punishes its own clanspeople instead. From the point of view of the emic approach, the very fact of having somebody murdered in the clan establishes a strong connection with the spiritual world for this clan and the consequences of this connection are imitations of the event that has already happened. Blood was shed and the spirit-bird '*takht* gains access to the clanspeople and drinks their blood' (Kreinovich 1973: 389).

Clan collective disease caused by its members excessively approaching the spirits

There are many other critical situations that draw the whole clan towards the spirits as the result of the deeds of one clansperson. The essence of any taboo is to keep people at a safe distance from the spirits. K. M. Rychkov considers that community of 'sin' is of high profile for the unity of a clan. By 'sin' the scholar means breaking taboos and different prohibitions in the religious and social domain. Not to follow taboos and prohibitions, as Rychkov writes, means not to worry about self-preservation and the well-being of the entire clan (Rychkov 1922: 137). The entire clan is endangered when its individual members do not refrain from deeds which may draw them towards the world of the clan spirits. If an individual commits a 'sin', it affects not only him alone, but all his clansmen. For example, an unnecessary dangerous connection with the spiritual world is established when animals are killed in too cruel a manner. Evdokiia A. Gaer relates the following story narrated by her informant:

> A hunter from the Malki village caught a hare. The hare was alive. He brought the hare home. He skinned it while the hare was alive. Then he let it go, without its skin. As a bloody dot the hare ran into the nearest forest. For long time people could hear its cry *'Singmal! Singmal! Mal! Mal!'* Crying like that the hare disappeared. The man jeered at his game. There were many people in the village, but soon all of them died (Gaer 1991: 17–18).

Gaer does not write that the inhabitants of Malki belonged to the same clan. But we can suppose that it was so, because of her conclusion: 'For cruel behaviour towards animals, the person might pay with his own life as well as with the life of his clanspeople' (Gaer 1991: 17–18). In the case of a murder, it is logical to expect that the spirits would also punish the guilty party and their clansmen with some misfortune and would feel sorry for the victim's clansmen. But as a matter of fact, it is the reverse.

Paradoxically, as already mentioned, it is the clan of the victim which is 'punished' with diseases and misfortune. The murderer's clan is also affected, but differently. The violence once committed has a tendency to continue, the situation has a tendency to repeat and multiply, and the murderer's clan becomes inclined to violence. The informants explain it in the following way: having committed an act of violence, a person communicates with the spirits of violence, *ochiki,* and gives them access to his or her entire clan. The murderer's clanspeople become inclined to aggression and this becomes apparent in increasing numbers of suicides and quarrels. Increasing violence is even directed against their own clanspeople.

If a man has murdered someone, *ochiki* will be transmitted to his children. His child will become evil and will be able to kill someone! [...] I remember [...] it even flashes my eyes right now. At first they tried to keep it back, they did not tell anybody anything about it. But then people nevertheless learned about it. (A boy) was an orphan and lived with his grandmother. They took him on a hunt as a cook. Then they noticed that when he was cooking [...] (The hunters thought that) he fed them porridge, but he himself secretly ate something different. He had put on weight. He was a good boy. (A hunter) said (to another one): 'Do you not notice it? Why does he give us bad food while he himself eats something better? Let us kill him!' Another (hunter) answered: 'I am not able to kill him'. Then the first one murdered the boy, ripped open his stomach and examined it: 'No, there is nothing except some flakes of leather!' Then they buried him and returned home. We lost (that boy). His grandmother cried. She went to a powerful shaman. She related what had happened. He (the shaman performed a ritual and) learned everything about it. All the men went (to those hunters to ask). They came in. The younger (hunter) said: 'I did not do it'. The older man said: 'That was me, I did it. I thought that he offended us, fed us poorly and so forth. We killed him and ripped open his stomach to see what he had eaten'.They forced them to go there (to the *taiga*) and to point out the place where they had buried (the boy). (Kada)

As the people learned about their clansman's crime, they did not punish him, but instead took some measures to prevent increasing violence within their clan. 'They shamanised to drive away *ochiki* (from their clan) so that his (the murderer's) sons and daughters should not become like him' (Kada). '*Ochiki* is like a man, but invisible', Irina explains. 'It forces people to kill each other. In the past it was also like that. People drank vodka and attacked each other with knives. *Ochiki* did it. When someone murders another person, *ochiki* appears. It inspires other people to do the same'. *Ochiki*, as our informants assert, cannot pass to unrelated people, but it easily passes to the clanspeople of the murderer.

Despite the fact that the Nanai have paternal affiliation, some signs of dual descent can be noticed. So, *ochiki* can be inherited not only through the father's but sometimes also through the mother's line and be transmitted not only from husband to wife but also from wife to husband. The shaman Ol'ga Egorovna's daughter knifed her first husband. Her second husband knifed himself in the presence of all the family. Commenting on this event, Mariia Vasil'evna states that *ochiki* have dwelt in Ol'ga Egorovna's family. In Mariia Vasil'evna's opinion, they originated not from violence as such, but from Ol'ga Egorovna's shamanic spirits.[30] These spirits came,

---

30   The Nanai word *ochiki* is probably a variant of the Manchurian word *vochko* which means spirits of the departed shamans that became the spirit-helpers of their descendants, the living shamans.

as she explains, to Ol'ga Egorovna's daughter and forced her to commit a crime. Then they passed through the daughter to the daughter's husband. 'That old woman's (Ol'ga Egorovna's) *seven* (spirit-helpers) have been passing on (to the next generation)', Mariia Vasil'evna says.

> You think what? Have they not been passing on? Everything is passing on through blood! Now my granddaughter makes a row and she does badly at school. My granddaughter or my grandson! It is my blood! Everything has been passing on! If I am a drunkard, my granddaughter is also a drunkard. My son is a drunkard too; it is going on that way! It has been transmitted through blood! (Mariia Vasil'evna)

So the idea of clan blood revenge probably arises as a result of some efforts of the victim's clanspeople to choose the lesser of two evils. An inclination towards violence is considered to be a less evil kind of misfortune compared with the fate of constantly being exposed to the danger of losing the blood of their clanspeople. In other words, clan blood revenge is nothing but an attempt by the victim's relatives to avoid the dependence on spirits that can multiply the number of sick and murdered clanspeople.

Dangerous intimacy with spirits also happens as a consequence of breaking exogamy. The Nanai consider that sexual intercourse usually entails a woman's communion with her partner's clan spirits. But when a woman joins spirits which are both her partner's and her own clan spirits, she doubles her dependence on them. As a result, her closeness to the spiritual world affects her entire clan. Incest creates an unsafe intimacy with the spirits not only for the direct participants, but for the rest of the clanspeople as well. The clan spirits acquire the means to influence this clan even more powerfully and dangerously. The Nanai say that the participants of incest even 'give birth' to some new clan spirits belonging to the category *saika/sadka*, which are 'blood-thirsty' and carry out great devastation. I. Koz'minskii wrote that people explain almost any death that happens after a short-term illness as the result of the interference by spirits born as a result of incest. These spirits are also believed to cause destructive epidemics (Koz'minskii 1927: 44).

The shaman Ol'ga Egorovna says that if someone commits incest, even secretly, all the clanspeople may gain numerous *amban* (evil spirits). 'A great number of such small *burkhan* (spirits) will appear. One (shaman) will not have time enough to kill them. [...] Children will fall ill, grow thin, just skin and bones!' Not only the children whose parent was a participant in incest suffer, but all the other children within the clan as well. 'Brother and sister give birth to lots of *amban*, which attack their clanspeople'. – 'They (*amban*) will disturb their clanspeople's children. The children will suffer from diarrhoea. [...] Small children soon die from dehydration caused by diarrhoea. There are such persons (spirits) [31] that disturb them and come out of the genitals of those who committed incest, the *amban* come out of their genitals. They also kill the old people' (Ol'ga Egorovna).

Because the entire clan suffers from the consequences of incest, the clan court is usually harsh. 'The old people met and discussed what to do with them. This one would say to kill them; another one would say to kill. So they killed them with lances' (Ol'ga Egorovna). From the emic point of view, it is explained that the entire clan depends on the deeds of any one member, since all the members of the clan are connected to the same clan spirits, which, in addition, are considered to be their relatives.

Kinship with spirits is, as the Nanai see it, the result of the spirits' ability to enter into sexual relationships with people which causes a close connection between the clanspeople and the clan spirits, not only for the shamans, but for all the clanspeople to a greater or lesser degree, depending on their spirit-relatives. 'Do all the ordinary people, who are not shamans, have *amban*?' the shaman Ol'ga Egorovna was asked. 'Sure', she answered. 'It is so because they have *amban* in their clan'. Sergei M. Shirokogoroff noticed that one of the decisive characteristics of the clan was their common clan spirits. He wrote: 'The clan is a secluded group of relatives on the paternal line. Besides being aware of their common origins, they consider that they depend on the common clan spirits' (Shirokogoroff 1919: 47).

Clan spirits affect relatives with a common male ancestor and with rare exceptions do not pass to other clans. 'The Onenko clan has its own *amban*. [32] Kile have their *amban*', Niura Sergeevna says. 'Khodzher have their *amban*, Bel'dy have their *amban*', the shaman, Toë Petrovna, says. Being so, it is probably not the social differentiation which makes people look for certain identifying marks, such as totem spirits, in order to fix the differentiation. On the contrary, their connection to the different zones of spiritual reality leads people to troubles that can only be solved by the collective efforts of the people who share the same troubles. This causes people to establish the given social units.

Common clan spirituality is expressed in the Nanai mythology by the clan's collective line (road) of life. The Ul'chi (another people of the Manchu-Tungusic group) call this line *musu*. '*Musu* is the united line of the close relatives' life. Each clan and family has its own *musu*' (Smoliak 1991: 173).

---

31 The fact that spirits represent animals is by no means always the case; they are often seen as persons. According to Anna Smoliak's data, spirits were anthropomorphic or zoomorphic, and many of them could change their appearance, for example, to assume the shape of people, of domestic animals, or of predators (1991: 68).

32 In such expressions the interchangeability of the emic terms *seven* and *amban* is especially clear. If the matter had concerned benevolence of the clan spirits, they would be named *seven*, but in this case it is a question of danger that clan spirits cause, correspondingly spirits are called *amban*.

Anna V. Smoliak reports that sometimes 'the Ul'chi invited a shaman for a special ritual to correct their *musu*': If there is a good *musu* in the clan, all the people
are healthy; they live in peace and friendship, have successful businesses, all of them
think and act together. [...] *Musunchu* is a lucky person who has a good *musu* inherent in one clan, family. But when misfortune, quarrel or disease appears in the clan
and the family, the old people said: 'It is time to correct *musu*' (Smoliak 1991: 173).
It is important to emphasise that using the idea of *musu*, the Nanai express shared
good fortune as well as misfortune, which, they believe, really exists and unites all
the clanspeople.

Social and spiritual sides of collective clan disease

Shirokogoroff's discovery of a collective shamanic disease was unjustly forgotten in
Russian anthropology, and this resulted in decreasing the chance of success in examining kinship in the traditional Manchu-Tungusic society. To explain the prevalence of unilineal descent, scholars mostly accent its social profit because it helps
to unambiguously assign each individual to a certain group of relatives. Murdoch
supposed that division into unilineal groups is needed to avoid confusion when it
comes to the distribution of rights and duties in society. Differentiation and classification of the kin into agnates and cognates is needed, as he wrote, to define juridical relationships with each relative, to know what relatives to help, who is good for
a marriage alliance, whom to leave inheritance (Murdoch 2003: 69–70). The social
side of clanship is interpreted in this explanation as primary and basic. In contrast,
the religious characteristics of the clan (the idea of common clan spirits, the totemic
name of the clan) are described as necessary only for the identification of members
of the kin group who live separately, because the religious specificity helps to main-
tain the knowledge of membership in the group (Murdoch 2003: 76). In other words,
the religious order is considered to be secondary and derived from the social order.
This version leaves some models of traditional behaviour with no real explanation,
such as why people neglect the close territorial connection with their close cognates
and choose distant agnates they have perhaps never met when they decide who to
help and who to refuse aid, who to avenge and who not. It also does not explain why,
in some cases, the purity of the clan may be more important than saving the life of
their children and why they prefer to kill a child whose mother conceals his or her
father's name and whose membership in the clan is unclear. According to A. F. Startsev's materials, the Udege killed a child to avoid possible future breach of exogamy,
which might happen when the child becomes an adult and searches for a spouse. If
the child was not killed, 'he was deprived of his rights and duties, he could not attend clan meetings, did not enjoy its support, could not take part in blood revenge.

Being deprived of his rights and duties, he was forced to commit suicide later when he became adult' (Startsev 2005: 224).

It's quite another matter if we take into consideration collective clan disease in its acute and chronic condition, and the entire clan's dependence on spiritual events which affect its individual members. In connection with collective clan disease, the cases listed above can be explained. Unlike distant agnates, close cognates are excluded from those who are prone to collective disease, which is why they are excluded from help and obligatory revenge.

Also, it would be dangerous to bring up a child who might belong to an alien clan and suffer from a different, alien clan collective disease, because one of the symptoms of such disease is unmotivated hostility against the alien clan's people. The Nanai say that they kill the illegitimate child because he is considered to be *amban*, a bearer of the alien, that is, evil spirit.[33] After the adopted children become adults, the Nanai assert, they quarrel with their adopted parents and their clanspeople and sometimes even kill them.

The certain clan rules (the system of prescriptions and prohibitions including exogamy) were aimed at adapting to communication with spirits and managing clan disease. It would be hardly right to say that transgressing clan rules inescapably provokes punishment by clan spirits,[34] and that establishing a number of rules would legitimate clan order by way of sacralisation. In reality the shamanists search for prescriptions and prohibitions in order to protect in this way their community against possible negative results of spiritual praxis. Shamanic praxis 'is not for joy and joking. People invented it weeping and they talked about it lamenting! They did it (shamanised) because of dependence on spirits (*baita*). They practiced it weeping! People who lived before us could prolong their lives a little, because they danced in a shamanic way, weeping' (Lingdze). Though clan rules helped people to manage with collective clan disease, they did not embrace the entire complexity of communication with spirits and did not influence some cases of individual spiritual troubles. 'Formerly, people did not pay attention to that (to spirits' influence on them), and they did not recognize the reason they died. They did not understand where they received their diseases from' (Ol'ga Egorovna).

Running the danger of collective disease, the clan looks for a means of defence, which entails religious instructions and prohibitions. Being aware of unilineal descent and of their own place in it, people may define the circle of possible persons

---

33 The spirit, which is inherited by that child, could be considered as benevolent (as *seven*) in case that child is born to his or her father's clan. But for his or her mother's clanspeople the same spirit is considered as *amban*.

34 Only uninitiated ordinary shamanists can believe in punishment for breaking clan rules. Shamans perceive clan rules as a means of adaptation: in some cases negative results can follow correct observance of the rules, and in other cases the rules can be broken without negative consequences.

who could be subject to the similar mental and other troubles and who should look together for the means of a cure. If it is so, not social, but religious signs of clan are primary and determinant. The spiritual harmony of the unilineal clan assists people to realise their social unity. Social characteristics are secondary and derivative.

Even in exogamy the social side might be secondary because religious ideas and religious experience underlie it. Leo Ya. Shternberg (1933: 159) wrote that 'there should be a powerful stimulus for creating such a strong and longlived unit as a clan'. He considered that such a powerful stimulus was 'commonness of sexual rights' (ibid.), that people were united into clans to get the guarantee and mutual control of observance of clan rules. At the same time it is hard to imagine that order is kept for the sake of order and nothing else, that there are not more real dangers in the breaking of rules than mere social disapproval. Generalising the field materials, it could be presumed that exogamy is not an end in itself. It might be merely a means and a way of adaptation to the dangerous spiritual reality, which can stir to activity in cases of disorderly incestual relationships. The real stimulus which does not allow people to forget about their clan belonging is their spiritual unity instead, some common spiritual invisible space, which is available only to them and not to outsiders, which involves them in shared night dreams and visions and which constantly threatens them with common troubles. The stimulus to remember their clan peculiarity and exclusiveness is their collective clan shamanic disease, which demands common efforts and actions for its avoidance. Exogamy is but one of such means and actions. Despite the fact that clan spirits can help, they are potentially harmful. Therefore there is a system of taboos and prohibitions which keeps people at a distance from their clan spirits in cases when there is no special need in spirits, and a system of rituals is needed to appease the spirits. There is also a danger caused by alien clan spirits which are considered to be evil just because they are outsiders. The system of taboos and rituals ensures that the clanspeople do not lose their main social and religious guidelines, their awareness of their clan belonging, which is important even when they live separately and take up residence far from each other. Social factors that unite the clan are secondary to the religious factors and represent merely social adaptation to the consequences of communication with spirits.

Affirming that traditional societies are holistic, one nevertheless would not be able to say that their social and religious domains are always interdependent and never appear separately. For instance, the social practice of mutual aid duty within the clan is not connected with any religious ideas. On the other hand, in traditional society, which is involved with shamanic practice, there also exists individual religious experience, and the content of the individual's communication with spirits could be secret and isolated from the rest of society. My informants affirmed that in the past the number of ordinary people (non-shamans) who practiced behind closed doors was so big, that 'in fact there were very few really ordinary people; almost everyone was 'a small shaman' or 'a shaman capable of merely self-help service' (*mepi saman*)' (Ol'ga Egorovna). What distinguished 'small shamans' from real ones was the lack of social activity. *Mepi saman* served only their personal needs (self-treatment, ensuring success in the hunt and in other personal activities). There were also shamans, not (yet) initiated and not recognized by a society. Therefore one can conclude that both social activities existed without any religious sanctions, and religious experiences (communication with spirits) existed among shamanists not only within society, but also beyond its framework.

One cannot also assume that there existed a certain unchangeable totality of spirits, which would be identical to a clan and which would be passed from one generation to another within the certain clan. Not all spirits were inherited; some of the inherited spirits could be 'lost' and the descendants of a departed shaman could never be able to communicate with them anymore. Sometimes it was dependent on the shaman's personal will either to go along the spiritual roads of the departed clan shamans (or which of those roads to choose) or not and either to gain the certain spirits belonging to those departed shamans or not.

> Earlier great shamans gained lots of spirits and after their deaths they were left neglected. But she (shaman Gara Kisovna) took some of those (spirits) to herself. She had not even dreamt them and simply started summoning them.[35] That is why she fell sick. [...] In the past shamans never acted like that. If spirits did not impose on a shaman itself, shamans preferred to neglect them and to close the deserted (spiritual) roads. They abandoned and closed everything, they tried not to even touch them (the neglected spirits and deserted roads). But she opened them, that was why she died. I do not know why she collected them. I told her: 'Why are you doing this?' – 'Never mind, that is all right!' But that was not all right. What can we do now? (Aleksei Kisovich)

In accordance with my own field data, Anna Smoliak (1991: 68) also confirmed that not all the spirits were inherited, that shamans constantly lost some of their spirits and met new ones. Shamans were also able to obtain the spirits of alien clans. That group of spirits (*dona* in Evenk[36] language) was described by Sergei Shirokogoroff (2001: 35). It affected the spiritual purity of a clan.

By their own initiative shamans also could gain ownerless spirits, which did not belong to any clans and which were independent of even any territory. Anna Smoliak (1991: 68) writes: 'There are countless numbers of spirits, which live independently of people'. – 'Each shaman had a multitude of individual spirits, which had only that shaman and no one else' (ibid.: 99). 'In addition to the inherited spirits, shamans

---

35 It means that initiative proceeded not from spirits, which usually force a shaman to accept them, but from the shaman herself.

36 Evenks, formerly known as Tungus, is a member of the northern group of Tungusic languages. Nanai belong to the southern group of Tungusic languages.

gained other spirits and the number of his or her spirits constantly rose during the time of his activity' (ibid.: 86). My informants often complained that it is not easy to control the number of their spirits and to serve each of them by making their image and by offering and worshipping. Shaman Gara Kisovna said that if she had made the images for all her spirits, 'those images would have filled her entire house and she would not have a place to sleep'. Nevertheless the field data collected among the Nanai allow us to affirm that in spite of the existence of individual and alien spirits, the inherited clan spirits represented the most important part of each shaman's personal pantheon. The existence of exactly that kind of spirits gives shamanists the opportunity to realize the phenomenon of collective clan disease and to adapt to it.

Field materials collected in Siberia by Russian anthropologists at the beginning of the twentieth century were at some variance with the sociological theory of the origin of clanship. Generalising from their materials, S. Brailovskii (1901: 355) wrote that Manchu-Tungusic clans 'represented congeneric-religious units', emphasising the religious components. Sergei M. Shirokogoroff (1919: 50) also wrote that not only one shaman is chosen by the spirits, but the entire clan is the spirits' elected representative. According to his ideas, shamanism is not a business for an individual, but a matter of the entire clan. Shirokogoroff (1919: 48) asserted that the clan is needed as a means of adaptation to the dangers of the spiritual world, as a way to defend people from the harmful influence of both the clan spirits and the alien ones, and my field materials, collected almost a century later, completely confirm his ideas.

HOW TO 'OPEN' MORE SOULS

> I nurse a strong grievance against those people
> who departed remaining unopened,
> that they never managed to be opened.
> That is just a mockery on their part.
> *(Shaman Marina Aleksandrovna)*

The outward reason for writing this chapter was an attempt to examine some characteristics of terminology used by contemporary Nanai neo-shamans. Nanai neo-shamans, who not only proceed with the traditional shamanic methods, but also arm themselves with the techniques of healing borrowed from other religious and healing practices, use the same term to denote both shamanic initiation and healing. In Nanai language, to get a shamanic initiation *nikheleuri* stands for 'to open'. To open a person as a shaman means to remove 'a cover' that screens the person from spirits, to unsheathe him or her in front of the spiritual world, and to make him or her accessible to spirits. In connection with shamanic initiation, they also use the expression *'angmani nikheli'* that means 'to open neophyte's mouth' in order to enable that mouth to become a channel between people and spirits. Thus, 'to open' a shaman denotes in Nanai both to open a neophyte for contacts with spirits and to expose spirits to a person.[37]

According to the terminology of the contemporary Nanai neo-shamans, some persons, who come for a shamanic healing rite (but not all of them), are also being opened without becoming shamans. In this context 'to heal' is to some extent equal to 'to open'. Telling about her successful experience of healing, neo-shaman Marina Aleksandrovna said:

> In my time they opened me as a shaman, and now I open other people (by healing them). I have opened three persons in Nanai region and one in Sovgavan. We have such a hierarchy. Such a hierarchy! That is the way! The centre is I, and there are two more people below and then some more below. I have also opened several persons in Dubovy Mys village, and they themselves do not know that. I am as if in the centre among them. (Marina Aleksandrovna)

Using the word 'open', Marina Aleksandrovna means that she healed ordinary people, not shamans, but while performing healing rites her shamanic spirits, according to her expression, 'impregnated her patients' aura', opening the access for spirits to those people.

Using the same word to designate such processes as healing and shamanic initiation helps us to accentuate not as much the results of healing, but the very essence of disease, which concerns patients' souls. Moving the accent from healing the body towards the state of the soul, which is a long-term result of healing, gives us the possibility to put a question of comparison of spiritual consequences of shamanic healing, on the one hand, and, on the another hand, of shamanic initiation.

Spiritual reasons for diseases

According to the shamanists' conception, any disease is caused by spirits, which come in touch with the human soul, and is dependent upon their presence (possession) or action (Waddle 1909: 224). That concerns both ordinary illness and shamanic disease.

In the process of becoming a shaman, a person falls sick because clan spirits start leading his or her soul along certain roads of the spiritual world, jeopardising it. Nikolai Petrovich considers that the attacks of his shamanic disease were provoked

---

37 The scholars explain the main task of shamans in much the same way, and sometimes use the same verb 'to open'. For example, Åke Hultkrantz (2004: 151) writes that the shaman's primary task lies in opening the road to the supernatural powers through the medium of ecstasy.

by his spirit-kids, which took him along such roads in his night dreams. 'I followed them everywhere, got into tight corners (on their roads) and fell sick. After that a shaman (during a healing ceremony) helped me out. Then I again followed them (my spirits) and again got into a scrape, and again a shaman liberated me'.

FIGURE 3: The shaman Nonna Dukhovskovna (in the centre). During the difficult delivery of one of her children, a shaman induced his *seven* spirits to pull apart her body from top to the bottom towards the sides, which is still seen in the line in her face that goes over her entire body. After this treatment Nonna became a shaman herself.

Not only shamans, as shamanists believe, but also ordinary people get sick because spirits take their souls into the dangerous places of the spiritual world, which they can learn from their night dreams. 'There are people who realise learning from their dreams, that their souls have left them, but there are also people who are not aware of that' (Lingdze). Starting healing an ordinary person (non-shaman), a shaman first determines the location of his or her soul. With that purpose the shaman figures out who of the patient's departed relatives (or to say more exactly, which spirits connected to those relatives) visited the patient with the disease. In some cases shamans can even see those relative-spirits. The day before the patient came to her, shaman Mingo dreamt three women-spirits that approached the wicket gate near her house and expressed their displeasure that because of Mingo's forthcoming shamanising they have to leave the patient's soul soon. During that shamanic ceremony Mingo sang, addressing her patient:

Those women (spirits) came here beforehand,
They probably know something about us!
They had learned that you were going to come here to shamanise;
and they passed ahead, they themselves beforehand came here.
That is interesting!
They came to look at us!
(Mingo)

In another case before healing Ella Ivanovna, the shaman Lingdze suddenly had a vision of the spirit, which guarded the entire Ella Ivanovna's patrilineage. Later she explained the case to Ella Ivanovna's mother:

I saw there was a boy lying on the apex of your roof. He was lying prone on the very top of the roof. [...] He did not show himself to anyone, hiding his face, but I could clearly see his body. [...] You asked me to shamanise for Ella Ivanovna. How could I refuse? I started working and saw that boy on your roof. (Lingdze)

Concerning dangerous places of the outward spiritual space where spirits bring human souls, shaman Gara Kisovna explained the following:

Anything can happen to *panian* (to a soul-shadow); (in the night dreams) it (human soul) can fly to the sky, to go underground and underwater. It goes around only because *amban* (clan harmful spirits) carry it along their own (clan spirit) roads. No one (soul-shadow) can go on its own. (Gara Kisovna)

Searching in her ritual for a patient soul's trace, shaman Gara Kisovna found in the ground something like a door. She decided that the patient's clan spirit, which had taken away her patient's soul, dragged that soul into the hole, covered by that 'door' and locked it there. Healing consisted in opening that door and letting the patient's soul go out. As shaman Lingdze explains, 'those patients fall sick because "children", the spirits which were "born" of their departed shamans-relatives, lasso their souls, wrap them, twist them round and bring them up'.

Disease in ordinary people, non-shamans, can also result from the fact that they are relatives of that one, who has been chosen by spirits as a future shaman. Having become free after the death of their servant-shaman, the spirits bring troubles and cause misfortune not only to the one of their future servant-shaman, but to the entire group of kinsmen (Heyne 1999: 380; Shirokogoroff 1999). According to the emic ideas, the spirits that accompanied a departed person (especially a shaman) during his or her life cause any diseases, including shamanic ones, to the entire (patri-) lineage. Shamanic disease can be characterised both by specific mental disorders, and also by ordinary somatic problems, which are noted for the fact that they can hardly be healed by means of allopathic medicine.[38] The spiritual factor, which causes shamanic and ordinary disease, is (from the emic perspective) the same: it is uncontrolled contact with spirits.

Meanwhile, there is an essential difference between shamanic and ordinary diseases. First, it relates to the factor of how far in the depth of departed generations the person's soul has been taken by spirits. Nikolai Petrovich explained that spirits can take the soul of ordinary persons not farther than two generations back, only to the generations of fathers and grandfathers. The ordinary person, non-shaman, 'is not able to go farther into the depth of centuries, but nevertheless he or she necessarily

---

38 In one of the cases known to me, shamanic disease manifested itself as heart disease, in another case the symptoms resembled long-term influenza.

goes along that (paternal) line'. Only shamanic souls can be led further and be put in touch with a larger number of the spirits, which were earlier mastered by his or her departed relatives. Second, according to the emic point of view, spirits differently use a disease as a means of forcing people to act in compliance with their intentions in regard to shamans and to ordinary people. They send disease to a future shaman, forcing him or her to accept shamanic service. If neophytes themselves wish to become shamans, the spirits have no need to compel them, and

> they become shamans with no disease; they simply have the special night dreams and become shamans. [...] The most powerful shamans were formed that way. For example, Chongida! He was not sick; he did not go out of his mind, there was nothing like that. But he could show any tricks. He was a great shaman! (Aleksei Kisovich)

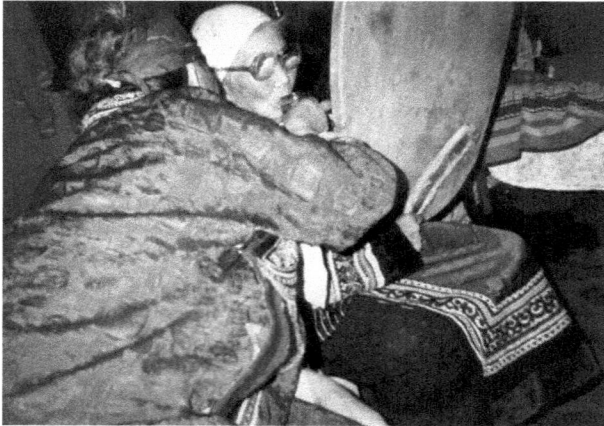

FIGURE 4: Sacrifice to the shaman's spirits during the ritual.

That is a totally different matter with ordinary people. Spirits send diseases to them, trying to draw their attention and to make them worship and sacrifice. Willing to urge a person to worship, as Ol'ga Egorovna said, 'A senior spirit sends *seven* (spirits subordinated to it): 'Go and get that person's soul!' So, they (*seven*) go. Like policemen they arrest that person',[39] tying him or her up with disease. To the question, where those spirits place the 'arrested' soul, Ol'ga Egorovna answers: 'They put them at their places', in those corners of the spiritual world, where they dwell themselves.

---

39 As Nanai represent not a small closed 'traditional' society, but at least since 1930s are included in a centralised state, the references to the notions of 'policemen', 'arrest', 'prison' etc. are familiar to them and are used in their everyday speech.

And that is the worst thing! They would place that person there, and he or she would be sick for years and suffer. They put (souls) in the bad places. There is a hot place and a cold one. You continue living here (in the physical world), but there is also a spiritual world with life just like here, (where your soul is taken). They would take a soul and torture it there (in the spiritual world), but a person would suffer (falling sick) here (in the physical world). (Ol'ga Egorovna)

Recovery in exchange for a contract about the long-term worship

If the reason for disease is installation or attachment of a spirit to a person, healing consists in driving that spirit away.

Another way of healing disease is taming disease-producing spirits and reconciliation with them. Taming is realised by means of making 'a new body' for that spirit that is a fabrication of its image. That healing delivers the patient from disease, but does not free him or her from the contact with that spirit. On the contrary, it reinforces and aggravates it. The cured person finds out that he or she is now permanently connected with that spirit and has got new a charge towards it. At the same time the patient becomes also involved with worshipping his shaman's spirits. As the shaman and the patient belong to two different clans (only an alien shaman can force a patient's clan spirits to enter into a 'new body'), the shaman's spirits are alien to a patient, but after being healed a patient must establish long-term worship and offerings to the shaman's spirits in addition to his or her clan spirits, which had caused the disease. Neglecting that charge results in the return and aggravation of disease. Even if the patient is not a shaman, after this kind of treatment, he or she discovers that the spirit placed in the new image penetrates into his or her night dreams and is expected to be dreamt for the rest of life. Thus, Evdokiia Chubovna got two spirit-'boys' as a consequence of the healing she received.

Wherever I was, I surely dreamt them. [...] Once I was travelling by a ship. I went to bed and fell asleep. They pushed me: 'Mum, well! You nearly left us on the beach!' I dreamt of them this way. I lay on the bench, and they pushed me again: 'Move a little, mum! You have almost left us on the beach, but none the less we had time to board to the ship! Now move a little!' I woke up and moved a little: 'Go to bed!' (I said to them). (Evdokiia Chubovna)

Despite the fact that Evdokiia Chubovna constantly communicates with her spirit-boys, she is not a shaman. The very fact that she is in contact with the spirits is only a result of the healing of her disease. The more often a person resorts to such kind of healing, the more images of *seven* spirits he or she collects and the more he or she is being opened towards the spiritual world.

Souls given up for temporary use

In case of another diagnosis, if a person is sick because the soul-shadow *panian* has left his or her body, the shaman's task is to search for the soul and to place it not always back into the patient's body,[40] but – it is important to notice this! – into a special depository *dëkaso* guarded by the shaman's spirit-helpers. That depository can be located in the patient's clothes, in vessels which are kept at the patient's place or in some distant objects like hills or stones; sometimes they are located even inside living creatures. One shaman had *dëkaso* inside a whale. Mariia Petrovna placed her patients' souls inside a fish, that fish swallowed the souls of her patients and for a while kept them safe. Common for all those locations is that they are outside the patient's body and that in each such location there is a strong presence of spirits which oversee the soul brought to them. The informant of Igor Krupnik describes the Yup'ik healing rituals, which include inserting the patient's soul into her dress outside her body.

> (The shaman said:) 'Now I am finding Aġnaġisiak's *(Аг,наг,исяк)* soul-shad-
> ow and bringing it in order that it won't leave her anymore (and she won't fall
> sick anymore)'. He (shaman) told my father: 'Keep a tight hold on her *kerker*
> (one piece suit) from one side; I am keeping it from another side'. We were not
> keeping it tightly; we were simply keeping that empty (*kerker*) hanging. [...]
> Suddenly, probably the very moment her shadow had been brought, it (the
> patient's shadow) went right into the *kerker,* and the *kerker* stood upright.
> But it was actually empty! I was very frightened; I seized it and did not let it
> go. It was shaking right in my hands and was as if firm inside (Pust' govoriat
> 2000: 482).

Andrei Popov's thorough translation of the texts of Yakut shamanic ceremonies also gives us information about the fact that in some cases the soul-shadow, after being returned, is located outside the patient's body and is given to the spirits for special superintendence in the spirit's nest, dwelling, or in its groin and armpits. In one of the ceremonies recorded by Popov, a shaman sings: 'Spirit of respect-worthy fire, menacing granddad, [...] staying in front of you, I am asking: Hide your child (the patient's soul), who you have been educating, into your warm groin and armpits' (Popov 2008: 209). There is one more similar fragment from a shamanic healing ceremony.

---

40 At least during all the numerous shamanic ceremonies where I was present, the patient's soul
    was never returned into his or her body. My informants found conceivable returning a soul
    into the patient's body, but could not remember any certain case when it actually happened.
    The patient's soul was instead placed into the special soul depository.

I have separated you (the patient) from *абаabы* (the evil spirit), and have sent you to the land (of good spirits)! [...] The spirit of respect-worthy fire, force him (the patient) to live in your durable dwelling, drag him along your nest of warm fur, smooth him with your warm palm and your woolly paw! Do not let that one which has warm breathing go out! Do not let that one which has cold breath get in! Do not expose him (the patient's soul) to winds and storms; let him recover sitting on the warm couch, luxuriating and being nursed! (Popov 2008: 254–255).

The patients' souls, which in the course of healing are not always returned to patients and are instead accumulated in the special spiritual depositories, become an essential resource for shaman's self-strengthening and empowering. As that issue is of exceptional importance for perceiving the objective regulations of shamanic practice, I will cite some more authors who dealt with this topic. According to Glafira M. Vasilevich (1969: 226), Evenk shamans preserved in *omiruk*, which is a box or a sac, not only the souls of their patients, but also the souls of the patients' relatives, and shamans of Ilimpiiski Evenks had similar depositories for souls, but into those *omiruk* they also placed locks of the patients' and of their relatives' hair. Yakuts gave up the souls of their patients to supreme deities (Popov 1949: 310; Vasil'ev 1909: 28). Vasil'ev (1908: 82) also writes that after a Yakut shaman takes a patient's soul away from a hostile spirit, the 'shaman does not return it to the patient, because otherwise it can leave again. [...] He must convey it to the supreme deity Ayaa-Toën and place it there on the sacrificial tree'. Ket shamans stored the souls of living people in arrowheads and in sticks' (Alekseenko 1967: 109). Khakass considered that the souls of children were kept in cradles in the mountain Ymai like in a temple (Butanaev 1984: 93, 97). Smoliak (1991: 116) reports that the most popular Nanai shamans stored up to a hundred souls in the special sacs (*somolakan*). Kenin-Lopsan (2008: 119) writes that during the ritual a Tuva shaman holds a rag of white cloth, and he places the patient's soul into that rag. The soul leaves a mark on that rag. Then a shaman turns the cloth over and makes a tight knot. After that *the soul is not able to go anywhere anymore and becomes the shaman's prisoner* (my italics).[41]

---

41 It would be necessary to emphasise that the examples given here are taken from different Siberian cultures. Everywhere one can find that shamanic spirits are considered to act often against human will and that is why they are perceived as sticking, importunate and sometimes even extremely uniquely coercive. Not only among the Nanai, but among the other peoples who practiced shamanism, healing resulted in long-term attachment to spirits, and neglecting those spirits resulted in the return and aggravation of the disease. It would be important also to notice that all the pleasant sides of shamanic and shamanic-like activity have also negative side as if their 'shadow' is caused by coercive spirit power. For example, successful hunting can have an obtrusive, coercive character. One Nanai hunter complained that he was doomed to kill a lot of bears. 'It was mischievous. If he did not kill a bear, it (his spirit) would punish him. But if he killed it, there were plenty of them anyway. They came to him as if to punish him and

Returning the shadow-soul *panian* back into a patient's body was also practiced but it was considered to be much less efficient. If a soul had left its body, it was inclined to go out of it again and again. Ol'ga Egorovna explained:

> (If a shaman returns a soul into its body) it will yet again leave it almost every day. Should I collect those (souls) every day?
> Is it more secure to bring it to the granddad (to the spirit)?
> Surely it is more secure! They will not be able to run away from there. If the person falls down in his waking hours, then his *panian* will try to run away (from *dëkaso*), but even then it (*panian*) will not likely manage to open the doors (of *dëkaso*). (Ol'ga Egorovna)

According to Nanai shamanists' ideas, *dëkaso* is a closed spiritual space. Sometimes, as they imagine it, *dëkaso* looks like a house (for example a house on animal legs), like a village or even the entire city. That spacious spiritual space can be located inside some physical objects or as if cloaked from outside. Shaman Kada's two-dimensional (spiritual/material) space was placed in the big stone in taiga, visible to everyone.

> In the forest side, far from here, there is a road on the slope of the high hill
> [...]. It is a very scary place. There is a stone there. It is always droning *gum-m-m*. People go there very rarely. I dreamt that stone, it was very smooth.
> Is it in reality?
> In reality! There is also a spirit master of that place and I can see it dreaming. (Kada)

Kada assures us that she can enter that stone.

> You cannot see any doors there. I just beg and beg (the spirits to permit me to enter) and then I see how little by little the doors appear and then they open [...]. There is the sun there; the place is similar to here. There is also the river, everything. It looks like a city and there are gates in front of it. (Kada)

In *dëkaso* shamanic spirits are supposed to nurse the souls, which they have picked up in exchange for healing. Shamanic spirits wash, warm and breast-feed the acquired souls.

---

he had to kill all of them. He lived near Lidoga village' (Ol'ga Egorovna). Coercion was also an integral part of human/spiritual cohabitation. Anna Smoliak wrote about Ul'chi: 'Women got "husbands" from the spiritual world; and they (spirit-husbands) called those women to themselves. A shaman could not heal such women: they committed suicide'.

Do not let that one which has warm breathing, go out! Do not let that one which has cold breath, get in! I beg you, do not take it into your head to make us a laughing stock for a vari-coloured dog and laughter for a grey one. (Popov 2008: 209)

In one of the recorded shamanic ceremonies, Mingo brings the patient's soul into *dëkaso* and instructs them this way:

I am seating the sick woman at the table.
I am seating her on the chair on the different worms spread on its seat.
I am seating the sick on that chair at the table
and putting a Manchurian toy *yagoran* in front of her.
I am putting (a toy) to make the sick one to sit (quietly) and to look (at that toy).
Let nine swifts guard her
not enabling anything bad to approach her.
If (something bad) approaches her,
let them remove it. [42] (Mingo)

The Nanai themselves translate the word *dëkaso* into Russian as *iasli, detskii sad* (nursery school), but also as *tiu'rma* (prison). Such translation can be explained by the fact that souls are kept in *dëkaso* under coercion, against their will, and they constantly try to escape. Nikolai Petrovich says that 'each *panian* seeks to leave *dëkaso*, it longs to go home and to join its body, but spirits *amban* catch it' on its way home and the person falls sick again. To compel the soul to be imprisoned in *dëkaso* and that way to preserve his or her health, shaman Kada, as she declared it, after inserting a soul into *dëkaso*, wound it round with a grass snake as with a belt. She says: 'I should tie it round like that, twist it around with snake. If a shaman makes it right, (the patient) will learn it from his or her body because he or she will recover'. The patient is healthy till his or her soul is located in *dëkaso*. Nikolai Petrovich relates that this way.

Let us assume that they delivered me (my soul) to *dëkaso*. I am supposed to live with no diseases until my death. If I am in *dëkaso*, I will live till I am one hundred or even one hundred twenty and not be sick. I am supposed not to have anything (bad), not to know anything and to die this way! (Nikolai Petrovich)

---

42 This is a fragment of a shamanic ceremony the author recorded in Naichin village, Khabarovskii krai, in 1991 and translated together with the performer of the text, Mingo Geiker and her husband Nikolai Petrovich Bel'dy.

Changes in the spiritual condition of the person recovered that way consist in forming a strong dependence on the spirits of that shaman who has healed him or her. It is expressed in the person's involvement with ritual and sacrificial practice of that shaman. If the recovered person refuses or simply is late in participating and sacrificing, it threatens him or her with troubles incomparably much harder than those ones which brought him or her to the shaman for the first time. Here is the case from shaman Ol'ga Egorovna's practice.

> If you do not feed shamanic spirits in time (after they have healed you), they will arrest your soul and imprison it! Once I shamanised for Aimar. He said that after that he became really well. Really, really well he was!

In spite of being cured, Aimar did not open himself up to Ol'ga Egorovna's spirits. Nothing has changed in his life; he did not keep his word, did not sacrifice and stopped visiting the shaman.

> Four years had passed. He and Sergei went fishing. After they drew out their fishing net, he suddenly began to pack his belongings. 'Where are you going?' 'Home! I have much work to do!' He left. After that Sergei returned and went to visit him. But he (Aimar) had already hanged himself. For no particular reason! His mother also hanged herself. [...] His two children remained orphans. (Ol'ga Egorovna)

Ol'ga Egorovna interprets the case that there were her shamanic spirits, which without her orders on their own initiative punished Aimar, because he first started shamanising and then stopped. Whereas the very fact that he applied to a shaman even once actually meant that since then he had to sacrifice yearly.

The patient healed is usually involved in the regular ritual shamanic praxis mostly against his or her will and this is only an outward expression of the person's subordination to the spirits, which dwell in *dëkaso*. Internal dependence on those spirits is expressed in a change of his or her mental condition. All the time patient's soul is located in *dëkaso*, he or she either does not dream anything or constantly dreams of the same closed room, where his or her soul is forcibly locked, in defiance of its longing to get out. They believe that for some people their souls' residence in *dëkaso* is so unconsciously distressing that they go out of their mind (Aleksei Kisovich).[43] In this case they can be healed if they rise to the next higher stage of intimacy with spirits, and became shamans themselves.

---

43 It is believed that patients' souls have in *dëkaso* great troubles especially after their shaman's death. Shaman Ol'ga Egorovna explains it this way: 'After I die, some of my patients' souls will not be able to struggle out of my *dëkaso* and they [the patients] will die. A shaman dies, and the people who he has healed remain there [in *dëkaso*]. If nevertheless someone's soul succeeds in getting out of *dëkaso*, that person can remain alive, though he will fall heavily ill'.

The soul's dwelling in the immediate vicinity of shamanic spirits results in the fact that the soul (and correspondingly its master) acquires some peculiarities of those spirits' behaviour. In Kada's *dëkaso* the souls of the healed people are guarded by her spirit-helper dragon *puimur*. Not to let the souls escape, Kada's other spirits tie them to dragon's legs. Kada assures that the person whose soul has been tied to the dragon, 'becomes as strong as that dragon is, and he or she moves, stirs and yanks as strongly as the dragon does'. Acquiring characteristics of a spirit-health guardian by an ordinary person is similar to acquiring the features of a spirit-helper by a shaman. In this respect the patient healed becomes 'a bit of a shaman'. The patient's convergence with the shaman's spirits starts in the moment of making a decision to apply to be a shaman. The very wish to get in touch with a shaman results in establishing that contact. If a patient doesn't invite a shaman, but on his or her behalf someone else does, that contact is founded for those who request a shaman. Mariia Innokent'evna relates that sometimes people saw spirits of the requested shaman before he arrived. She remembers that each time, after people invited a famous shaman, they saw a red snake, one of his spirits, which appeared 'among the racks right in the yard' of those who invited the shaman.

> There were poles on both sides of the house, and that (red snake) wrapped itself round those poles. It wound them around with red. So if people went to a shaman and he agreed to cure them, they could see his *seven* in their yard. How frightened they were! Later during the ceremony that shaman sang: 'Half of snake! Red neck!' People saw that *seven* with their own eyes. It appeared before them in their waking hours. After they saw that red snake they knew that soon the shaman himself will come, that people have already been taking him. His *seven* advanced him. (Mariia Innokent'evna)

Hired body

Healing by means of placing the soul into a special depository is applicable exclusively to the ordinary people and is impossible for both neophytes and experienced shamans. Nevertheless, if we concentrate on the spiritual consequences of healing as resulting in convergence with shamanic spirits, in some respects we can compare healing with shamanic initiation. After being healed a patient recovers, but his spiritual status changes, which can be expressed in forming spiritual dependence.[44]

---

44 That dependence can manifest itself in the following way. Staying in the special shamanic depository, the souls find themselves being in captivity of a shaman's spirits. In case that a shaman dies, the people whose souls remained in his or her *dëkaso,* are exposed to danger. Ol'ga Egorovna explained that in that case a person would fall sick, and being powerless to get out from *dëkaso,* can die. In that case people resort to the help of another shaman, who can open

Similar to that is the central moment of shamanic initiation. Everything that can seem to be important in shamanic initiation – change of neophyte's status (from being possessed to possessing one), change of social status and even temporal 'death' – all that is, from emic perspective, only the result of another central event. That event is the replacement of human soul-shadow *panian* by shamanic spirit (or totality of spirits), which is named *niokta*. According to Anna V. Smoliak (1991: 132–154) and to my informants' explanations, from that moment when a person has been opened, he or she has no soul *panian* anymore and only has shamanic spirits instead. Smoliak's informant Molo Onenko said that during the initiation ritual, the shaman's soul 'turns over, as if from back to prone and is transformed, changed' (Smoliak 1991: 144). From the time of initiation the shaman's body becomes a depository, where spirits dominate, supplant his individuality and his own soul, and that differentiates the shaman from the ordinary people. One of our informant-shamans confessed that sometimes his body becomes 'a container for spirits'. 'Spirits can use a human body as a container to live in. At the certain time they start drawing his attention and totally ruling his brain. [...] As soon as evening comes, that is it! Look, eyes are being changed!' But in the morning, when spirits go to sleep he (the shaman) again comes to his senses. Another shaman told me about himself this way:

> I am duplex! When it (a spirit) appears in me, my muscles are strained in a different way. [...] When it happens, a kind of switching occurs and instead of saying 'I' you start saying 'he'. You yourself notice it, but your interlocutor does not usually notice anything.

There is another similar statement of a young woman-shaman:

> Of course, shamanic disease is frightening. The most frightening is the feeling that you don't exist. It is as if someone else is living inside of you. After the disease you don't remember anything that happened. It is as if everything was erased. (Tkacz 2002: 14)

According to Valentina Kharitonova's data, 'during a ritual against his own free will, a shaman can repeat some information which was not even known to him earlier. It accompanies the feeling that he is not able to say anything from himself. His

---

that *dëkaso* and take out the patient's soul. I can also refer to the praxis of shamanic conflicts, when a shaman could use his patient's soul hidden in his *dëkaso* as a necessary resource of defence in case of an alien shaman's attack. A shaman could give to his or her enemy the soul (and it means also a life) of his or her former patient in order to preserve his or her own life instead. Thus the price of the patient's healing was his or her closeness to shamanic spirits and at the same time giving the shaman and his or her spirits the right to dispose of that soul using his or her own discretion.

own thoughts became 'closed', a person either forgets them or they temporary as if go out of his personal knowledge. That condition is also conducted with the sense of the impossibility of ruling over their own personality, at least to rule it painlessly' (Kharitonova 2004: 34). The presence of an alien spirit, which replaces the shaman's individuality, is vividly perceptible during shamanic ritual. Starting the ritual, a shaman lets the spirit have his body as a container and returns into his or her own body after the ritual is over. That fact probably explains the typical shamans' complaints that they poorly remember or completely forget what they have sung and told during the ritual. A Nanai neo-shaman told me about how she danced while she was consecrated into the shamanic state. 'Girls, you know what! My eyes themselves closed! I wished to close them so much, but still I could see even with closed eyes. That was scary! I was afraid of myself!' I also quote another of my informants, a Buriat neo-shaman's statements. That shaman uses the popular word 'trance' for an explanation of the independence and even isolation of an alien personality, which replaces the shaman's individuality during the ritual. This word 'trance' is popular among the neo-shamans newspeak, which expresses the emic idea of presence of a spirit in (or near) a shaman's body; that presence can be so powerful that it can even replace a shaman's individual soul for a while, his or her personal perception of the environment.

> I start shamanising (in the room) and suddenly find myself somewhere in the field! It means I have fallen into a trance. When my soul flies out, I find myself in the field. There is wheat being in the ear, at a distance there is a house. I walked up the porch, opened the door and suddenly went out of the trance. But there (in the physical world) half an hour has passed. I do not know what they talked about that time, and who came. [...] Another time I have such a feeling that (having started a ritual) I suddenly see a basement opened. I jump there and someone closed the cover over me. It is dark, groping my way I try to move, but it is dark, and I cannot see anything. While I was feeling my way with hands, whoops, I went out of the trance! The entire hour has passed! But I do not know what happened (to my body in the physical world).
> But while you were out, your body continued performing the ritual and kept on talking and singing?
> Certainly! My spirit told (in place of me) while my soul was travelling in austral and did not know anything about where and what. I do not know anything about what my body said, and what the conversation was about!

This informant compares the shaman's body with a cover or a coat, which the shaman can take off and lend to a friend. 'You left your coat for your friend' and you know nothing about 'where she walked in your coat, who she visited'. The same is with your body. For a time of shamanic ritual you leave your body for your spirit, and you yourself go out; that is why 'you know completely nothing about who came during the ritual and what people were talking about'.

Certainly my informant tells about the most extreme manifestations of spirits' supplanting shamans' personalities. Even during the ritual, spirits do not always push shaman's individuality aside from his or her body to such an extent that the shaman remembers nothing that happened in the physical word. Nevertheless, in the literature there is some data that in fact a shaman cannot be responsible for what spirits have done after borrowing his or her body. 'During rituals and in the moments of ecstasy, shamans were not charged with their deeds, because not they, but their spirits, which entered them, actually acted. Shamans' deeds were unconsciousness, they merely submitted spirits' (Khangalov 2004: 152).

Spirits *niokta*, which use a shaman's body as a hired coat, usually leave their master not long before his death. Losing it, the shaman becomes weak and feeble and soon dies (Smoliak 1991: 144). Simultaneously with loosing *niokta*, the shaman again obtains soul *panian*, which he or she left during initiation. After death that *panian* goes to the world beyond *buni*, but *niokta* as the totality of spirits which replaced the shaman's soul during his or her activity, 'never died, but passed to the future shamans' (Smoliak 1991: 144). It is *niokta*, which is then inherited by the shaman' descendants.

Unlike a usual person, the shaman fell ill not because he or she lost his soul *panian* (the shaman does not have it), but because *niokta* sometimes leaves his or her body. Both the shamanic disease of a neophyte and the following diseases of a mature shaman can be manifestations and relapses of the same shamanic disease, which can be healed by means of searching for and returning *niokta*. Directions of actions during healing the ordinary person and the shaman are opposite (moving a soul into the spirits' dwelling in the first case and inserting spirits into the body in the second one), but despite this fact the essence of healing is the same. It consists in drawing the person nearer to the spirits. In this respect any successful healing shamanic ceremony opens a person to spirits and resembles shamanic mini-initiation.

At the same time the healing of an ordinary person differs from initiation with less radicalism. Shamanic initiation decisively brings a person nearer spirits, which results in radical transformation of his or her mental world. It represents the final and crucial renovation, which does not leave the neophyte any possibility to shift his or her ground. On the contrary, the ordinary person's convergence with the spirits, who received shamanic treatment, can only be a temporary compromise. Even after that deed he preserves the opportunity to avoid intimacy with the spirits and to keep from further contacts with them.

When the steps towards opening to the spirits are exhausted

It is important to emphasise that recovering can be reached only in the case of a person paying for it by new steps on approaching the spiritual world. If he or she has been already staying in certain contact with spirits, but does not undertake any further steps, the means of healing that recently seemed to be reliable stop helping.

> Sometimes I weep and cry (shamanising), but a person, who came to me (to be healed) feels release only for one or two days and not longer. However powerful the shaman is, can the patient be saved from death? Even if you yourself became a shaman, would you not die, when your time came? If you became a superior, would you be saved from death? [...] Could (a shaman) Gara Kisovna say that nobody died of those whose souls she searched for? Despite the fact that she treated them, people later died. She herself also died. How can a person dying be kept? There is no use in shamanising, and my shamanising is also for nothing. [...] Why do shamans die? Nobody revives after death. They took (shaman) Mingo before her death to Troitskoe (hospital) and to Naichin, but all the same she died. If a shaman saves people, why does he die himself? [...] Why did Mingo not recover? She was singing in the shamanic way for months. (Lingdze)

In that moment the methods of healing, which recently helped, stop helping both shamans and ordinary people. Earlier it was only important to follow your dreams, make spirits' images at the right time and sacrifice to those images. But then, as Lingdze complains, 'no matter how many images you made, you could fill the entire barn and entire yard with those images, but if the time to die came, you would never survive!' Earlier it was enough to bring the patient's soul into the reliable 'prison' *dëkaso*, and not to forget to sacrifice in order to be sure that you would not be sick till your death. But in the moment the shaman learns that the patient's soul is not able to sit in *dëkaso* anymore, those spirits which guarded it, for some reason disenthrall it in spite of regular sacrifices. Worrying about her daughter Ella Ivanovna's health, Mariia Vasil'evna took Ella Ivanovna to different shamans, to Lingdze, to Mingo. They placed Ella Ivanovna's soul into *dëkaso*. But each time soon after the treatment Ella Ivanovna's soul left *dëkaso*.

> (Spirits) take her away. Despite the fact that she (shaman) located her *panian* into *dëkaso*, in spite of the fact that she closed everything and instructed the spirit grandma to keep (Ella Ivanovna's soul) in that *dëkaso*, all the same, soon they took it (her soul) away from there and the disease returned. Is it not interesting? She (shaman) had locked her *dëkaso,* but nevertheless they took it away! [...] Spirits quickly took it away, probably because they wanted to crush her! (Mariia Vasil'evna)

One of Mariia Vasil'evna's versions is that the shamanic spirit-guard does not manage with its duties anymore.

> If it managed, it would not let them (souls) go out. Shaman taught (her spirit-guards): 'Keep them, feed well, nurse!' But she (spirit-guard) does not manage. [...] It does not matter how the shamans do it, all the same, (souls) escape from *dëkaso*, and a patient falls sick again. *Amban* (evil spirits) take it (the patient's soul) away. They want to kill (the patient)! (Mariia Vasil'evna)

Answering my question concerning the reasons why souls leave *dëkaso,* Vera Chubovna said: 'Is it good to be imprisoned? Surely they (souls) try to escape!' Nikolai Petrovich, reasoning about spirits' inconsistent behaviour (first, they guard souls and then they let them go) said: 'For spirits it is probably such fun!'

When the previous methods do not help anymore, shamanists resolve for additional steps in moving further into the spiritual world, in getting in contact with senior spirits and in 'opening' wider to the spiritual world. Shamans are not able to give orders to the spirits, which have a higher position than the guarders of *dëkaso*; they can only beg and implore them. Chapaka Danilovna said that her daughter Liliia had been sick since she was born. 'For ten days she is well and then sick again. After shaman Ildenge treats her, she is well no longer than a month, and then again

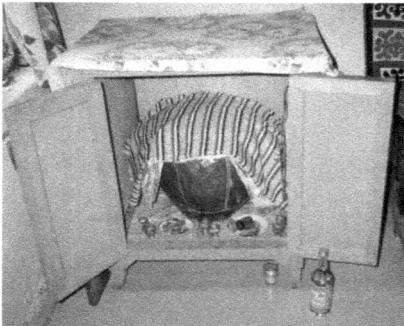

FIGURE 5: Offering to *saola,* a clay vessel in which, according to the belief, the spirits of a dead shaman live.

she falls sick. He could not cure her in any way'. Being tired of uselessly repeating the same ceremonies, by this time Ildenge brought the soul of his little patient not to *dëkaso*, but to a special large earthenware pot *saola,* where was placed, as it was believed, the most powerful spirit *Sagdi ama* (old father). When Ildenge was bringing Chapaka Danilovna's daughter's soul there during the ceremony, she, as Chapaka Danilovna recollects, began to go out of her mind. Liliia was two years and six months old at that time, but two adults could hardly manage to keep her.

Who would ever have expected such strength in that little child?' The shaman's wife could not bear that any longer and began to cry to her husband: 'Why do you do it that this little child goes out of her mind?' – 'Let her go out of her mind! Let her know how to go out of her mind!' (Chapaka Danilovna)

But after the shaman's spirits reached the village, where *saola* was kept, opened the pot and threw Liliia's soul there, the girl raged, suddenly fell on her back and dropped off to sleep. She was sleeping the entire next day and since then she stopped being sick. Her mother said: 'She did not cry, did not go outdoors. No diseases touched her! There was never either influenza or anything else!' Chapaka Danilovna explained that as the shaman gave Liliia's soul to the senior spirit, it became inaccessible to those ones, which took it from *dëkaso*, and that is why Liliia did not fall ill for several years.

Despite the high efficiency of such treatment, it is not popular among the shamanists and is only used in extreme cases. Its danger consists of high risk that against the background of complete health at any moment the person healed that way can suddenly get grave disease and perish. Well-informed people told Chapaka Danilovna that she must not keep her daughter's soul in such a place for long. So later Chapaka Danilovna asked the shaman to perform another ritual and to take her daughter's soul away from *saola*. She said: 'Liliia could fall gravely ill and there would not be any means to save her, if her soul would stay longer in that *saola*. That is why I asked (Ildenge) to take her soul out of it'.

Despite the fact that Liliia's soul is not in *saola* anymore, deep intimacy with those powerful spirits, which she had earlier, resulted in her getting unusual abilities, visions and hallucinations. Even after she became an adult, Liliia, as her mother says, 'knows and sees everything, and she is not afraid of what she sees'. Irina Torokovna, Liliia's neighbour, relates that once Liliia went to visit her sister. She did not know that her sister was not at home and that the house was locked. According to Irina Torokovna's words, Liliia herself told the story this way.

I knocked and knocked at the door, but no one opened it. Probably there was no one at home? I went to the window to knock on it. She approached the window; someone raised the curtain and there was a woman behind the window looking at me, she said. I thought, she said, that there were probably some guests there, and was still surprised why they did not open the door. I thought that way and was not scared. Later I asked my sister: 'Who was at your place?' – 'There was not anyone! The house was locked!' Another time she went out at night to empty the bucket. It was dark, no moon. As soon as I opened the wicket gate, she said, I saw a man standing there; he was big like a giant. I could not see his face, only his body! I felt displeased'. All the same she quickly emptied her bucket and ran into the house, it gave her the creeps. (Irina Torombovna)

There are lots of similar stories about Liliia. Her ability to see spirits is a consequence and price of her recovering.

Disease as a coercion to converge to spirits

According to shamanists' opinion, the more a person undergoes a cure, the more he or she is drawn to spirits. Diseases are considered to be a means used by spirits in order to establish contact with people and in that way to force them to worship and sacrifice. Sending disease, spirits attract a person with temporal release from the disease and then, alternating relief and exacerbation, they subordinate the person more and more, and that person in turn is more and more 'opened' to spirits. One can conclude that healing is the final aim only for the patient, for the spirits healing is merely a way of 'opening', attracting and collecting people's souls.

Not only usual diseases, but also shamanic ones are a means of involving people in worship. In those rare cases, when someone accepts a shamanic call readily and at once, he or she does not suffer from shamanic disease.[45] A neophyte falls sick in case he or she either resists his call or is not able to cope with spirits. 'He falls ill because he does not want to become a shaman' (Nikolai Petrovich). 'It does not matter whether you want it or not! They will force you! I permanently had a headache and my entire body hurt. Everything hurt as if it were an influenza. I was sick for a long time, for almost three years. Then I decided, all right! And I began dancing in the shamanic way' (Niura Sergeevna). As in the case of ordinary disease, a shamanic one can be healed by means of contact with spirits and agreement to obey them. Otherwise if a neophyte does not pay attention to his or her disease and does not try to get in touch with spirits, as Nesulta Borisovna said, 'the spirit, which had selected that person as a future shaman, can get angry and kill him or her. If you are not going to obey, the spirit will kill you. The spirit starts harming and kicking you about'. Treatment of shamanic disease consists in taming spirits which bother him or her and forming future relationships.

By the end of life the utilitarian urge for health sinks into the background for a shaman. The shaman has been open to spirits to such an extent, that contrary to logic, the only craving that remains is thirst for *seven* as such. Nikolai Petrovich told me about the competition between him and two of his sisters for the ability to own a spirit inherited from their departed mother-shaman. He complained that his sister Toë Petrovna lured that *seven* by the inadmissible means of sacrifice blood. 'After that spirit tastes blood in Toë's place, it will stay with her forever and will turn into an evil spirit'. I ask Nikolai Petrovich whether that spirit will serve Toë, and he answers: 'It will not serve her! It will try to lead her faster to death'. I was surprised at why then she lured it. 'Because of her old age, other spirits, strong spirits are leaving her', and she thinks: 'Let me have at least that one! I would better become *amban* (malevolent spirit) myself and will be able to harm you!'

---

45   My informants could remember only one Nanai shaman-volunteer, Chongida Onenko.

Multiplicity of initiations

Repeated shamanic treatment sometimes brings an ordinary person so near the spiritual world that he or she obtains some abilities similar to shamanic ones. Vladimir G. Bogoraz and another researcher mentioned that among the indigenous peoples of the North-East of Russia practically everyone is a shaman to a certain degree. There is no similar information published about Nanai and other Manchu-Tungusic peoples. Probably it can be explained by the presence of especially powerful shamans among Manchu-Tungusic peoples that is by the availability of such persons who were a cut above the rest of the population in their right to call themselves shamans. Meanwhile, as my field material shows, and as was already mentioned, the Nanai also consider that almost all the ordinary people, non-shamans, are possessed of capabilities similar to shamanic ones. They assure that earlier, when the traditional setup was still preserved, each Nanai could shamanise a bit, while not being a real shaman and not being able to accomplish public service. The ability of persons, 'who could shamanise a bit' was limited to the capacity to heal only themselves. Ol'ga Egorovna said: 'Earlier there were very few ordinary people here. All were shamans! But most of them could only treat themselves and no one else'.

FIGURE 6: The cap of Mariia Innokent'evna Tymali, although not a shaman herself, shows images of her personal spirits.

Almost every non-shaman, in the issue of being shamanic patients, had images of personal spirits *seven* and regularly sacrificed to them. A lot of ordinary persons (or, as some informants assure, each adult Nanai) had spirit-cohabitants, which they met in their night dreams. That especially concerns the Nanai clan Zaksor, which has a reputation for inclination of all its members to shamanising. The members of that clan are believed to have such powerful shamanic-like abilities that they do not need to go through the initiating ritual to become shamans.

In spite of the border between shamans and ordinary shamanists being quite sharp,[46] the gradation of different conditions concerning human/spiritual relationships is complicated and varied. Astride that border there are grade levels which correspond to the different conditions, which indicate to what extent an ordinary person is close to spirits and to what degree a shaman possesses more and more powerful spirits. In some cases even a person who has passed through shamanic initiation is not able to become a shaman. Ol'ga Egorovna's father was paralysed for three years and that disease was considered to be a shamanic one. When they were initiating him into shamanism, and when the shaman and other people who were present danced in shamanic way, they gave a drum to Ol'ga Egorovna's father. He got up, 'grasped the drum and started running around! He was paralysed, but began running! [...] For three years his arms did not move, his legs did not move'. Next day he recovered and began working in the collective farm. But he flatly refused to shamanise. He gave his drum and other shamanic paraphernalia to the clubhouse. According to the materials of Matvei Khangalov, pretty often Buriats also perform the ritual of shamanic initiation, but do not start practicing as shamans. Khangalov explains it in the following way.

> If a Buriat, who descends from shamanic lineage, and does not intend to become a shaman, suddenly falls sick, he usually applies to a shaman with a request to practice some sorcery. But the shaman explains to him that, as he belongs to a shamanic lineage, he should perform a ritual of 'washing the body' (a shamanic initiation) and then he will recover. Perforce they accomplish that simplest ritual of washing the body, but after recovering he does not become a shaman and remains an ordinary Buriat. (Khangalov 2004: 131)

As opposed to the case of a person not becoming a shaman after initiation, one can make examples of the cases, when, on the contrary, the ordinary person gets some shamanic abilities with no initiation. Sometimes an ordinary person can visit in his or her dreams spiritual territories and even act like a shaman there. Thus we can tell of an intermediate state, which can be either completed or not completed in the forming of a new shaman.

Shamanic initiation decidedly brings a person closer to the spiritual world and considerably changes his or her social status. But even initiation is not a final stage in forming a shaman. Closeness to spirits continues to gradually increase during the years of shamanic praxis. For years the shaman gains more and more spirits, including those which change his or her opportunities dramatically. Shamanic dis-

---

46 What distinguished the shaman and constituted his being 'unusual', were certain extraordinary capacities, qualities, and abilities (Heyne 1999: 391).

ease is not only an episode in the very beginning of a shamanic career; it remains in remission and can become aggravated. In the process of obtaining some new spirit, shamanic disease can return and in order to cope with it, a shaman needs a new mini-initiation. The scholars have already attended several shamanic initiations (Kister 1999; Khangalov 2004). But, as I know, nobody wrote about the multiplicity of shamanic initiations among Manchu-Tungusic peoples. Probably it can be explained by the fact that, for example, in Buriat and in Korean tradition, each shamanic initiation has its own name, which makes their multiplicity noticeable. But Manchu-Tungus do not have such names, although they actually also experience several initiations. The number of such initiations varies. Among the Buriat, each initiation is accompanied by rituals in which the community participates. Mätyäs Balosh (2007: 91) writes that Buriat shamans can be initiated 12 plus one times during their lives. According to Matvei Khangalov's (2004: 128) data, to become a powerful shaman, one had to pass nine grades, one after another, nine body washings, that is, nine rituals of initiation. 'Those Buriats, who descended from shamanic lineage and who were gifted enough [...] reached the highest position *galši*, [...] but those who were weaker and did not have any special vocation, remained on the second or third level, in the lower positions'.

Each initiation was provoked by the fact that some new spirits got into contact with a shaman and the necessity appeared to tame and possess them. 'Having more initiations confers more magical power. Stronger shamans meet stronger spirits, and they can be attacked by stronger malevolent spirits as well. With each initiation their paraphernalia becomes more and more sophisticated in order to give them more protection' (Balosh 2004: 91). Shamans experience dissection of their body, which is famous due to the Yakut materials collected by G. Ksenofontov (1992), not only during their first initiation. The Nanai shaman Lingdze experienced it several times. She told me that her spirits 'murdered' her when she was starting shamanising.

> They dressed my body, cut off my legs and arms, they cut everything off, then they boiled (my body), there steam was rising, this way they did it. Crying I was sitting near my body. I was sitting near myself murdered and crying. For a long time I cried or did something else. Then I started singing in the shamanic way. My body began to stink. (Lingdze)

Later, when she was already a practitioner, the dissection was repeated several times. Here is her description of one of her later experiences.

> I dreamt that I died and they were dissecting my legs. They threw me onto the stove and dissected my legs. My legs hurt to such an extent that I could not walk. There were red marks left (on my legs), because they cut them. (Lingdze)

If a shaman met new spirits but missed performing the rituals for them (that is in fact missing the next initiation), his or her disease is aggravated. Lingdze missed several such small initiations and her disease has gone too far.

> I live with suffering. In the morning I cannot even make a fist! What is it with me? While I hang about, it is all right, but after I have sat, it becomes ouch! [...] My bones, head, legs, everything hurt. Today I am better. Three days ago I got up, but before I could not be planted on my feet and I could not get up. [...] One problem stops, but another begins. How is that? (Lingdze)

Using buzz words, Nanai neo-shamans interpret healing-opening in the context of building contact between people and 'cosmic energies'. They insist that people must become more and more open and accessible to those energies. Shamans' urgent need to heal people is actually their need to open to spirits as many people as possible.

Shamans practice not only because of their altruistic wish to help (their earnings are usually incommensurably lower than their work performed), but because their spirits do not let them stop. It is spirits which force a shaman to heal:

> 'Come on, work! Save people! Do something, do not sit around!' If you do not want to work, your spirits will punish you. All shaman's spirits, his entire team is sitting idle! They are sitting, but they are supposed to work! They are supposed to eat! If you do not feed your spirits (do not sacrifice to them), they will kill you. They start gnawing you. 'You yourself make me gnaw you! You do not want to feed me!' (Ol'ga Egorovna)

Nanai neo-shamans have similar problems. Their need to heal is so inevitable that in the case of the patients' lack they try to heal (to open) people secretly, against their will. One neo-shaman confessed to me that 'if her acquaintance does not want her to heal, she herself without being noticed comes and – whoops! – does something to her!'

Trying to explain why the necessity to heal and to open patients is so urgent and immediate, neo-shaman M. told me that it is important for her to manage to open her patients before they die. She says: 'You do not know that gods do not permit (people) to go there (to the world beyond) if they have not been opened. I must open him!' She says about those people who died before she had the opportunity to heal and open them, who left with closed *chakras*: 'I feel strong offence and bear a grudge against them, because they left being unopened; they were not able to open themselves'. M.'s patients are convinced that the call for people to get to be opened was issued not from the shaman, but mostly from his or her spirits. One of them relates one of M'. ceremonies:

I am not silly, I understood that it was not she herself speaking, that there were (other creatures) who were speaking through her mouth. [...] She took a drum and started talking. [...] How interesting it was! Let be our nature, ecology, everything! And that it is really urgent to open more and more people, to open those who could become shamans. She was talking that way, [...] she was talking with her drum. Not on her own! (Ella Ivanovna)

Using the same term 'to open' both for naming shamanic initiation and for curing indicates the fact that being treated by a shaman to some degree means being initiated. Indeed, a salient feature of any initiation is some experience, which leads to the modification of the religious and social status of a patient, changing his or her position regarding both spirits and people. Shamanic initiation leads to establishing close ties with spirits and gives the ability of new social activity. But the mini-initiation received in the process of healing gives an ordinary person a similar experience, though a much less spiritual one. Recovery leads to change of religious status: the former shaman's patient becomes involved in the ritual praxis (he or she must regularly sacrifice), his dreams are changed and in some cases he or she even gets visions. To some extent social status is also changed. After being healed the patient turns out to be a member of a certain shamanic congregation, and his participation in certain rituals becomes his or her duty, which becomes an addition to the patient's usual religious duties regarding his or her own clan. But as shamanic treatment opens a patient to spirits and changes his life to a much smaller degree than shamanic initiation, it can be named merely 'mini-initiation' as it is only a minimal step towards opening to the spiritual world.

WHICH SHAMAN IS BETTER

> That is interesting that one shaman always stigmatises another shaman
> and says that he himself is better, but another one is evil.
> I have heard it since I was a girl:
> 'Why do you consult that shaman? He is bad!
> That one is so-and-so and another one is also so-and-so!'
> None of them gave praise to their colleagues.
> They never spoke of the others with praise.
> *(Larisa Ganzulievna)*

> Why do shamans compete?
> There is such a *seven* (spirit) at work. It forces them to fight!
> *(Ivan Torokovich)*

Rumours which form shamanic hierarchy

The complicated and elaborate traditional classification of Nanai shamans is based only partially on formal titles, which are arranged according to a shaman's specialisation (shaman-healers, shamans who deal with the souls of the dead, and so on), and which are legitimised in certain rituals. Shamans also have other titles that are changeable and depend on public appraisal of shamanic power (strong and weak shamans). Belonging to a certain rank does not give shamans any tangible social or financial benefits. Payment for their treatment is small, almost token. Shamans are not only socially recognised, but also feared. But the advantage of belonging to the highest levels in the shamanic hierarchy goes beyond observable economic and social rewards. It gives them the privilege of being more popular and of collecting a larger quantity of clients than their rivals, other shamans. The more patients a shaman heals, the better he or she feels. As the shamans themselves explain, if they do not practice enough, their spirit-helpers 'stay hungry and start eating their own masters', as if to force them to cover a wider number of people in their healing practice. Another situation in which shamans are pressured to get a larger number of clients is shamanic spiritual 'warfare'. The more clients a shaman heals, the more clients' souls she or he may collect in her or his personal spiritual 'depository'. After healing clients, a shaman receives a certain power over those souls and can use them as a resource in spiritual battles. The larger the number of souls the shaman has collected, the more chances he or she has to conquer rivals (alien shamans) and to win.

   Some of the criteria that help people to evaluate a shaman's power are objective: they are the shaman's previous successes in healing and also her or his ability to demonstrate miracles (to make their spirits visible, to stab themselves without harm, to move things at a distance). Shamans themselves feel that they rise to the higher levels of hierarchy by virtue of gaining additional spirit-helpers, which gives them some extra abilities. But the social component of their success and building their popularity is also of high importance to them. They never keep their achievements secret, but try to make them noticed and appreciated by the public. Those shamans' triumphs add support to the main criterion of their power evaluation, which is subjective, namely common talk and rumours about 'little' and 'big' shamans. As this criterion is unreliable, unpredictable, and changeable, it is also not measurable, and the Nanai do not link it to the special rituals. Rumours and common talk about shamans' power are important means of forming public opinion concerning the shamanic hierarchy, which deals with the very core of determining shamans' relative status within a society. The different subjects of that emic discourse about shamans' merits and defects (shamans' clients and the shamans themselves) have different, often conflicting aims; most of the talk is typically biased and contradictory, and it makes the formation of a definitive public attitude toward shamans also conflicting and complicated.

The reason why shamanists' judgments about shamans are so subjective is probably that speakers usually depend upon the shamans about whom they are speaking. Speakers realise their words can influence their relationships with shamans, and as a result they try to influence those relationships in the direction they need. The truth of the speakers' utterance is not what is important to them, and neither is the coincidence of their message with real facts. What is important is the effect this statement will produce on their listeners. Therefore, in the emic discourse about shamans' qualities, the communicative situation influences the content of the statements to the highest degree. In each communicative situation, who exactly is speaking, who the listeners are, and the purpose of the message are all facts of special importance.

When speaking about the virtues and shortcomings of different shamans, the same person can have different and even contradictory opinions when addressing different audiences. If, for example, a shaman speaks about himself to potential patients, he praises his own merits. But if he speaks about himself to his adversaries or to dangerous spirits, he either exaggerates his strength to frighten his potential enemy or, on the contrary, he hides his real qualities and pretends to be weak and feeble in order to provoke his adversary into taking hasty and incorrect actions.

Lay shamanists are very interested in discussions about shamans because they are in need of information to help them choose a proper shaman in case of need. Shamans are also attracted to such conversations because they see themselves as the most appropriate source of information about their colleagues; in addition, they participate in those debates to influence their clients' opinions. In my fieldwork among Nanai shamanists, I did not plan to research emic discourse about shamans' qualities, but as that discourse was extremely popular, I collected information on this subject in the process of investigating other topics.

Besides interpreting shamans' qualities in conversations about both their useful and harmful abilities, the bearers of Nanai tradition 'measure' the power of shamans and use these evaluations to rank them. To rank shamans according to their power is not a feature unique to Nanai shamanism. Åke Hultkrantz (2004: 152) describes how other Arctic peoples 'prefer to grade their shamans according to their powers rather than their functions. The Samoyed thus classify their shamans in strong, wonder-working shamans, medium shamans and small shamans; a fourth category are the dream-readers and soothsayers'.

According to Bäckman and Hultkrantz (1978: 63–64) Yakut shamans are divided into three groups: The great shaman – *ulahan-oiun*, the middling shaman – *orto-oiun*, and the little shaman – *kenniki-oiun*. The Enets, a Samoyed group, placed their shamans in different grades and used names which announced their status: shamans of the first class (the greatest) were called *budtode*, the second class, *dyano* and the third, *savode*. In the Nanai tradition there is even a special terminology that makes it possible to measure shamans' power. The powerful shamans are called *dai saman* (big shamans), and weak ones are *nuchi saman* (little shamans). Scholars usually considered the folk classification of shamans, based on the measurement of their power, as an inconsequential expression of personal attitude toward shamans, and unfortunately they have shelved discussion of this topic. Even Anna V. Smoliak, one of the most competent researchers of Nanai shamanism, did not address this ranking of shamans' powers. In her influential book *Shaman: Personhood, Worldview, and Functions* (1991), Smoliak pointed to the four categories of Nanai shamans. They are *mepi saman*, the shamans who are able to treat only themselves; *taochiko saman*, the shamans who heal others; *khergenti saman*, the ones who are able to perform funeral repasts; and *kasatai saman*, who send the souls of the deceased to the beyond (Smoliak 1991: 51). Eight years after Smoliak's publication, Ol'ga A. Bel'dy suggested her own variant; she repeated some of the categories from Smoliak's classification, but she also included *dai* shamans, who have a strong magical impact on humans and on the *seven* 'executors'; and the *nuchi* 'ordinary, beginner, simple shamans' (Bel'dy 1999). Unfortunately, she limited herself to those few words and did not elucidate on emic evaluations of shamanic power.

In the emic discourse, there is usually a greater degree of consensus on shamans' power or weakness than there is concerning their good or evil nature. Most people usually agree on which of the shamans are 'big' and which are 'little'. At the same time, people consider shamans' power to change through different periods of their lives; they can both increase and lose their strength over time. People always talk about shamans comparatively. When they approve of certain shamans, these statements usually go together with disapproval of other shamans. The following conversation is typical:

Speaker 1: Lingdze started shamanising long ago, she is a hereditary shaman. She knows more than Mingo. Mingo has been shamanising for much less time. What does she know?

Speaker 2: But all the same, Mingo does not want to be lower than Lingdze! All the same, people think that she is lower than Lingdze, that she is a weak shaman. Nikolai Petrovich said about her: 'I think that she (Mingo) is not a very powerful shaman. But concerning Mariia Petrovna, one can say that she is a real shaman! Regarding Toë Petrovna, one can say that Toë Petrovna does not have much shamanic power, everything that she has is just trickery'. Nikolai Petrovich also blamed Lingdze, he said that all her shamanic stuff is merely deception.

This is not an unbiased statement; other people have quite different assessments of those shamans' capabilities. In order to have grounds to compare shamans, people demand that shamans perform public miracles as evidence of their shamanic power. For example, a shaman who wished to become a *kasatai saman* (one who can send deceased people to the beyond), was expected to vomit a bronze disk *toli* before the eyes of the public. 'If you are such a shaman, prove it!' Mariia Vasil'evna said. 'Show us that *toli* can come out of your mouth!'

The classification of 'big' and 'little' shamans does not imply that there are only two big groups of shamans with a well-defined boundary between them. On the contrary, there are many intermediate positions, although they are uncertain and are not defined with special Nanai terms. Some Nanai compare the hierarchy of shamans with a military hierarchy. Mariia Vasil'evna says:

Servicemen have a soldier, an officer, a colonel. Shamans have the same differentiation. At first the one is an ordinary shaman [...] but with the passage of time [...].

Ol'ga Egorovna continues:

With the passage of time, he becomes a big shaman; he turns into a 'god' (a spirit-man). The little shaman would never become a god! Not every shaman can grow to be a god. There are a lot of jobs for a shaman. There are both hard jobs and easy ones. A shaman must work and conquer everything. [...] If you win, it will be good for you. You have been working and working and at last you have nevertheless won it! You have risen higher. Probably you are already a lieutenant or a sergeant! Higher and higher!

Shamans assert that they are all classified into ranks and categories in the invisible spiritual world and that no two shamans are equal. Shamans say that in the spiritual world there is a shamanic tree (see FIGURE 7, 8) which all shamans can see when they shamanise. Having assumed the aspect of birds, they perch on the tree's branches to look around at their familiar companions, the other bird-shamans, who are also perched on the same tree. On that tree the shamans can find out which of them are currently stronger or weaker. The weaker shamans alight into the lower branches of the tree, but the more powerful shamans are able to reach the higher branches. 'A lot of shamans alight into the shamanic tree', Nikolai Petrovich told me, 'Some of them perch lower. Those little, small shamans alight on the lower branches. The middling shamans alight higher. And higher and higher, there are those who are the biggest shamans, who are really big and more acknowledged'.

Some of the successful shamans perched on the higher branches are not able to resist the temptation to express their scorn toward shamans who are perched lower. Ivan Torokovich condemned one shaman-woman:

She told us that she perched high and that from her high branch, she dropped her excrement onto those who were lower [...]. She considers herself to be

FIGURE 7: Zinaida Nikolaevna Bel'dy is demonstrating the image of a clan tree on the bride's dress.

FIGURE 8: Coat-tail of another bride's dress with the representation of the clan tree.

better and higher than the other shamans, because she could alight higher, not lower. She explained it to us that way. She perches there and drops her excrements onto the rest of the shamans! (Ivan Torokovich)

According to Chapaka Danilovna, one shaman woman told her that when shamanising she perched on the shamanic tree higher than the famous shaman-man from the Dada village. The next day, when they were awake, that shaman from the Dada village visited her. He told her, 'You are a woman, you should be more modest! Why did you alight higher than me?' Shaman answered, 'But what about *boa ibakhani* (a mythical bird)? Where does it fly?' Chapaka Danilovna narrated this story with a bit of deprecation, as she felt that that shaman overestimated herself by affirming that she was a mythical bird.

Despite the belief that in the spiritual world there exists a tree which, it seems, could resolve all doubts concerning shamans' relative power, information about exactly which branch was reached by this or that shaman and who exactly was higher was sometimes inconsistent, and public opinion about shamans' power was always changeable. That fickleness, which grows sharper, is the result of the endless contradictory gossip and discussion about shamans. We are not able to understand the reasons why shaman-birds are placed in the shamanic tree in this or that way, but we can try to analyse one of the most decisive factors that can influence the content of emic discourse on shamans' qualities. Those factors are the communicative situation and the roles of its participants, both speakers and listeners.

Shamans talking about themselves to non-shamans

The content of shamans' utterances about themselves depends on whom they are addressed to. If a shaman speaks to uninitiated shamanists or to scholars, she or he is inclined to praise her or his own power and pre-eminence over the rest of the shamans. Among my numerous recordings, I could not find even one self-condemnation addressed to such an audience. Shaman-woman Mingo boasted of her ability to fly in her dreams: 'What do you think? I flew (in my dreams) like a pilot! No Russian is able to win such a victory (over spirits that give ability to fly in dreams)!' Mingo also bragged that she predicted when the Second World War would end. After that Andrei believed in me. He said: 'You are a real shaman!'

Another shaman-woman, Kada, said about herself:

I am *tudin* (a clairvoyant), I know everything! I know when the hunters return from the taiga. Who will die soon, I know! I knew beforehand about Valia! I knew when they were going to bring her corpse here. She died in Troitskoe village, and I told Galia, 'Galia, today they are going to bring here someone's bones'. Valia died! When I visited Valia, she was still well. But on the very same day in the afternoon, they brought her dead body. (Kada)

Shamans also praise their own ability to sing and dance like no one else. 'During the war, when I shamanised, lots of people came to listen to my voice', Mingo says. 'If it is necessary to sing in shamanic way, I can sing! If it is necessary to dance in shamanic way, I can dance!' Shamans like to retell flattery from their patients concerning their shamanic skills. Toë Petrovna repeated the words of the people who listened to her shamanic ritual: 'They told me, "This old woman shamanised that way!" Oh! It made us feel creepy all over!'

From an emic perspective, the ability to sing and dance in a shamanic way is given by the spirit-helpers. Thus most of shamans' boasting expresses not only their satisfaction with themselves, but also their pleasure in their authority over the powerful spirits. One of the abilities that contact with shamanic spirits gives is the capacity to see spirits. As this capacity is not given to all the shamans *pari passu*, it becomes a matter of competitiveness. Nikolai Petrovich is not a shaman, but having inherited some shamanic spirits from his mother, he boasted of his ability to see spirits:

I saw a lot of them. I knew a lot, when they shamanised, and I could even give a hint to a shaman about anything. Once I was lying in my room, but they were shamanising over there (in another room) [...] The old man shaman was dancing, dancing there. He began to gather all the *amban* (evil spirits) together into one cart. He was gathering them and gathering. Then I saw from my room that the main one was left and something else was left with it. I felt it! Even in my eyes it became like that, as though it had remained under the bed. That bed was in another room behind the wall! How could I? You know, I cannot see through the walls! But that time I saw that creature lying over there. It hid. And with it [...] it also kept a baddie under itself. I shouted from here, 'The main being has been left!' But he (the shaman) did not pay any attention. It was useless to tell him! He just knew his own stuff! He was already driving it away (the cart with the spirits collected). Well, I thought, all the same you would have to be back, there's nothing you could do! He drove away.³ I do not know how long he was driving, but then he stopped. '*Khekhei!* I left the main one!' An old woman and another old woman told him, 'Nikolai Petrovich told you about that long ago, when you were still gathering them (those spirits) into your cart; he said that you had left the main one'. [...] (The shaman) left part of his *seven* to guard (the spirits that were caught), and took some of the most powerful ones back. He returned and grasped that one (from under the bed). 'Now all of you are in my hands!' Then before he left he said, 'Ask that one who saw if something else is left'. – 'Yes, there is something else!' I said. 'It is at the same place, under the bed, but in the very corner! A

black creature!' He returned, took that one and left [...]. Such a devil I was!
(Nikolai Petrovich)

Another quality often praised by shamans is their fearlessness in the face of evil spirits. Nikolai Petrovich's words about his own bravery are also rather typical of shamans.

I am not frightened, neither by *chert* (the devil), nor by *podia* (the spirit of fire), by nothing! [...] Try to understand me, since I was a boy I was afraid neither of darkness nor of anything else! It was all the same for me! The people got together to drive *amban* (the evil spirits) away. The people were driving the spirits from one place to another, but I needed to go out. When they drive away *amban*, no one is supposed to go out from that place. But for me it was easy! Just as you like! Drive the *amban* as much as you want! But I am going out! I went out and returned back. For me it was worthless! My mother also knew that [...] 'That person', she said about me, 'he is not frightened of anything!'

If shamans or visionaries attend a ceremony performed by other shamans, they rarely resist the temptation to demonstrate their better (as they usually think) abilities, as compared with those of the shamans performing the ceremony. Intervening in this way is an opportunity to praise their own endowments. Vera Chubovna consulted one shaman-woman about her sick sister, but she did not like the way that person shamanised. She said:

You know, when she was shamanising, I was so impatient! I nearly grasped her drum away from her! I would have done it better myself! [...] I was sitting like that and trembling! That is how I was trembling! Why, I thought [...] I should not have trembled, if you had been doing it right! (Vera Chubovna)

Vera Chubovna's emotions were so strong that the woman performing the shamanic ritual could not continue and stopped. She complained that barriers and obstacles appeared on all her spiritual roads and she was not able to struggle forward. Vera Chubovna asserted that it was she who made those obstacles.

Rival shamans sometimes meddle in the ceremony and afterward tell people that their actions were (or would have been) more successful than the actions of the shaman who was performing. That opposition becomes a kind of self-advertisement to impress people with the rival shaman's authority and increase the number of his or her clients. Several times shaman Kada told me about how in her youth, when another shaman was performing, she was the first who could tell that the patient present in the same room had died. Despite the fact that she was not yet a shaman, she could prove her superiority over the two shamans at the ceremony. The ritual was performed for her uncle, and a shaman followed his *panian* (soul), which was supposed to leave his body. Such rituals are performed in the darkness, and nobody can watch the sick person. Suddenly Kada approached her uncle, touched his hand and his feet and ordered that the ritual be stopped because he had died. Several years after that case, she was still proud that it was she, and not the shaman performing the ceremony, who had first noticed the change in the condition of her uncle's soul. 'I told them', she said, 'turn on the light! That is interesting, why did not you learn that he is already dead?' She explained that 'the *panian* (soul) of the dead person becomes completely different', and that she learned about her uncle's death because she was the first to notice that change. She remembers with pride and satisfaction that after the ceremony, when they laid out the body of her deceased uncle, people said, 'There were two shamans here, but neither of them noticed that the patient had died. It was only Kada who understood it [...]. When she becomes an adult she will not be an ordinary person!'

Non-shamans about shamans

The content of uninitiated peoples' utterances about shamans also depends on whom they are addressing. If they speak directly to a shaman, they prefer to flatter them. From the person's point of view it is especially important to flatter the shaman if they hope to get some help from them. One woman who came to shaman Lingdze for a ritual told her, 'Those beings (spirits) want to put all my children into the ground, and crying I came here [...]. She (another shaman) is not able to perform either *epili* or *teuchi* (ceremonies) like you; you are the only one who can do it! All the elders know about that'.

        Uninitiated shamanists can criticise shamans only behind their back, and even this is extremely rare. One of the negative opinions about shamans I recorded concerned shaman Ol'ga Egorovna. A woman who consulted Ol'ga Egorovna considered that she did not perform, as she said, in a traditional way. This is unlikely to be correct, as Ol'ga Egorovna is a very old and popular shaman who hardly even speaks Russian. Nevertheless, in her agitated and incoherent story, the informant described Ol'ga Egorovna as follows: 'She is doing terrible things! [...] There was something mystical, almost contemporary (in her ritual)! It was like in the books! [...] My hair stood on end, and it sent shivers down my spine! [...] Don't dare to consult her! If you are fated to die, so die! Die like that! Why do you bring misfortune upon yourself and upon your children?' These kinds of utterances are very bold. Only shamans, if they feel their superiority over the other shamans, can criticise them. Non-shamans rarely dare to do it because it can be unsafe; shamans' spirits are believed to hear all the offensive words said against their master and to cruelly avenge them. 'If I am not guilty, but someone said anything bad about me', shaman Kada explains, 'I feel unwell at heart, and all the same something bad will happen to that person. If they say something bad about me, I will never say anything to them, but my heart bleeds about that. [...] How many people are around in this village, but no one says anything bad about me! They all praise me!'

Shamans unanimously say that someone who criticises a shaman inevitably will be punished by shamanic spirits. Thus Ivan Torokovich said, 'Nobody dares to criticise a shaman! They are scared, because (a shaman) can crush you!' His wife, the shaman Mingo, added:

Try to offend a shaman! You will see what will happen! [...] You must not ever offend a shaman! Never! Neither being drunk, nor being sober, must you not say a single bad word against a shaman! (You will beg me) on your knees! [...] Wait a bit! You will come (to me) to cry! (Mingo)

It is considered dangerous to express a negative attitude about shamans instead of praising them. First, even if a shaman knows nothing of the negative rumours, it is believed that the shaman's spirit-helpers will find out about it and will punish the unwary gossips even without their master's knowledge. 'Let us suppose that you criticise me', Nikolai Petrovich says, 'my *seven* [...] will certainly hear it. It will approach you and harm you [...] Not the shaman himself, but his *seven* will punish you'. In addition, some shamans have special spirit-informers that bring them the news and gossip and let them know who has said something bad about them behind their back. Shamans are believed to both stay at home and to invisibly visit those places where people criticise them, which is why they learn about each word uttered that could hurt their pride. Once, Niura and her husband Chinchika stayed at home. Chinchika said that shaman Mariia Petrovna had not been visiting them for some time, probably because she fancied she was a shaman. Niura asserted that Mariia Petrovna's spirit-helper, Armokii, retold the conversation to Mariia Petrovna:

'He said about you so and so!' Armokii said (to Mariia Petrovna): 'As a punishment I am not going to let him sleep tonight! I am going to wake him up all the time!' The next day Mariia Petrovna visited us and asked my husband, 'Uncle, why did you condemn me?' – 'No', he said, 'I did not condemn you. When did I condemn you? I just said that you fancy yourself that you are a shaman and that because of that you stopped visiting us'. – 'Well, could you sleep this night?' – 'No, I could not, it was as if someone pulled my feet all the time'. (Niura Fedorovna)

I asked Niura, 'Was it Armokii who pulled him?' She explained, 'Yes, it was Armokii who pulled his feet. It said, "I am not going to let him sleep". It was like that. Whoever criticised her (Mariia Petrovna), Armokii retold her everything'.

As it was believed that spirits could actively meddle in communication, negative utterances about shamans were very rare. Instead, communication favoured the formation of public opinion for the benefit of shamans. 'Everyone tries to play up to shamans', Chapaka Danilovna said. 'In general, you should not establish any contacts with shamans', contradicted Irina Torombovna, who listened to her. 'No, you can come in contact with shamans!' Chapaka Danilovna corrected, and Irina immediately agreed: 'In a hostile way you should not! In a friendly way you certainly can!' – 'That one who dares to blame shamans is going to be unwell!' Chapaka Danilovna continued:

> Even if (a shaman) is sleeping, how can we learn what is happening to him this moment? He is probably conversing with his *seven* in whispers, he is maybe doing this and that, and they (his spirits) are also doing something! They can have revenge upon us, and after that we will not even learn about where the misfortune came to us from. (Chapaka Danilovna)

The talk of shamanists about shamans does not usually reveal their true attitude. Not only do they flatter shamans speaking directly to them, but even in shamans' absence they exaggerate shamans' high points and try not to talk about their low points. They believe that even if the shaman is absent, his or her spirit can hear their words and either report to their master about critical opinions or punish too-truthful talkers.

Shamans talking about themselves to other shamans

Both people talking about shamans as if they were in their presence and the shamans themselves when they are addressing ordinary people (non-shamans) support the same legends about shamans' exaggerated positive qualities. The case is somewhat different when shamans speak about themselves to other shamans or about other shamans to someone else. When shamans address their colleagues, they are not self-laudatory but self-deprecating. They are as little concerned with unbiased self-certification as when they praise themselves in front of their patients. They usually inform other shamans that they are weak, fail to possess the needed shamanic abilities, and do not take advantage of the proper spirits' support. If shamans praise their spirits they might rouse the envy of their colleagues, who in turn might steal some of those spirit-helpers. Self-deprecation was therefore a means of defence against such robbery. The beginner shaman Alla Kisovna told another shaman-woman about her dreams and unusual abilities, which she later regretted:

Why did I say it to her? I opened my heart too much! They are able to steal it! Not they themselves, but their *seven* (spirit-helpers) can steal. Mikhail Pykevich told me, 'You see, I never tell anyone about myself!' He knows it! [...] He does not say anything about himself, but I am a fool, I tell everybody, and people can take everything away from me. I am losing and losing everything and that is why I am so sick! (Alla Kisovna)

Afraid that their spirits can be stolen by their more powerful colleagues, shamans try (at least for some time) not to disclose information concerning their spiritual experiences and abilities. I met several shamans who for a long time kept secret their ability to shamanise, even from close friends. Thus for several years I worked with the shaman Nesulta Borisovna, and for the entire time she did not say anything about her abilities to me or to her fellow villagers. 'She hid her shamanship, being careful not to pass it unwillingly to someone else', her neighbour told me. 'She thought that if I heard that she was shamanising, I could take her shamanship from her. That is why she kept it secret. She did not say anything about it, (she thought that) people would envy'.

Shamans' secretiveness is one of the means of their inter-shamanic competitive activity. For example, some shamans pretend to be weak in order to deceive their competitors and provoke them to take imprudent actions. Shamans say that when they meet each other in their dreams and visions, they can assume the aspect of a feeble, sick person or a weak animal. Shaman Ol'ga Egorovna says, 'Shamans are artful! You will never guess who of them is a big shaman! You are not going to guess it! He is walking as (assuming the aspect of) a decrepit doggie'. – 'Does he pretend to be weak?' I ask. She replies:

Yes! Artful! I am a fool, I went, saw (him) and what did I do? I either tread upon him, or struck him a blow or something else [...]. We are fools, I think, I am a hero! Let me try to crush him! That is why shamans get enemies [...]. The big shamans wander having assumed the aspect of a decrepit doggie. Another shaman sees that he is weak and it is possible to do anything with him. He tries, but that doggie abruptly attacks him. Only then does he realise that it was a big shaman. Shaman-enemies hide that way. (Ol'ga Egorovna)

Secretiveness and false demonstrations of weakness are shamans' means of defence; these techniques provoke others to get involved in conflicts that are not to their advantage.

Secretiveness and false allegations about supposed weakness are also typical when shamans address the spirits. In the beginning of their rituals shamans usually utter the following phrases:

You can't get any sense out of me. (Lingdze)

Wherever I go, I would not be able to do anything better but just to lose my way. (Lingdze)

Having started shamanising, I will shamanise. Having started telling lies, I will tell lies, I am going to talk just nonsense and rot. (Mingo)

Now having been seized by fear I will grasp and bite something. But whatever I will grasp, I would perish! (Lingdze)

Do shamans really question their power when they start their rituals? Do they actually consider themselves not to have strength enough to manage their job well? If it were so, it would contradict the boasting that the very same shamans perform in other communicative situations, especially when they are facing their relatives and clients. Shamans usually complain about their false weakness at the very beginning of their rituals, when all necessary spirits are already present but the ritual itself is ahead of them. They say false declarations are needed not only to mask them from possible enemies but because they actually feel fear as they face their spirit-helpers and start the ceremony. 'When I am frightened', shaman Lingdze confessed, 'I say to them that I am stupid and that what I am singing is only nonsense'.

Addressing their colleague-rivals, shamans are especially careful not to give any true information about their abilities and problems in order to disorient them and not make it easy for them to excel. Rivalry, competition, and even enmity with other shamans precludes the possibility of telling the truth.

Shamans about other shamans

Talking face-to-face, shamans usually avoid making judgmental statements about each other. But *in absentia* they often estimate each other's abilities. I succeeded only once in recording the cautious praise given by a shaman to her colleague. The shaman Niura Sergeevna said:

The main shaman is Ol'ga Egorovna. There is someone in Upper Nergen village who can manage a bit. How can you gather only those who are good? This is a secret matter! Ol'ga Egorovna knows everything, even about those people who live behind Khabarovsk. There is no one in Dzhuen village, but in Achan there are some who know, who are able. (Niura Sergeevna)

Aside from this, all the shamans' opinions of each other that I recorded were critical. The reasons for criticism were different. Sometimes they blamed colleagues because they were allegedly untalented and did not have enough shamanic power. 'They write in the newspaper that Kada is a big shaman. That is wrong!' said shaman Ol'ga Egorovna. Alla Kisovna suffers from shamanic disease, but shaman Lingdze said she has no proper shamanic abilities. Alla Kisovna's relatives reassure her, saying, 'You are probably more powerful than her. Your shamanship is stronger than hers and she envies you'. Alla Kisovna herself thinks about their relationship in the same way: 'Lingdze understood that I was stronger than her. She did not want me to become a shaman, because otherwise she would get a powerful competitor'.

If shamans attend another shaman's ritual, later on they usually criticise their colleague for taking the wrong actions and for their lack of knowledge. 'That shaman (Kada) was very interesting', Chapaka Danilovna said. 'She shamanised, but she did not have either *dëkaso* (storage for the clients' souls), or anything else. She brought the client (the client's soul) and threw it right in her yard. When I listened to her, I did not understand anything [...]. It was just funny!'

Another common point of criticism is the erroneous selection of spirit-helpers and the number of them. Thus Mingo, who listened to a recording of Lingdze's ritual, seemed to have heard the incongruous words '*Sinda mama*' (the old woman of the village Sinda) instead of the real expression '*Kinda mama*' (the fragment of an old woman). When guests arrived, Mingo began to laugh at this in their presence. She unjustly reproached Lingdze for allegedly having only four spirit-helpers, the absurd '*Sinda*' among them. Quite popular is the accusation that a rival shaman's spirit-helpers are evil and only capable of harm. Indeed, alien spirits possessed by another clan's shaman are always unsafe. For any shaman, her or his own spirit-helpers are *seven* (good) but foreign spirit-helpers are *amban* (bad). Lingdze is one of the most popular shamans. As she successfully treats many people, and I recorded mostly positive opinions about her helpfulness and skills. However Ol'ga Egorovna denounces her, saying her spirits are evil, which explains why when 'feeding' one of her *seven*, Lingdze chomps and drinks raw blood. Shamans often advise people not to consult other shamans, who they say have evil spirit-helpers. Ol'ga Egorovna told me the following about one of shamans: 'If you want to shamanise, do not go to her. She has a lot of *amban*. [...] She has three big spirit-balls and she shamanises with them'. It is interesting that other shamans impute the same fault to Ol'ga Egorovna. Evdokiia Chubovna says that in Ol'ga Egorovna's clan there are lots of *amban*: 'She does not have any honest *seven*, she has only harmful ones. It is good for her, but for people! [...] No!' – 'Is it bad for people who consult her?' I ask. 'Right', she replied. 'There is nothing good for them! But she herself is a nice woman!'

Shamans' accusations are usually mutual. Mariia Petrovna's widower tells about his departed wife:

> She considered a lot of people to be fools. In any event she felt that she was stronger than both (shamans) Toë Petrovna and Nikolai Petrovich. She always

laughed at him (Nikolai Petrovich) and especially at that one (Toë Petrovna). 'Why does she (Toë Petrovna) take a drum? [...] What exactly does she take a drum for? She must not take it!' [...] In her selection of people, in communication, she was very strict. (Robert Salkazanov)

But Toë Petrovna, Mariia Petrovna's elder sister, who was criticised so strictly and who probably did not even suspect that she was the object of such a critique, made a similar accusation against Mariia Petrovna:

I thought that I would go to my sister, but my sister has a lot of *amban* (evil spirits). She has lots of *ochiki* (evil spirits). One should shamanise (to drive her bad spirits away). (My sister's spirits) are afraid of me. [...] She has a lot of *ochiki*, it is more than people can bear! Even in the street in darkness, (her spirits) show themselves to people. Is it good? (Toë Petrovna)

Classifying other shamans' spirits as evil, this critique is transferred onto the shamans themselves. If, as was said, the spirits were evil, their master shaman could not be good. Lingdze said about one shaman:

People did not like looking at him. You looked at him and felt that he was in company with the *amban* (evil spirits). Such a person he was! He was certainly a human! Surely a human! His body was human; there was nothing, no *amban*. But in my thoughts it was as if he was a person with *amban*. I did not even like to glance at him. He lived in his village, I lived in my village. There was nothing interesting! (Lingdze)

A final reason for criticism is the collaboration of shamans with the first researchers and participants in the Soviet anti-shamanic campaign. It was not only scholars and communists who labelled shamans as deceivers and charlatans who merely did magic tricks and cheated the public and who did not have any real support from the spirits. Molo Onenko was an informant for Anna Smoliak, the famous researcher of Nanai shamanism. When I asked Nikolai Petrovich about Molo, he said: 'Neither shaman Mariia Petrovna nor Ivan Torokovich appreciated him. They said that he just told lies! They said that too many liars had appeared and he among them. [...] They did not believe in him'. Trying to explain why such an expert as Anna Smoliak, who worked with him for long time, did not notice any 'deception', Nikolai Petrovich said: 'He wanted to be distinguished by a researcher-Muscovite and to show that he knew his business well'.

Ordinary people who hear how shamans criticise each other are usually afraid to retell anything to the offended shaman. But if a shaman does learn about some critical conversations, they can come into conflict with the offender. One such conflict arose between two shaman-women. Lingdze described it this way:

My sister has a small son [...] He spent a night at that shaman's place [...] Then he said: 'The shaman said that you were an *amban*, a strong *amban*. She talked about you this way'. After that I met her and asked: 'My friend, when did I become an *amban*?' She laughed, 'Ha-ha-ha!' I said: 'That boy told me that, when he returned home in the morning'. 'No', she said: 'No!' 'Did not he understand? He goes to school, he understands everything!' When they hurt other people in truth they hurt themselves! (Lingdze)

Mutual accusation is typical of shamans' interrelations; it separates them and does not allow for joining together in lasting unions. The Nanai artist Larisa Ganzulievna tells that shamans never spoke of the others with praise. I asked her: 'Is it because they compete in their healing proficiency?' She replied: 'It is not because of healing proficiency, but each of them tried to raise himself at the expense of the others'.

Shamans condemn and denounce their colleagues in an effort to form listeners' opinions in their favour, to show them that other shamans have the wrong spirits, that their knowledge is not sufficient and their deeds are wrong. Such talk consists not so much of warnings but rather as hidden persuasion to use only their own services.

Shamans talking to each other

Shamans' mutual criticism in each other's absence and addressed to relatives, friends, or to real or potential clients is so widespread that one could expect all shamans to be incapable of mutual friendly communication. But it is not so. When I asked shamans whether they quarrelled when meeting each other and whether they criticised each other in person, they answered that it does not usually happen. Shamans can fight and even wage spiritual wars against each other, but it occurs only within the spiritual world they penetrate in their dreams and visions. They never quarrel in the real world, and when they meet, nobody notices their mutual unfriendliness. Shamans' mutual hostility is usually expressed only in their intention to avoid each other. If possible, each shaman tries to take up residence far from the other shamans. I worked with two shamans who were sisters as well as with their brother, who also had shaman-like abilities, and each lived in different villages. 'The shamans', Ivan Torokovich said, 'are not able even to sit together. They will not sit down at the same table, because each of them has his own pride'. But nevertheless when they met, they were outwardly friendly to each other. 'In public they were quiet and silent', Niura Sergeevna said. 'They did not say anything bad to each other'.

Some rare skirmishes between two shamans could happen. Alla Kisovna remembers a case when two shamans quarrelled in her presence. 'The day when S. drowned', said Alla Kisovna:

Shaman L., I and some other people were in the kitchen, but shaman M. was in the living room. L. said: 'Is M. your aunt?' I answered: 'Yes, she is'. – 'Your aunt said this and that', she said, and at this moment my aunt M. came into the kitchen (she had heard our conversation) and immediately [...] it wounded her pride and she began to argue. But arguing is not allowed! Shamans must not wrangle! 'Why do you speak about me this way?' M. said. It offended her! They are like that, I have noticed. Usually shamans sit peacefully, but some of them [...] no! It looks like they have such natures. (Alla Kisovna)

Despite the fact that shamans were almost always well-mannered to each other, they were usually suspicious of colleagues' behaviour. V. was becoming a shaman when she spent a night in shaman N.'s house. 'When I came to her place', V. said:

She told me, 'I can't for the life of me find a place to lay bed for you. That is where! Go to my bed, but I will lay on the couch!' So we lay. Why did she lay on the couch, though she has a bed? I think: 'I know that she is a big shaman. What is she going to do with me? Will she disturb me or what?' Early in the morning I woke up. Nothing! I was not frightened, I was not scared, I was not afraid of anything at night. 'Did not you dream anything?' N. asked. 'I did not. Your *seven* did not touch me', I said.

If there is no need, shamans do not attend rituals performed by their colleagues. If they did, they might disagree with some detail and they might not be able to resist the temptation to put the colleague right, which could cause a tense atmosphere. Alla Kisovna remembers one shaman-woman performing a sacrifice:

The Nanai were listening, but the grandfather got up and said, 'I am not going to come here any more!' He got up and left. 'I will not come here again!' As it turned out, he heard that she asked her spirits to give health to her. Only to her and that is it! He did not visit her any more. (Alla Kisovna)

However, there were some situations when shamans could not manage without other shamans' assistance. If a shaman fell ill and could not cope with a particular difficulty, she or he had to consult colleagues. Sometimes they helped each other, but it was also not unusual that they refused to help, such as this example of Lingdze:

When she (shaman Mariia Petrovna) was in a bad way [...] she called me [...] to come to the hospital. She wanted me to come there and to make *pergechi* (guesses). I did not agree and did not go. I do not know anything about my own life. How will I make *pergechi* for the others? When something suddenly happens to you, you do not know whether you are going to die or not. How will I manage to live today? I do not know what will happen tomorrow. (Lingdze)

Besides the necessity of communicating in case of illness, shamans sometimes performed joint rituals, which were considered especially effective in cases when several shamans had similar difficulties and could combine their efforts against common alien shaman-enemies. In the face of a common danger, any disagreements were very much unwanted, but even in this case the shamans could argue. Shamans G. and Lingdze were supposed to perform the ritual *taochi*, to look for a client's lost soul together. But at the moment when Lingdze was ready to join her in singing, shaman G. suddenly grasped Lingdze's drum and tied a cord round it. The Nanai believe that anything that happens to the shamanic drum affects the shaman themselves. Lingdze told me that at that moment she felt as if she herself had been tied up. She was frightened that it would limit her shamanic abilities. 'When they brought my drum and my shamanic belt, she tied a cord around my drum this way, back and forth. Twice back and forth!' Lingdze said: 'I asked her: "Why have you tied my drum up?" – "How do I know about it?" she said. "I do not know!"' Lingdze believed that G. could tie up her drum unconsciously under the influence of her spirit-helpers, but it did not lessen her offence. Lingdze reported that she said to G.: '"It is like someone pulls my body in a thousand different directions! I live not for being tortured! Why are you torturing me like that?" I said it to her in a friendly way'. Mariia Vasil'evna, who was listening to Lingdze's story, exclaimed: 'That is interesting, a shaman torments another shaman! They offend each other!' Lingdze continued:

> I said to her, 'Why are we killing each other? Why do you offend me?' […] She was sitting silently and did not say anything. I told her, 'From now on I will not know what to beat my drum about, what to sing about! You have tied up my entire drum! Have you tied up my drum or my *seven*?' […] Since then I am sick. I always have a bitter taste in my mouth. I am unwell. I do not want to talk about anything! (Lingdze)

Another inter-shamanic conflict took place in the course of a ritual performed by three shamans. Starting the ceremony, Pilkha, who was the eldest, sent the youngest shaman, Molo, along the invisible spiritual road to search for the client's soul. But instead of helping him, Pilkha, as the informant expressed it, 'sent some sort of a dream in front of him':

> Molo's companions began to vex him […] Molo stopped singing and sat down. Was he not frightened? Surely he was very frightened! It had become dark, very dark as if a kind of fog had appeared! Kolia (the middle-aged shaman) said to Pilkha: 'Why are you torturing a man?' Pilkha – 'ha-ha-ha' – was just laughing. It was Pilkha's tricks. How angry did Molo become! He threw away his drum, he threw away everything! Will it please someone? It was Pilkha who made darkness in front of him. See! There you are! Molo sat down; 'I am not able!' He said: 'How can I go, if they are going to do that?' Kolia said:

'Why do you offend a man?' [...] They quarrelled this way, but after that they nevertheless did everything needed. They did everything in order to help (the client). Nobody is going to tolerate it if someone offends him that way. Even an ordinary person would not tolerate it. If you are doing something, you should do it correctly. But they offend some people, they torture some people. You are a big shaman, therefore you understand more? But he is a young shaman, therefore he understands little? Why do you offend him? You must not!

Such behaviour among shamans is nevertheless rare. Conflictual discourse can result in dangerous enmity, which shamans try to avoid. They prefer to communicate in a friendly way, at least for the sake of appearances. It is known that listeners, hearing some report, perceive the information in light of their own circumstances and therefore interpret and understand it in their own, unique way. The active reciprocal position of the listener is inherent to any act of communication. But when the information concerns the appraisal of shamans' merits and demerits, the role of the listener becomes especially apparent. Mikhail Bakhtin (1979: 246) writes: 'Understanding of any lively utterance is always actively reciprocal, though the degree of that activity can be different; any understanding is fraught with answer and by all means causes in a more or less degree: a listener turns into a speaker'. The act of cognition and understanding happens, according to Bakhtin, in the process of dialogue: the activity of the one who is cognising corresponds to the activity of the one who is offering the information (2000: 227). Such activity is inherent in any holistic cognition:

'When a listener perceives and understands meaning in speech, he takes an active reciprocal position with respect to it. He (completely or to some extent) agrees or disagrees with it. He supplements it, applies it practically, prepares to execute it, etc. That reciprocal position of the listener is manifest in the course of listening and understanding from the beginning and sometimes from the first word of the speaker. The vivid trinity appears: the person who perceives the information is a part of that information, of the whole text perceived'. (Bakhtin 1986: 494)

Thus, the dialogic meeting of two consciousnesses is bilateral. Not only is the listener a part of the information perceived, but the speaker can change the content of his report under the influence of his suppositions concerning the possible reactions of the listener.

Because the content of the evaluating utterances in shamanic emic discourse profoundly affects the participants in that communication, in some cases the reciprocal reaction of the listener can be hostile. This forces the speaker to adapt his or her utterance according to the listener's preferences and abilities. The listener in turn initially reacts to the utterance not only with words, but sometimes with actions. Thus there are three levels of communication: first, the subjects (speaker and listener); second, the text reported/apprehended; and third, the action actuated by this text. In discussions about shamans' qualities, the third level of communication is the most important. The speaker's goal is not simply to convey unbiased information about a shaman; usually the speaker wants to urge the listener to a certain action corresponding to the speaker's personal interest. In turn, the listener's goal is to make the right choice about how to act according to the information received. In emic discourse about shamans, the choice of the listener's action and the speaker's participation in this choice is much more significant than the objectivity of the information. It increases the subjectivity of this information and decreases its correspondence to reality.

By telling (potential) congregants about his helpfulness and outstanding shamanic abilities, a shaman urges them to make a decision to remain (or become) his clients and not to look for help from other shamans. When a shaman condemns a competitor-shaman, he has in mind the same purpose: to distract clients from his rival and to win them over to his side. When a shaman reports to other shamans, his potential opponents, about his false weakness, he tries either to avoid a spiritual attack on himself or to diminish their vigilance in order to weaken them before his own spiritual attack.

Valuation arguments are actually a means of indirect pressure brought to bear on the listener. In emic discourse about shamans, the indirect nature of this discourse is inevitable. Let us imagine that a shaman openly invites people to a consultation and healing and frankly confesses his troubles and weaknesses to them. Let us also imagine that when in conflict with a rival, a shaman informs him exactly what advantage he has and where he is unprotected and defenceless. All those frank and direct statements would weaken the shaman. Clients would avoid him because they would fear being involved in the honest shaman's troubles and not receiving proper healing. In the second situation, the opponent would receive valuable information on how to conquer and ruin that open-hearted shaman. That is why shamanists use public relations techniques. They do not directly invite clients; they advertise instead, and it forces clients to make the crucial decision to come to them. They do not confess their vulnerability to rival shamans, but they spread false rumours both about themselves and their opponents, which helps create their popularity and beat down their rivals.

This examination of shamanists' evaluations enables us to find out what shamans' main values are and what they most argue about. The shaman's superiority over his colleagues is mostly concentrated in the possession of shamanic abilities (such as the ability to sing and dance in a shamanic way, to see spirits, not to be afraid of spirits, and to use those spirits efficiently). In other words, their entire polemic mostly concerns the ability to get into better contact with the best shamanic spirits who are able to bestow all these abilities upon effective shamans.

Mutual agreement of some participants in emic discourse about which shamans are in the proper contact with the best spirits unites those participants into certain groups. On the contrary, disagreement on this issue separates them from others and establishes the boundaries between those groups.

Thus harmonious communication usually exists between a particular shaman and his or her congregants or clansmen. Within one of these groups the shaman is praised regardless of who expresses this opinion. The same information is true even if the communicative roles change and the speaker becomes a listener and vice-versa.

The durability of the groups formed around shamans is thereby partly based on disinformation. Shaman's self-certification usually contradicts the appraisal given to him by his rivals. Blameworthy information about another shaman and self-adulation is an integrated, double-sided phenomenon.

In contrast to the close relations between shamans and their groups, contacts are broken or are even absent between different shamans. This is shown first in shamans' tendency to avoid mutual communication. Second, when the communicative roles exchanged (when the speaker becomes a listener and vice-versa), the evaluation of the shaman is reversed so that a positive assessment is replaced by a negative one, and which shaman is praised and which is criticised depends on who is speaking.

In the traditional Nanai society one clan is opposed to another clan and one shamanic congregation confronts another one. To some extent, this is connected to the peculiarity of emic discourse on shamans' qualities. Those inter-clan confrontations and other social relationships of the shamanists are not only accomplished and realized in ordinary social practices; they are also dynamically mediated in rituals, which are in their turn inseparable from narratives (including tales), dances and other arts. In the next chapter we will try to look at how shamanising by arts guides, arranges, and stimulates people's customs and expectations.

3 SHAMANISING BY ARTS

WHY TALES HAVE HAPPY ENDINGS

The birth of a folklore (verbal) plot, motif, character, composition of an integral
text, and also formation of the certain folklore system with a number of genres,
codes, ideas and relations represents one of the greatest riddles of culture.

(Putilov 1994: 117)

A tale as a road

Nanai shamans conceive of tales as roads. The literal meaning of the Nanai expression 'to tell tales' is: 'to walk along the road of the tale'. When someone knows the tales, he is described as the one who 'knows where the tale walks along'. The idea of a 'tale road' is a shamanic one. Shamans are believed to penetrate the spiritual world in their rituals and in night dreams and to walk along the same spiritual roads, along which 'the tale goes'.[47] Both the tale and shamanic roads are called by same word *dërgil* and both the tale and one of the shamanic genres are called by the same word *ningman*.[48] The Nanai saying *'Enei dërgilbi chava ningmandi'* means: 'He tells the tale about the *dërgil* (shamanic road) which he goes along'. – *'Mene dërgilbi chava ningmandi'* means: 'He tells people about his *dërgil*, which he sings (shamanises) along'. – *'Mene yai poktova ningmandini'* means: 'He tells (as a tale) his road, which he sings (shamanises) along'.

Boris N. Putilov, researcher of Slavonic epos, considers that 'the storytellers never thought that behind the world of epic stories there is another 'reality'. The special

---

47 Here is one of the examples of how shamans describe their spiritual travels. 'Wherever a shaman directs his steps, there is a road that comes to light. He wants to go there, and there appears a road, he wants to go along another side, and there also appears a road. Either up or down. It is not a wide road, it looks like a cord. There are no wide highways over there. [...] It is dark around, but that road is like a ray of light, and he walks long it. He walks and walks and then he reaches a city. Then he can see the entire city at once' (Ol'ga Egorovna).

48 Among the different tale genres, the closest to shamanic practice is the genre *dërgil ningmani*: tales about travelling along the invisible shamanic road *dërgil*, overcoming obstacles on that road, fighting enemies, and getting revenge for the murdered father. (The hero's) father goes ahead and fights, fighting, he makes headway, but he meets an enemy who is stronger than he, and that enemy kills him. But when his son (the hero) grows up, he will learn everything about his father and he will go searching for the murderer. He will go looking for his enemy. That is what the tale usually narrates (Ol'ga Egorovna).

epic history is for them actual reality, and the improbability and incredibility of it is out of the question' (Putilov 1999: 89). Nanai material, with its living shamanic practice, gives us a chance to look at that issue from a different angle. Unlike Putilov, shamans are convinced that the tale does not recount some fictitious plots, but it narrates real events,[49] and that the tale actions do not represent an unreal world, removed in space and time, they are topically actual and can happen to each of them at any time. Therefore, what the bearers of the tradition consider to be true stories is from the point of view of researchers, a narration, 'fictional, impossible in reality and opposite to what is evident' (Putilov 1999: 95).

Such a discrepancy of opinions is a result of the fact that the researchers look for correspondences between the epic plot and events of the physical world (the *ilu*). But for the storytellers all epic events are happening in the real (for them) but invisible (for others) spiritual world (the *dorkin*) where shamans go in their dreams and rituals. A tale, from the emic perspective, is a repeated trip along the same road, which has already been visited by a shaman. The objective reality of the spiritual roads is not called into question; from shamanists point of view, it exists regardless of whether one of them has already narrated the certain tale plot or performed a shamanic ritual visiting that territory or not.

Nevertheless, storytellers and shamans use spiritual territories differently. When travelling along the spiritual territory, the shaman threads among some unfamiliar objects, feels his way, groping along. He cannot know what is going to happen in the next moment, what is behind the corner and he asks his spirits to find out about it. In the tale it is told differently. The storyteller can see the entire road at once, from its beginning to its end, because he has already travelled along that road.[50]

The similarity between the tale and the shamanic practice is so obvious that it is discussed not only by researchers but also by the bearers of the tradition. On their own initiative storytellers and shamans like to compare tales and shamanic ceremonies.[51] Shaman Kada confirms that when she is shamanising she visits the

---

49 Shaman Lingdze affirms that 'the stories of how people lived in the past turned into *ningman*'. Another shaman Ol'ga Egorovna explained it this way: '*Ningman* tells about life as it was before. Maybe some day there will be tales of how we lived. *Kolkhozes, sovkhozes*, how we were working, [...] it will be a tale one day!'

50 'It means that you or someone else has already visited the place which became a tale road. That's why you know what you can meet on this or that length of road. But when you perform a ritual, you can bump into anything unexpected and unknown at any turn of the road' (Nikolai Petrovich).

51 Here is how shaman Kada describes her ritual travel, which is close to some tale motives. 'Do you mean motifs?'
    When you heal a person, you go as if you go along a *ningman* [a tale].
    Yes, I go as if along a tale.
    One can tell about your shamanic stuff that it is like a tale: now you are a bird, now you turn into a fish!
    When I am searching for a soul-shadow of my patient, I look for his traces. [...] Following his

same village, about which they narrate in tales. The characters of Nanai tales seem to shamans to be real spiritual creatures; and some of them are even considered to be familiar shamanic spirit-helpers, which actively help shamans in their activity.

> To shamanise is like to narrate a tale. The shaman has (spirit) dogs, *mokto puimur* (half of a dragon), and *simur* (serpent), [...] and there are also many Nanai tales about *puimur* and *simur*. (Kada)

For shamanists a tale, like a shamanic ritual, is a means to communicate with spirits. That's why while performing a tale a shaman can suddenly turn it into shamanising. Niura Fedorovna observed a shaman when she was telling a tale. Suddenly the intonations of the storyteller changed and she continued reciting the tale in a shamanic way. 'It happened because her shamanic spirits came', Niura Fedorovna explains. In Dada, also 'a blind shaman-woman was telling a tale, suddenly she began to tremble and continued singing the tale in a shamanic way, because her *seven* (spirits) came' (Nikolai Petrovich).

Encoding and hiding information by means of telling tales

The moment when the connection between a tale and a shamanic ritual becomes most apparent is the tale's first performance, when the certain text is performed as a tale for the very first time. It is considered that each tale (of the correspondent genres) is created and performed for the first time by a shaman, and only later is carried on by other people. The source of a tale can be shaman's night dreams. Mariia Innokent'evna told about her husband a shaman: 'What my husband saw in his dreams, he narrated later as a tale. Several such dreams – and he got a tale'. The connection of tale and shamanic praxis is indicated in the name of one of the tale genres: *dërgil ningmani* (tale about a shamanic road *dërgil*).

When a researcher tries to find out why a shaman tells about his secret shamanic road, pretending that it is a tale, a mysterious phenomenon comes to light. It appears that for a shaman it is very unsafe to tell such an encoded story. 'He can tell people about his shamanic *dërgil* only in cases in which he was tired of life' (Nikolai Petrovich). 'He does not talk about his *dërgil* very much. It happens very rare. If he told

---

traces I become a dog, then a pike. I have more than one *seven* (spirit). How could I cross a river? On that pike I cross the river. [...]

When you work your way through thick bushes, and cannot manage, how does your bird help you out? Your bird is small, but you are big.

When I follow the trace, do you think that am I walking on the ground? No, I am flying and passing the tree branches. Then my children-spirits, a girl and a boy, sail a boat together with me. How do you fly, do you turn into a bird?

No, I fly right by the boat; [...] that boat has wings.

about his *dërgil* too much, he would soon die. I also can see different dreams, and if I relate everything [...]' (Chapaka Danilovna).

Narrating about his shamanic roads can result for a shaman in a tragedy. Ol'ga Egorovna watched how a woman narrated about her shamanic road *dërgil* pretending it was a tale.

> She was talking for a long time, but then, in the middle of her story she suddenly stopped and said: 'Something dreadful is going to happen to me! I won't live anymore'. Her whole body started trembling. And she died soon. She should not have related that story! (Ol'ga Egorovna)

If a shaman tells a tale about his own spirits, and people guess that it is not a regular tale, they, as shaman Lingdze affirms, would say: 'If he began playing with his own *seven* (spirits) like this, he would die soon'.

However those shamans who know about the sad destiny of their predecessors nevertheless again run risks telling people about their shamanic roads, creating in that way a new tale and die after that, as if creating a new tale is an odd method of suicide. Investigating that riddle is complicated by the fact that the circumstances, which force the shaman to talk to people about his or her *dërgil*, refer to the most secret spheres of shamanic activity. Even the very fact that a tale, when it is performed for the first time, is not yet a real tale, but merely a shaman's story about his own *dërgil*, is also a secret.

When a shaman tells people about his *dërgil*, he prefers to lead his audience astray and to present his narration like a common tale and to hide its true meaning. It complicates understanding a tale as an encoded, encrypted narration. Thus he talks about himself in the third person and names himself *mergen*, a fine fellow (or, if the shaman is a woman, she calls herself *pudin*, a beauty). The other shamans and shamanic spirit-helpers are also *mergen* and *pudin*. This way (with few exceptions) any names in the tale are avoided. Hiding the real personality of the characters under those uncertain names is one of the components of that code, which the shaman uses for ciphering his narration. By doing this he uses the special methods of encoding. As there can be several *mergen* and *pudin* in the same tale, it is not always easy to distinguish between them. So deciphering a tale always includes determining the identities of the tale's characters from their generic names *mergen* and *pudin*. The tale 'Mergen and his sister' (*Nanaiskii fol'klor* 1996: 243) is about the kidnapping of the *mergen's* sister, searching for that sister and punishing the kidnapper. In the beginning the tale says that a *mergen* and his sister live together in the taiga alone:

> Once in the morning the *mergen* was going to hunt. His sister was warming up the *boda* (liquid cereal). 'My brother', his sister said, 'my brother, I saw a bad dream this night. My brother, stay at home today!' – 'It is impossible!

Since I was born I don't know and I don't understand how it can be possible
to stay at home during day time! *Khere-e-e, undisi,*[52] but his sister, *khere-e-e,
undisi,* was turning over two fire-brands, she was stoking the fireplace and
warming up *boda*. So half-heartedly was she doing that! Her brother got
angry. Going out of the house, he kicked and turned over the pot with the
boda. Then, *khere-e-e, undisi,* he put on his hunting equipment and went to
hunt. (Nikolai Petrovich)

After coming back the *mergen* saw that his sister had been kidnapped, and he
went to look for her. This beginning is quite typical of many tales. According to the
storyteller's explanation, the sister was not a human (though nothing in the text
indicates it), but *mergen's* spirit-helper. In the physical world (*iludu*), this *mergen*
actually lives in the taiga absolutely alone. He is a shaman and he names his spirit-
helper his 'sister'. Although he goes hunting every day, one day he got a foreboding
feeling that something evil would happen that day, and that it would be better not
to go anywhere.

The bad dream he saw that night also told him the same thing. In shamanic
tradition it is usual to interpret dreams and presentiments as messages from spirit-
helpers. So, the hero's dream was interpreted as a message from an invisible 'sister'
who warns the hero and asks him to stay at home. Because of the foreboding of evil
the shaman has no heart to do anything. That is why, according to the storyteller,
the hero-shaman turns the pail with *boda* over, he just bemoans what has happened
and does not know what to do.

According to Nikolai Petrovich's explanation, if the shaman had considered his
premonition (the message of his 'sister'), had not gone to hunt and instead had begun
to shamanise to try to guess the reasons of his bad mood and his dreams, he would
have been able to prevent the kidnapping of his spirit 'sister'. The elliptical telling of
the story, the reservations and obfuscation and the use of the special code in order
to hamper full understanding of the text occurs because the authentic meaning of
the tale is partly hidden. The teller prefers to conceal rather than reveal the content
of the tale. For example, hardly anyone of the listeners of Nikolai Petrovich's tale
is supposed to understand him- or herself the real nature of the hero's 'sister'. The
audience that listens to the tale takes for granted the incomprehensibility of some of
the tale's fragments.

---

52 The phrase '*Khere-e-e, undisi*', is performed in a singing voice and means word for word 'oh,
    tell (me)'. It is one of the word-tunes, which have almost lost their verbal meaning. Nanai tales
    are filled with such words and that is why they sound so melodious.

Tale as a meeting place for enemies

Let us now try to clarify, why the first narration of a new tale is for shamans unsafe. Narrating about their *dërgil* shamans neither fear punishment from spirits for revealing their secrets, nor refuse from life by that original method. On the contrary, they tell a tale because of having realised and trying to escape the mortal danger, which they met on their *dërgil*. 'For example, in case I am about to die', Nikolai Petrovich says, 'I begin to tell a tale about my *dërgil* (to save myself)'. The reason why a storyteller shaman may nevertheless die after telling a tale is because the tale as a last resort in fighting against an enemy does not always help. Telling a tale can end not only in victory, but also in defeat. Once in the presence of shaman Mingo the conversation turned to this topic: why a shaman, when he 'is to die soon' and 'has too little life ahead' suddenly begins to tell people story about his *dërgil*. Mingo let out that secret: 'He tries all sorts of attempts to succeed. He does it on purpose trying to win!'

Examining in the field those shamans who agreed to share what they know about tale code, I try to penetrate into tales' hidden content and understand what kind of mortal danger shamans try to escape from by means of their tales and why such a tale is concluded with the hero's final victory and always has a happy ending. It is especially interesting if one considers that the shaman who creates a tale intends that its hero be himself and not somebody else.

The tendency to come to a happy ending characterises not only tales, but also shamanic rituals during which a shaman travels along his *dërgil*. Both the tale's hero and the shaman go along the similar roads and on those roads both have to win. 'A shaman goes along a road *dërgil* looking for a patient's soul-shadow; he goes as if along a tale road and then he wins!' (Niura Sergeevna).

Dërgil ningmani tales are a means to fight against hostile alien clan's shamans, and a means of winning over the enemy to cure himself. Shamans, who are at warfare against each other,[53] do not usually meet, but fight exclusively in their night dreams and in their rituals. (Stealing spirit-'sister' in Nikolai Petrovich's tale is an episode of inter-shamans fight). After a shaman has dreamt the enemy's attack he performs *ningman*, a ritual of divination. (It is significant that the name of that ritual is the same as the name of a tale). In the process of that ritual shaman, as he explains it, penetrates into the 'space' of the dream, where he has just returned from, to find out more concerning his enemy's intentions. In case the results of divination are unfavourable, he has to undertake specific actions to defeat the threat.

Having found himself in danger and in a desperate situation in which there is no hope for help from anywhere, shaman has one last resort. After performing *ningman* divination, shaman starts telling people a special tale (in Nanai it is also called

---

53 My informants affirm that practically all shamans are struggling with each other.

ningman) about himself, and that tale becomes for a dangerous weapon, which can strike either his enemy, or himself. Telling such a story shaman 'walks' along the same road in the spiritual world, invisible by eyes, where he has already been both in his unfavourable dream and while performing *ningman* divination. Sometimes he begins from the afar events, which preceded his today problem, and his travel-story can start from any point on his shamanic road, since any moment of his shamanic biography (the tale can even include information about how he has become a shaman, got his spirit-helpers, and how successful he was before). The tale finishes with the latest episode of inter-shamans warfare and with the current difficult situation, which is now the greatest threat. Everything in that narration is true, and the only episode invented is shaman's final glorious victory over his enemy. The shaman adds this invented but desired happy ending with the purpose that being narrated and accepted by his auditory the happy ending will be realized and as a result of his narration will be an actual victory over the enemy.

However, the tale-invocation does not always lead to success, and shaman-narrator can suffer a defeat. (His stronger enemy can feel danger and also can start telling a story!) As a result of the tale-battle one of the participants is believed to die: either the shaman's enemy or the shaman-narrator. Some storytellers died, as my informants reported, right in the process of telling a story.

Presence of audience strengthens the efficiency of the story-ritual and plays a significant role in the outcome of tale-battle. (The same is true of other shamanic rituals as shamans need some sympathetic but passive participants in the rituals which include some conflicts and fighting). This audience is supposed to perceive the story as a regular tale, to accept a happy ending, not calling in question the possibility of the hero's (actually the shaman-narrator's) final victory and it must not guess the actual meaning of the story.

> So the story is going on, and nothing is noticeable! Those who do not know shamanism, those who have not intercommunicated with the elders would never suspect anything! If someone nevertheless guesses what the story is actually about, the narration would never achieve its goal and the probability of the shaman's defeat and death increases. The shaman is telling about his own *gora* (road). Everything goes as if it is nothing else but a tale. (Nikolai Petrovich)

The explanation for the Nanai tale's optimism, its happy ending and the victory of good over evil (to be exact 'our' shaman's victory over the 'other' shaman) is a result of the fact that the *dërgil ningmani* tale is a kind of shamanic ritual, a means for the shaman to overcome his enemy and a part of the shaman's strategy which helps him to strengthen himself in the community.

VIOLENCE IN FAIRYTALE MARRIAGE

(My uncle) said that (his spirit-lover) was calling him,
[...] and he rushed right into the water.
He wanted to drown himself.
It was (his spirit-lover) that pulled him along!
If he had drowned, he would have joined with that creature (spirit-lover).
It was calling him! That is scary!
Those who do not understand it,
are puzzled by why all that happens exactly like in a tale!
(Konstantin Maktovich and Zinaida Nikolaevna Bel'dy)

Vladimir Propp (1996: 298), in his analysis of Russian fairy tales, noticed that the bride in these tales just seemed to be 'a cordial lovely girl, of unspeakable beauty', but actually, as his research showed, she was 'an insidious, vindictive, and black-hearted being, always ready to murder, drown and rob her groom'. The image of the cruel bride is also known in Nanai folklore, especially in the 'heroic tales', which narrate blood revenge. Unlike Russian tales, with their focus on cruel brides (not grooms), in Nanai tales brutality is a characteristic of brides and grooms, wives and husbands. What is more, in Russian tales, the bride's brutality is mediated through and allied with the difficult tasks that she assigns her groom. As the groom is not able to perform these tasks, it seems not to be her fault but his when he perishes. On the contrary, the Nanai bride acts much more openly. She herself engages her groom in competition. As her groom is usually depicted as inferior to her in strength and cleverness, she usually executes him with her own hands. In Aleksei Kisovich's tale, for example, a beauty plucked at two mens' hair and dragged them towards her house because they could not outrun her while she was skiing. 'Look, dear!' She said to her youngest sister. 'I have caught them by their heads and was carrying them when their heads tore from their bodies! It's a bad job! What to do?' – 'Okay', the elder sister said. She tied the heads and put them on the threshold: one inside and the other outside. 'Let everybody know what I have done! Now everyone will come here themselves!' After that the elder sister called men to contests every evening, and the losers and all their neighbours moved to her place after each competition.

Such competition with her grooms is, for a woman, a way to find a proper husband. She marries only a man who is not inferior to her in strength. In Nanai tales, violence against a person of the other sex is not usually explained or motivated. In a tale recorded by Valentin Avrorin, after a beauty came in:

A man got up, pulled out his knife, knocked down this alien beauty. He stuck the knife in to the depth of one finger, slashed with the knife, but she did not shout: 'Painful!' The man stuck the knife into her heart to a depth of two fingers, he thrust it – and she did not shout: 'Painful!' (Avrorin 1986: 195).

Even after lovers have lived together for a long time, one of them may suddenly and hardheartedly begin to beat the other one with no explanation or reason. In a tale recorded by Orest P. Sunik, a wife says to her husband:

'My dear, I would like some raw fish, go fishing!' But when her husband returned from 'fishing', he brought a faggot instead of fish. He caught the beauty's hair, and she began to laugh. 'My dear, what are you doing?' The fine fellow started beating her. He was beating her unmercifully until all the switches were used. After that his wife told him: 'When I asked you to fish, why did you feel so annoyed? If you don't want to fish, can you not coax the fish to the surface? But now, let not one rat, not one bird come here during the next three days! Let all food disappear from the grange!' She left her husband; for several days he could not find any food around and died of hunger. Then his wife came back, restored him to life, and they began to live happily. (Sunik 1958: 136–139)

A tale such as this does not usually elucidate the reasons for such cruelty and violence against a future or present lover. But one can find its explanation in the shamanic ideas still topical for some Nanai. Note should be taken about the problems shamans have in their everyday life and in their own marriages.

Vladimir Propp (1996: 298–299) distinguishes between two types of bride fairy tales. There are tales about meek brides (whom the hero rescues from a serpent) or about athletic brides (whom the hero takes by force). Nanai tales also include two types, but they are rather tales about two different types of violence in shamanic marriage. There are also two different types of lovers (or potential lovers): one of them is cohabitation of a human with a spirit, and the other is a marriage of two humans who somehow are connected with spirits; that is, at least one of them is a shaman. The first type of marriage tale will be analysed in this section, and the second in the next one.

The spirit-cohabitant as bait

The tales about conflict within relationships between a human and a spirit in cohabitation are in their turn divided into two groups – the tales that speak about violence as a means by which a human successfully tames a received spirit-helper (the spirit is a threat, it is tamed and becomes a helper), and the tales in which spirits tempt a human and threaten him or her with mortal danger, in which version the taming of the spirit is unsuccessful or it is not planned.

In both tales and shamanic practice, the notion of seeing a beautiful woman (or for a woman, seeing a handsome man) and the wish to have close relations with them serves as bait, with the invitation to have contacts with the spirit possibly finishing tragically for the tempted person. In the tale 'Coffin' by Nikolai Petrovich Bel'dy the hero sees: 'Oh, oh, nine *pudin* are bathing, chattering loudly'. When he passed them he hears: 'Our friend *mergen*, come to bathe with us, have a rest with us bathing'. So they are shouting, laughing and playing. *Mergen* says: 'Oh, cute ladies, delightful *pudin*!' Uttering these words he fainted. After some time he woke up with his eyes full of worms'. According to the interpretation by Nikolai Petrovich, the female spirits, met by the hero, could become his helping spirits if the hero is able to tame them. The same happens in shamanism 'if (the shaman) cannot take a good *seven* (helping spirits)', says Nikolai Petrovich. In a vision, an analogous case to that in the tale was seen by the famous shaman Dekhe, Nikolai Petrovich's mother. She had a vision that in the form of a bird she, together with other shamans who looked like birds, flew onto a tree branch on the bank of a mountain river. From that place they could see that in the river a person got into an accident; the woman-shaman sees that 'person' in the river as a handsome man, but at the same time for a man it seems to be a beautiful woman. One and the same attractive spirit of the opposite gender is seen in those visions by several shamans while each tries to outdo the other and get a new helping spirit-cohabitant, which will make the shaman stronger than his or her less successful competitors.

> On two banks of the mountain river there are trees and on both sides shamans are sitting on the branches of trees. They are sitting and looking and each one is envious (of competitors who are able to get attractive spirits for themselves). Each one is envious! (Nikolai Petrovich)

The shamans realize that that one, who would succeed in that adventure helping 'the person' from the river, would get it as a spirit-cohabitant and helper.

> The man looks, but a beautiful woman shouts: 'Is there anybody, come and save me!' It ('a woman') was caught here (points under the chin). It is hanging on a hook. There is a mountain river with a quick current. And across the river a rope is pulled. And it ('a woman') is hanging in the middle of the rope. That's it! Every shaman knows, if he wins here, takes the woman, he will get the best spirit *seven*. If he saves (this 'woman'). 'And my mother says', Nikolai Petrovich continues, 'I was also caught. Caught!' she said. 'It was too bad!' she says. 'For a woman an extremely handsome man is hanging. But for a man an extremely beautiful woman is hanging'. It would have been enough just to wish to get that *seven* and you are also hanging on the hook. She (Nikolai Petrovich's mother) says: 'I only could say it and at the same moment I myself

was hanging on the hook'. Other shamans said: 'So sorry, she was a good shaman, now she is perishing!' And then she speaks, as if in the tale an old woman (a spirit) appears, looks and says: 'Ah! Ah! You were caught!' And it (an old 'woman') tells the old 'man': 'So-so!' They had a boat, boarded it and began to row to my mother (to Nikolai Petrovich's mother). The old 'woman' was at the oars, and the old 'man' was pulling the rope (on which Nikolai Petrovich's mother was hanging). They come closer and closer. They reach the place; the old 'man' gives the rope to his old wife, takes a hammer and wants to hit the person who is caught on the rope. She (Nikolai Petrovich's mother) sees what is happening, sees that soon she will be dead. At the same moment she called her spirit-helper. She called it at the very moment, when the old 'man' wanted to hit her head. And immediately it (her spirit-helper) comes to the surface of the water, almost making the boat capsize. Instead of mother (of Nikolai Petrovich's mother) the old 'man' hit (his own wife) the old 'woman' and broke the rope on which she (Nikolai Petrovich's mother) was hanging. She (Nikolai Petrovich's mother) swam away and also she had time to take that handsome 'man' (which was hanging on the hook and which attracted her in the beginning). (Nikolai Petrovich)

Nikolai Petrovich affirms as a result of his mother's success she got that handsome 'man' as her new helping spirit, but unsuccessful attempts to get such a spirit usually lead to the real death of the shaman. 'Who is beaten by a hammer perishes. That's all! Comes home and immediately dies!' Other informants also told me about similar ways of getting attractive spirits as cohabitation partners. According to the shaman Toë Petrovna Bel'dy,

the shaman Chongida Mapa was walking in a dream and (in his dream) came to some small river. He sees that 'a woman' with long hair is swimming. It is impossible to look at it, it is so beautiful. This was a *seven*! Chongida Mapa hugged it and became very strongly attached to it, could not free himself. He called endlessly for his *seven*, but nothing happened. Then he called (his family spirit) *Khodzher Ama*. And only *Khodzher Ama* freed him. (Toë Petrovna)

As in shamanic practice, cohabitation with a spirit (and also other forms of contact with spirits) is very often accompanied by the danger to the shaman's life, and the motif of death caused by an attractive 'woman' (or 'man') is confirmed in the tale.

Beating the shamanic spirit-cohabitant

In a tale recorded by Valentin Avrorin, a boy trying to reach his fallen arrow sat on a tree that had fallen in the water. As the boy was on the tree, it suddenly broke free and began to float towards the middle of the river and then to drift downstream, while staying away from the shore. When at last the tree came ashore on a beach, a beauty came out of the tree. On the beach the boy's elder brothers came as if from nowhere and nine hunchbacks also appeared. The brothers killed the hunchbacks and filled a trough with their blood. Then they caught the beautiful woman in the floating tree: 'They dragged her to the floor and forced her to drink the blood out of the trough. The eldest brother caught and mauled the beauty. While he was battering her, she disappeared'. Then the brothers went searching for her. When the boy met her at last, he said: 'Why have you escaped? I'll kill you now!' She answered him with astonishing words: 'Well, my friend *mergen*! If my head had been in order like it is now, would I have made you work so hard? Well, let us make up!' They reconciled and got married (Avrorin 1986: 54–56).

I asked some shamans to interpret this Avrorin's tale. According to their explanations, the boy in the tale is actually a shaman in the making, and the beautiful woman is not a human; she is his spirit-helper *seven*. She herself had chosen the boy as a future shaman and took him (not his body actually, but his *rapuap*, soul-shadow) somewhere away on the floating tree while his body remained sick at home, having lost its soul. Then the boy's brothers (shamans) helped him to establish contact with his spirit-woman to make him a shaman, too. For this purpose, they offered a sacrifice to his *seven* (fed her with blood), beat her, and after she had left, they searched for her and gave her to him as a spiritual 'wife', a shamanic spirit helper. One can see why such a spiritual cohabitant might have to be cruelly tamed in light of shamanic ideas about the initial stage of the neophyte's contact with his or her shamanic spirit-helpers.

Neophytes inherit most of their shamanic spirits. That means that almost each *seven*, which comes to a neophyte, previously served someone else, and it carries a certain message remaining from the previous shaman. That message also includes a memory of past fighting against shamans of certain clans. It means that the spirits inherited inevitably contain cruelty, which was accumulated by them in those fights, and each shaman, who used those spirits, added cruelty to them.

> The *seven* gets into all the stuff around, wanders everywhere; it needs everything! (Lingdze).
> A *seven* becomes dirty after it has been serving (the other person). If you haven't washed yourself for a long time, you also become dirty. The *seven* is like a human who sometimes has to have a bath and change his/her clothes. It (the *seven*) is probably dirty (when it has first come to the neophyte)! Its (the *seven's*) hands are possibly bloody up to the elbows, because it could catch and murder some people (while it was serving its previous master-shaman)! Has it become (evil) like an *amban*?
> Yes! And one must wash it clean after that. (Nikolai Petrovich)

That circumstance is considered to be one of the main reasons for the famous phenomena of shamanic disease (usually a mental disorder) which strikes almost every shaman in his or her initial stages.[54] 'The *seven*, which served another (departed) powerful shaman, (now) drives the other one mad, that one who has to become the next shaman (after the deceased one)' (Mingo). Trying to manage these problems, the neophyte has first to tame his/her spirit-helpers before using them. One way this can be accomplished is through dreams. The shamans 'work themselves in their dreams' intending to win and domesticate their spirits. 'One has to win against their own spirit-helpers, and having won, go (along the invisible shamanic roads). Only after that does one become a shaman. They must get over it in their dreams!' (Aleksei Kisovich).

A different kind of taming takes place in rites. In the rite of initiation an experienced shaman, who is invited to assist the neophyte, is supposed to take away the neophyte's inherited spiritual 'bad stuff'.

(An elder shaman) removes those *seven* who hinder the neophyte, gets (the neophyte) rid of *amban*, bad *seven*.[55] He takes all of them away and picks up only nice *seven*. Only after that does (the neophyte) start shamanising. Only then is he a real shaman! (Mingo)

Nikolai Petrovich told me about that period in the following way:

A lot of work and a lot of suffering! The people around are tired of looking at it (at the neophyte's suffering with shamanic disease). But they can open[56] a neophyte as shaman only after (his spirits') dirtiness is driven away from him or her. Each *seven* has a lot of griminess and trash. When the *seven* are cleaned up, they become kind and helpful, and after that a person turns out to be a shaman. (Nikolai Petrovich)

Anna Smoliak relates similar information among the Nanai about the positive and negative characteristics of spirits during the initial stage of shamanising:

Before the shaman inserts the spirit into the image (dwelling), he/she has to annihilate its negative attributes (*okhoku*), which bring diseases. Most of the Nanai informed me that *okhoku* is a harmful, negative *seven's* offshoot, its bad qualities. The most 'stubborn' spirit *seven* (and especially *amban*) could have a lot of such qualities. A shaman should not ignore even one (of these qualities)

---

54 Another cause of this disease is the neophyte's unwillingness to become a shaman.
55 In the original text, it is *'eden seven'* which means 'fool *seven*'.
56 'To open a shaman' (*'samamba nikheliuri'*) means to 'open his mouth', to give him the possibility of singing in a shamanic way.

but must strive to extinguish all of them (all spirits' bad traits) up to the last one, to clean the spirits *seven*, to make them harmless. But the weak shaman (performing the ritual) could miss one of (the *seven's) okhoku* and to place into the figure of a *seven* a 'spoiled', a not 'clean enough' spirit. (Smoliak 1991: 75–76)

One of the ways to clean up such 'dirty' *seven* is to drive it by force from one place to another. Anna Smoliak (1991: 76) says that the shaman sang and danced for a long time, 'driving a spirit all over the world until 'dirtiness' (its evil qualities) would have fallen off it'. During a ceremony, the shaman drove those harmful qualities into a special grass figure and then threw that grass statue away toward the North. 'When they open a shaman, they take away all their bad stuff', Nikolai Petrovich said. 'They (*seven*) have a bad retinue, you know! All that bad entourage must be driven away'. Smoliak (1991: 142) also wrote that a shaman drove spirits inherited by a neophyte from place to place in order to clean them up.

But the other means of 'cleaning up' the neophyte's *seven*, used at the same time, was beating them. Some of the shamans' spirits are their cohabitants or potential cohabitants, so the violence against the spirits, including the spirit-cohabitants, was thus necessary in that period.

When you are becoming a shaman, you may go out of your mind; you may stay insane for ten years[57] until they (the other shamans) kill all your bad *amban*. When you are mad, they perform a rite *koaldosi* to murder and take away all your *amban*. (A shaman) would kill one *amban* using an axe, and hammer another one.

(The shaman) goes along the (invisible) roads, where the *amban* live. [...] They partition those *amban* roads. If they succeed in winning against the majority of them, they can leave (for the neophyte) just the nice stuff.

(An old shaman) can be shamanising all day long till five a.m. They both (the old shaman and the neophyte) are 'walking' along the (unseen) road,[58] along which the neophyte is becoming a shaman.[59] He (the old shaman) [...] clears this entire road and leaves just the yai beings (those spirits who would help the neophyte to sing in a shamanic way). The neophyte also knows everything (sees the spiritual shaman's travel, follows him along the spiritual road beyond) and even helps the old shaman (gives him advice). (Mingo)

---

57 Mingo affirmed that she herself was out of her mind for ten years.

58 Such an invisible road is considered to be inherited from the departed shaman; the neophyte is not able, for the time being, to 'walk' along this road because he or she cannot cope with the 'dirty' *seven* who dwell there. The elder shaman walks there first to tame the spirits and to put everything in order.

59 In Nanai language it is possible to say 'to become a shaman along the invisible road', 'to sing along such road', 'to tell a tale along the road' and so on.

Alla Kisovna remembers a *koaldosi* rite performed for her elder sister Gara Kisovna.

Before the ritual, people brought big stones inside the house. Gara Kisovna's husband went in the morning and filled the entire corner of the room with those stones. At night after the old shaman Samakan caught one of Gara Kisovna's bad and dirty *seven*, he inserted it into a stone and began to hammer that stone. He hammered it this way until the stone broke. In the moment when the spirits were driven into the stone, Gara Kisovna started to shout in different voices. If there was a spirit-dog, which was supposed to come into the stone, she recognised it, exclaiming: 'It is my dog!' and whined like a dog so plaintively that sometimes I felt like crying of course! When another spirit came into another stone, Gara Kisovna said, for example: 'It is an old man!' And she spoke like an old man and cried.
– Did the shaman beat the stone all that time?
– Yes, and the stones were smashed into smithereens! This way he (the shaman) left the good beings for her and drove all bad ones away. He smashed them! He broke the stones. [...] Whatever voices she (Gara Kisovna) shouted! If he said: 'It is my dog', she barked like a dog, or (if it was a cat, she mewed) like a cat. How interesting it was for us! We listened to it. (Alla Kisovna)

According to the different explanations, those evil beings the shaman beat were considered to be either the negative characteristics of the neophyte's spirits or independent unambiguously evil spirits *buchile*, which go together with those which are to be taught to help.

Hammering the stone, the shaman kills those *buchile*.[60] He kills the beings which cause (the neophyte's) disease. *Buchile* is evil spirit who kills people by making them become emaciated. The person (who is becoming a shaman) is wasting away; just a bag of bones is left! They are sick for a long time. What people call *buchile* are like animals, like foxes, polecats and the other ones. They are different from the other shamanic spirits, and an older shaman kills them. But some *buchile* are (the neophyte's) 'mothers' and some are their 'fathers',[61] and when (a shaman) was killing Mariia Petrovna's *buchile*, she was crying that he was murdering her mother. In all seriousness! When he was killing her 'father' *buchile*, she was crying that he was murdering her father. In earnest! She was wailing about it at the top of her voice! When he was

---

60 Killing a spirit is a relative thing because the spirits are considered to be immortal. After such 'killing', they can appear somewhere else and start tormenting another person.
61 *Seven* and *buchile*, which a shaman calls fathers and mothers are considered to be spirit-cohabitants for his or her predecessors.

killing her 'child', she was crying that he was murdering her real child. The most wicked beings are killed this way. (Chapaka Danilovna)

Only after that ritual could the figures of shamanic spirit-helpers be made. A shaman caught the good neophyte's spirits that were left (or according to other explanations, the spirits were cleaned of their bad characteristics), and inserted them into the prepared figures. In this case the shaman was supposed to have only 'good' and 'clean' spirits, but that idyllic circumstance was achieved through violence.

Beating is used not only in the *koaldosi* rite. 'Beating' the spirits, which cause disease, is also a widespread method of healing as a particular case of widespread shamanic exorcism. Trying to drive away a spirit that is responsible for the disease, shaman makes a statue of grass as tall as a man and massacres it. 'My granny was out of her mind', Ivan Torokovich remembers:

> They usually tied down her arms and legs tightly, but she tore free and ran outside. We could not catch her. We were tormented this way for half a year. Then two shamans together began to (heal her). They were drumming and drumming all night long. They gathered all their spirits, and called: 'Come on, come on!' (Her spirit) did not want to be caught by any means. They (the shamans) grasped it anyhow and inserted it into the *euni* (the big grass statue). (Ivan Torokovich)

At the moment when the spirit was believed to have come into that figure, people started to beat the figure with the sticks and continued doing so until just a heap of grass was left. Then they threw that grass away toward the North. 'In the morning', Ivan Torokovich continued, 'the sick woman was quiet at last! But before she had been sick for years!'

The spirit-cohabitants, which come to a neophyte, must be (according to the traditional ideas) tamed. This explains the Nanai tales' motif of taming the lover with violence.

Threat of violence from the non-shamanic spirit-cohabitant

Not only a shaman but also a regular person-shamanist was often supposed to have a spirit-cohabitant in his or her sleep. A woman had the jealous spirit-cohabitant *khoraliko,* which she usually dreamt of at night (in Nanai *khoralsi* means 'to be jealous'). This spirit was considered to feel jealousy towards the human woman's husband. As Anna Smoliak (1991: 74) writes, the *khoraliko* chose a woman and touched her in order to draw her attention. As a result she fell sick.[62] Smoliak affirms that in the past every woman had at home a figure of such a 'lover'. Smoliak has traced examples of spirit-cohabitants among all the groups of the Nanai. The Ul'chi and the Orochi named it *'khuraliku'*, that is 'jealous tiger' or simply *'puren ambani'* – 'the evil spirit of the forest' or 'tiger' (Smoliak 1991: 75). Another kind of spirit-cohabitant is the *busu* (or *buseu*), who takes away young women's souls. The women fall ill and get 'lovers' in the world beyond. Such 'lovers' are believed to constantly 'call' their human wives (Smoliak 1991: 77). The jealous spirit was believed not to like its 'wife's' human husband, and when, during the shamanic ceremony, they brought the figure of a *khoraliko* spirit of a woman into the room, her human husband went to the other corner of the room because the spirit felt jealousy towards him and did not like to see his 'wife' next to her human husband. At the same time that spirit (the forest being) was believed to help her human husband in hunting. Anna Smoliak (1991: 75) writes that hunter Oto Geiker attributed his hunting success to the *khoraliko* spirit of his wife. To express his gratitude for this help, Oto fed the figure of the spirit, changed the shavings on it and had made for him a new 'hut' instead of the old one.

Being tricky creatures, the *khoraliko* spirits were not considered to be constant in their sympathy. The most strongly pronounced sequence of cohabitation with a spirit was the sudden death of a human involved in it. In some cases it happens that a husband of that woman who has a spirit-cohabitant dies. If after that such a widow remarried, his or her next husband also died. Chapaka Danilovna explained it this way: 'If a woman married, but her husband died, if she then married another man and he died as well, it meant that a tiger had marked that woman as its wife; it was it (the spirit-tiger), which killed all her husbands'. To stop such deaths of spouses required the taming of the spirit-cohabitant.

Another possible tragic conclusion of such cohabitation was described by Anna Smoliak, who confirms that sometimes it was a hopeless task for a shaman to try to heal the human lovers of some spirits. According to her data, persons, who have spiritual cohabitants, often committed suicide by hanging themselves. *'Pasiku amban* (hung evil spirit) flew around with a rope'. Smoliak (1991: 77) writes, 'and threw it onto his lover's neck. Such a person, with an invisible rope thrown on them, felt that rope on their neck all the time, and, as Nanai believe, will unavoidably hang him/herself'. In Konstantin Maktovich's Bel'dy novel, there is a similar real case describing how a spirit-cohabitant first helped Konstantin Maktovich's uncle to hunt successfully, and later forced him to commit suicide by hanging (Bel'dy 2009: 243). Taming spirit-cohabitants is not always a successful attempt to escape the troubles caused by human/spirit cohabitation.

---

62 The spirit mates were also believed to cause gynecological disorders among women.

CRUEL BRIDE FROM A FAIRY TALE

> She wheedles, surrounds you by her spirits, sits next to you,
> talks heart-to-heart and suddenly grabs (steals your spirit).
> There are a lot of such artful ones: the entire village; all are the 'shamans'.
> *Ol'ga Egorovna*

After examining the plots connected with the cohabitation of humans and spirits, let us pass on to another type of the tale plots that speak about the marriage of two people and in which the cruelty of the bride is usually expressed by the perishing of the bridegroom, who loses a pre-marriage contest with the bride or her relatives. Consider that for shamans a tale *ningman dёrgilni* (a tale about the shaman road *dёrgil*) is a true story about the events that are really taking place in shamanic praxis, we can look at tale plots in the context of shamans' experience in the invisible spiritual world and of those social relations that are formed in the course of their practice. Shamanic traditions, as well as the story telling traditions, which have been preserved among the Nanai to the present day, give the researcher information that is inaccessible in the European material.

Studying the Russian tale, Vladimir Propp complained that the habitual practise, which according to his opinion had once served as the basis for generating tales, was lost irrevocably in the European material. Propp proposed that the sources of folklore plots should be studied on the basis of this material, in which they interact closely, in particular on the basis of the material of the shamanic tradition of Siberia and the North, places where the complexes of habits and oral poetic tradition are of a productive character and can be recorded by ethnographers in their live environment. Propp had particular hopes in studying shamanism, which, according to his thought, would help in comprehending the fundamental nature of the fairy tale. He considered that 'when collecting shamans' stories about their rituals, of how the shaman went to the life beyond the grave searching for souls who helped him, how he crossed (the border between the worlds), and when comparing these stories with the wandering and flight of a fairytale hero, some conformity is found' (Propp 1966: 360). He stressed that the study of fairytale plot sources can be extremely productive if shamanic materials are used.[63]

---

63 His wish was adopted and today several research papers have appeared dealing with the inter-relations of tales and shamanism using the latest studies on shamanism. Some researchers started to look for conformity in the essential features of tales and the heroic epos, and shamanic rituals (Taube 1984: 350). The conformity of tales and rituals was very often seen in the tales of the ethnic groups who practiced no shamanism that is to say in non-shamanic tales (Balzer 1995a). Other researchers turned to strictly shamanic folklore. In this way the objects of attention for Åke Hultkrantz (1995) were not tales, myths or legends, but those stories that spoke about shamans and the shamanic spirits. *The rite and folklore in the Siberian shamanism* by Elena S. Novik (1984) became one of the most profound studies of the structural conformity

In spite of the changes in Nanai society that have taken place over the last decades, for all the traditional shamans the tale remained, until recently, part of their own practice, and at the same time information understandable to them about the shamanic practice of their predecessors. At the same time for the majority of other tradition carriers, including some storytellers (because of the confidentiality of information connected with shamanic practise), for whom the tale is simply an interesting narrative. In my research I tried to reveal how the Nanai tale *ningman dërgilni* is seen not just by any storytellers but by devoted experts who may be either shamans or people with basic knowledge of shamanism. [64] Trying to understand how the tale is seen by devoted listeners and narrators, i.e. the shamans themselves, I have discussed with them both the published tales and those which they themselves narrated. The present chapter shows how shamanists interpret the tale motif of violence in the marriage, and how these plots are compared by tradition carriers with analogous situations within shamanic practise.

'Amotivational' cruelty

In the tale told by Aleksei Kisovich Onenko, the bridegroom appears before the bride in the form of a bear and unexpectedly attacks her. Then the bride, taking her spear, thrusts the bridegroom into the earth. Keeping her spear to support her, the bride jumps over the bear, hits him and injures his back. The bear disappears. From some place underground the voice of the bridegroom – bear – is heard: 'I do not die of your wound, this way you cannot kill me!' At another time the bride strongly grasps the future husband, whose wound has healed, and pushes him onto sharp stakes in the earth so that he is below and she is on top of him. The wounded bridegroom dis-

---

of the tale and the shamanic right within the single cultural complex.

64 When we speak about the tale as a sacramental message to the spirit, as a partner in the communicative act, we are passing over information recorded by us from shamans. When we transfer to the tale the attitudes of tradition carriers, such as epic narration, which are kept away from the audience with the frame of the plot, we demonstrate how the tale is seen by non-shamans. In this way part of society (the shamans) is involved in the process of generating texts, while the other part (the listeners, the storytellers, those who adopt tales from shamans as ready-made tributes) don't always see in them (add to them) the same content that was added by the creators. This is demonstrated by different interpretations of one and the same text by different tradition carriers. Here we confront the typical multiplicity of complicated conceptual structures that characterise different groups in society. The majority of structures are placed on top of each other or simply mixed up (Geertz 1973). For the devoted listener or narrator, the tale is a means to achieve a certain magical aim. Its artistic features are secondary, constituting simply an additional way to more effectively achieve the same magical aim. According to Vladimir Propp (1996: 354), the fairy tale it is a 'product' of 'free' artistic creation for the undevoted person. The undevoted person can accept artistic action as a ritual. Some travellers in past centuries saw shamanic rituals in this way.

appears again and the bride hears his voice from underground: 'This way you cannot kill me!' After some time, when the bridegroom is healthy again, he is boating on a river and again meets the bride, who is boating in his direction. The bridegroom offers her the liver of the elk he has killed in the forest. The bride comes to his boat, takes the liver from him, eats it and then, pushing her own boat away, throws her harpoon into the groom. The wounded bridegroom remains alive. After that they join forces to kill the enemy who had killed their fathers and get married. In some tales the bride's cruelty affects not only the bridegroom but also other people around him. In the tale *There Were Two Pudin (Beauties)*, written down by Valentin Avrorin, one *pudin*, having seen such a handsome man that seeing him 'the tears were coming from her eyes' (1986: 140), noticed that one of the man's wives was cutting a fish, taking a piece to her mouth to eat it. Then the *pudin* 'scraped (dirt) from under her nails and flicked it in the direction of the woman, who was eating. She choked and died'. The *pudin* killed the attractive man's other wife in exactly the same way, 'then set the man's house on fire. But because of the fire the house became iron and was sealed (no entrance, no exit). The man could not find the place to come out'.

However, the man did get out and his future bride took with her all the people in the man's village, making them her slaves. When the man marries once more, again not the heroine of the tale, the future bride comes to visit the man's new wife. 'Eh, my friend, where do you go, why did you come?' asks the attractive man's wife. 'I move among people with no business', says the *pudin* cunningly. The *pudin* eats the refreshments offered by the wife, then takes the tobacco pipe from her and slips it into her bosom. 'The pipe was turned into a snake, which killed the man's wife'. In this tale not only the bride is cruel. The bridegroom, as if not planning it and against his will, uses violence in relation to her. Having met her future husband when he is fishing, 'the woman slaps the back of her head and becomes a bear. Then she jumps into the water. The man says: 'Oh, a bear! It must be killed!' He took an arrow and shot it. Killed it and brought it to the shore. Looked: he made a mistake and killed a woman. He began to weep. Then the woman came back to life. When she was alive, the man married her. They went home together'.

The tale motif of the cruel behaviour of the bride does not in any way reflect the real habits of the Nanai people. Not a single researcher mentioned the cruelty of women. Above all, cruelty, if it happens in the everyday family life of the Nanai, can be connected with men who sometimes treat their wives roughly, although not women in general. The researchers confirm that the woman in the Nanai family is not without rights and is not oppressed. The cruel behaviour of the husband against his wife was criticised (*Istoriia i kul'tura nanaitsev* 2003: 51). It is also characteristic of the Nanai that brides who cause suffering to their bridegrooms do so – apparently – against their will and, as is stressed in some tales, feel remorse for their behaviour and sympathy for the bridegroom they have made suffer. This way the bride from Aleksei Kisovich's tale, who had hit her bridegroom-bear with a spear, can neither work nor sit calmly when she comes home. She thinks about her wounded bridegroom-bear and grieves: 'Perhaps he feels bad, the wound is serious!' In the tale *There Were Two Pudin* (Avrorin 1986: 138) the wife, who is beaten by her husband and so lets him starve to death (as a result of her conspiracy the food store in the granary disappears, and wild animals in the forest that could be hunted disappear) weeps for her dead husband: 'Who listened to my voice and made even the taiga animals disappear?' She supposes that she herself was not to blame but her shamanic helper *pudin* Simfuni, whom she did not always please. In addition, despite the cruel deeds of the future married couple mentioned here, Nanai tales are full of the motif of bride and groom helping one another, as well as the married couple's joint fight with their enemies. However, the motif of the cruel bride is not only imaginary; it undoubtedly has sources in the real life of the Nanai. The present chapter is devoted to revealing the ethnographic realities behind these issues.

Hard tasks for the bridegroom

In the tales that tell of the marriage of two people (rather than of a human and a spirit), the cruelty of the bride is very often seen during the pre-marriage contests that take place between bridegrooms to win the right to take a bride. If a bridegroom loses the contest, he may be killed by the bride, as was mentioned in the tale about a woman who pulled two of her bridegrooms – neither of whom could win her outright – by their hair so hard that their heads were pulled away from their bodies (*The Two Sisters*). In the best case, the losing bridegrooms remain alive but become the slaves of the prospective bride. They give her and her father their villages with all the people under their power. In the tale called *There Lived Two Sisters* the bridegrooms who lose the contest tell the bride: 'As you beat us, we will be living according to your wishes. Whatever you do, we will not argue' (Avrorin 1986).

The pre-marriage contests 'between the wife's brothers and her husband' took place not only in tales but also in the practical lives of the Nanai and other Manchu-Tungus peoples.[65] In Soviet ethnographic literature it was a tradition to explain this as the bride's brothers wanted to find the best and the strongest bridegroom among the suitors. Valentin Avrorin supposed that such contests were the survival of the matriarchy tradition 'when the brothers had more rights on their sister than her alien husband'. Apart from that, from Avrorin's (1986: 219) point of view, the contests were limited to hunting and carried out to give the husband the opportunity to prove his 'superiority over his brothers in endurance and hunting skills, thus confirming his right to have their sister for his wife'. Arkadii Anisimov has written about similar contests based on Evenk material.[66] 'Between the son-in-law and the male popula-

---

65 Such contests were rare and constitute an exception to the rule.
66 The Evenks as also the Nanai belong to the Manchu-Tungus language group, but differently

tion of the wife's village a real competition begins' – he writes. Sons-in-law 'hunted from dawn to dusk to win the name of good hunters' (Anisimov 1936: 36).

Exaggeration of the material content over the spiritual role was characteristic of Soviet ethnography, which was oriented to materialism and sometimes, as in this case, was in contradiction to the peculiarities of the studied culture. In this way, Valentin Avrorin's (1986: 216) opinion of the pre-marriage contest as a means of finding a successful son-in-law and hunter is summarised in his comment on the tale 'Palim Podo' in which the brothers invite their sister's husband to hunt: 'Let us see who is stronger and more skilful'. With the purpose of winning, the son-in-law asks help from a shamanic spirit called the sea shell who not only kills a whole sounder of wild boars for him but also makes a handsome man out of this formerly 'bald and snotty' man: 'Such a white man, so handsome, not bald, without skin boils, without sniffles, nothing […]. It is nice to speak about him. To write about him – one cannot stop'.

The supposition that the task of the contest is to find the worthiest suitor is in contradiction to the fact that sometimes in a tale the plainness of the winner and selected bridegroom is especially stressed. The character of the tasks in such contests, which are not limited to hunting and exceed the realistic human physical abilities, speaks about the fact that contests are held not to test the bridegroom's personal qualities and hunting skills but his shamanic abilities and his contacts with spirits. These tasks are not, for example, meant to lead to the hunting and killing of an elk (as expressed, for example, through the tale by Ol'ga Egorovna Kile called *Yurgi megren*) (Bel'dy and Bulgakova 2012: 146–153). The hero has to run long distances, either by an agreed route – as in Aleksei Kisovich's tale *The Two Sisters* – or for a long time after an unnaturally flying ball (as in Kisovich's tale *The Horse's Son*, ibid.: 62–89). A task in the contest may be a test of skill, for example jumping into some fantastic cradle in the middle of the sea (as in *The Horse's Son*). In one of the tales it was necessary to beat the spirits in a game of bones (Avrorin 1986: 189), in another to beat them in the contest with a woman who 'throws enemies so that the hip or the hand may break' and kills the suitors of her hand (as in *The Horse's Son*). Fulfilling each of these tasks is possible only if you have superhuman strength, and even then it is necessary to use the help of spirits.

In this case it was possible for the bride to select the strongest shaman from among the contestants. However, we have to give up this supposition if we pay attention to who is competing with whom in such competitions. The bridegrooms do not compete with one another but with the bride, although in some tales a bridegroom's brother competes with the father or the unmarried sister of the bride. In this way the bride is not simply looking for the strongest at the shamanic contest but for such a bridegroom who would exceed her in shamanic power or on a broader scale: for a man who would be a more powerful shaman than the shamans of her family.

from the Nanai, to the Northern subgroups. The Nanai belong to the Southern subgroup of the Manchu-Tungusic group.

Therefore, harm is not caused by the bad character of the bride but by the contest between family shamans and the establishment of possible mutual assistance between shamans of the different families who would join together as a result of the marriage. In shamanic society, governed by contact with family spirits – the spirits believed to be in family relations with humans – contact with another family's spirit carrier, that is with alien and potentially dangerous spirits, in itself raises problems. Even the arrival of guests, the representatives of another family, was accompanied by certain 'safety measures' in traditional society. Moreover, such measures are significant in such an important case as the introduction of the bride, the representative of another family, to her new family.

Shooting as a defence against the bride's spirits

Traditional Nanai marriage was carried out at the patriarchal locality. When the bride moved to the bridegroom's family, certain rites were performed with the purpose of protecting the bridegroom and his relatives from the bride's spirits, whom she involuntarily brought with her and who, according to the Nanai, could cause different unpleasant things to happen to both the bridegroom and his relatives. To avoid this danger, the spirits of the bride's patriarchal line[67] were frightened off during the wedding ceremony. When the bride's cortege left her father's village, the men of this family fired shots into the air in the direction of the bride 'driving away her spirits, forcing them to remain in the village'. The shaman Ol'ga Egorovna explains: 'The bride, for example, my daughter, leaves and our *amban* (spirits) go with her. Men with guns are shooting and driving *amban* away'. Vera Chubovna Geiker says: 'Take them away and shoot, so that devils, not a single one, (did not go after her). Drive away, shoot to allow the bride to leave calmly'.

In addition, taking the bride away from her father's home, they turn to the wooden image of the home spirit *diulin* and ask it not to follow the bride. Moreover, the legs of the spirit's image were tied to keep the *diulin* from going after the girl.

> This is how the spirit stands in the corner with the tied legs. They tied (its legs), and left it there. Only then (the girl from this house) was given to the bridegroom. Otherwise the spirit would untie itself, follow the girl and would not allow her to live in peace. Later the spirit's legs were untied and it was told: 'Don't go after her, she has already gone away. Now she is already a stranger to us. Protect us here. If it is necessary, you can go and see how she lives'. This is how they spoke to the *diulin*. I remember it very well. (Vera Chubovna)

---

67 For the Nanai and other peoples of the Manchu-Tungusic group, the patriarchal line is characteristic in the families.

When the bride's cortege came closer to the village of the bridegroom, already a group of other male relatives of the bridegroom came to meet the bride, shot into the air driving away her father's spirits.

When they reach the other village, people also shoot in the direction of the arriving cortege. It is like a war! When my mother's sister married, there were Chinese soldiers, a military unit. People say that they were shooting together with the village people. They were helping. Oh! Like a war! Shooting! (Ol'ga Egorovna)

Ol'ga Egorovna remembered a bridegroom who considered this measure insufficient. To have more safety and reliability, he put the barrel of the gun on the arriving bride's shoulder and shot again. It is true that in some cases people believe the danger of the spirits who are brought with the bride can be extremely great. For example, marriage to a widow is dangerous because the spirits who had killed the former husband could also kill the new bridegroom. Vera Chubovna remembers that at the wedding of an old woman a real salute was arranged. 'Everything burnt in fire!'

Together with this there were also opposite cases in which wedding shooting was not too good. Ol'ga Egorovna remembers the wedding of a shaman's daughter (who was not a shaman). This wedding was held without the traditional shooting. As she remembers, the shaman, the bride's father, had banned shooting. 'He said: "Shooting is not allowed! You may hit gods!"' Among the spirits accompanying the bride there could be – so he thought – his helping spirits.[68] It is possible that similar problems could sometimes appear if the bride could have become a shaman, and her helping spirits were consequently the spirits of her father's family. To cope with such a bride, it was necessary to have a bridegroom who could outstrip the bride's shaman spirits. The search for a more powerful bridegroom-shaman became more acute when the shaman-bride, or the shamans of her father's family, had a *baigoan*, i.e. a shaman from another family as her enemy.[69]

---

68 As a bride inherited her father's spirits, they are supposed to follow her.
69 Shaman conflicts and wars mainly take place in dreams between people who, in real life, have not met but at the same time have the most serious influence on people's lives. A person who was killed in a dream by a shaman also dies in real life, while a bridegroom-ally found in dreams also appears in real life. 'Shamans have quarrels with their helping spirits, a seven against a *seven*', says Chapaka Danilovna. 'The fight is not real. The *sevens*' fight is against each other. In dreams they meet *sevens* and quarrel. Everything takes place in dreams. The winner is decided, the loser is killed. True, if the *seven* is killed, the master will die. A similar contest to those of tales takes place in dreams!'

The bridegroom able to survive takes a gratuitous bride

The bride had always been considered to a certain extent dangerous for the bridegroom and his relatives; in certain cases the danger presented by the bride was considered so great that the bride's relatives refused to take the bride money (bride price) for finding a bridegroom and gave the girl free of charge. The amount of the bride money that they refused to take was rather large. (See for example: *Istoriia i kul'tura nanaitsev* 2003: 52). According to Ivan Lopatin's data, at the beginning of the 20th century a bride was always found by financial transaction; the price for a bride was 'too high and for many men it was beyond their means'. As a result, 'some poor people work until old age and cannot collect enough money to pay for a wife. This is why among Golds[70] there were very many men who were, against their will, unmarried. On the other hand, rich Golds buy several wives for themselves' (Lopatin 1922: 149). Against the background of such an attitude to marriage, if the girl's parents announced a pre-marriage contest with a free bride as the prize, it was evident that they had a benefit in mind that exceeded the sum of the bride-money to a significant degree.

This situation, which seems strange, requires explanation. In the pre-marriage contests described in Nanai tales, the loser rather than the winner celebrates victory. In the tale recorded by Orest Sunik, the shaman asks the people present to attack him. No one could beat him. 'Kochalan and Tugdelen began to attack him. Tugdelen says: 'Shaman, attack me!' The shaman invited the strongest spirits and attacked him. Kochalan's hand broke. Tugdelen's breast was crushed. Now they began to look for another man to fight the shaman. The shaman's daughter was in tears: 'Instead of these men, will you, please, come up! *If there is not such a man found, my father will die because there is no one who can win the fight with him*'[71] (Sunik 1958: 115).

It seems that the shaman and his daughter should have been glad that there was nobody with stronger shamanic power. On the contrary, they grieved. The absence of a shaman-bridegroom who was stronger than the girl's father presented a deadly danger for the girl's father. This is why the shaman offered his daughter to such a man – if there was one – free without a bride price. When this tale was discussed with shamans and the question of why the girl's father dies if nobody can beat him in the contest arose, I received the following answer. The shaman, the girl's father, is in a state of invisible shamanic war with some of his colleagues; that is, he has a *baigoan* (shaman-enemy) from another family, a family of greater shamanic strength than his and who can therefore vanquish and kill him. As shamans themselves say, such shaman killings take place later. The loser and the shaman killed by the spirit usually die unexpectedly and without a clear reason. Understanding that the shaman himself may not be able to cope with the enemy, he uses the additional chance he has to

70 Golds – former name for the Nanai people.
71 My italics.

save a life – he looks to marry his daughter to a shaman who is stronger than he and his enemy and who could become a powerful ally. Then, with the bridegroom's help, the shaman can get rid of his enemy. This effort from his son-in-law is so important to the father that he frees the son-in-law from paying bride price. If this man does not become son-in-law and family member of the shaman in danger, the strong shaman may instead become one more dangerous enemy of the girl's father.

The means for finding a shaman who could be made an ally was a pre-marriage contest, which attracted men (both married and unmarried, because the Nanai practise polygamy) who were willing to compete for the prize of a free bride. According to Ol'ga Egorovna, the bride in the tale 'wants to find a good man for herself to save her father and protect him from *baigoran*. The girl wants to have a strong helper for her father, who organised the contest to find such a young man. In the tale analysed by Avrorin, the shaman needing a bridegroom's help is the bride's father. In other tales such a shaman is the bride herself. The pre-marriage contest is not always an episode in the shaman 'war' and the bride, or one of her relatives, does not always risk losing this war. In some tales the bride suffers significantly because of her own spirits. This is also a problem that she cannot solve unless she finds herself a suitable bridegroom. For example, in one particular tale a woman is laying in an iron cage 'tied nine times nine' struggling here *kingiar* (the iron cage clanking) – and there – *kingiar* as if she is mad or *amban* (as if the evil spirit had gained the upper hand over the woman). The hero of the tale tells her: 'The woman [...] nobody could win in the contest with you to get married to you. Why did you become an *amban*, unwilling to have a husband? You began to kill the people in the village, began to eat them and became a mad *amban*' (Avrorin 1986: 148).[72]

The contest is a fight with this woman who 'throws (the contestant) so that his hip or hand is broken' (ibid.). Here the aim of the contest is to find a shaman-bridegroom who is able to cope with the spirits torturing the woman.

It is possible that such tales reflect the Nanai understanding that if a man without enough shamanic power marries a woman with some serious spiritual problems, he perishes because these spirits gain power over him. This way the tale bride does not kill anybody, the bridegroom dies as the result of his efforts to marry her. In one of the tales the story is told not about the contest but about some men who spend a night in the house of a single woman. One man stops the others, who are trying to go to the woman 'to get married'. He warns them that approaching the woman may kill them: 'Do not go to the *pudin*, do not marry her because she has not yet got rid of her enemy'. The shamans whom I questioned about this tale confirm that this woman is a shaman with a *baigoan* who is stronger than she is. I asked Niura Sergeevna Kile, 'Why wasn't it possible to marry the woman from the fairy tale?' She answered: 'Because she was a shaman and she had *baigoansal*'. – 'She was a shaman

---

72   In this tale the contest is not finished with a wedding but only with the recovery of the woman.

and fought with shamans of some other clans', confirms Ol'ga Egorovna. 'At the beginning (with the help of the bridegroom) it is necessary to kill this *baigoan*; only then they marry. It is like that in the tale and in real life'. Niura Sergeevna confirms that she 'had also heard about it. If the bride had a *baigoan* it was not recommended to marry her. I do not know why the man is afraid to marry, but if he marries, he is afraid he will be killed'. – 'If a man marries such a woman, the *baigoan* kills him', (Kseniia Ivanovna Digor). If the man who did not allow the other men to go to the woman marries her (he is stronger because he could foresee everything), his helping spirits would help the woman's helping spirits. In the pre-marriage contests, the winner is not only the man who voluntarily helps solve the bride and her family's problems, but also the man who, having received the bride free of charge, survives.

Marriage as a truce in shamanic war

If a shaman cannot beat an alien shaman from another clan, marriage can become a means of getting a strong ally – a son-in-law who is able to help. Another way of getting rid of enmity is a marriage between two shamans who are at war with each other, or between their close relatives. In the tale recorded by Valentin Avrorin, the shaman Saksi together with the *mergen* 'began to push each other. The *mergen* pushed the shaman Saksi so that he fell. Later he kicked the shaman so that the shaman flew to the sky. [...] Somewhat later the shaman Saksi fell on the ground and stuck there. Shaman Saksi says: "You won, I give my daughter to you"'(Avrorin 1986: 152). When the hero of the tale kills an enemy who had killed his father, in some cases he marries the enemy's daughter bringing a temporary cessation of enmity between the families. In the tale 'Fox', a *mergen* is fighting with another shaman. When his enemy understands that he has no strength to beat the hero, and that he will soon perish, he says: 'Don't reach my soul-shadow. Good, together with my village I surrender to you, with all my property I shall follow you. I shall give my beloved sister to you free of charge, without a bride price'. The *mergen* accepts his conditions and stops fighting (Avrorin 1986: 189).

> Earlier clans were enemies. Earlier they lived this way: they did not approach each other to say let us fight! They fought with spirits (that is, they did not meet each other in reality). The unfamiliar shaman comes here (i. e. remaining at his home, he sends his spirits here) and kills children in our village. But our shaman also goes to his village and kills people there. When will it stop? Shamans fight this way. But if a man fights with a woman, and if they make a deal with a spirit, they can stop fighting and marry. If they marry, the enmity will be over. [...] Nobody touches anybody else. It happened. In the tale it was really so. (Ol'ga Egorovna)

In the same tale called 'Fox', the *mergen* disputes the right of seven spirits *ngeven* to have the master's daughter as a bride and wins a game of dice (Avrorin 1986: 189). As a result, the *ngeven* do not 'take away the old man's daughter without a bride price' but rather the *mergen* gets the right to become a bridegroom. However, he does not marry the master's daughter immediately. First the *mergen* goes on a trip, during which he kills the enemy who had killed his father. During this trip he meets his bride, several times refusing closeness with her as it seems to be dangerous for him. Within this time a big snake attacks him four times during the nights. ('The snake crawled to him, as an arrow piercing his breast'.) When he eventually comes to the house where his wife-*pudin* lived, she 'only flashed him a look out of the corner of her eye'. – 'After that she did not look at him', (Avrorin 1986: 189) which meant that a relationship between the bridegroom and the bride has not yet been established. Then some beautiful woman appears and, as the storyteller explains, she was the same snake who attacked the hero. When the beauty spoke with the hero's bride, the hero 'stood up, took out a knife and fell on the *pudin*-guest arrived, striking her with his knife. He stuck the knife in to a depth of one finger, then to a depth of two fingers. When measuring a quarter of the knife, he wanted to (thrust it and to) kill her, the woman (the bride) stood up and took the man's hand: "My friend *mergen*, if you kill this *pudin*, you will also kill me"' (ibid.).

Only after this do they make peace and get married. Such a long delay before the wedding of these tale characters can be explained by the following: The *mergen* cannot marry the *pudin* immediately after having won the contest because they are both shamans who are in hostile relations with each other and their helping spirits cannot immediately get along with each other. In this way, the hero is unable to fight the snake-woman (who is not a human, but his bride's spirit). The Nanai believe that the helping spirit forms an integral whole with the human whose servant it is, and that the injuries made, for example, to the pictorial image of this spirit are at the same moment transferred to the human. Hence the woman's words to the bridegroom, when she explains that killing the snake-woman would threaten the life of the bride herself. However, the hero must be violent with her to tame her and ensure his own safety.

This why, despite the fact that the marriage between the characters was predestined at the beginning of the story (after the victory in the game with bones), the marriage could take place only after the victory over the snake-woman, the bride's helping spirit, who was dangerous to him. 'When shamans get married, they are unable to immediately make peace between their *seven*' (Chapaka Danilovna). In 'Two Sisters' (Bel'dy and Bulgakova), the contradictory emotions of the girl, who fiercely attacks the bridegroom, inflicting deadly wounds while at the same time feeling sorry for him, can be explained by the fact that her helping spirits continue without the girl's will to wage war on a man with whom the bride has fallen in love and considers her bridegroom. The activities of the girl's spirits are in contradiction to her usual human feelings. The mutual enmity of the shamans who have already lived for some time in marriage can be renewed on the initiative of the spirits, who may not have finally made peace with each other, as happens in the tale about the woman whose helping spirit Simfuni *pudin* made her husband starve to death against the woman's will (Avrorin 186: 138).

But even the marriage of the shamans, who were earlier at war, does not guarantee the end of their enmity. In some cases even after being married in dreams they continue to quarrel. At the beginning of their marriage, the wife's spirits may kill someone from her husband's family. In their turn, the husband's spirits will continue, against his will, to kill the family of his wife. Such killing is understood as a spiritual attack which inevitably results in the real death of the person assaulted. 'In reality they do not kill anybody, although those persons die anyhow' (Chapaka Danilovna).

In other cases the enmity of the married shamans stops right after the wedding: 'the spouses live together, and their *seven* also begin to live together. They live together and during shamanic activities help each other. The enmity between them comes to an end' (Niura Sergeevna), often turns into an alliance against another hostile shaman.

> Then male shaman fights together with his wife. If an alien shaman attacks a wife, she says to her husband-shaman: 'Will you help me! It is necessary to drive him away! Help!' Immediately they start their shamanic activities together and drive him out'. (Ivan Torokovich Bel'dy)
> When it is hard, spouses help each other. [...] When they perform their shamanic activities, they call each other to help. Only in the case of marriage can a shaman give his helping spirit to his wife for an extended period; and only the husband gives his helping spirit to his wife, not the other way round. (Niura Sergeevna)

If hostile shamans cannot marry among themselves, they can ensure that their children marry in order to stop hostility.

> It is so that I, for example, have a daughter and my *baigoan* (a hostile shaman has) a son. Then they give the children to each other for marriage. They will live together peacefully; their life together will be good. Shamans will not fight with each other. [...] (For the sake of peace) I give you my daughter without a bride price! There will be peace, everything will be alright. (Ol'ga Egorovna)

Unreliability of the marriage truce

Unfortunately, the marriage truce can be unreliable and brief; it can stop enmity for only a limited time. The agreement to have marital relations could be risky for one of the former enemies and result in his or her death. The point is that the success of such a marriage depends on the will of that spouse who supposed that his or her shamanic power is greater. Forgiveness of the former offence and peaceful coexistence characterises the weaker spouse, while the other one, who feels his or her power, could at any moment restore enmity unexpectedly and insidiously.

> I know about it. The future husband loves the woman but she does not want him! But anyhow in her body she felt pain and she does not want to make peace. If he had killed anybody in her family, in her soul there is still some pain and she does not want to find peace. If the woman agrees, she will tell all her *seven* to act peacefully and there will be peace. But if she does not want that, there can be no peace. (Chapaka Danilovna)

The shaman Miraka lived in the village of Upper Nergen; her grandfather, a shaman, was in hostile relations with a shaman Khodzher from the lower reaches of the Amur River. As this enmity resulted in sacrifices among Khodzher shaman's relatives ('the Khodzher's family began to die'),[73] in order to stop the deaths, the shaman from the lower Amur gave his granddaughter to Miraka to be his son's bride. They married and the enmity stopped. But later Miraka could not resist the temptation and was again engaged in shamanic activities, at which time she rejected the truce and restored enmity. They say that after the restoration of enmity, Miraka saw the shaman from the lower Amur in a dream. He asked her: 'Let us become friends, there will be peace!' Knowing about the restoration of enmity, Miraka's relatives began to persuade her to forbear from it. Ol'ga Egorovna said that her husband began to scold Miraka for her hostility.

> He said: 'Make peace! When you beseech your spirits, ask them to make peace with you. [...] There is no life without peace, you will die anyhow!' Miraka said: 'What the deuce do I need with peace? She did not want it!' Egorovna's husband told her: 'Make peace [...]. It is necessary to speak (with the lower Amur shaman) to make peace, not to compete with anybody'. – 'I do not want to! What the deuce do I need with it?' says Miraka. (Ol'ga Egorovna)

According to Ol'ga Egorovna, Miraka's sister told her:

---

73 To be safe when defending themselves from the attacking virtual enemy, shamans usually give their enemy the *panians* (soul-shadows) of their relatives or patients.

Make peace! Let us conclude an agreement with the lower Amur shaman! You will live in peace and all others will have peace!' But she (Miraka) does not want this. Her competitor learnt in his dreams (that she does not want peace). Only two years after that the same Miraka was alive. (Ol'ga Egorovna)

As a result of the continuation of the shaman war, the participants and some of their relatives perished. In the beginning, Gosha, Miraki's youngest son, perished in a traffic accident. Then Klava died, the daughter of Khodzher shaman, who was given to marry Miraki's other son in order to stop the enmity.

I saw Klava, loved her. She was a shy girl, not swearing. Slim, not tall [...]. She worked at a hospital. Once she woke up in the morning, prepared food, fed her children, and said: 'Now I go to work. I do not know whether I come back or not'. She went out and fell. Simply fell and died. She fell in the porch. There was a loud noise. People ran out but she was already dead. She was a good girl, I loved her. Miraka herself also did not live long. (Ol'ga Egorovna)

For a male shaman the possibility of a marriage truce is more complicated because of the insidious deception of a female shaman who is weaker than he, and who, under cover of the wish to have a marriage truce, may conceal her true aggressive intentions. 'If a woman cannot cope with a man – her enemy *baigoan* – she will suck up to him. The female shamans are very sly' (Nesulta Borisovna).

Sometimes a man also can use such a method, but it is more characteristic for women. 'Women-shamans have more slyness and deception, men have less' (Ol'ga Egorovna). One of the methods of such deception, characteristic of women, is to attract a man for temporary cohabitation; then during sexual intercourse she steals from him that spirit, which, she considers, is the most dangerous for her and at the same time the one she most desires to have.

Obtaining such a spirit, the woman turns the man's own strongest weapon against him. As a result of such a theft, a weak woman becomes stronger than her contestant, and the male shaman may fall seriously ill and even perish from the loss of his spirit.

If two shamans begin cohabitation, the woman may steal the *seven* from the man. She steals! It happens! I understood it when Aunt Olgoni told me that to steal a man's *seven* it is necessary to have sex with him. When a woman sleeps with the man, he does not expect, or think, that she may steal; he thinks that she loves him. He does not think that she could play dirty tricks on him. But at the same time the woman takes away his *seven*. Only after that he understands (what had happened). Nevertheless, she will not give (the *seven*) back. Or if she has among her own *seven* such a *seven*, which is not very good and

not important, she may suggest as an exchange and give her bad *seven* to him.
(Ol'ga Egorovna)

In Upper Nergen village there happened a case, in which a theft of a spirit almost
took place:

> Here we had a female shaman and a blind male shaman. [...] The woman
> wanted to take something away from him (to steal his spirit). They two re-
> mained alone together and she began to make proposals. She wanted to take
> away his *seven*, but the man began to suspect it. Suspecting, he came to us.
> He was silently sitting. I asked him: 'What are you grieving about? About the
> road back?' He says: 'No! Not about that. Your female shaman wants to take
> away my *seven*. She does not leave me for a moment. She follows me all the
> time. Is it good to allow this? I have only the one *seven*. If I give him away, how
> could I live? How could I remain alone? I live with this *seven* as if with my
> own face'. This man loved children. He loved children. He was a good man.
> When Soviet power was established, the collective farm was established. He
> worked in the rural municipal council at Bolan. I have forgotten his name.
> In spring his eyes became painful. He told his story: 'I went to the doctor;
> she dropped some acid into my eyes, one after the other. I was all in tears
> when my eyes were painful – this is how my eyes were destroyed. Both eyes.
> Another doctor, who was older, asked the younger one: 'Why did you do it?'
> She answered: 'I mixed up two medicines'. – 'There was a label! You should
> have read which medicine to use!' She had burnt both his eyes and he became
> blind. Poor man! He walked slowly, with a long stick. When you look at him,
> he seems rather young. This female shaman wanted to take away his *seven*.
> She lived at Lidoga village. The man did not approach her, did not come close.
> He did not speak with her. [...] So he went away from the village. The man
> says: 'If she follows me to my house, I begin to quarrel with her'. But this
> female shaman did not follow him. She understood. It was dangerous to go
> to the lower Amur. *Baigoan* (hostile shamans) almost always come from the
> area of the lower Amur. She did not go after him. Later, when he had gone
> away, she said: 'If I had been a young woman, I would have had sex with him
> and taken that *seven* from him'. (Ol'ga Egorovna)

A truce achieved as the result of a marriage of hostile partners is reliable only
on condition of mutual agreement between the future marriage partners and their
aspiration for peace. We know of many cases when shamanic marriage was successful and did not result in the revitalisation of enmity. However, sometimes such an
agreement is not eternal and can be broken for different reasons. Then the enmity
of families, united as a result of the marriage, may be renewed with fresh strength.

The violence connected with marriage or cohabitation, which Nanai tales relate to us, is practically always based upon shamanic practice. If one of the cohabitation partners is (according to the interpretation of the shamans) not human but a spirit, violence is either necessary for the human as a means to tame the spirit, or that human must survive in a dangerous situation, enduring the violence of the unpredictable spirit. When the tale marriage partners are human, violence is caused by the fact that either both or one of them practises shamanism. Shamanic characteristics of the woman (or of close relatives like her father or brothers) decrease the possibility of her marriage because, through marriage or even through a short cohabitation, she may involve her partner in the spiritual troubles of her family. As a result of cohabitation, a hostile shaman may affect both partners. The hostile shaman may constantly attack the family of someone who practises shamanism. If a person under attack does not have sufficient shamanic strength to cope, he or she perishes.

It is important to note the asymmetry of marriage problems. Tales talk about the danger to men of cohabitation with a female shaman, but not the other way around: they talk about cruel brides but not about cruel bridegrooms. Evidently this can be explained by the fact that the transfer of spirits takes place in marriage – as the Nanai confirm – from a man to a woman, but not the other way round. In a happy shamanic marriage the man can give his wife the possibility of temporarily using his shaman spirits, although the wife cannot give her spirits to her husband. It is possible that such movement of spirits from men to women is connected with the patrilineal organisation of the Nanai family. Unfortunately, the information I received from my informants is not satisfactory to confidently speak about these issues, and is even partially contradictory. [74] (My informants told me, for example, that the helping spirit is transferred from the man to the woman, while at the same time speaking about the fact that as a result of cohabitation the woman is able to involve the man in hostile relations with her own enemy – a shaman who will now attack not only her but her cohabite as well). Nevertheless, it is possible to presume that the tale motif of the cruel bride (but not the cruel bridegroom) is connected on the one hand with the cruelty of spirits and the danger in communicating with them, and on the other hand with the definite laws of primary movement – the transfer of these spirits from the man to the woman and not the other way around.

---

74 As a result of changes which have recently taken place in the Nanai culture and in the culture of other nations of Siberia and the Far East, it was difficult to find informants who were conscious of the links between the shamanist practice and the laws of the traditional family organisation.

SPIRITS AS DANCING MASTERS

> When I went to dance, my eyes themselves began to close.
> It was that I cannot stand not to close my eyes,
> but even with closed eyes I can see everything.
> That is what horror is! I am scared of myself.
> *(Ena Kile)*

> *Seven* itself sings through you
> and despite the fact that you do not know how,
> you will also start singing.
> *(Mingo)*

In traditional Nanai society there were no other dances besides shamanic ones, because shamanists believed that rhythmical body movements accompanied by corresponding rhythmical drum beating and rhythmical clanging of metal pendants could easily connect people with spirits. So dances were only used in the certain cases when communication with spirits was needed. Those dances mostly consisted of rhythmical moving the hips, which made metal pendants on a belt clang; in shifting one's feet from one to the other and in beating a drum or rhythmically banging the floor with a stick. Not only shamans, but also most of the other participants of the ritual gave in turn the spirits their personal dance-offering. They danced one at a time and never together. For dancing each of them in turn fastened to him or herself the belt with metal pendants, which belonged to the shaman (to the master of this ceremony) and took the shaman's drum, and after finishing the dance he or she passed the drum and the belt to another participant. Nanai believe that at least nine participants must dance before the shaman takes his or her belt and drum and starts the main part of the ritual.

Formerly men competed as to who would dance better and funnier. Some women tried to dance beautifully and others preferred to do it in a funny way. There were a lot of children who came to watch; they sat around. Some old man could at one moment beat by his drum stick in the drum, and at another on the crowns of the children's heads while dancing. He could send a woman to fetch him some water, but while she was walking past, he drummed at one moment on the drum and at another on her bottom. When they started doing that, all the children ran away in order not to let him reach them. There was such laughter! It was such fun, you know! [...] First he (the dancing man) would approach the young people and hit their heads with a drum stick. They rushed to push other people off and to run away. Especially the girls rushed to run away. There was a big table. [...] Isara Onenko from Dada village could pass under that table without stopping drumming and without interrupting his dance. His drum did not stop and the pendants on his belt did not fall silent! They did it like that! They competed with each other, as to who would dance better, who would dance finer, everybody in his or her own way. When there were shamanic dances, it was a real feast!' (Nikolai Petrovich)

FIGURE 9: Shaman Gara Kisovna Geiker (1981). It is said that she was lifted up from the floor, as her head is in one line with the door.

Examining the shamanic ritual techniques among Evenks and Nanai, Anna-Leena Siikala (Siikala and Hoppál 1998: 35, 37–38) noticed that during rites, in which the shaman's spirits are thought to depart for the shamanic journey, the shaman creates an image of the role performances of his spirits helpers purely verbally, in which case only the shaman is regarded as 'seeing' or 'hearing' the spirits during the rite. The other technique, the shaman's complete identification with the spirit role, is used in another kind of rite, where the shaman, instead of departing for the other world, brings the spirits to the physical world and lets them possess him. The field materials allow me to assume that dancing is typical for the second type of rituals, when the shaman identifies him or herself with spirits mostly in sacrifice. In talking about the shaman's role, we compare him with an actor playing on stage and assume that he imitates the presence of spirits trying to have an effect on his audience. At the same time the bodily movements of dancers are believed to be manifestations of *seven's* presence and means of *seven's* self-expression.

Seven obedient to the shaman

In the rituals connected with a shamanic journey, divination and exorcism, the shaman is more active than the spirit-helpers; he or she makes all the arrangements and gives orders to the obedient and even passive, lacking initiative spirits' helpers.

Only concerning those rites one can say that '*seven* immediately executors orders of its governor' (Kile 1994: 67). Once Chapaka Danilovna asked shaman Ildanga about how obedient his *seven* were to him, and he answered:

> *Seven* stay around and look at their shaman. If the shaman did not appeal to them, they would never do anything. They don't do anything on their own initiative. They just stay and look at the shaman's mouth. That's why all the words must be uttered: 'Take that item! Go there! Take other goods!' They are waiting for the directions! *Seven* are like that. They are standing and staring at shaman's mouth. If you tell them to do something, they will do it. If you don't tell them, they won't. (Chapaka Danilovna)

They are like soldiers waiting for commands. (Irina Torombovna)

Not only speaking, but also beating the drum is regarded as a means to bend *seven* to the shaman's will. 'While you are beating (the drum), *seven* stay here and work. But as soon as you stop, they fall down and do nothing' (Chapaka Danilovna). But sometimes *seven* are indifferent and do not pay any attention to their shaman despite all his words and drumming. In this case the shaman uses foul language and 'shouts at them: '*A, masilaoru!* (Come on!) Do it quickly, right away!' And they hasten to do it' (Chapaka Danilovna).

Sentences in the imperative mode, giving orders to *seven*, prevail in the texts of shamanic rites, as in the following extract from the healing ceremony.

(Shaman Mingo to her spirits:)
Khere, khere, khere, khere! [75] Try to guess it! Are they in the Amur River under the water? My dad, try to guess it well!
Hey! My mum, my dog *Sembele!* [76] Why are you dawdling over there, on the curve of the river?
Is it (the soul of a sick person) there, indeed?
Well, *khere!* Get up quickly, my dads! What are you pottering on that place about?
Khei, khere! Amichoni! [77] You are just useless guys! *Khei, khere!* Go into (that cliff) quickly!
Veiu (group of spirits), don't fall behind! Come on into that mountain!

Not only in rites, but during all the period of serving the shaman, the *seven* are believed to be obedient to their master.

---

75 *Khei, khere* are typical for shamanic singing words, non-semantic and untranslatable.
76 *Sembele* is the name of the *seven* dog.
77 *Amichoni* is a foul word.

My *seven* is like a dog. It sleeps under my window (outside). When I am in need, I can call it and we'll go together to fetch someone's *panian* (soul) or to do something else. My (*seven*) can guard some person if I order it to do so, (for instance) a *panian* (soul-shadow) in *dëkaso* (depository for souls). I can send it to accompany someone who is leaving for the city. It can guard (people) for a year. (Nikolai Petrovich)

Shaman subordinated to *seven*

Obedient to their shaman, *seven* cannot nevertheless allow him the main choice; they can neither permit him to refuse the shamanic gift at the beginning of his activity nor to cease shamanising after he has become a shaman. Sometimes shamans have not much desire to perform the healing rites, but they do so just because, as they say, their spirits force them to.

> *Endur* (the spirits, which are supposed to govern *seven*) punish those people (shamans), who don't perform shamanic rites and don't pray to them. They send *seven* to go and capture the souls of those people! They (*seven*) go and arrest such people like policemen. It is all the same!
> Where do they put those (souls)?
> In the place (where the spirits themselves are supposed to dwell)! It is the worst thing! They put you there, and you will be sick and suffer for years!
> (Ol'ga Egorovna)

Answering the question if a shaman is able to refuse people who want to be healed, Nikolai Petrovich said: 'If he refuses, his *seven* will begin to pull him about, and he will fall sick. Anyway, he will (cure people)! They (*seven*) will force him! The *seven* want to work. They don't want to sit without a job!' Aleksei Kisovich's opinion is even more determined: 'When people come to a shaman, he is not able to refuse (to shamanise) for them. It is impossible. Otherwise, he can die. If he refuses, he will die. It is necessary to go (with them to shamanise)'. Gavriil V. Ksenofontov wrote that if a Yakut shaman Matrëna K. did not shamanise for 20 days, her cattle began die, because her dissatisfied spirits began to exterminate them (1992: 56). Lingdze, who sometimes refused people (she practiced in the years when the authorities prohibited shamanism), experienced how her *seven* punished her for that.

> If you reject people and don't drum for them, you can fall heavily ill. If you perform the rituals for them, you'll be better. If I sit at home and don't shamanise, everything irritates me, hurts. But after I have shamanised, I feel much better.

Shaman Ol'ga Egorovna also remembers the case when she turned down a man who wanted her to heal him.

> B. came to me, but I told him: 'I have no plan to shamanise today!' He left, and after that I saw in my dream that my (*seven*) 'grandfather' and 'grandmother' tore me to pieces for that. 'What plans did you have?' they say. It is interesting! It is impossible to refuse. 'I don't want to do it anymore! I'm bored to death with it!' I said. 'I will relax!' But they forced me. In my dream they told me: 'If next time you do like that, you'll come to a bad end'.

Seven's demands in offering

According to the traditional view, offering and especially sacrifice is the rite in which *seven* put a shaman under their supervision to the greatest degree. The Nanai believe that *seven* sometimes long for offering even for no particular reason. For example, when some technical equipment (e.g. a camera or television) went out of order, shaman Lingdze said that '*seven* broke them begging that way for some offering'. People must make small offering *seven* some vodka. '*Seven* make us do it. If you don't feed them they will get angry with you!' (Ivan Torokovich). Nikolai Petrovich narrated what once happened to him when he forgot to make such an offering:

> If we do not put (vodka) in the corner, (the *seven*) take offence at us. Once it happened to me. I had been drinking and came home with a bottle. I sat at the table, opened the bottle. Was I not young that time? I poured (some vodka) for myself, but did not put anything in the corner (for the *seven*). I drank it and went to bed. How it hit me at night! I was just shaking! It came over me so suddenly! But what could I do? There was no vodka at all. I had drunk everything, I had not left anything. That time I was learning in my dreams (how to shamanise) and I always shamanised while sleeping. It hit me like that! I understood that I must find (some vodka) somewhere. It was night. Masha (my wife) ran to V. S.'s wife, who always had something in store. She brought a bottle, poured some glasses, put them in the corner and I fell asleep. In the morning I woke totally healthy and went to work. (Nikolai Petrovich)

Shamans are supposed to permanently have a vodka offering for their *seven* even with no positive reason. The shaman Mingo once forgot to renew the offering for her spirit helpers. This is her story:

> I forgot to put (vodka for my *seven*) and nearly died because of that. I sank some pasta into the boiling water and did not even have time to put the lid

on the saucepan, when I fell down and lost consciousness. The doctor came and gave me an injection. It was useless. (Nikolai Petrovich) ran to the shaman, V. S.'s wife. She shamanised and said that we must put three glasses to the corner. *Zaksor ama* and *Zaksor enie* [78] (Mingo's main spirit helpers) had taken offence at me. In fact I actually had not put (any vodka out for them), I forgot. I had a bottle. Can you remember everything when you are so young? You never know where your *seven* can come from. And if there is no offering prepared for it, it will (hit you). (Mingo)

FIGURE 10: Sacrifice. Nesulta Borisovna Geiker attaches at three sticks a cloths which is watered with the blood of a sacrificed cock. Three glasses with sacrificed vodka are on the little bench.

The shaman's dependence on his or her spirits also manifests itself in the fact that in missing offerings and sacrifices, the shaman loses the ability to heal and becomes sick or even risks dying. Chapaka Danilovna explains it in this way: 'If (a shaman) does not have an animal (for sacrifice), they (his *seven*) do not do anything (do not help him heal people). Only if there is an animal, only in that case will they start (helping). If (the shaman) tries (to perform a rite) with no animal, they (his *seven*) will kill their master. *Seven* are like that!' Irena Torombovna, who is listening to her, adds: 'It is necessary to pay for their job'. Chapaka Danilovna proceeds: 'They kill because they consider that their master has deceived them (has not paid). It is impossible without (sacrifice)'. A shaman and his congregants must pay *seven* for those acquisitions (recovery, finding lost values, etc.), which they received with their help.

---

78 *Zaksor* is the name of Nanai clan, *ama* is father, *enie* is the word for 'mother'.

Usually Nanai perform big sacrifices once a year in the late autumn. But *seven* are also thought sometimes to force people to give them a sacrifice involuntarily and unexpectedly, transgressing the established order. Ekto was carving a wooden figure of a *seven*, when he accidentally stuck the knife into his own hand and cut it. His blood poured onto the *seven* which had been just carved. The whole *seven* was anointed with blood. According to Ol'ga Egorovna's explanation, that *seven* could not resist the temptation and asked to eat some human blood right after it had been carved. The *seven's* impatience was considered to be a sign of its evil nature and a reason for the soon-to-come death of the couple.

> Who could guess (that they would die so soon)? (Ekto) was such a strong and healthy old man! He suddenly fell ill and died. She (Gara Kisovna) continued to feed that *seven* and also fell ill. She lived very little (after that) and died, too. The people do not walk down her street. They are scared. They say: 'We can see someone who is standing near her door on the porch'. Nobody walks there at night. They go along the other streets and then through the vegetable gardens. (Ol'ga Egorovna)

Seven's activivation during sacrifice

Seven are believed not only to urge people to sacrifice, but during it, unlike in the other rituals, they become active, intense and sometimes possess their master. Nanai annual sacrifice to shamanic spirits is called *undi*.[79] Its final episode *samamba mepi khorichiori* (literally: 'shaman heals himself') is the most remarkable one from the point of *seven's* activivation. Feeding his *seven*, the shaman calls them by drumming and by inviting them to a sacrifice. The shaman brings one *seven* after another. They are thought to enter his body by turn, to speak and act through him. Each *seven* is believed to come with its own melody and behave in its own way, and the shaman correspondingly changes his singing and plays the role of the newcomer like a good actor. Thus one of shaman Gara Kisovna's *seven* ('granddad') was thought to be always drunk, and when it came, she also behaved as if she was drunk for several minutes. Her other *seven*, the oldest 'granny' was believed to be very weak, and when it 'arrived', Gara Kisovna suddenly fell down. Nikolai Petrovich explained it in the following way:

> It ('granny') has come from afar and is very tired. It is an old hag indeed. That's why it is more tired than other (*seven*). It has come from afar and falls down. But it is actually a cunning person. (It wants) people to wait on it.

---

79 *Undi* is the annual sacrifice ceremony, at which the shaman goes around to his congregants' houses.

The shaman's songs during this part of the rite also contain imitations of the sounds of animals (zoomorphic spirits), and are usually interpreted as ventriloquism. Anna-Leena Siikala emphasises that in such moments of the rite the shaman feels the expectation as he concentrates on his performance (Siikala and Hoppál 1998: 35). By his sounds and movements the shaman indicates that a spirit is present, and the rite takes the form of a great show (ibid.: 37). Åke Hultkrantz (1996: 20) shares this opinion and is reminded of the well-known psychologist Oesterreich's conclusion, who went through the ethnographical material of Siberian shamanism and did not find there any certain evidence of possession, although the dramatic, mimic representations of meetings with spirits which the shaman performs, and in which he imitates the voices and behaviour of spirits, may be interpreted as relics of ancient possessional states.

However, not everything that Nanai shamans perform during sacrifice can be explained as skilful theatrical play. Nanai believe that *seven* not only possess the shaman during sacrifice, but sometimes become visible apart from his body, as if they were some independent subjects. Dancing, drumming and clanging with the metal pendants on his belt, the shaman meets one of his *seven* that came to the feast at the door and 'leads' it to the small table in the corner laid especially for *seven*. Drumming and dancing without a break, the shaman eats what his assistant puts in his mouth and then returns back to the door. But the shaman Chongida Onenko did it differently. People turned off the light; he sat down on the floor in the middle of the room with no drum and called his *seven* by turn, inviting them to the feast. The *seven*, which came in, were visible to the audience.

> 'Come on!' (Chongida shouted at his *seven*). 'Whoever wants to, you may come here!' The door was opened and closed (on its own, and the *seven* came in). There were people sitting around, old men, and other shamans. 'You just try to touch it (a *seven*)!' (Chongida) said. They were such *seven*! The very moment when (Chongida) called them, they opened and closed the door and came in. Though it was dark, people could see (them). When people held out their hands (for a *seven*), it (the *seven*) hit their hands with something. It hit those who wanted to pick it up. The shaman told them: 'Guys, leave it alone! You'll never grasp it! Never! What is the need to touch it? Don't!' The door was opened and closed. And they (the *seven*) were eating (the sacrifice food). In the twinkling of an eye they had done it, finished, and left. (The people) turned on the light. It was clear that they (the *seven*) had eaten something. The food had been touched. And there was no blood (in the bowl) left! They had drunk it all up! (Aleksei Kisovich)

The overwhelming majority of the stories about how *seven* become visible and audible tell us about sacrifice. It does not usually happen in the other rituals. For example, in shamanic travel in the spiritual world, the manifestations of the physical world are supposed to be reduced: it should be dark in the room; the shaman keeps his eyes closed and does not move around. On the contrary, the sacrifice is supposed to involve spirits in the physical world. So it is performed in the light and is full of motion and different manipulations of things. Furthermore, sacrifice is believed to be a special joy for *seven* that 'are overcome with emotions and not able to restrain themselves'. – 'An animal is sacrificed for them! How glad are the shaman's *seven*!' (Aleksandr Sergeevich). Shaman Mingo affirms that sometimes when a shaman opened his mouth to get some sacrifice food for his *seven*,[80] fire came out of shaman's mouth and went back again. 'It is a *seven*, who catches its food in the air. The *seven* sometimes plays with its shaman this way'. Earlier Nanai had windows of fish skin instead of glass. Aleksei Kisovich said that Chongida had such a *seven*, which 'flew to the sacrifice like a bullet, tearing up the skin on the window'.

In some cases the audience was also convinced that they watch spirits. Sergei M. Shirokogoroff (1999: 331) wrote that the state of many participants could be near to that of the shaman himself, and Vladimir Basilov (1990: 22) added to it that important to understanding the nature of ecstasy is the fact that it may affect not only the shaman, but also other participants of the ritual. However we cannot completely accept the thought that the shaman tries to work more miracles because it is advantageous for him. Not all the cases which we meet in reality can be explained from this point. Thus, the Nanai consider that the *seven* around the shaman sometimes become visible against the shaman's will. Several people reported that they saw the 'snakes' which came out of shaman Mariia Petrovna's mouth when she was dancing, performing the sacrifice.[81] 'The snakes came out of Mariia Petrovna's mouth. Then

---

80 Shaman's assistant pinches off some sacrifice food and put it to shaman's mouth, while shaman himself continues to drum.

81 Remembrance of Mariia Petrovna, which includes evidence of her ability to emit snakes out of her mouth, was published in M. P. Passar (2010). It consists of the following author's recollection: 'Once I came to visit her. [...] Suddenly I heard Aunt Maro's mumbling and moaning. She was sitting squatting in front of the stove. Her eyes were rolled up; there were only whites of the eyes visible. I stopped dead in my tracks: a snake coil, a finger thickness, was hanging from her mouth. Then the snake fell down onto the newspaper that was lying there. My aunt fast wrapped it and threw it into the stove. [...] At last she signed and glanced back at me. [...] With my help she hardly dragged herself to her bed and fell asleep. My cheeks aglow flaming because of what I saw. [...] Then I ventured to approach the stove and open it, I took out the crumpled newspaper and unwrapped it. But there was nothing inside. Being astonished, I was standing like that for a long time'. Mariia Petrovna was not the only shaman who had such experience. According to Toë Petrovna's words, 'when shamaness Kiakta drank alcohol, the snakes came out of her mouth. They appeared, she took them and threw them away. They appeared again and she again threw them away. It was when she was drunk. We were interested to see that something alive came out of her mouth and she threw it away. We went there, where she threw them to look, but there were not any snakes. You see how she throws them, hear how they fall with a plop. But when you go there to see, there is just nothing! It disappears'.

those snakes returned back to her mouth. It means she was a powerful shaman' (Valentina Sergeevna). Mariia Petrovna's *seven*, snakes, were believed to come out to get the offering. Her sister Toë Petrovna saw those creatures falling out of Mariia Petrovna's mouth into the bowl with the sacrificial drink.

> People put near (Mariia Petrovna a bowl with) some Labrador tea and blood. Only then did they (the snakes) begin to fall down. After they had fallen (into the bowl), people took (the bowl) outside and poured it out. At that moment the snakes disappeared. They disappeared as soon as they fell (to the ground). I saw it myself. They were like snakes. Some of them were yellowish. First they came out of her mouth and then went back in. Then she ate *kala* (sacrificial food), she ate raw meat and drank raw blood. Her *kolia* (snakes) actually ate it (instead of her). (Toë Petrovna)

Mariia Petrovna was said to suffer from her *seven'* performances and tried to stop them. At first she decided not to give her 'snakes' any sacrifice food, but it became even worse. Her *seven* appeared, 'took offence', returned back to her mouth, and then she fell ill because of it. In other words, the *seven'* volition was considered to prevail over their master's wish, and she could not manage with them. Later Mariia Petrovna made another attempt to get rid of her 'snakes'. Instead of feeding them she began to throw them into the fire.

> I saw how Mariia Petrovna flung them into the fire. She was shamanising and when the *kolia* (snakes) appeared, she threw her drumstick aside, but kept on holding her drum. Then she pulled the *kolia* out of her mouth and began to drum with them. After that she flung them into the fire. (Nikolai Petrovich)

Shaman Lingdze considers that attempt to be in vain, because it was not up to Mariia Petrovna to stop her *seven's* tricks.

> She threw them into the fire on purpose. She tried to burn them down. She was supposed to put on a saucepan, to pour in there some water with Labrador tea and, when *kolia* appeared, to sink them into it. But she (instead threw them) into the fire. She became worse, fell ill. (She did it because she) did not want them to go out (of her mouth) again. That's why she threw them into the fire. But it was useless. Such things will never stop while you are alive. [...] Mariia Petrovna fried (her *seven*), that's why it turned out so badly with her. As she cooked *talgachi*[82] (fried her *seven* as if they were fish), now she cannot sing (in the shamanic way). Her mouth is full of something. She flung all (her *seven*) into the fire! She'd better ask someone to pour some water and put

---

82 *Talgachi* is a Nanai traditional dish of fried and mashed fish.

there some Labrador tea. People would feel sorry for her; she would sink (her *seven* into that water) and they all would disappear. But she instead threw them into the fire! Now (her *seven*) have entangled her. Who will be able to help her? (Lingdze)

Seven's activation after sacrifice

The Nanai believe that *seven*, which energise during sacrifice, continue their activity for some time after it. They consider that *seven* keep on sacrificial dancing and eating for several hours after the people have finished the sacrificial ceremony.

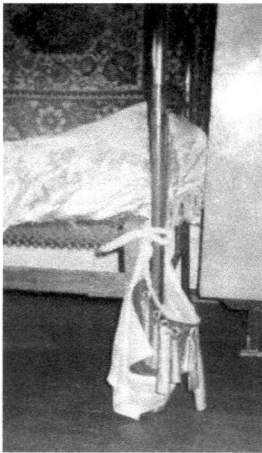

FIGURE 11: Shaman's belt with metallic pendants *yangpan* that is tied to a corner of the bed for the night.

Shamans affirm that they do not know all the spirits that they possess, and inviting them for sacrifice, they are never able to list them all. Some of the *seven* are thought to remain unfed and unsatisfied when the ceremony is finished. That's why at night, when the participants of the ritual fall asleep, the spirits, who have not 'eaten' yet, are thought to come and to continue the ritual on their own. They imitate peoples' drumming and dancing. For example, during the ceremony people tie on by turn the shamanic belt with metal pendants, and dance, drumming and clanging the pendants. At night in the deserted room, the latecomer *seven* are believed to proceed by tying on the shamanic belt, drumming, and dancing. That's why after the sacrifice is finished people don't put away the shamanic belt; they instead tie it around a leg of the bed and leave it like that for the entire night. The drum is also left in that room to be available for the *seven*. The people put the drum into its cover, leaving the mouth of the cover half opened to help *seven* to get the drum out easily.

The drum, the drumming stick, and the shamanic belt continue to work all night through. That's why the cover of the drum should be left half opened. [...] They (*seven*) keep on working. The drum is rumbling (by itself); the pendants are clanking; they (*seven*) are dancing till broad daylight. When a lot of people (*seven*) come, they are dancing till broad daylight. They (*seven*) continue doing it; they do not sleep. (Nikolai Petrovich)

The *seven* are supposed not only to dance, but also to treat themselves from the deserted table. They continue to have sacrificial food despite the festival being finished and all the dishes taken off the table. The shamans consider that *seven* eat from the reflection of the past feast, from invisible imprints of the dishes which recently were on that table. This reflection is called in Nanai *armol*. Nikolai Petrovich said: 'They (*seven*) keep on having food. They don't sleep, they continue to eat'. – 'But there is nothing on the table now!' – 'There is nothing on the table, but the *armol* (of the dishes) is still over there'. Trying to explain the meaning of the word *armol*, Nikolai Petrovich pointed at the cheval-glass:

> If I took this mirror away to the yard, its *armol* would however remain here. Do you understand it? The cheval-glass would remain here, after I have carried it out to the yard. We believe so. This is another example. I usually lie on this sofa all day long. This night I'm going to go fishing. I'll go fishing, but my *armol* will stay here on this sofa. I'm here, despite the fact that I'm actually fishing outside! And everything that was on the (sacrificial) table remains there, in spite of the fact that the table has been cleared away. (Nikolai Petrovich)

Thus, the *seven*, which come to the feast after it has been finished, are satiated with *armol* of sacrificial food and dancing. At the same time the shaman and some other people watch in their dreams what is going on in the deserted room, where the drum in the untied cover and the shamanic belt tied to the leg of a bed have been left. In the morning they share their dreams and discuss what other *seven* came to the feast at night.

We can assume that such an invisible sacrificial party is merely a 'mirror image' in human's minds of real events that happened in the normal world, just as an *armol* is a reflection of a material item. But the Nanai shamans' conception is different. They believe that, on the contrary, not people, but *seven*, are initiators of sacrifice; that it is not people who ascribe to *seven* ability to act in human way, but *seven* themselves who teach people how to act performing rituals. Probably people do merely what spirits want them to do. That's why shamans try to learn beforehand from their dreams what the ritual acts should be like, what kind of sacrifice food should be prepared, and what kind of wooden sculpture the *seven* would agree to be incarnated. If a shaman takes no heed of such kind of edifications, his *seven* will punish him with diseases and other troubles.

Dance as a kind of *seven's* behaviour

Leopold Shrenk affirms that according to Giliak (Nivkh) ideas, shamanic spirits fulfil their duties always dancing, and that this corresponds to the dances of shamans themselves. The thing is just that the spirit's appearance and its dance is not visible to anyone else but a shaman (Shrenk 2011: 123). One could suppose that it is shamans, who ascribe to *seven* their own ability to dance. But shamans themselves believe that *seven* use dances on their own, independently of people. Dancing is thought to be a kind of *seven*' usual behaviour. Not only in dreams but in reality are drumming and dancing *seven* believed to become audible, as if they themselves are performing some kind of ritual.

Nesulta Borisovna said that her son Misha was on the hunt inside his winter hut when he heard from outside the sound of drum and pendants on shaman belt. The sound was coming near and then someone seemed to drum and dance right behind his door.[83] 'He could go off his head! It (the creature behind the door) was dancing like that: *dung-dung, kalia-kalia*. It did it like that. What good was in it? (Misha was) alone in the taiga, in wilderness! How frightened was he, poor thing! He put his knife on the ground near the stove'.

Not only the Nanai, but also their neighbours, people of other nationalities, who don't practice shamanism, sometimes hear *seven* drumming and dancing. Zinaida Nikolaevna talked about some Russians who heard such sounds in a deserted house.

> In Sinda village, the Russians told the Nanai: 'Why don't you believe in your spirits? We've learned how frightful they are. We do not tell about it because of shame. People may decide that we are also believers!' It happened that those Russians had gone fishing. They stayed at night in a deserted house. They went to bed and heard on the garret something like a small bell beginning to roll over, here and there. Some voices were heard, and then a resounding drumming, a clanging of pendants on a shamanic belt, and yells (as if someone was dancing). [...] The fishermen jumped up and ran to the Amur (River), leaving all their stuff (in that house). (Zinaida Nikolaevna)

The fact that the Russians, who did not know anything about Nanai beliefs, heard in the uninhabited places the same sounds which the Nanai themselves heard is for the Nanai an indisputable argument proving the existence of the spiritual world. The spirits are thought to drum and dance in the shamanic way on their own, and people either imitate their behaviour or are possessed, giving to spirits their physical bodies as temporary vehicles.

Seven are also believed to pass the ability to dance from shamans' ancestors to their descendants. Each neophyte learns his own manner of drumming and dancing from his dreams. In Mariia Innokent'evna's story the *seven* took a shaman beginner in his dreams to the Land Yaoka Mountain, where his ancestors lived, and taught him how to drum and to dance.

---

83   *Dung-dung, kalia-kalia* are the words signifying the sound of the metal pendants on the sha-
     manic belt.

I dreamt that an old man came to me. There was a drum in his hands. As soon as he came, he began to sing in the shamanic way. He was (sitting and) performing some kind of ritual, and I was watching him in silence. Then he got up and began to dance. He was dancing and drumming like that *nam-mo, nam-mo!*[84] I told him: 'Where did you hear someone who would drum this way *nam-mo, nam-mo* dancing?' Probably people (other *seven*) taught him in his dreams to drum and dance like that *nam-mo, nam-mo*. I did not hear what he answered. I woke up. (Mariia Innokent'evna)

Chapaka Danilovna was called to be a shaman and met in her dreams the dance teachers, her *seven*:

In my dream I had climbed the hill. There was an old Nanai house on the top. (I came in). There was a stove, a copper. The people were stoking it. The steam was rising. There were plank beds. My (*seven*) 'mother' was bossing it. She told me: 'Dance!' I answered: 'I can't. I've never danced before. I can't. I don't want to'. – 'If you can't, look how other people dance!' I looked: My 'mother' was dancing with a drum and shamanic belt. She had the shavings on her head. Someone said to me: 'You should do it the same way as she does'. They gave me a drum; put everything (shamanic belt) on me. But I could not! I was pacing like military people pace. I was pacing so funny: *tuk-tuk!*[85] 'I am not able to dance. I can't'. How they wanted me (to dance)! But I did not want it, however! I will never become a shaman. I don't want to. (Chapaka Danilovna)

Seven, which call people for shamanic practice, are considered to be first of all the dance teachers. This teaching is usually reinforced with threats in case of refusal. The shaman Kada remembers that her 'teacher' said, if she declined, she would die. 'Dance!' it said. In case the neophyte accepted the shamanic call, performed the sacrifice and danced, his *seven* gave him (especially for the first time) unusual strength and cured him of his diseases. Ol'ga Egorovna reported that her father was paralysed and could not get up from his bed for three years. Then he agreed to become a shaman.

My father could not dance. Then they raised him. One man bore him from behind, two other ones from the sides. That way they danced (all four together) three rounds. But as soon as (the *seven*) came, my father ran on his own. The men let him go, and my father was running, running, and running. Then he fell down and said: 'I cannot any more. I'm old'. [...]
But his legs were paralysed!

---

84 *Nam-mo* is the word signifying the rhythm of drumming.
85 *Tuk-tuk* is the word signifying the sound of Dusiia's paces.

All the same, he got up. After he finished, he fell down.
How was he able to get up?
His *seven* was probably carrying him. (Ol'ga Egorovna)

The significance of dancing, which is thought to be a usual behaviour of *seven*, differs in various shamanic rites. Dance is used in several of the rites, but for most of them it is not a necessary part. Sacrifice, and especially its final episode, *samamba mepi khorichiori* ('shaman heals himself'), cannot be performed without it. Maybe that's why the name of that episode is often replaced with the word *'meuri'* ('dance'). In everyday speech when people want to say something about sacrifice they mostly use the last word. They can speak about sacrifice this way: 'They killed the animal and danced'. – 'The shaman fell ill, he has to dance'. – 'The shaman has got into trouble, that's why he is going to dance'. Talking about her shaman father, Ol'ga Egorovna could say: 'When he fell ill, my mother told him: 'Come on! Dance! Maybe you'll recover after that!' They argued. But he never danced until he died'. In all such expressions 'to dance' means 'to perform a sacrifice'.

According to native Nanai ideas, *seven* can dance independently of a shaman, and it is they, which force their shaman to dance together with them even under his protest. They have their own will, which can be subordinated to a shaman's in some rites and they always impose their will on that shamanists who refuses to sacrifice and to dance with them.

SHAMAN ON THE STAGE

(Shamans) must not perform on a stage, because *seven* does not like it.
Otherwise it attacks a shaman, and the shaman feels sick right away. Very sick.
It is because his *seven* does not want to shamanise in vain, to no purpose.
Seven does not want him to perform on the stage for nothing.
(Ol'ga Egorovna)

At present, while the traditions in the North are rapidly being destroyed and the ethnic identity is being lost, bringing back shamanic practice is perceived as an integral part of ethnical revival. 'Ethnic mobilisation as a global phenomenon everywhere actively used religious markers, which became one of the demonstrable determinants of the development of society' (Glavatskaia 2010: 240). Shamanism is often understood now as 'one of the most important elements of the culture of the indigenous peoples of the North, which not only marks the uniqueness of each of them, but also constructs their circumpolar unity (Popkov 2006: 235). Meanwhile, because in many places in the North shamanism in its classical variant is lost, the actual 'preservation or reconstruction of traditions' has become impossible and now we are dealing with creating new ones. 'The new social conditions led to a cardinal change of the shamanic praxis forms; they partly transformed functions of today's (neo-) shamans and even caused some super-new and original personages among the adherents of shamanism. But the idea of a person-shaman was proved to be not only not unchallengeable, but it acquired new content' (Kharitonova 2006: 6). By 2013 there was only one traditional Nanai shaman left, Ol'ga Egorovna, who because of her age (born in 1920) has not been practicing for long time.[86] At the same time new (neo-)shamans appear who work in a completely different way (laying hands, massage, etc.).

In the short period of change from classical shamanism to neo-shamanism there was an interesting phenomenon – presenting not actors, but real shamans on the stage. It happened from the mid-1980s to the mid-1990s because on the one hand, during that time there were still some real classical Nanai shamans practicing, and, on the other hand, there was a need to fill with some material those numerous performances and cultural events which were called to demonstrate the activity of preserving the culture of the indigenous peoples of the North. There were specialists whose job it was to show the native folklore on stage, explain it, the cultural establishments, the system of boarding schools and the administration, which helped them to organise the Soviet festivals, or just national festivals (as it is now called), put them before the necessity to step onto the stage (Ol'zina 1997: 10).

During that time requests were received to perform folklore on stage. But there was not (with some exceptions) a good professional base to satisfy these requirements and to arrange the folklore. As a result, such pseudo-folk compositions appeared on the stage, which have almost nothing in common with authentic folklore. The simplest way for the organisers of the festivals was not to think about any arrangements for the stage, but simply to bring to the stage authentic folklore as it was, not arranged at all and not adapted to the conditions of the stage. It happened when not actors and singers, but bearers of the tradition themselves went on stage. 'In contrast to the European peoples who bring to the stage arranged folklore', writes Ol'zina (1997: 10), 'we have brought to it a part of our own life which is authentic folklore'. At the same time as shamanism was becoming a popular fad, the real shaman, practicing in traditional surroundings, was also appearing on the stage as the performer of folklore and sometimes even as the performer of real shamanic rituals right on the stage. Sometimes the shaman was presented as a lecturer, to popularise his shamanic activity. Real shamanic actions were performed at folklore festivals, because their organisers had started to include shamanic sacrifices in the programmes. Thus the phenomenon of the appearance of a shaman on the stage has become widespread.

---

86 Ol'ga Egorovna died in March 2013.

More widespread, mass healing has also led the shaman on stage.[87] It was not a long phenomenon, as on the same sites this was rapidly replaced by neo-shamanic, as by the new, modernised form of shamanism (like the shamanic theatre, which has been opened in Yakutsk). The essential peculiarity of all the new forms of (neo-) shamanic practice is that they are not naturally developing from tradition, but being introduced from outside, borrowing from other cultures or being artificially created by local workers in the field of culture.

> They select from the past a segment which is suitable – or at least, seems to be suitable – for expressing and maintaining, with vital intensity of feeling, the emotional ties of attachment to the ethnic group. In other words, this neo-shamanism could be an excellent symbol – and, at the same time, technique – of the reproduction of ethnic identity in a postmodern milieu' (Hoppál 1992: 201).

The phenomenon of classical shamans (not yet neo-shamans) on the stage becomes a transition from classical to neo-shamanism. Just the fact that a traditional shaman, invited to a public performance, is not supposed to perform a ritual (or does not perform just a ritual) on the stage, but to demonstrate in public[88] his art of singing and dancing has changed the habitual stress. The stage or just the presence of onlookers can correct the content of the ritual performance. Using the concrete material collected among the Nanai, let us examine to what extent stage shamanism promotes the preservation of the identity of the culture and how the tradition bearers and the shamans who practice in their habitual surroundings, treat these new forms of shamanism.

Shaman as an actor

Bringing 'a piece of real life' to stage guarantees the essential attribute of a performance, its true cultural authenticity. But at the same time it leads to some special problems. As the practice has shown, the authentic performance is alien to the stage laws that are to hold the audience's interest. There is then no stage presence, no excitement. Authentic folklore, which existed well in its natural surroundings, was badly perceived by uninitiated onlookers. It has turned out itself not to be real entertainment, not good amusement (Ol'zina 1997: 10). What is more, they have not succeeded in turning shamanic ritual into a variety show, because their spirit-helpers,

---

87 Bat'ianova (2004: 251) reports that 'inefficient attempts at reviving the traditional beliefs and the intrusions of ignorant activists upon the sacral sphere resulted in an increase in suicide'.

88 The audience is not just a group of passive onlookers. They do not only watch the ritual. The presence of everybody supports the shaman and is believed to have some mystical meaning.

FIGURE 12: From the festival 'Living thread of times', Khabarovsk, 2010. (top)
FIGURE 13: The Nanai language teacher Marina Aleksandrovna El'tyn performing at the festival. (left)
FIGURE 14: Nowadays shamanic dances on stage. (right)

as the shamans affirm, come to them even on the stage, so they have to communicate with them right before the onlookers' eyes, who do not even suspect it. That's why most of the shamans treat that experiment badly. The untimely communication with their spirits is objectionable to the shamans for the shamans realise they must not arouse their spirits as mere playthings. For shamans, not all the world is a stage.

Not only on the stage, but also in their everyday lives, the shamans are scared of their spirit helpers. They are frightened to take a false step to irritate them and so to be punished. 'If you laugh at the *endur* ('the spirit')', the shaman-woman Niura Sergeevna said, 'you will die straight away!' – 'If a shaman is silly', said she the next time, 'and gives away too much, he won't live long. He must not say too much!' The ritual for show could make the shaman forget about caution and cause the unpredictable reaction of his disturbed spirits. The same Niura Sergeevna said: 'Once some people from Leningrad came to my place with Valerii Ivan Torokovich. He told me: 'Well, put on your dressing-gown of fish leather and let you dance in the shamanic way round your house!' I told him: 'I must not do that! Nobody must do it like this! I can dance just at home, but if I do it like you want me to, I'll fall ill and die!' So I did nothing for them that time'.

There is a fragment of another shaman Lingdze's ritual, in which she boasts that she has yielded to no persuasion and has never taken part in any contemporary cultural programmes:

How many times they tried to drag me by force everywhere,
They (wanted to) take me away!
As long ago as when Kaplan [89] was here, she wanted to take me away.
But I don't sell myself for a ruble or for two.
And after her there were some more people,
I don't remember where they came from.
They made me *yai* ('sing in a shamanic way') about everything,
They made me do some *erde* (tricks).
However many hundred, however many thousand rubles
people would get out,
that's all the same. It would not attain my *ergen* (soul);
it would not reach it, and it would not reach my heart either.
I don't want it [...]
It's impossible to live, as the other people will tell you.
I cannot live according to the other people's words. (Lingdze)

Lingdze has actually never travelled anywhere and has never stepped on the stage. In 1991, she nevertheless agreed to be the head of the ritual *kasa* [90] ('sending souls of the deceased to the other world') that was performed in front of the video camera. The ritual was considerably changed in comparison with its traditional variant. We

---

89 Mariia Abramovna Kaplan was a researcher of Nanai tales, a research worker of the Russian Museum of Ethnography in Leningrad and a worker of *Krasnaia Yurta* (Red Yurt) among the Nanai.

90 Officially, the ritual *kasa* has not been openly performed since the 1930s. Some people affirm that it was secretly done through up to the 1960s.

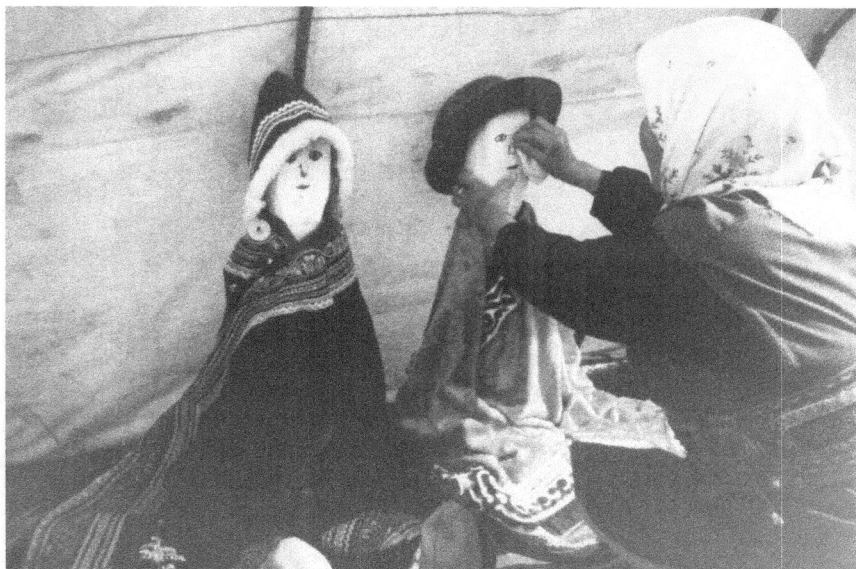

FIGURE 15–17: The *kasa*-ritual, the dolls representing the souls of the departed.

FIGURE 18: As in the world of the dead there is an opposite season of the year, the ritual is executed in early fall. Therefore the shaman wears a winter-dress and uses a sledge for the transport of the souls. (right)

can see this, judge by how much it was cut (several hours instead of three through seven days as in traditional ritual). According to some participants' replies, they were always aware of being in front of the video camera (they worried, for example, if the ringing of the small bells on the shaman's hat was being recorded well). They also did not forget that they were acting against the tradition and exposing themselves to danger. That's why, when Lingdze began the ritual, she sang, appealing to her spirits:

Let nothing bad happen to the people who have come to shoot a film.
Let nothing bad happen either to grandfather or to me,
no matter what we are saying. (Lingdze)

Several days after they performed this ritual, Lingdze said: 'It was ridiculous what we were doing! Vexing and ridiculous! We were performing, but I turned aside and asked (the spirits): 'We are making such noise, such hubbub! But spare us!' And she concluded: 'Maybe some of us will fall ill now!' Later she actually affirmed that just because of that ritual performed in front of the video camera, one of its participants died, the son of another one also died and her own pig with all its piglets died, too.

Nowadays, in the programme of different festivals held in Nanai district, like everywhere in the North of Russia, they began to include the 'local ethnographic material'. The old people who know the traditions well are invited to perform traditional rituals before the onlookers. But the old people themselves usually treat this innovation with suspicion. Mariia Vasil'evna has been a worker in the field of culture all her life. That's why, on the one hand, she is in sympathy with those who try to organise such arrangements. On the other hand, she has lived a long life and knows the traditions well. Like the other aged people, she fears the contacts with the spirits not planned by the organisers of folk festivals. 'At the festival', she said, 'they made us bow to *temu* ("the spirit of water"). They made us feed the water. They took me with them in order that I would bow, too. But two women (who were invited with the same purpose) refused to bow. Well, will I bow alone? And we told the chief of the cultural department: "We won't go to the beach!"'[91]

Today the request for those shamans, who agreed to show their art before an audience, has become nevertheless so big, and the opportunities opened before them have become so tempting, that some could not stand their ground. Thus in 1994, a shaman woman, Mingo, agreed to go the United States, where she showed her art in Seattle Unity Church and on Bainbridge Island (Washington State), where the special seminar was conducted (Bel'dy 1999: 15, 17). Great success and the presents turned her head. She told me after she had returned: 'I have conquered America!' and recollected with exaltation how one of the Americans even bowed before her. But she was already sick that time. She fell ill right after she returned home. Then

---

91 Later Mariia Vasil'evna agreed to perform this ritual.

she had an operation and died soon afterwards. Mingo died right after she returned home. According to Chapaka Danilovna's words,

> having come back, she fell badly ill. Her eyes hurt, she even lost consciousness. That's how (her spirits) punished her! (Her spirits meant:) 'She was travelling all around chattering and did not pay any attention to us!' Her own *seven* spirits have tortured her to death. Her own *seven*! Like other the shamans who have gone somewhere, she died. They travel and die. I pity them! (Chapaka Danilovna)

The reason for Mingo's death was explained by her trip to the United States. 'She danced and sang in the shaman way on the sea shore in America', Nesulta Borisovna said. 'And the people filmed her. She fell ill right after she was back. Such grief!' The tours of the other Nanai shamans also ended tragically. As far as in 1983, shaman woman Gara Kisovna went to Moscow to the festival of the Art of USSR's Peoples. After she returned home, her husband Ekto died. She lived a little more than a year after this trip and also died. Lingdze explained both these deaths with Gara Kisovna's appearing on the Moscow stage. 'Gara Kisovna came to Moscow', she said, 'and something bad has struck her. She shamanised just like that, playing with it. She travelled and shamanised. Do they like it? Do her *amban* ('her spirits') like it? The word sung in the shamanic way is not a joke! Wherever they have taken her! Wherever they have carried her! Everywhere she danced in the shamanic way. (Having returned,) she told me: 'There was nothing bad in it!' But the *amban* does not like it when people shamanise in vain!'

Shaman Mariia Petrovna's death is also considered to be the sequel of her tour to France and Italy and of her performances there. [92] Mentioned here, Mariia Vasil'evna went there with her. She remembers that dancing with a drum on the stage, Mariia Petrovna herself feared that something bad could happen. 'She was just dancing on the stage', recollects Mariia Vasil'evna, 'but she was afraid to sing in a shamanic way. She was chanting just two words: *"Mimbive aiasigoando!"* ("Let me be well!") She

---

92 Another explanation of why the shamans die after they have come back is that the spirits from the other lands follow them, but the shamans do not know how to cope with such spirits. According to Dusiia's words, once Mariia Petrovna, who had returned from the trip, was shamanising at her place. Suddenly she said that she sees a person who is standing behind the door. For the other participants of her ritual this person was invisible. Dusiia was also there and she speaks about it this way: 'Mariia Petrovna asked Niura, what she would advice her to do. 'What must I do?' she said. 'He wants to come in. He is standing behind the door'. I did not like it', said Dusiia. 'Why would she bring this spirit in? But Niura told her: 'Well, bring it in!' And she had brought it in. It came to her place because it caught the smell of the sacrifice animal she fed her *seven*. This food had drawn its attention. And it began to harm Mariia Petrovna. It had not gone anywhere. That is why she had problems with her head. That is why those shamans who have visited other countries do not live long. They die'.

repeated only these two words. She did not sing much. One must not (shamanise) just in jest! But she is playing on the stage! If she does it playing, she'll fall ill. Her *seven* will punish her'. – 'In general, shamanic matter is a fearful one!' In this way Mariia Vasil'evna concludes her reasoning. But just the same as Mingo and Gara Kisovna, having come home, Mariia Petrovna, was overwhelmed with impressions, recollected her trip with delight and even thought to change her life in order to continue singing and travelling round the world. 'When she was back from her trip', Nesulta Borisovna said, 'Mariia Petrovna told me that she is stopping shamanising and is becoming an actress and a singer. After that she did not live long. She fell ill and died and did not become an actress'. When I brought Lingdze the news about Mariia Petrovna, who had just died in the nearby village and had not yet been buried, Lingdze took her drum; she began to cry about her and to sing, recalling also Gara Kisovna, who died before.

> They were crying and when I stop crying I don't know [...]
> Poor thing! Why were not you ashamed? [...]
> You lived that way to be like you are now, with no breathing [...]
> You went to the city and sang there and made such noise
> that the ground cleft, and your cry (went in) there.
> What have they covered it with? What have people let you go with?
> You should not have permitted them to torment you like this!
> What did you want to become living this way? [...]
> What did Gara Kisovna and you find there (in the city),
> if you agreed to give away your own breath (for this)?
> (Gara Kisovna also) went to make noise (to shamanise for filming) to an island.
> What was good in it? (Lingdze)

'People took her all over the taiga and the meadows', Lingdze recalls Gara Kisovna, 'they tormented her in such a way that her old disease recommenced. She would have to say a million times, a thousand times: 'I don't want! I don't want!' I feel sorry for her!' – 'She went so far', next time Lingdze says. 'The people asked her to say different things. It was as if they hurt her making her say different words. It was as if they tore her body asking her to tell. And she told. She applied to the sky, to something else and asked for mercy'. – 'They took Gara Kisovna to different places. They took her to the taiga and made her dance in a shamanic way. It would have been better if she shamanised on the floor (in rooms), but they took her everywhere. And she could not bear it any longer. If she had lived quietly, she would be still alive. They had just taken her to the hospital and she died at night. She did not know what else she could do for herself (how to help herself), so she went to the hospital. When she came to my place before it and I made *pergechi* ('foreseeing ritual') for her, her *panian* ('soul') was already dead. How could I tell her: 'You have already died!' It is impossible to tell people such things. Despite this it was not possible to shamanise then, I tried to do everything according to her wishes. I felt sorry for her! I feel sorry for everybody! People cry before their death. Although he cries, how can you save him! Your time has come and you die!'

> If you have shamanised in the right way, you would be still alive [...]
> Being occupied with such a matter,
> permitting people to take you everywhere,
> have you earned much money?
> Were you so merry because of a ruble or two?
> You had enjoyed yourselves so much that (you let them) take your breath away!
> You bring so much junk, that you are not able to carry it in your rucksack.
> But I ask people nothing! (Lingdze)

After Gara Kisovna returned from Moscow, Lingdze dreamed of coming to Lingdze's home and saying:

> My sister, none (of my spirit-helpers) has stayed with me [...]
> All my *seven* ('spirits') have been left in Moscow,
> Because I shamanised in the wrong place,
> played the fool and made noise. (Lingdze)

Lingdze dreamt the same about Mariia Petrovna, who had just returned from her trip:

> Marus'ka ('Mariia Petrovna') went to the city.
> When returning, she sat behind my (closed) door and
> peeped through the chink.
> Seeing her while she was peeping, I asked her:
> 'My sister, why don't you come in?
> You were able to travel all over the different countries.
> Why cannot you also come to my place?'
> But she never came and went away.
> She thought I would tell her something.
> Oh, my friends, I feel sorry for them! (Lingdze)

According to traditional ideas, when a shaman performs on the stage and unwillingly calls his spirit-helpers, these spirits don't wish to appear to give the shaman an opportunity to demonstrate to an audience (who don't really perceive the essence of what is going on) just the character of the traditional ways of singing. If they have come, they want to do something habitual and get a reward for that. These presentations follow the common idea that shamanic spirits cannot work without profit.

'The *seven* (spirits) force their master to work all the time', says shaman Ol'ga Egorovna. 'Come on, work! Heal people! Do something! Don't sit like this! Come on, work!' If a shaman doesn't want to work, his *seven* would punish him. His company doesn't wish to sit inactively. They are sitting whereas they must work! Because they want to eat! If one does not feed his *seven*, it will kill his own master. It will start to crunch him. 'It is you who forces us to crunch you! You don't want to feed us!' – 'We', Ol'ga Egorovna continues, 'work in the *kolkhoz* in the same way. If the *kolkhoz* pays us nothing, we abuse our chief as well!'

The unlucky shaman-actresses also perceived all this. As long as both Gara Kisovna, who had just returned from Moscow, and Mariia Petrovna, who had not yet travelled anywhere, were alive, the latter discussed Gara Kisovna's trip this way: 'Gara Kisovna took her drum to Moscow with no certain purpose. The master of the drum (spirit) wants to heal, taking into account that the people being healed would feed it then. The master of the drum thought to profit by this. But it did not get any prey!' So Mariia Petrovna decided that a disappointed spirit chose a victim on its own. He chose the chief of the Communist Party, Leonid Brezhnev, who died exactly during those days when Gara Kisovna was in Moscow. 'On the way back', continues Mariia Petrovna, 'it was the same. (For her spirits) it was travel in vain with no work and no gain. So in Daerge (where Gara Kisovna lived) they (her spirits) chose the old man Innokentii as a victim. After Gara Kisovna came, Innokentii died'. According to Chapaka Danilovna's opinion, shamanic spirits could leave their masters alone only if they would be successful in turning their trips into big rituals and involving in them all the onlookers.

Continuing to shamanise, Lingdze sees Gara Kisovna's spirit-helpers, which are invisible to us and which she had not been able to overpower.

Gara Kisovna, the *diaka* (your spirits)
Are behind you, bristled up and spread wide! (Lingdze)

Those, who organise shamanic performances, consider them to be just a cultural component, a chance to demonstrate the ethnic identity of traditional art. But this thought is in sharp contradiction to the traditional ideas, according to which any word sung by a shaman causes contact with spirits, sometimes really unsafe ones. In some cases it was possible to change the mind of some shamans for a while and to induce them to go on a tour, the other shamans, who stayed at home, reproached them for desacralisation of the ritual, reducing it to a mere variety show, dangerous, because *seven* oppose it. Filming shamanic activity on stage can promote the preservation of the memory of the traditional art and fix it by documentation. But the question is still open if they actually help to preserve this art by bringing to the stage a 'piece of real traditional life'.

An actor performed the role of a shaman

Another phenomenon widespread recently is the role of a shaman performed by an actor, an uninitiated person, who does not believe in any spirits and is not afraid of anything. But even in this case, as the bearers of tradition affirm, if an actor sings in a shamanic way quite accurately, he inevitably brings the spirits to the stage and it happens irrespective of the actor's convictions. As the contact with spirits is believed to be unsafe even for the shaman, moreover it is considered to be fraught with danger for the uninitiated one, who does not know how to cope. There are many stories about such performances. 'One guy performed a shaman', Nikolai Petrovich said, 'and at that moment got very ill, he fell down right on the stage'. His wife, shaman Mingo, listening to him, clarified: 'One must not sing in the shamanic way without a reason. Otherwise he will fall and die. The *seven* ('shamanic spirit') comes to you, but you have no special *yai seven* ('the *seven*, which permits you to sing in a shamanic way'). What will you do when it jumps upon you? Of course, you will die! If you are not a shaman, you must not sing (in a shamanic way)! You can go out of your mind or fall ill and then die!'

Meanwhile some resourceful Nanai have however found a means to earn money using the request for shamanic singing. They go on tours, even abroad and don't expose themselves to the danger of contact with shamanic spirits. The bearers of tradition explain that it happened because such actors listened to the shamans and learned what means they can bring into play and in what way they must not perform as a shaman. The most effective means to draw spirits is shamanic singing, that is, the special incantation of special words. The certain elements of shamanic dress are also important because spirits can be embodied there. On the other hand, dance is a quite neutral element of the ritual. During the traditional rituals, most of their participants (not shamans) take turns on the drum; wear the shamanic belt with its metal pendants, and dance. But they dance in silence and they don't wear any shamanic cloth. Therefore, while dancing they don't draw spirits, and merely confirm their devotion to the shaman, the main performer of the ritual. Following this example, the actors, who have to perform a shaman on the stage, intentionally distort the most effective, they believe, elements of shamanic behaviour and hope to relieve in this way the ritual from its dangerous strength. Wearing the dress, which we would not call ethnographically authentic, they dance, beat the drum and clang the metal pendants, but either do not sing at all or sing some innocuous words with some lyrical tune. So they overcome the fear of performing as a shaman by using purposefully wrong words and wrong intonation. In this way, the traditional form is intentionally changed. Mariia Vasil'evna remembers that in 1950 they put a drama on the stage and offered her the part of a shaman there. Dancing with a drum, Mariia Vasil'evna repeated only the words *'Piktesi aiagoando!'* ('Let your children be healthy!'). 'I could say just these words', she explains, 'I must not say anything else during all the performance. Otherwise I could fall ill. If I had repeated what the shaman actually sings, the *amban* would have heard me! They are always nearby, as (the shaman) Lingdze says! They would have heard me and I would have fallen ill. It would have been bad for me! Why would I repeat it? I would not have been well. (It is not safe) for those who are not able to repeat the shamanic words. No, of course, I fear!'

According to the traditional presentations, the most effective in the shamanic ritual is a special word chanted in a special way. Just words, intoned in a certain rhythm, draw the spirits. Putting on the real shamanic dress is also considered to be dangerous. But anyone can dance with a drum. That is why those who have to perform the role of shaman are not afraid to beat a drum and dance. But they intentionally pronounce 'wrong' words, which are chanted in a way unlike a shaman would intone them, but like they sing their everyday lyric songs. When some reporters came from Khabarovsk to film a shaman, Mariia Vasil'evna, who wanted to earn some money, agreed to dance like a shaman round the fire. Before going to the beach where the fire had been made, she asked Lingdze what she should change, to distort in her performance to guard herself against contact with the spirits. This fact is quite significant for our topic. How can such a performance be a means of maintaining the ethnic uniqueness, if (according to the traditional ideas) actors can secure themselves against the spirits only having refused to adopt the authenticity of what they are performing? Artificial growth of 'secondary' staged shamanic folklore hardly can be considered to be a reliable means of preserving ethnic identity.

Ethnic mixing in the image of a staged shaman

Probably just that causes such typical mixing of different ethnic features in the image of a staged shaman. [93] This image is quite common for different peoples of the North of Russia. [94] Now such an 'international' shaman appears not only before those who would like to see a show, but also for those who want to be healed. Following the numerous healers and extra sensors, some 'shamans' come to the stage to heal members of the audience. But we should find out at first if they really are shamans, to what extent they are bound to the tradition, and if their action is effective in preserving

---

93 Amateur talent activity, which was organised in the North by the Soviet Rule, elaborated a model of how to sing and dance. That model was common for all the peoples of the North of Russia. Yurii I. Sheikin, who investigated this amateur talent activity in the North, noticed how similar and ethnically neutral were the songs of the different peoples of the North, which they perform on the stage. This fact will impress us even more if we know to what extent their traditional songs differ (Sheikin 1996).

94 Shamanic dances on the stage can significantly differ from their traditional variants. They are performed not by one at a time, but collectively, and are mostly based on newly invented choreography. But rhythmically beating the drum in the rhythm of body movements constitutes their main element.

ethnic identity. We have never heard about a traditional shaman who made up his mind to change the methods of his activity and go to the stage. In our view, it is impossible because all this activity is really connected with all traditional surroundings. Only some shaman-innovators and autodidacts can do that. They often have shamanic inheritance and so can demonstrate some unusual abilities. But they use new forms borrowed from the contemporary reality, not traditional ones.

Young representatives of Northern peoples identify shamanic activity with the work of a contemporary healer, because they consider shamanic spirits to be that kind of energy which the healers use as well. Quite significant recently is the appearance of a dissertation, in which the author for the first time, as she writes, has formulated the concept that 'Nanai shamans use extra sensory abilities'. Here we have an author who considers herself the bearer of Nanai language and culture, so we can look to her point as typical of today's generation of the Nanai (Bel'dy 1999). As young successors of the shamans don't care now which cultural form they should choose to demonstrate their shamanic abilities, we have to raise serious doubts that this new revised shamanism is the most important means of preserving the ethnic identity of Northern peoples.

'Last summer', Ol'ga Egorovna relates, 'a man came here. He was a Nanai. His wife was a Tatar. He said: 'I grew up in a children's home in Komsomolsk. I have no parents'. He does not understand a word of Nanai. The newspaper *Tikhookeanskaia Zvezda* ('The Pacific Star') published an article about him. (In the photo there) he is with a shamanic drum wearing not Nanai dress but some other nationality dress, but a shamanic one and the shamanic hat with fringe. And the title: 'I am studying to become a shaman!' How can one become a shaman if the spirits won't punish him? (She laughs). 'I am studying to become a shaman!' He will surely be a shaman! Some bad *ambashki* ('evil spirits') will come to him and he will shamanise with them. They (the spirits) need to eat!' (Ol'ga Egorovna)

Contemporary artificial revival of shamanism is happening, as a rule, not in traditional surroundings. Adapting to these new surroundings, a shaman on the stage either avoids contact with spirits (shaman-actor) or, on the contrary, uses this contact for his purposes (shaman-healer). But in both cases he is not able to use the traditional forms of shamanising. The reason is these forms are closely connected with the traditional way of shamanising.

Traditional shamanism, if one can find it now, is inseparably linked with other elements of traditional culture, which makes a single, indivisible system. This makes us doubt that one can use any isolated element of this system as a means of preserving the identity. It is well known that the phenomenon of national self-consciousness can hardly be connected with just one isolated element of the culture (for example,

164

with a language or with a religion). Not only shamanism, but also language, folklore, ritual system, norms of behaviour and some other forms to express ethnic, national self-consciousness fulfil the functions which help us to differentiate one *ethnos* from another. It goes in accordance with the traditional ideas, which are still kept in the North of Russia, and which say that it is impossible to isolate an element of shamanic ritual and to show it on the stage for exclusively art value. The neophytes who want to practice shamanism like a kind of healing, are not able to return to the traditional shamanism anymore. (Dramatic changes in the way of life made it impossible.) They prefer to adapt to the new conditions and to borrow some contemporary forms of analogous activity. Both for the shaman-actors and for the shaman-healers, the new variant of shamanism has some distinctive traditional features, but is not according to the traditional practice at all. Thus shamanism, all the more, cannot be an effective means of preserving identity.

Despite the fact that 'ethnoreligiosity' now became one of the most widely available and recognizable brands of ethnic identity, one would not say that it has dealings with the ethnographically correct restoration of shamanism. Not only the reviving of the ethnic culture by means of shamanic practice restoration can be considered to be doubtful; some researchers call into question the very possibility of the restoration of shamanism as such: 'It is a very strange undertaking to revive shamanism. Only external stimulation of some processes is possible, but not revival. [...] Interfering with the deeply inward and esoteric life (if we mean to revive really sacral practice) is hardly achievable. If nevertheless some attempts are made from outside, they merely lead to some strange deformations' (Kharitonova 2006: 259). A shaman on the stage is now rather a generalised symbol of indigenous culture, which blends all the Northern cultures together with unified contemporary mass culture.

Shamanism applies not only to tales, art and dances, but also to all other spheres of society's life. Blacksmiths, unusually successful hunters, and traditional judges were believed to be connected with the spiritual world. The traditional economic and power strategies were sometimes determined by persons who were dependent on communication with spirits not less than shamans. That dependence, adaptability and flexibility of the traditional spiritual practices becomes more noticeable in periods of socio-cultural change. In the next chapter and in the epilogue, there will be provided a comparison drawn from ethnographical descriptions concerning pre-Soviet, Soviet and post-Soviet data. The first sections of chapter 4 are devoted to vengeance relationships between clans and to the shamanic judiciary system concerning pre-Soviet times, since the Soviet regime put an end to such local practices, and the epilogue briefly concerns present-day neo-shamans.

4 POLITICAL AND LEGAL LABOURS RULED BY SPIRITS

THE SPIRITUAL NATURE OF JUDICIAL AUTHORITY

> In the court the judge made a mistake with his words and died right afterwards.
> If he had pleaded that case right, he would not have died.
> How can it be that a person died because of what he said?
> *(Chapaka Danilovna)*

The traditional Nanai social system was notable for its internal order and external lack of any special power-holding structures and apparatus of coercion, which would keep people within legal boundaries. The scholars observed that all the public agents they met were actually the representatives either of Russians *(starshina)* or of Chinese and Manchurians *(khalada* and *gasianda)*. The social institutions they represented had nothing to do with clanship, the main authentic social structure of the Manchu-Tungusic peoples. Besides that, the public agents placed from outside 'did not enjoy prestige' among the native people; 'on the contrary, they were disregarded'. But the 'clan as such did not have any established power-holding structures' (Shternberg 1933: 109). Vladimir K. Arsen'ev mentioned the absence of power-holding structures among the Udege, one of the Manchu-Tungusic peoples. 'Never had the idea entered anyone's heads', he wrote 'to predominate over the others'. – 'In any business, the leaders appear themselves. When the Udege go to hunt, the most experienced one places himself at the head of the others. He makes the arrangements and everyone obeys them, because they know, it is his business. When they sail a boat, the deciding vote belongs to the person who is famous for being a good sailor' (Arsen'ev 1926: 17). [95] The absence of any external coercion and hidden order seems to be so attractive that it produces an impression of a perfect democracy. Democracy is, for example, for Viktor A. Zibarev, who considers that among the indigenous peoples of the North the power is expressed in the common meetings' resolutions and is based on the authority of customs and principles of morality. In other words, as he believes, the bearer of authority is the entire society (Zibarev 1990: 33). I take leave to doubt the truth of this statement. It seems to me unconvincing whether in the society which practiced slavery, which was notable for permanent inter-clan tension and other social disharmony, a method of collective elaborating of resolutions with equal

---

95 K.M. Rychkov (1922: 137) also wrote about the lack of power-holding structures among the Evenk people.

influence of the entire community on the result of the process could be operated. There existed a strong power-holding structure among the Nanai and the Manchu-Tungusic peoples, but it was hidden from the observer because of its spiritual nature. I am going to show it in the example of the traditional Nanai court.

Coexistence of potestative and political systems

For a long time, the traditional power strategies coexisted among the Nanai with the Russian state political system.[96] Before the revolution (1917), the operation of the general state regulation on peasants was extended to the Nanai. Their villages were included in the structure of Russian *volost'* (small rural districts in old Russia) and ruled by *starosta*. The official administration was often represented by indigenous people, but that fact did not bring the official authority closer to the indigenous people's traditions, thus those two systems were very different (Rychkov 1922: 137). As Vladimir K. Arsen'ev (1926: 28) wrote, the indigenous people met all the requirements honestly, they elected the indigenous *starosta*, but with the profound belief that they themselves didn't need it, whereas the Russians did; and they continued to live according their old customs and laws. In turn, the Russians 'were completely indifferent to the indigenous peoples giving them carte blanche, if only they did not disturb the peace in Russian villages' (Shrenk 1903: 32).

Concurrently with the traditional court before the revolution, there existed the so-called indigenous court of the princes, which acted according to the initiative of the Russian administration. The representatives of the indigenous peoples elected a prince from among themselves for a period of three years. But those elected princes, *starosty* and elders, were not grateful for their nomination. On the contrary, they felt their duties to be a burden and tried to avoid them. Even their privilege as administrators did not attract them. It could be explained by the fact that the indigenous administrators understood the essence of authority differently from the Russians, who met among them 'the unknown kind of social organisation' and who 'tried to indicate the territories, population groups and clan elites using their own ideas' (Zibarev 1990: 54). As a result, a certain resistance against the official court appeared among the indigenous population, and the official indigenous judges themselves did not tend towards jurisdiction (ibid.). I. M. Suslov writes about the Evenks (Tungus) that such an indigenous prince 'single-handedly gave punishment on his own direction. There were no appeals. [...] The Tungus knew the prince could do anything

---

96 There was instituted a court of elders with the chairmanship of a foreman. 'Each village, which had not less than 15 families, had the special clan direction of a foreman and one or two his assistants who were chosen from the foreman's most honourable and best clansmen' (Soliarskii 1916: 21). Several villages were governed by an indigenous board which consisted of a chief and two elected persons (ibid.: 22).

with them including flogging in front of the community. They realised the unfairness of the punishments, which sometimes resulted from bribes and they felt powerless' (Suslov 1928: 58).

After the revolution, attempts to create clan Soviets and clan courts were no more successful. Estrangement from the state authority took place not because the government pursued its interests without regard to the indigenous peoples, but because their perception of the essence of authority was too different from the traditional one. One of the main reasons for such incompatibility of state and traditional ideas of authority was based on the fact that the traditional power strategy was connected with shamanism, the predominant ideology, which underlined the very core of the indigenous culture and penetrated all its domains. The resources of the traditional authority were charismatic, shamanic ones. This fact also explains the 'invisibility' of traditional power strategies, which existed for a long time simultaneously with the official power without being noticed.

The traditional conception of authority

The traditional Nanai court is a part of shamanic culture and, on the contrary, some aspects of shamanic practice itself are potestative. Anna-Leena Siikala's (1978) classification of shamans' role in the community and Sergei M. Shirokogoroff's (1919, 1924) data on the connection of shamanism to clanship bring us closer to understanding the phenomenon of hidden shamanic power.

The social stratification of the Nanai community is fixed terminologically. The people who have neither authoritative nor spiritual advantage are called *solgi nai* (ordinary people). To indicate the initiated ones there were several terms: *saman* (shaman), *diangian* (judge, chief), *bator* (warrior), etc. According to the traditional Nanai ideas, any authority is of spiritual nature. People could acknowledge the leader's right to make arrangements only if they believed that he or she enlisted the spirits' support. The nature of shamanic authority manifests itself not only in shamans' activity, but also in the power of any other leaders up to contemporary political figures.

Uniting shamanic and political power is famous among different peoples. Vladimir Basilov, for example, reports that shamanism among the ancient Turkish people was practiced as a state cult and the shamans participated in the public administration. The sovereigns had court shamans and sometimes the sovereigns themselves could perform the role of shamans. Shamans had great influence over state affairs and at their instigation people were murdered and without their approval warfare was not waged (Basilov 1992: 16–18). Among the Nanai that unity of power and spirituality is less visible because the authority manifested itself only periodically in case of urgent need; obscurity of the traditional authority was also conditioned by dispersed settlement.

Civilian authority manifested itself among the Nanai exclusively as juridical authority and the traditional Nanai court was a court of mediators. The judge-mediator, in Nanai *diangian* (Naichin dialect) or *manga* (Gorin dialect) dispensed justice practically single-handedly. The term *diangian* is borrowed from Chinese, where it means 'chief, officer, or functionary' (Zolotarev 1939: 83). V. A. Zibarev (1990: 45)notices that none of the peoples of the North had native terms for the designation of rulers, and all the terminology which indicated the indigenous administration *(kniaztsy, toëny, shulengi, dargi, dzhanginy)* was borrowed from Russians, Yakuts, Buriats, or Manchurians. At the same time the term *manga*, which was used by Gorin Nanai and by Ul'chi, is certainly of local origin (*'manga'* in Nanai means 'strong', 'brave', 'fearless'). [97] The Nanai elders did not accept the translation of the word *'diangian'* as 'judge', because *diangian's* function was not actually to judge, but to bring the conflicting parties to agreement. Eloquence was *diangian's* essential quality. [98] Leo Shternberg (1933: 22) wrote that *diangiansal* [99] were valued as good orators, their tongues, as his Orochi informants said 'rotated as fast as a mill-wheel'. Besides, *diangian* was any person put in a position of authority and also the spirits at the top of the hierarchy.

The judge's spirit-helpers

In Nanai mythology shaman and *diangian* are of similar essence. According to one myth, the Moon is a shaman and the Sun a *diangian*. *Diangian's* spiritual call was considered to be even more unavoidable than the shaman's and his dependence on spirits was believed to be stronger. *Diangian's* spirits were inherited like the shaman's, and sometimes *diangian's* spirits passed into the next generation and formed not a *diangian*, but a shaman. Like shamans, *diangiansal* dreamt their spirits and could talk and sing while sleeping. The elders affirm that like shamans, *diangiansal* have the special zones of the spiritual world, which are hidden inside some physical material objects (hills, stones, trees), where their spirit-helpers dwell.

In the traditional trail system there were even more strict gender limitations than in shamanism. Shamanism was characterised by rather specific gender roles with no strict gender prohibitions, but for the traditional court there were really harsh gender proscriptions. Only men could become a *diangian*, and women were not even allowed to be present at the trial until the moment when the final decision was accepted. At the same time the position of *kasatai* shaman (guide of the souls of the departed), which was considered to be appropriated mostly by men, in some exclusive cases could also be taken by a woman. Women were strictly prohibited

97 The other meanings of the word *'manga'* are 'disaster', 'trouble', 'violence'.
98 *'Diangariori'* in Nanai means 'to talk verbosely', 'to talk profusely', 'to blab'.
99 Plural of *diangian*.

from being present at a trial practice, but at any shamanic ceremonies women could be freely present. The elders considered those limitations to be of spiritual nature; the spiritual laws of patrilineal inheritance of *diangian's* spirit-helpers were much stricter than in shamanism.

Like a shaman, *diangian* dreamt of a 'person', [100] who instructs him in his activity, and like a shaman, *diangian* carves a figure, which represents that 'person' and from time to time offerings are made to it with vodka, porridge etc. (Shternberg 1933: 506). Like a shaman, *diangian* had a sacrifice place *toro* as a tree or a pole with images of his spirits on it and he regularly sacrificed pigs and roosters to his spirits there. Each time before going to the court, *diangian* had to put some vodka in front of his *toro* and bow there, and only after that could he say at the trial what his spirit cuckoo prompted. Regular *diangian's* sacrificing for his spirits was mentioned by Leo Shternberg (1936: 69). During the court like during a shamanic ceremony, the sacrificial vodka was also poured and put out for the *spirits*. Leo Shternberg also reported of the blood sacrifice, which *diangian* accomplished after finishing judging. He wrote: 'The day after the court *diangian* pierces a pig's ear and splashes its blood toward East and West, and then he makes up a feast' (Shternberg 1933: 505).

My informants confirmed that everything that *diangian* said at the trial, he said not according to his own reasoning, but as a result of spirit-helpers' suggestions. This peculiarity was also noted by Leo Shternberg, who wrote that *diangian's* main spirit-helper gave his master the gift of eloquence and at the trial *diangian* suggested all the appropriate ideas and words. According to Nanai expression, those suggested thoughts become his voice (Shternberg 1936: 69). Similar information was found by Leo Shternberg among the neighbouring people, the Nivkh. He wrote that the Nivkh 'хлај-нівух' (the same as Nanai *diangian*) is chosen by the special spirits which constantly inspire him, dwell in him and suggest to him fine and convincing speeches, which have an irresistible impact on his audience. *Diangian's* speed of speech, ability to speak smoothly and fast during a long time, irrespective of the content of speech, was considered to be a special spirits' gift (Shternberg 1933: 101). The outward sign which proved that *diangian* spoke under the influence of spirits was the fact that he usually trembled and twitched while speaking at the trial, whereas after he finished his speech trembling and twitching left him. So *diangian's* activity is not only of a social nature, but mostly of a religious one. The traditional court, which presupposes *diangian's* contact with his spirits, is actually not only a social agency, but predominantly a ritual.

During court, *diangiansal* used different magic methods. For example, as Leo Shternberg writes, some Nanai *diangiansal* were 'mue mokholiandini diangian', that is, *diangiansal* connected with the spirits of water. Talking and investigating someone's conflict, those *diangiansal* drew something with a stick on the surface of water,

---

100 Like a shaman's spirits, the spirits of *diangian* could take the form not only of an animal, but also of a person.

and in certain moments of their speech bubbles rose from the depths and burst. It meant that spirits reacted with those bubbles to their words and influenced their final decision, which should be pleasing to the spirits (Shternberg 1936: 69). When Ul'chi discussed a murder case, they put in front of a *diangian* 'a wooden cup with water and put a small piece of coal in it, the coal symbolised the soul of a murdered person, who demanded revenge' (Zolotarev 1939: 80–81).

The invisible roads where people are murdered

Leo Shternberg (1893: 11) wrote that, while at trial, *diangian* wore a special costume and had bow, arrows, lance or sabre, which are not used but probably have symbolic meaning. Sometimes shamans also use arrows or lances for shamanising instead of a drum. [101] The bearers of the tradition consider those arrows and lances to be spirits which are met in night dreams, while a *diangian* or a shaman walks down the *dërgil* 'roads' of the spiritual world. As shamans explained, they can penetrate into the *diangian's* spiritual space, and vice-versa. They are the spiritual territories, where they murder people using those lances and arrows. Aleksei Kisovich tells about it this way:

> There are bows and arrows on those roads, and *diangian* can see them. […] (Some of them) are the *dërgil* (spiritual territories) which belong to Khod-zher clan's father (clan spirit). They are the *amban's* (evil spirits') roads where people fight. Lance, knife, bow and arrows are *ochiki* spirits (that provoke violence). It is worth seeing! First you must conquer (those spirits) and pass down those roads. Only after that will you become a shaman. It is happening in your dreams. […] The *goria* (mentally ill) people also walk there, along the *ochiki* paths; they walk only along the bad roads, even along those roads which make you wish to commit suicide. (Aleksei Kisovich)

Bow, arrows, lance or sabre are often mentioned in the rituals as weapons against both people and spirits. According to A. M. Zolotarev's (1939: 78) data, Ul'chi put an iron hatchet, Japanese sabre or lance under the sick person's pillow to frighten the spirits responsible for disease, and at the same time any of those weapons could be used by a judge while speaking at the trial. A Nanai judge also used a wooden rod at the trial. Leo Shternberg (1933: 22) wrote that such a rod represented a stick with something like a human head carved on its top. Vladimir K. Arsen'ev (1926: 30) mentioned the same carvings on the tops of Udege judge's rods.

---

101 Concerning the use by shamans of a bow and arrows instead of (or together with) a drum, see: Potanin 1882; Yakovlev 1900; Potapov 1934; Shirokogoroff 1999; Anokhin 1994.

Sergei Bereznitskii (2001: 21) considers that the similar rod used by an Orochi judge symbolised his domination and authority. But this assertion contradicts the data which was collected by his predecessors. Thus Leo Shternberg (1933: 505) wrote that the rod *beregde* with an image of a leg on one end and a head on another was the judge's paraphernalia, a receptacle of his spirit-helper *marna*, which assisted him to try to reconcile the conflicting parties. The face carved on the rod depicts the spirit, which inspires a judge and helps him to convince other people (ibid.: 101). Vladimir K. Arsen'ev (1926: 30) also noticed that according to Udege ideas, in the judge's rod there is the power of his spirit-helper, which through the speaker-judge induces the conflicting parties and decide the fates of the guilty ones. As Leo Shternberg's informants said, not the judge's competence and ability, but exactly his rod, which is brandished by a judge, while he is asserting his claims, plays an enormous role in the reconciliation of the parties. Precisely in that rod is contained the *diangian's* and his relatives' fate (Shternberg 1933: 22). A. M. Zolotarev (1939: 76) reports that *diangian* brandishes his rod with the aim to cleanse his spiritual road. The more complicated the matter is, the bigger should be the lance.

The judge's rod's connection to the spirits is also proved by the fact that Nanai *diangiansal* put it under their heads before sleeping for inspiration. They did it in order to meet 'persons' in their dreams, who were their spirit-teachers (Shternberg 1933: 506). It is that spirit which instructs *diangian* what he must say and what to demand at the trial (ibid.: 505).

The trial resembles shamanic ceremonies in many ways. Both the trial and the shamanic ceremony are performed in darkness. Niura Sergeevna recollects:

> They brought two *diangiansal* from the Amur downstream. Then at night they started the discussion. There was night! Silence! They lighted a camp fire; there were lots of mosquitoes, in summer mosquitoes bite. [...] They never had trial in the daytime, only at night by a fire. [...] When *diangiansal* speak, people do not let their children go out (to prevent them from making noise). There was such a law. If a child was little, they did everything to stop it from crying. Mothers constantly suckled them. To prevent dogs' barking they constantly fed them and took those dogs which bark a lot deep into the forest. Probably it would have been bad if they had barked during the trial. (Niura Sergeevna)

Niura Sergeevna had a little baby when the trial was in her village; she said that at night silence was needed and she gave the baby the breast in order that he didn't cry. She said that 'the baby behaved quietly and did not fall ill, nothing bad happened to him'.

Behaviour management during the trial was much stricter than during shamanising. Kseniia Ivanovna says: 'When a *manga* (judge) is trying, no one in the entire village is permitted to sew or to do anything else!' Trial discussions never took place inside, but only outside at night, that is in the time and in the place when and where 'the spirits' souls could be seen' (the spirits roam about). Special importance was attached to fire, which could be in the centre of those who were at the trial. 'Dicta die all the participants gathered near an elder's yurt. They lighted a campfire. Then they interrogated a complainant and listened to the elder from the defendant's clan' (Lopatin 1922: 187). The fire was considered to be a place for the spirits. My informant Niura Sergeevna recollected:

> They never entered the house. They lit a campfire outside. It was strictly pro-
> hibited even to overstep a hot coal. (If you step over it), you could get sick or
> else! There was one man who jumped over a hot coal (while they were having
> trial). He did not die, but his leg was taken bad. His leg bent and he could not
> walk anymore. (It happened because) he jumped over a hot coal! He did not
> actually jump over it, but simply stepped over it, and he became like that! At
> the time of the trial, when they discuss the case, nobody could even step over
> a hot coal! (Niura Sergeevna)

Election of a judge

In Soviet times it was appropriate to consider that 'only the most honourable members of society were elected to be judges, and then as a result of numerous trials
those judges acquired authority first among their fellow villages and then among the
neighbouring population' (Narody 1985: 86). Leo Ya. Shternberg (1936: 69) also believed that only those with faultless personal reputations and 'with outstanding gifts
and intelligence' became *diangiansal*. Taking notice that *diangian* is not a position of
trust. Aleksandr M. Zolotarev (1939: 76) suggested that a person of generally recognised authority, one who is gifted with eloquence, intelligence, who knows customs
and has influence, becomes a *diangian*. Counter to Zolotarev's point, Arkadii F. Anisimov believed that a *diangian* among Evenks was elected. The details of his description of the election process are especially interesting. If we do not pay attention to
his style, borrowed from communist party bureaucratic character ('the candidature
was minutely discussed at the general clan meeting and then approved' etc.), we will
see that the main part in the election was played by a shaman.

As Anisimov writes, the clan shaman performed the rite of testing and initiated
a new judge. He reported to the spirits about the choice of a new judge and asked
for their opinion. Anisimov considers that if a shaman said that the spirits were
against a new candidate, he actually lied, hiding in this way his own antipathy to
a neophyte. If the spirits agreed and thus approved a candidate, the candidate went
through a public test which was accompanied by a shamanic ritual. During that

test a subject had to jump like a flying bird, to sing like a swan and so on (Anisimov 1936: 87–89). Anisimov explained it as an inspection of the physical development of a candidate and his hunting skills. It is doubtful whether the ability to cry like a swan indicated certain skills. But it could be evidence that the candidate possessed spirit-helpers in the guise of birds.

My Nanai informants confirmed that there were people who first pointed the candidate out to judges and only then did the shaman perform a ritual of initiation. But those people did not choose a *diangian*, they did not discuss his candidacy, but merely noticed some peculiarities which were symptoms of choosing by spirits. Not people, but spirits choose *diangian* and the ability to be *diangian* is inherited. 'An ordinary person is not able to become a *diangian*'. Only those ones, who have special dreams and who have a cuckoo spirit-helper, who have a *toro* (a pole as a sacrifice place) in their yard, become *diangian*. He places a pole with an image of a cuckoo on its top. Only such a person is a *diangian*' (Niura Sergeevna).

Diangian formation was similar to shaman formation and went through a special shamanic-like disease, which was caused the inherited spirits. Like the shamanic disease, *diangian's* disease resulted from the neophyte's resistance against his mission and from the spirits' enforcement of its acceptance. Sometimes that opposition between the neophyte's and the spirits' wishes caused the neophyte's death.

> Nina Bogdanovna was married to Ivan Danilovich (*diangian* Danila's son). He (Ivan Danilovich) was also bound to become a *diangian* to replace his father, but he did not want to. He had convulsions for three years and then he died. When he died his children did not recognise that. Their mother came and they told her: 'Our father is probably drunk! He has fallen asleep!' But he was already dead. […] He (Ivan Danilovich) died because he did not want to become a judge. He said: 'What should I get that *toro* (a sacrifice place) for? People will laugh at me!' But what! He had better put a piece of wood (a *toro*) and place (a sculptor of) a cuckoo over there and he would be alive! But he did not want to. (Ol'ga Egorovna)

After people noticed that someone was suffering from *diangian* (shamanic-like) disease, their task was not to report to the spirits about their decision, as Anisimov writes (1936: 87), but with a shaman's help to learn from the spirits whether they actually intended to make this person a *diangian*. A shaman performed a ritual *pere-chi* (divination) and then during the initiation ritual helped a *diangian*-neophyte to manage his spirits.

The traditional court as a clan institution

All the scholars who wrote about the traditional Nanai court noticed that it was a clan institution.[102] Clan was always on the side of a kinsman no matter if he was a victim or a person responsible for crime. In case both a criminal and a victim belonged to the same clan, the crime did not have any aftermath. Leo Shternberg (1933: 97) wrote about the Nivkh (Giliak) that murder within a clan went unpunished. Besides, K. M. Rychkov reported that Evenks (Tungus) let intra-clan murders ride. He wrote that the brothers 'Чívумане', who murdered their father, were left unpunished. He also reported that Tungus Komba killed his brother and cut out his scrotum in order 'not let his soul hide in that scrotum'. However, the kinsmen hid that crime and did not punish the murderer. Rychkov also wrote that Tungus Pompota murdered his mother and burnt her corpse in fire because she wanted to sell the sables she hunted at her own discretion. But clansmen also hid and let that extraordinarily brutal crime go unpunished. At the same time that would be another matter between people of different clans. In that case only in extreme cases would a murder be substituted for ransom (Rychkov 1922: 136).

A crime against a person from an alien clan resulted in inter-clan conflict and in order to reconcile a dispute they invited a judge-negotiator. The scholars underline that a judge *diangian* should be from a neutral clan[103] (Zolotarev 1939: 76; Shternberg 1933: 22; Melnikova 2004: 89). Sometimes they brought two, three or even four *diangiansal* (Melnikova 2004: 89). Niura Sergeevna recollects that to discuss a case of fire in Dzapi village they brought two *diangiansal,* one from the Gaer clan in Omi village and another from the Bel'dy clan in Naichin. The contestants were Dzapi and Khodzer and in their village there were neither Gaers, nor Bel'dys.

Viktor A. Zibarev (1990: 104) considers that choosing judges from the neutral clans guaranteed their neutrality. Partly it really was so; Shternberg's (1893: 11) explanation is also right: clan relatives are not able to go to the victim's clan to negotiate because they would simply murder him in revenge. But nevertheless, there are correspondingly some other reasons for such a choice and they are conditioned by the deep connection of the *diangian's* institution to clanship and clan spirituality.

Diangian is not able to judge his own clan just as a shaman cannot heal his kinsman. The bearers of diseases are clan spirits, which cohere with shamanic clan spirits, and the shaman is not able to oppose the spirits of his own clan in healing his own

---

102 Ivan Lopatin emphasised that the nature of Nanai court was purely tribal (Lopatin 1922: 186).
103 Ivan Lopatin's stated that *diangian* was assigned from the victim's clan and that beside them one more elder was needed (Lopatin 1922: 187). But this has not been corroborated, neither with the other scholars' data nor with my field research. First, *diangiansal* were not assigned, they were chosen among those who went through the hard trial of shaman-like spiritual formation. Second, despite both the victim's clan and the defendant's clan being represented by some elders, they were not *diangiansal. Diangian* was invited from a neutral clan.

clansmen, and only shamans of other clans than the patients can heal them. The same concerns the traditional court. Having committed a crime, a person becomes connected with special spirits *ochiki*. These spirits can be later inherited and can cause violence among his descendants. Trial supposes opposition of a judge and a criminal on a spiritual level if they belong to different clans. The judge who arrived could not use the dwelling and fire from the new place which belonged to an alien clan. Leo Shternberg reported that Nanai judge *marna* does not live in the adversary's yurt, but in his own tent. He drinks and eats only what he brought from home and burns only his own fire (Shternberg 1933: 506). Nivkh (Giliak) judge lights his pipe only from his own fire (ibid.: 104). If relatives of a victim accompany a judge, they carry their own water and food, because they cannot drink from the river where the defending party lives. Neither can they hew, fish or hunt there (Arsen'ev 1929: 29). It can be explained by the newcomers' aim to be isolated from the alien spirits which could attack them through fire, water and food, which is especially topical within the trial environment.

Trial as replacement for blood revenge

For the bearers of shamanic culture, each crime caused not only material, but spiritual damage and it was spiritual loss which was considered the most dangerous for a victim. Precisely because of the idea of spiritual harm, which can be caused not only to a victim but to the entire victim's clan, the list of crimes includes such actions which we would label as merely petty misconduct. They are 'overturning of a birch bark scoop with water in somebody else's place, leaving an arm in somebody else's place, taking by dispersion someone else's tobacco pouch, falling down in somebody else's place, not entering through the door if it is wide open' (Arsen'ev 1926: 31). Spiritual harm which threatens with misfortune was estimated as the most significant and it demanded reflex actions which could be not only revenge, but buyout. Shternberg noticed that in Nivkh (Giliak) language the word *jus kind* 'to pay' originates form the word *us kind* which is a synonym of '*uxskind*' – 'to fight, to be at war'. Unpunished inter-clan crime causes blood revenge. It was supposed that from both sides an equal number of victims should be murdered. If it seemed to one side that they lost one person more, revenge went on and often took such a scale that entire villages were devastated. Leo Shternberg wrote: 'Revenge didn't always result in a few victims; there are some cases known when entire clans were extinguished, and only women were left alive' (1933: 99).

Blood revenge is based not on emotional, but rather on religious reasons. They believe that relatives' bones must be raised. Leo Shternberg's informants explained to him that:

[...] the soul of the person who met a violent death is not able to move to the 'village of the deceased', where it could continue the same life as on the earth. Until it had been avenged, until the murderer's blood had given it strength to raise its bones, it is not able to leave the earth and has to whirl in the air in the appearance of a bird-avenger, which utters scary screams at night. [...] That scary and miserable bird [...] yells of revenge and it itself can enact dreadful revenge upon the clansmen who forget their charge. Even if the case is closed with redemption, it remains dissatisfied. It needs a dog sacrifice. They give a dog's heart to that bird in order to prevent it from enacting vengeance on both contestants (Shternberg 1933: 505).

Leopold Shrenk wrote that each person who did not execute the precept of blood revenge inevitably pays for that omission with misery or even death, and that this popular belief has powerful decisive meaning for discharging blood revenge (1903: 21). To discharge revenge a victim's relative must have killed either the murderer or someone else from his paternal relatives. 'Fury of revenge is so big that even newborn babies are not spared. [...] Only women are excluded from revenge' (Shrenk 1893: 11).

For revenge they often chose the moment when an adversary did not expect any attack. Shrenk (1903: 25) wrote that Nivkh could 'deliver a blow at that time when his challenger was light-heartedly sitting next to him eating or smoking a pipe', because it was considered that it was in the interests of the attacker to act from an ambush in an underhanded way and as fast and suddenly as possible. Ivan Lopatin affirms that blood revenge was widespread among the Nanai. After the Amur region was joined to Russia, the Nanai began to be concerned about Russian authority and justice and they thoroughly hid any traces of blood revenge. However, Lopatin (1922: 187) met some blood revenge cases even in the early 20th century.

Viktor A. Zibarev (1939: 82) considers that the traditional court replaces the institution of blood revenge. Besides, if *diangian* did not interfere, the law of revenge came into force. Traditional court also included fighting. Thus, before the contestants in Orochi and Nivkh courts are reconciled, they fight a duel, using sticks and bows. Such a duel can result in someone's death (Shternberg 1933: 22). Shternberg also points to the fact that if blood revenge was replaced by court and buyout, they offered bloody sacrifice to spirits. He writes that they kill dogs, offer their hearts to the bird-avenger and then eat their meat (ibid.). To all appearances, that sacrifice prevents the spirit 'bird-avenger' from causing misfortune to the victim's clan.

Among the Nanai the court never finally supplanted blood revenge. Blood revenge was not only included in the process of trial, but also forestalled it. Chapaka Danilovna narrates one such case, which took place in Gordoma village:

When my father married my mother, she had already had a child (a boy). [...] My father went fishing, but then turned back halfway. People saw how he turned back halfway. He forgot a gun, he returned for a gun. At home he took the gun and started checking if it was charged or not. His gun shot and the bullet went through the boy who was sitting on a chamber pot. He dropped dead. (Chapaka Danilovna)

The boy's mother was from the Possar clan. So after that accident the Possars, most of whom lived in Torgon village, went to Gordoma village in order to kill Chapaka Danilovna's father. But Chapaka Danilovna's father's clansmen had gathered even faster and in one night they built a wooden fence around the murderer's house.

There was a law at that time: that one who destroyed such a fence would be guilty himself. There was such a law! So a lot of Possars came, all of them were with lances. But it was banned to destroy the fence. In this way they saved my father. They (the Possars) lay a fire on the high bank of the river and started calling my father: 'Come here!' But people were guarding him, they did not let him go out. [...] They defended him. Those people with lances came to murder him to take revenge for the child's death. But his fellows did not give him to them. Then the Possars went along the beach, sticking their lances into sand, challenging Chapaka Danilovna's father to a fight, (but he did not come). (Chapaka Danilovna)

Only because the attempt of blood revenge was unsuccessful, people resorted to organising a court. They brought a *diangian* from the Zaksor clan in Dondon village. All the people from the neighbouring villages gathered at the court. The *diangian's* decision was that Chapaka Danilovna's father was not guilty, because the gun itself accidently went off. Attempts at blood revenge were suppressed. Similar attempts at blood revenge forestalled few other cases.

Approval of impunity and neutralisation of complainant's aspirations

Diangian was usually invited not by the victim's, but by the criminal's kinsmen, because the main task of the court was not to punish the criminal, but to neutralise the conflict, and it corresponds to the defendant's interests and contradicts the complainant's interests. Only in case the defendant's side had brought a *diangian* and only after that, relatives of the victim also invited another *diangian* to defend their interests. Usually the contestants negotiated the buyout (*mangaladiori*). To replace the murder the defendants usually gave to the victim's relatives some money and goods (mostly expensive silk dress length or sheep fur coat). But in case there were no suitable expensive goods, they gave one of their clansmen to the victim's clan, and the complainants preferred to take women to marry them. A. M. Zolotarev describes Ul'chi court this way.

> (*Diangian* says:) give (to the complainants) a girl, give them a chain mail, a silk dress, give them a bear not to leave any traces. Then the offenders answer: 'As we are guilty, we will become marriage brokers and we will live in peace with no quarrels'. [...] Then a judge goes to the offended ones and says: 'Well, my friends, things are on the mend, they look pretty much like the last of peace time. Everything goes according to your wish. I put my back, my entire life into completion of this case. And do not answer me back!' After that the case is considered to be closed (Zolotarev 1939: 81).

Evdokiia A. Gaer noticed that if a woman was murdered by her husband, her brother could demand that the murderer's sister marry him. That woman (the murderer's sister) was named *sirbogokha ekte,* that is, paid off for the murdered one. There was a belief that that woman did not die a natural death (Gaer 1991: 65).

A judge did not always search for a suitable buyout for damage. Quite often the case went unpunished and as a result of the judge's activity, complainants stopped trying, either for blood revenge or for buyout. Sometimes there was nevertheless a buyout fixed, but it was too small in comparison with the loss caused or nobody controlled the execution of judgment and as a result it came to nothing. Such was a case of Kseniia Ivanovna sister's death.

> My sister drowned in the Nana River. Then my father and I went hunting and my sister stayed at home. In the morning people took her fishing. After they rode off for half a kilometre, the sledges went under the ice into the water. When the sledge was falling into water, the man who was sitting behind her on the sledge fell down on her, he weight down onto her, and she drowned. That case was discussed at the trial. (Kseniia Ivanovna)

The victim's relatives asked for a young woman as a buy out. The woman, received from the defendant's clan, was pregnant and she lived in the new place for a very short time. She went home to give birth. Then she returned but soon after that she left again and never came back, but nonetheless the trial did not recommence.

The traditional court's aim was not so much compensation of loss, as neutralisation of indignation of complaints and elimination of their wish for revenge. It can be confirmed by the fact that in many cases, according to *diangian's* decision, compensation was not required. It was *diangian's* ability to suggest an idea as if there were no crime committed at all. Ol'ga Egorovna remembers Ivan Danilovich's father, who was a *diangian*:

When someone committed a murder, he negotiated the case in such a way that no one committed any crime. That is why they fetched him from afar, from Nikolaevsk to Khabarovsk. [...] Both Nanai and Russians applied to him. If someone murdered another person, someone's husband or son, serious conflict arose there and the defendants fetched him. All the people around knew about him. And he conducted business in such a way that it was as if there were not any murder at all! Whatever he said, there were no objections. (Ol'ga Egorovna)

The trial's decision could be implemented only if both sides came to agreement. *Diangian's* made every effort to reach such an agreement. His decisions were considered to be final and were not subject to appeal, because they were fixed by *diangian's* spirits. Niura Sergeevna relates an unpunished case of arson.

It happened that my brother occasionally burnt all the houses in Dzhuen village. [...] People stayed on the beach and looked at their houses burning. When the fire went out, they began blaming my brother. After that they went for a *diangian*. And nothing happened! Nothing bad happened to the person responsible for the fire. He was not punished. (Niura Sergeevna)

The trial's focus on neutralisation of the complainant's claims was expressed in special terminology. If a *diangian* succeeded in reconciling the contestants it meant he succeeded in 'raising the case'. If he had to pass any sentence, people said that he 'lowered the case'. In Niura Sergeevna's story about fire it was expressed that way. '*Diangiansal* came to us, invited people, sat down the way we are sitting now. They sat down and began talking about that fire: how it happened, what had been burnt and what they should do, either they should lower the case or raise it.'

As the trial was not oriented towards punishing the defendant, but towards the elimination of the plaintiff's claims, not the plaintiff's, but the defendant's kinsmen were interested in calling a court. Leo Ya. Shternberg (1933: 506) reports that almost always not the injured party, but the criminal and his relatives were searching for a judge. Inviting a judge, the defendant's party sought to prevent blood revenge, to lessen reparations for damage or even to leave the case unpunished. Not restoration of social justice and not prevention of further crime was the task of the court, but making peace at the expense of suppressing the victims' resistance and indignation, because, as my informants affirmed, such was the will of *diangian's* spirits. It was *diangian's* main spirit-helper cuckoo, which exculpated the criminal, freeing him or her from blame.

Democracy or 'spiritocracy'?

Shternberg and Zibarev considered that the traditional court of the indigenous peoples of Lower Amur region was democratic; they supposed that the entire society ruled at such trials (Shternberg 1933: 108; Zibarev 1990: 33). Zibarev (1990: 66–67) believed that indigenous courts in Siberia expressed the will of all the people, and was based on fairness and that the canons and norms of that fairness were formed by the people themselves. Proof of its democracy was, according to him, such peculiarities as publicity of legal procedure, permission for almost everyone to be present and to participate and the decisive role of public opinion in the passing of sentences and decisions (ibid.: 68). Traditional legal procedure was public indeed, and with the exclusion of women everyone could be present at trial. But none the less its democracy seems to be questionable. Those, who were present at trial could pass their opinion, but only *diangian's* opinion played the decisive role. Our field data did not concur with Shternberg's (1893: 23) words that after the discussion, they collected the opinions and in the capacity of the final and decisive one they chose the opinion of that person who reasoned most soundly, even if that person was young. On the contrary, my informants attested that nobody dared to contradict the last *diangian's* word. That obedience was explained by the fact that *diangian's* words issued not from him personally, but from his spirit-helpers. 'No one opposes *diangian*. Never!' (Niura Sergeevna). Arsen'ev also wrote about men who were present at trial: 'There is trouble brewing, if they would be intractable and would not make concessions'. *Diangian's* authority was indisputable, his word was irrefutable and was accepted by everyone. Ol'ga Egorovna said: 'Everyone obeyed *diangian's* words. When he starts talking, all the attendants are sitting quietly! Nobody would ask a question! Nobody would say a word against him! His every word will be implemented'.

It can be proved that, according the informants' point, not only those who attended at trial, but also *diangian* at trial had no possibility to express his own opinion. Neither his will, nor his understanding and interpretation of a case decided it. There is a superpower above him, which issues not from people, but from spirits. At the trial *diangian* himself served those spirits who rule over all his words and actions. The contestants actually fear to contradict not so his words, but the will of his spirits, which is expressed through his words. Any *diangian's* decision was accepted because people were afraid of dealing with his spirit-helpers.

All my informants emphasised *diangian's* lack of freedom and dependence on his spirits. Nesulta Borisovna said that *diangian* learned from his night dreams about where people were going to invite him and how he must judge. 'If he does not obey and act on his own will, he will get troubles; he can fall ill and die'. Presiding over a court, *diangian* like a shaman permanently feels the presence of a 'person' (of a spirit), which instructs him in his activity. Presiding over a court, *diangian* was not unrestricted to decide a case at his discretion, however he liked. Having sacrificed for his spirits before the trial, he had to say only what those spirits suggested he say. Shternberg (1933: 506) reported that before leaving for a trial, *diangian* gave some vodka to the image of his spirit-helper and said: 'I have carved you the way as I dreamt you and now teach me well'.

> *Diangian* always knows what to say at the trial. His *seven* (spirit-helpers) let him know what to say. If he expresses what he himself thinks (if his words do not correspond to what his spirits suggest he say), people will immediately recognise it. If he has too high an opinion of himself and says something from himself, people will understand it at once. He is prohibited to let his tongue run away with him. If a shaman begins speaking for himself, he will die! He will probably die not at once, but in two or three years. The same is with *diangian*. If he says something wrong 'that is something according to his own will', he can die. He himself knows it! He knows everything, but in spite of this knowledge, he does not say it, and when he speaks, he only says a little. (Niura Sergeevna)

Diangian must not err in a single word. If he said something against the spirits' will, he himself got *baita,* that is, he became dependent on spirits, which had dangerous power over him. Nesulta Borisovna tells of it this way: 'If he (*diangian*) said something wrong, he could even die! If he obeyed (spirit-helper) in the wrong way, if he did something erroneous to his *seven*, then [...] the spirits always watch him!' Then she narrates of a *diangian,* who said in the court something self-willed, judging according his own discretion. '*Diangian*, Shurka's father grew old unnaturally fast (in spite of being still of a young age). He suddenly became grey-haired! He died five days after Shurka was born. He saw the face of his son and died. That *diangian* lived in Torgon village'.

What is more, people did not expect *diangian* to think and to find a fair decision. They only required from him words, which would correspond to the spirits' will. Niura Sergeevna explained:

> If a *diangian* said wrongly, people would simply deprive him of dignity. He has his root *dachan* (the clan spirits are considered to be his root). That *dachan* beforehand knows everything about everything. It was a *dachan* which made him a *diangian,* and for *diangian* there is no getting away from it. They are his forefathers (spirits) who tell him about this and that (and prompt him while he is judging). (Niura Sergeevna)

If people realise that a *diangian* began expressing his own opinion, instead of uttering the thoughts which are suggested by his spirits, 'people would never invite him to judge again'. Next time there is a need, people will ignore such a *diangian*.

In spite of this, such a *diangian* still preserves his *dachan,* and spirits still show him everything about the case, but people do not want him to reason, to discuss and to judge them anymore'. Only this can be said about *diangian's* authority. *Diangian* is not free in his words, but is dependent on spirits, and that represents rather the spirits' authority.

It happened that the injured party did not want to accept *diangian's* decision and to leave the crime unpunished or almost unpunished. In that case a *diangian* used the special means of pressure, which were given by the same spirit-helpers.

> ʒ*anginje* should not return with no result. At the worst, if he saw that all his efforts were ineffective, a last means was used. He raised his stick and said: 'Now there remained one thing to do. That is to break my stick, but whatever happens to me or to someone of my clanship after that, you who will be responsible for that'. According to their belief, if a ʒ*anginje* breaks his stick, he will incur god's anger and trouble for himself and for his entire clan. If later someone of ʒ*anginje's* clan dies, that person, who made him break a stick, is considered to be responsible for that. (Shternberg 1933: 22)

As there is an image of *diangian's* spirit-helper on his stick, to break it means to incur that spirit's punishment, to originate a new case, and the new defendant will be the former stubborn plaintiff. But it is important to specify that spirits' anger does not deal with the *diangian* as such. He accomplishes what the custom directs him to do. *Diangian's* threat to break a stick is so effective because the opposing side scares his spirits and expects new troubles.

> When the other side exhausts *marna's* patience and raises a quarrel, he throws his stick onto the ground, and everything immediately calms down. [...] In the overemotional moments he threateningly brandishes it, he swears that in case his reasoning remains unsuccessful, he will break that stick and incur punishment both for himself and the obstinate opponent. (Shternberg 1933: 505)

Vladimir K. Arsen'ev writes about the Udege contestants: 'They are not able to talk among themselves and they pass their demands and excuses through their chosen ones [...]. According to the custom, argument should be as long as possible and the speaker should several times pretend that he wants to break their sticks, which could even open hostilities' (1926: 31).

Leo Ya. Shternberg, trying to find 'the motive force of the powerful clan institution' and to open the secret of the wonderful combination of the close alliance and the lack, as he considers, of any despotism, guardianship and regulation, of preserving personal freedom and lack of any pressure', named religious worldview to be such a force. It is true that religion is the force at the very base of the traditional or-ganisation of the indigenous peoples of the Amur region. But it is doubtful whether one could say that such an organisation is free from compulsion and despotism, that 'religious worldview spontaneously and with no outside pressure leads everyone's will and action to the harmony of the common interest' (Shternberg 1933: 111). Com-pulsion and despotism exist in shamanic cultures, but it is only barely noticeable, because it is accomplished on the spiritual level. It exists, and no one, including *diangian*, is free from it. Bocharov (1992: 25–27) subdivides coercion, which supports authority, into physical (state apparatus of coercion) and socio-psychological. The coercion which we face in shamanic culture is of another, third type. It is a specific spiritual coercion. In fact the content of this coercion boils down to a question of disassociation from judicial authority. The traditional court does not search for the ways of fair punishment of the criminal, but to the elimination and cancellation of the claims of the aggrieved party. Such a court advocates for the criminal and for nonintervention into freedom for criminality. Without taking into consideration the specificity of such coercion, we could, follow Shternberg, romanticise the traditional regulatory bodies and would not avoid their extrapolation into the contemporary state-legal reality.

SACRIFICE INTERPRETED AS ROBBERY

The reader is probably amazed by all that absurdity of shamanic 'diseases'
and by the naïveté of those people who permit (shamans)
to rob them so impudently.
(Revolutionary) Khudiakov 2002: 139

Bogdan was about to die because people did not give him (pigs for sacrifice);
for several days he lay unconscious. [...]
That is why he went to rob (pigs). [...]
It was right that he robbed.
(Shaman) Ol'ga Egorovna

As worldviews vary in different societies and cultural groups, they can cause dis-similar and even contrasting attitudes towards the same phenomena. In the 1930s, atheistic propaganda was aimed at convincing indigenous peoples that spirits didn't exist and that shamans were in fact 'predators' and 'exploiters' who deceived people in order to extort 'sacrificial' animals from them as gifts. While some indigenous people started following this atheistic doctrine, other parts of the indigenous population remained attached to traditional shamanic worldviews. As a result, neighbouring peoples began interpreting the same events in very different ways. This led to mutual misunderstandings that had tragic consequences. In one such case the misunderstandings resulted in the imprisonment and death of Bogdan Onenko, a Nanai shaman. [104]

Shamanic congregation compelled to sacrifice

Bogdan successfully provided shamanic services to a number of Ul'chi,[105] who he later robbed. All of these Ul'chi patients recovered from their illnesses and, according to the tradition, were obligated to sacrifice animals to Bogdan's *seven* (shamanic spirit-helpers). In other words, the Ul'chi who he robbed were not strangers; they were members of Bogdan's congregation and, as such, they had certain obligations towards him, or, to be precise, towards his *seven*. However, this was the time of Soviet struggle against shamanism as 'an obstacle to building socialism' (Suslov 1932), but in the interval after Bogdan's rituals and before the necessary sacrifice, Bogdan's congregation had accepted the Soviet's atheistic ideology. They had joined the revolt against shamanism. This was also a time when people associated shamans with the bourgeois class and blamed them for exploiting people, stating that shamanic activity 'harms [...] the development of the national economy and heavily imposes on the budget of the working indigenous people' (Suslov 1931: 132). It is likely that Soviet agitators had time to convince Bogdan's congregation that they should not sacrifice to his *seven*, because *seven* do not exist. Thus, making a sacrifice would only mean paying an exploitative shaman by giving him their property.

To get a better understanding of what such a refusal meant according to the traditional worldview, let us turn to the relationship between a shaman and his believers. First of all, believers are both patients and customers. As a strict rule, a shaman does not intervene for people of his own accord. He only acts if the sick person or their close relatives ask him directly.

> 'They come from afar', explained Lingdze, 'and urgently ask me to bow before my *seven* or otherwise to do something for them! And I do what they ask. Can I do all that on my own? (No,) only at their request! It is not I who make people do it!' (Lingdze)

---

104 Bogdan Onenko is also famous because he helped the ethnographers Albert Nikolaeevich and N. A. Lipski, who worked among the Nanai in the 1920s and 1930s. He was Lipski's guide and travelled together with him.

105 The Ul'chi is a people neighbouring the Nanai and closest to them by language and culture.

It is significant that shamanic intervention requires initiative from a congregation member. They must take the initiative not only in asking for the performance of a ritual, but the believers also take an active part in performing it. When healing sick people, the shaman promises his *seven* that they will receive an animal sacrifice in exchange for curing. In cases where shamanic treatment does not heal people or help them locate a lost item, etc. the patient is not obliged to give anything to the shaman's *seven*. Such people are not yet a part of his/her congregation, despite having come to him as a patient. In their quest for help, such patients may visit a number of different shamans until they find one who is able to help them. However, if the shamanic ceremony was successful, the patient becomes bound to the shaman and his particular *seven* for a long time.

There are special mechanisms which bind congregants to one another and to their shaman. Such mechanisms consolidate the group into a stable entity whose members return to seek their shaman's advice again and again. For example, after a successful ceremony, the congregation finds itself involved in sacrifices to the shaman's *seven*, and the preparations require the group's care and feeding of the animals, preparation for the sacrificial ceremony, etc. Yearly, each shaman must perform a ritual *undi* [106] crossing from house to house, visiting the patients they have helped in the past year, who are also the ones to make sacrifices (Smoliak 1991).

Sick people come and ask me to pray to my *seven* (for them). I bow (before my *seven*) and they (the patients) bow together with me. After that, her patients must return to make sacrifices to her *seven* that demand to be paid. [...] Who will work with no salary? Nobody will agree to work if the *kolkhoz* stops its payments. The same is here (in shamanic practice). No one is supposed to avoid payment-sacrifice. (Ol'ga Egorovna)

People believe that in the case of non-payment, it is not the shaman but *seven* themselves who will harm the

FIGURE 19: Sacrifice with a rooster.

106 The *undi* ritual is described in detail by Anna Smoliak (1991).

patient and this even against the shaman's will. Yet, not every patient who refused to sacrifice actually suffered mischief; and there were many who refused. Ol'ga Egorovna is indignant about that, saying:

> I rescue people, but they don't give anything for sacrifice. They just don't want to! How many years I have been working (as a shaman)! For more than 20 years! (They give) nothing! No rooster, they bring me nothing! Only when they need something, they ask me to pray for them! (Ol'ga Egorovna)

At our next interview she continues:

> Some people do not want to sacrifice anything after they have recovered. Spirits punish them. They fall sick again and hurry, run back to the shaman. There are lots (of such people). When a sick person comes and asks for help, I cannot refuse. I shamanise and ask the *seven* to have pity. Sometimes, if someone is badly sick, I have to shamanise for nine days and nights. So, don't forget when you are better! Some people do it (properly). Having recovered, they sacrifice a rooster or a pig right away. But other people have recovered and think that they will never become ill again. (Ol'ga Egorovna)

Aleksandr explains in Russian: 'If you need (to be healthy), you should kill a rooster in a civilised manner (*kul'turno*). If you don't do it, you will certainly die. A rooster or a pig! It's necessary! Without fail! If not, you will die'.

The troubles inflicted upon a patient who doesn't pay are mainly spiritual. Being keen on spiritual phenomena due to her shamanic capacity, Chapaka Danilovna tells about how sick Katia became when she didn't perform her obligatory sacrifice on time.

> Suddenly Katia got sick. She began to convulse. At night, they sent her to Troitskoe. I poured some vodka (for the *seven*) and bowed before them on my knees. I was beside myself with worry, I could not do anything. Everything was trembling inside me. I was shaking. It appeared, in my thoughts, as if a tousled woman was pursuing the car (where Katia was being driven). (The woman) was hurrying, running, catching up with the car! Already she has overtaken it! (Chapaka Danilovna)

A careless patient is not believed to be chastised immediately, but it is believed that bad luck (either the return of the previous illness in a more serious form than before, or a sudden and as if groundless death) usually happens anywhere between two to four years after the transgression.

Shamans compelled to sacrifice

The promise to perform a sacrifice is given in the course of ceremony, but if broken, both the offending patient and the practicing shaman may be adversely affected. In the decisive moment of a ritual, the shaman asks the patient to promise to perform a sacrifice in exchange for their own healing and well-being. However, it is not the patient but the shaman who makes this promise to the *seven*. It is the shaman, not the patient, who becomes the hostage in that contract. Asking to release the soul-shadows of his sick patients, the shaman becomes subservient to the spirits that have captured the ill person. The shaman remains in that position until the recovered patient brings the sacrificial animals to the *seven*. Ol'ga Egorovna explains making a deal with the *seven*:

> It is as if we had negotiated with a chief, asking him to release a person from a jail. The person recovered (after shamanic treatment), but neither said nor gave any thanks. But my word (promise) had been left there with a spirit! That's why it (the spirit) punishes me for that. It often happens like that. (Ol'ga Egorovna)

A sacrifice is needed to act as a substitute for the shaman and thus 'to raise a shaman from kneeling' in front of his or her spirits. Otherwise, as Chapaka Danilovna says, 'for several years you can remain in such a state as if your soul has still been on its knees before spirits. It is because spirit *Khodzher ama*[107] is wandering around (those places) and kicks you when passing by that the shaman's knees become bent and gnarled'. The ramifications of ignoring the injunction to sacrifice seem to be unjust as they are more severe for the shaman than the neglectful patient.

> If I bowed (before the *endury* and *seven*) and then nobody did anything in a month or in a month and a half, if the person does not sacrifice according to my promises, I'll get into trouble. (But) the patient who does not come (back with sacrifices) also has to look out for trouble. It is really bad! Too bad! There are people who don't come. Is it my fault that they don't come? I'm not guilty! It is he who is guilty! If that person does not come, the shaman's soul (*panian*) remains in the middle world (*iludu*) as an invisible reflection of a visible phenomenon, which has been taken away (*armoldu*). My *armol* is still there on its knees before spirits! Kneeling, and waiting for people to come (with an offering). If I fall ill while (staying like) that, nobody would be able to do anything (to heal me). It would be their own fault! Because of their empty words,

---

107 *Khodzher ama* is a spirit of the Khodzher clan. The legend says that this *ama* (father) was a shaman and lived in the late 19th and early 20th centuries. *Khodzher ama's* helping spirits still worship under his name.

because they do not do anything, I'll get in trouble! I'll die! That person, who made a promise and recovered, then forgot about his promise. Nobody believes that (the promise matters)! I don't like it! That's why sometimes I refuse to shamanise. I was sick all winter through, and all summer too, but nobody comes to make a sacrifice (for my spirits). (Lingdze)

The shaman's unfortunate position as scapegoat may be unfair, but it is not illogical. *Seven* are much closer to their shaman than to his patients, so it is easier for them to exert influence over him. Ol'ga Egorovna complains that 'if you are not feeding (your *seven*) you'll fall ill. It is a special concern for us shamans! They (*seven*) act like this: You ask for pity, and they take pity [...]. If you have made a promise to repay them for their pity, you should pay them back! Otherwise (*seven*) will take us (shamans) away! That's why I'm afraid to help people. I'd rather sit silently!' One of the results of the failed sacrifice is that disappointed *seven* stop serving their shamans and these shamans lose not only their health, but also their shamanic abilities.

If only they'd bring me a small pig! You may call and call for your *seven* when you need to shamanise, but they never come. Some shamans refuse to shamanise because (the cured people) do not help the shaman in return. 'We have been working but have not received anything! So we won't work any more!' The *seven* say this. And then they no longer come to work. You may cry, if you like, but no one comes! I'll fling my drum away and go to sleep! To hell with it! When (a person) is sick, he says 'For sure, we'll find a pig (for sacrifice)!' He says it once, twice, three times and then the *seven* refuses to come. Nobody pleases the *seven*! Nobody gives! (Ol'ga Egorovna)

The *seven*'s refusal to obey to their shaman is a serious threat to the shaman's health in any normal situation, but particularly in the case of neglected sacrifices. In this case the relationship becomes more complicated because the *seven* fails to receive a sacrificial animal as substitute for the shaman and so ends up forcibly devouring their own shaman as they are the only sacrificial being to which they have easy access.

If a shaman has shamanised for someone who had many evil spirits (*amban*), a sacrificial animal is necessary. If he (the patient) has promised and a shaman has removed his *amban*, and if the shaman's spirit-helpers get impatient waiting for the sacrifice to be performed, they will attack his owner! In one stroke, the shaman will lose consciousness! Such is a shamanic law! (Chapaka Danilovna)

The shaman's disease is understood, in this case, as a means of coercion used by *seven* to force their shaman and congregation to worship them.

If they have shamanised and a sick person has recovered, but they have not fed the *seven*, the shaman will fall ill. You (a sick person) were begging him (shaman), and the shaman has been drumming for you. You have got better, so you should dance (and make a sacrifice)! A rooster or a pig is needed! If you have not done that, the shaman will fall ill. The *seven* demands it! You must work and feed the *seven*! If you do not feed the *seven*, it will fly into a rage! (Ivan Torokovich)

The *seven* needs to eat something! If my *seven* have not eaten, I become sick. If you do not feed spirits, you are sick. But how can I find something to feed them? Using only those words that the *(seven)* taught me, I wail and sing. I have to live like that! I wail for a while and then finish it! Weep and finish! Such is the way of my living! Nobody will feel sorry for me, nobody will hear my wailing! How could it happen like this? I have begged my *seven* for every-thing, for everybody, but nobody has done anything for me. Fine, I'll perform a divination to find out information about the patient coming *(ningmachi)*! Let me do *ningmachi* and a healing ceremony *(taochi)* for everybody, regard-less of the number of people who would come to me! Let twenty people come if they want! But who has returned to me (with a sacrifice)? Is it good? We bowed to the sky and asked for happiness. Were they just words? Nobody sees those *(seven)* and nobody comes after that to sacrifice *(tagoadachi)*. Fine then! I will die! No matter how bad it gets! I don't care! (Lingdze)

Ol'ga Egorovna also complains about this unjust shamanic law. 'I am working and working and helping everyone, but nobody from the countryside helps me! I'll fall ill and die! That is the law!'

Shamanic measures of self-defence in case the sacrifice failed

The mortal danger that threatened shamans as the result of the failure to sacrifice led them to keep their congregants under close watch so that they remained obedient. If they were not successful in it, they could shamanise again but that time, with the aim to defend themselves by means of transferring the blame from themselves to the patients who had neglected their sacrificial duties. In this case, the shaman will recover from the *seven* rage, but their guilty patients fall ill and die instead.

Sometimes the (shaman) shamanises for someone, but that (patient) does not bring the animal's blood as promised. Then the shaman will be taken ill. If a shaman has an animal, but that cured person does not, the shaman will make a sacrifice instead, but in doing so saves only himself. He (will sacrifice for himself and) finish with that. He only avoids the *seven* curse himself! But that person, who has failed their duties, will fall ill and die. (*Seven*) will attack the person who was treated by their shaman, if he has no sacrifice. (Chapaka Danilovna)

By sacrificing instead of their patients, shamans realise that they condemn their patients to death; however, few are willing to endure their own torture and death in order to shield their congregants.

I'll stop being sick, but that one (who did not sacrifice) will fall ill. Then he will remember! Should I die for them, should I? I also want to live! To be alive! It is a shame to break promises. If I keep silent (about my illness) nobody cares about me. If they would have come on time (with the payment), there wouldn't be any grief for either of us! (Lingdze)

Another way in which shamans protect themselves from these occupational hazards is to perform a ritual that represents an inversion of the ceremony during which the vain promise was made. In this ritual, shamans order their *seven* to annul the results of the previous healing, to return the souls of the patients to that place of the spiritual world from where they had been taken in the previous healing ceremony.

I returned two people back. They did nothing (after recovery). Let them, who act like that, take their words back! I told my *seven*: 'As they do not care to bring me (a sacrifice animal), let all the previous stuff go back to them!' I did it like that and those two persons died. They lived over there in Bolon. (People) blame me now. But what could I do? It was necessary to relieve me of my promise to the spirit! I had conjectured, how to heal them, bowing before the spirit. And then my knees began to hurt, and my legs began to hurt. If it was going to be like that, I could fall ill myself! I only returned two people! How can I endure such a supernatural disease? I cannot! Nobody will rescue me! (And the *seven*) will punish me to death! But it is not actually my fault! I merely asked (my spirits) to feel sorry for those two persons and promised them a sacrifice. But then they (my patients) were sitting in silence! Bolon inhabitants criticised me severely after that. Well, shall I help you (next time), if you are criticising me? (Ol'ga Egorovna)

Robbing as a display of mercy

As Bogdan Onenko's congregation came under the influence of communist propaganda, he was one of those first shamans who had to deal with the mass rejection of sacrifice. As a result, not Bogdan's patients, but he himself fell seriously ill. We can judge how badly the shaman suffers in such a situation, from Lingdze's complaint to her patients who do not bring her an offering:

> Do I need other people's stuff? If I want (something), I can find it anywhere! If I am dying because of that (failed sacrifice), nobody will be able to save me! I save everyone else! Will anybody feel sorry for me? Why can't they come here and bow (to my *seven*) for me? Why should I be the only compassionate one? Just me? They don't love me! I have a bitter taste in my mouth. It is as if I have been covering with scales! (Lingdze)

Shamanic spirits are not supposed to help people for free; in exchange for their service they demand worship. But forcing people to pay they exert influence firstly not upon the shaman's clients, but upon the shaman himself. Because spirits have easier access to a shaman than to his patients, they make him sick and suffer, and the only way for the shaman to recover is to force in his turn his patients to participate in sacrifice and worshipping his personal spirits. That is why it is considered that after being healed, the shamans' congregants must bring to the shaman some animals for sacrifice in order to heal that shaman. 'They ask the shaman to dance and wail and heal their illnesses. If they did not sacrifice, it would be very bad for a shaman. It is a very, very bad and serious thing! That's why it is so' (Aleksandr Sergeevich).

But Bogdan was deserted by his congregation and left to deal with his angry *seven* on his own. His disease was so serious that he was near death.

> Nobody gave him anything and he fell ill. He was about to die because they did not offer him (a sacrifice). For several days, he was at home unconscious. There were no doctors at that time. Who could help him? And the elders began to say that he must be helped. An animal was necessary! [...] He has shamanised all over the village but nobody had given him anything. (Shamans) have children (spirits), they must be fed. If nobody offers anything, the *seven* gnaws us (shamans) instead. Such is the law! (Ol'ga Egorovna)

Later a few of Bogdan's patients agreed to sacrifice and he became better. 'There were some people in the village who were able to help him. Some gave a pig, others offered a rooster. He shamanised for himself and recovered' (Ol'ga Egorovna). But those sacrifices were not enough to satisfy Bogdan's spirits. It was necessary to make all the patients participate in a worshipping ritual and pay the spirits back for their service. Bogdan decided that in this case payment could be taken from his debtors by force. After he recovered, he came to Ul'chi district and began to 'rob' his disobedient patients.

Those people who had two or three pigs soon found out that they had none because he took them away! People who had good dress material – he seized that, too. Well, he did it purposely and in the presence of the owners. Then he said: 'Do not say that I am guilty! I was near death because of you, but other people revived me'. (Ol'ga Egorovna)

Nevertheless, the shaman's debtors started believing the new popular ideas of atheistic propaganda, which convinced them that spirits do not exist at all, and that the shaman simply wants to profit and to make good at their expense. That is why they complained to the bearers of the new ideas, to the Soviet administration about Bogdan interpreting his actions as robbery. Since that moment the interpreters of Bogdan's behaviour among the indigenous population were divided into those who considered it robbery and those who still believed it was a sacrifice and the honest collection of debt. Bogdan was arrested. People said that in the moment of arrest Bogdan allegedly pulled snakes out of his mouth and spewed fire out of his mouth, but did not manage to frighten the policemen (Aleksei Kisovich).

From the traditional point of view, Bogdan's action was humanistic and good not only for him but for his congregants as well. Being faced with his patients' refusal to sacrifice, he had another option besides 'robbery'. After healing his patients he had power over their souls (*panian*), which were placed in his personal 'soul depository' (*dëkaso*). It was at his mercy either to leave their *panian* in that safe place or to return them to that dangerous sphere of the invisible world from where they had been taken by him in the previous healing ceremony. The practice of returning the souls of the patients, who do not hurry to worship shamans' spirits, was known to Nanai shamans. It resulted in the sudden death of a disobedient patient, but it seemed to be fair because in that situation, not a shaman, but a patient was considered to be guilty.

Bogdan could also return (and kill that way) the *panian* of his stubborn patients. But he chose another option, preferring to take payment from them by force, which both would help him to recover and would leave his patients alive. From the traditional point of view, it was not Bogdan, but his Ul'chi congregants who instigated the conflict, it was they who sought his help, accepted certain obligations and then failed to meet them, thus putting him and themselves in danger. Yet, from the point of view of the atheist congregants, who were relying on the logic of Soviet criminal codes, Bogdan's actions were clearly criminal and motivated only by the desire for personal, and trivial enrichment.

SPIRITS AGAINST THE SOVIET RULE: ANTI-SHAMANIC PERSECUTIONS

Let us hope that this young man will not become a shaman,
as there is a centre of cultural work
organised by the Soviet Rule at the mouth of the Kochechumo River;
and it will be able to deter all the spirits *aiami, khargi* and *kheven*,[108]
which are trying to settle in him.
(Suslov 1931: 126)

In spite of anti-religious and anti-shamanic persecutions, which (with changing intensity) lasted during almost the entire period of the Soviet Rule, shamanism was not eradicated; it has survived in Nanai villages, though the number of shamans has gradually decreased. The shamans themselves explained the shamanism's power for survival by the fact that side by side with the persecution by the Soviet rule, they were also oppressed by their own spirits, which forced them to continue shamanic practice counter to all prohibitions.

Beginning of persecutions

Indigenous peoples of Siberia at first benefited from the Bolshevik revolution. 'Some Bolshevik theoreticians treated non-Russian nationalities, including indigenous Siberians as victims of tsarist imperialism. [...] At first, communists and their sympathizers rarely crusaded against shamanism, preferring mainstream Christianity as a target for their attacks. In such a climate, practicing shamanists felt relaxed. Moreover, many earlier indigenous converts to Orthodox Christianity found it possible to return to their polytheistic spirituality (Znamenski 2007: 328). Soon after the establishment of the Soviet Rule some shamans were even elected into the local government bodies for leading positions, which was done in the course of the experiments made to merge the traditional authority with the new one (Bogoraz 1932: 143; Vdovin 1981: 215). In some singular cases there were even some attempts made to establish collaboration between communists and shamans. 'Some shamans actively helped Red Army soldiers establish the Soviet Rule and in the suppression of counter-revolutionary actions' (Vasil'eva 2000: 29). In their turn there were some communists who applied to shamans for healing. Thus, in the report by the Yakut regional committee of the Communist Party (December 1926), it was noticed that 'shamans still enjoy indisputable authority, [...] and some communists resort to their help'. For example, in the spring of 1926, a sick Russian communist, Novgorodov, 'in-

---

108 *Aiami, khargi* and *kheven* are categories of spirits.

vited four shamans at once, and their shamanising just contributed to Novgorodov's early death' (Vasil'eva 2000: 60).

Nevertheless communists' collaboration with shamans was very brief; the experiments on involving shamans in politics failed, and, as the scholars affirm, some shamans themselves became staunch opponents of the Soviet Rule (Vdovin 1981: 215). I.I. Vdovin (1981: 216) writes that 'the most violent shamans' actions against the Soviet institutions of local governing began after they (shamans) were removed from those institutions'. According to Evgeniia A. Alekseenko (1981: 96), the Soviet administrators of the settlements told of indigenous people complaining about shamans' moral pressure, threats to inflict illness on those whose actions the shamans disliked.

N. Gutorov (1932) reports that since 1921 in the village Karaga, Kamchatka region, there appeared even an organisation of several shamans, which was led by shaman Savva. That organisation existed and was strong until 1932 and 'only after the Koriak national region was established was Savva's activity brought to naught' (Stebnitskii 2000: 159). Concerning the activity of that organisation, Gutorov writes in the following way:

The head of that organisation, the old shaman Savva [...] taught people how to live. [...] His main ideas were that people should not buy the imported food, because such food is not really nourishing. He also taught that it is prohibited to use the bathhouse, because there are evil spirits which dwell there and which can bite to death that one who comes there. He strictly prohibited teaching children in the schools, because children learn literacy in the school, but literacy teaches them how to steal. Savva also banned meetings, because the evil spirits are always present there. [...] He ordered any Russian clothes to be thrown away. [...] When people gathered around the shamans, the shamans ate fly agaric, became drunk on it, and after that they began to shamanise, to dance and play the drum under Savva's guidance'. (Gutorov 1932)

Sergei Stebnitskii reports that almost all the students who came from the village Karaga complained that the shaman did not let children go to school. According to him, 'the student I. Gutorova, who studied at the Institue of the Peoples of the North in 1937, wrote: 'Shaman Savva said that if children start studying, their arms will fall off [...] and the entire population believed Savva' (Stebnitskii 2000: 159). Ya. F. Samarin reports about another case of anti-Soviet activity by a shaman. 'In 1931 in the Uelen village (Chukchi region – T.B.) a young Chukchi, T. Elkov, wanted to shoot himself'. When they asked him about the reason, he said the following:

When I went to study courses with my wife, there was a shaman, who campaigned against the Soviet Rule. At a meeting I made a speech against that

shaman. [...] When I returned to Uelen, my wife died. The shamans told
me that it happened because I opposed them. [...] Even before, when I was
returning to Uelen, shamans frightened me, saying that I was going to die.
There was also Remeren, who went on that trip together with me. He also
spoke against shamans. Under the influence of their threats he shot himself
in Anadyr. [...] I also wanted to shoot myself, because Remeren was my best
friend. [...] But then I decided that there would be too much to gain from it
by the kulaks and shamans, that is, by my own enemies. (Samarin 1935: 90)

However, persecution of shamanism started not because of the weak and spontaneous 'resistance' of some isolated shamans. It was part of a wider anti-religious
campaign. Shamans were called 'the obstruction of socialist construction work'
and the fight against shamanism was proclaimed to be 'one of the spheres of class
struggle in the North' (Suslov 1932: 17). In 1924 the Presidium of the Central Executive Committee of Sakha adopted a special resolution 'On the Measures in the
Fight against Shamanism', which cited as the main measure the elaboration of mass
cultural-enlightening work, and for the fight against shamanic blackmailing and
point-blank deceit – also administrative-legal measures (Ocherki 1957: 118). The first
stage of the anti-shamanism repressions was quite peaceful. On the official level the
events taking place at this time were interpreted as if the shamans themselves, being
under the power of the Soviets, in a spell of enthusiasm renounced their shamanic
practices. I. Suslov (1932: 157) wrote: 'In different places all over the territory of Siberia, shamans voluntarily give up their practice, hand over their drums and robes to
the local village Soviets and renounce shamanism altogether'.

In the 1930s a universal process of eradicating shamanism took place. By the
order of the regional committee the members of the *Komsomol* organised a
meeting in the village of Ukhta, Ul'chi district, where the number of shamans was especially great. They (the members of the *Komsomol*) gathered
one day and went there – to the village of Ukhta – from Nizhnii Gavan and
(the village of) Bogorodsk. Young people, members of the *Komsomol!* Let us
go! They searched through all the attics of the houses where the Ul'chi lived,
and collected all the idols. Earlier on, when a shaman was buried, the *seven* [109]
belonging to him or her was put on his or her tomb. They (the members of the
Komsomol) collected everything also from there (from the tombs), then piled
them (all the *seven*) up and set fire to them. (Konstantin Maktovich)

---

109 *Seven* here it denotes an image of a shamanic spirit.

Aleksandr Sergeevich recalls an analogous case also in the village of Dzhuen.

People came to Dzhuen on a cutter. They convened a meeting, did not argue, did nothing. But after the meeting they started going from one house
to another, collecting drums, shaman's belts, and *seven*. Everybody knew already beforehand that they were going to come and collect these things. The
only things left were *edekhe* (metal images of the *seven* worn hanging around
the neck) – these were the only ones people were able to hide! (Aleksandr
Sergeevich)

Niura Sergeevna also confirms that after the meetings the members of *Komsomol*
went around the houses, they collected drums, shaman's belts, *seven*, [...] wherever
the lights were on, they entered and asked, 'Are you practising shamanism here?'
And then people hid from them the cock meant for a sacrificial ritual. They thrust
it in the stove. Hid it this way! A Nanai – member of the *Komsomol* – crushed the
drum, completely, trampling on it! What can you do about it? Everybody kept silent'. In Naikhin wooden poles with carved images of spirits were set on fire in the
street. Aleksandr Sergeevich recalls that in the village of Dokiada there was a big
saola.[110] Until the period of repressions, 'people from all over the region constantly
came there with pigs' in order to offer sacrifice to *saola's* spirits, and 'the Executive
Committee of the Nanai District decided, that it was necessary to fight against that.
'Down with it! We'll liquidate all that! It is the Soviet rule now! The Soviet rule does
not allow practising shamanism!' They did it. They did away with everything' (Aleksandr Sergeevich).
     But the fact that the ritual requisites were taken away from shamans exerted the
least influence on maintaining the shamanic tradition. Practically immediately after
shamanic equipment was taken from them, the shamans made new drums and new
images of spirits and secretly continued practicing. In some houses people practised shamanism even despite the fact that they did not dare to restore the drums.
The practice of using pot lids instead of drums that became known all over Siberia
also dates back to this period. 'Anyway, people practised shamanism at night', Ivan
Torokovich says, 'clanging the pot lids! Anyway!' – 'But where did they put their
drums?' I asked. 'What drums! They were all taken away! They were prohibited! If
you happen to have a drum, you will be arrested!' The practice of replacing drums
with pans that survived among the Yakuts until the 1990s was also described by
Marjorie M. Balzer. According to the words of one of her friends-assistants, a true
shaman was able to turn the drum-pan into a real drum during the shamanic ritual
(Balzer 1995b: 26).

---

110 *Saola* is a clay vessel in which, according to the belief, the spirits of a dead shaman live.

The shamanists hid everything they could from the *Komsomols*; the rest of the things were restored after some time and taken into use covertly. So in the past all Nanai used to have *mio* (a cloth with the names of deities *endur* written on it in Chinese). 'When people were prohibited to practise shamanism, they hid *mio*, but after some time took them out in private, talked to them (performed a ritual), and then hid them again. Now everything has been liquidated, but at the same time everything still exists! Only now it is not kept in a special outbuilding but right in the dwelling' (Aleksandr Sergeevich).

If the shamans maintained that the image of the spirit that had been thrown out and crushed in the course of the anti-shamanism campaign was not empty, but there was a spirit residing in there, that image certainly had to be restored in secrecy. So in Dzhari village was restored a *saola,* a clay vessel in which, according to the belief, the spirits of a dead shaman live.

Besides destroying shamanic equipment there was also anti-religious propaganda. Today Nanai elders remember that when they were children they demonstrated and disclosed 'miracles' in front of shamanists in order to convince them that spirits do not exist.

We were ardent Young Pioneers and we derided shamanism. When people were shamanising in a house, we arranged (mockery). There was such propaganda at school. In the village, there were authoritative persons who agitated (against shamanism). So, what did we children do? We cut a human face on a pumpkin and put a candle inside the pumpkin. Then we went to the place where people were shamanising. They surely were frightened; they thought it was an evil spirit. Had it not supported propaganda? (Zinaida Nikolaevna)

The administrative measures aimed at the eradication of shamanism resulted in the passive resistance of the shamanists to the measures taken by the Soviet rule: a low percentage of participants at pre-election meetings, systematic non-complete classes at indigenous schools due to parents' refusal to send their children to boarding schools; refusal of any medical or veterinary help (Suslov 1931: 128). After some time had passed, the initiators of repressions started to recognise the ineffectiveness of demolishing the shamanic requisites as well as the prohibitions on shamanism. I. Suslov wrote: 'I have learned about a great number of cases when shamans have handed over their robes and drums to the medical doctors or instructors of the Soviet construction work, promising to give up their practice forever. The instructors described it in their reports as a victory on the anti-religious front. However, when checking on it later on, it turned out that as soon as the instructor had left, people made a new robe and a drum for the shaman, but they did it secretly' (Suslov 1931: 128–129).

Arresting of shamans

Concerning the arresting of shamans, the informants gave me contradictory infor-mation. On the one hand, they tended to generalise and obviously exaggerate and scale up the persecution, affirming that almost all the shamans were arrested and shot; on the other hand, they gave very few concrete names, and it would be difficult to say that we have reliable data about arrests of shamans just for their activity.[111]

Here I cite some of my informants' utterances about shamans, saying that sha-mans were arrested and sentenced to death:

> They assaulted shamans; they used to call it a *troika* (the representatives of the official power who did it usually acted in groups of three). They 'purged' shamans! Arrested them! Shot them! This is what they did. And now what! A shaman! How can you practise shamanism? Why did they do it? It is not good, is it? Many shamans were imprisoned. That's why only a few (shamans) were left on the Amur River. (Ivan Torokovich)
> Shamans were arrested, taken away and quite a few of them were reported missing. (Lingdze)

The mass arrests of shamans (the so-called purge), about which some informants talk, are nevertheless not mentioned in the literature. With confidence I can only speak about the tragic fate of shaman Bogdan Onenko, whose case with 'robbing/ sacrifice' was described in the previous section. He was arrested and did not return home, to all appearances sentenced to a prison camp, where he died. But it is im-portant to notice that Bogdan was arrested not because of shamanising as such, but because of forcing people to sacrifice pigs to his spirits, which was understood by the authorities as robbery.

Another name of a shaman-victim was reported by Ivan Torokovich; that was Sangila from Dzhari village. Sangila lived long. 'He had neither a daughter nor a son. Lived with his wife only. They came and took him, and they did not even put him in prison. They shot him somewhere'. Ivan Torokovich emphasised that the main rea-son why Sangila was arrested and not another shaman, was that Sangila did not have relatives who would be able to take revenge on him.[112] According to his words, the

---

111 Some my informants rejected the idea of mass arrests of shamans. They name shamans who practiced during the entire time of the persecutions with no harm to themselves. Sofiia Sergeevna affirms that there were no arrests in her native Naikhin village. Nikolai Chubakov-ich does not know about any cases of arrests which happened in his native village Bolan. 'I lived in Bolan, there were shamans, but nobody was arrested'. He also argues that there were no serious anti-shamanic repressions at all, if not to take into account anti-shamanic pro-paganda and destruction of shamanic equipment. Sofiia Sergeevna also confirms that 'there were no persecutions in which (shamans) were imprisoned, no!'

112 The matter is that in this case revenge is understood not as physical, but as spiritual action.

authorities had a plan to arrest shamans and they chose Sangila to arrest as it seemed to them to be less dangerous for them.

One more case, people remember, was the arrest of a shaman right in the middle of performing a ritual called *kasa* (seeing the dead off to the beyond).

It happened during haymaking. We were just making hay in the *kolkhoz* in summer. Then he performed the *kasa* (sending the souls of the departed ones to the beyond). (Nesulta Borisovna)

I remember it as well. We were going through the *kasa*, it had not been completed yet, when people came and arrested the shaman, and they took the old man away. (Lingdze)

I went into hiding and saw everything. (Nesulta Borisovna)

Unfortunately, I did not ask my informants about what happened to that shaman next, but the common practice was to arrest a shaman and right after that to free him.[113] Nina Vasil'eva also affirms that she can name only several Yakut shamans against whom criminal proceedings were initiated, but at the same time 'who did not necessarily serve their sentences'. Sometimes the court confined itself 'to the imposition of a prohibition to practice shamanism' (Vasil'eva 2000: 59). But even a short time in jail left painful memories, as in Ivan Torokovich's story.

My grandfather was also a shaman. I was working in a lumbering camp far in the taiga. I came home. We finished work in April. We used to start in November and finish in August. The *kolkhoz* had sent us there. I arrived home, and my grandfather was not there. 'Where is Grandpa?' – 'Well', they say, 'we do not know if he is alive or already dead. They arrested him and took him to Khabarovsk. But at that time, in Khabarovsk, the jail was overcrowded. So whether you want it or not, you will plead yourself guilty. They beat them there! Sign it and that's that! They present a written indictment and make you sign it'. But he (the grandfather) says: 'You can kill me, but I am not going to sign it! Because I did not do it!' Then a commission came from Moscow. They started working. They were sent especially from Moscow here, to Khabarovsk Krai. The jail was overcrowded. And they let all of them go. And our grandpa also came home 'Well, how was it?' we asked him. 'Oh', he says, 'if they had not come from Moscow, I would also have been [...]. They drag somebody (from the interrogation), throw them down on the floor, and that's that! They won't stand up any more! Dead already!' So this was how it was! It was the work of the Central Committee, the NKVD, Yezhov! Beria, Yezhov – it is them! The things they did! (Ivan Torokovich)

---

113 From my informants I learned about four Nanai shamans who were arrested and the reliable proof that one of them, Bogdan Onenko, served a sentence.

It should be noted that the prohibitions and destruction of shamanic requisites and even some arrests *did not even decrease* the dimensions of shamanic activities. Only mass open rituals, which earlier concerned lots of people, stopped being performed, and shamanising as such never stopped, it just began to be completed secretly. In spite of the slackening of warnings against 'sheer administration' and 'harmful administrative oppression' in the early 1930s, which only produced an outward effect and yielded no positive results, the next step in the fight against shamanism was recommended to be taken. There was a plan given to local authorities to arrest a certain number of shamans.

On the one hand, the local authorities had to fulfil the plan, but on another hand, there were some reasons which prevented them from arresting shamans. It led to the widespread practice of attributing the name of a 'shaman' to those indigenous people who were not actually shamans. It was mostly those guiltless persons who were arrested and suffered for the sake of fulfilling that plan.

> In 1937 there was a 'troika' working in each village. They did whatever they wanted! They could write that a person was a shaman and a vermin, and that was that! People came after them from the NKVD, took them and that was that! Shot them! (Ivan Torokovich)

Trying to provide proof to the authorities about their active and successful activities in liquidating shamanism, the members of 'troikas' did not strive to be very objective and, under the pretext of shamanism arrested just any person for their own private reasons, such as to square accounts with them. In his novel, Konstantin Maktovich Bel'dy remembers the real case of how his father Makto was arrested because a communist (also Nanai) fancied Makto's gun, which he managed to 'confiscate' in the moment when Makto was arrested (Bel'dy 2006: 303). That way the Nanai shared the fate of the other peoples of Russia, who suffered during the time of terror.

> A great many people were arrested at that time. In Dzhari there were no elderly people left. [...] In the summer some old men were taken away. After that some more followed. Sandila, Kiachka's father, Korka. How many of them were there? Four or five, perhaps? They were taken on horseback, two together, barely alive. They were put in prison in the village of Troitskoe. How we cried when they went on foot! They were hardly able to walk, they were so old! They had to walk as far as Khabarovsk. They were not able to do that. People were criticised and tortured at that time! Do any of the shamans torture anybody like that? (Lingdze)

Like many other ordinary Nanai, my informant Ivan Torokovich was also arrested when he was young, though not in connection with shamanism, but for his supposed belonging to the class of middle peasants. At that time he was engaged in logging work and was one of the most leading/advanced workers. One day he was asked to come to the settlement of Troitskoe, the centre of Nanai district.

'Where do you work?' – 'In Troitskoe forestry enterprise to fulfil my plans'. – 'What did you give to the *kolkhoz*?' – 'Me and my father had two horses, we gave those. And four nets. Now I fulfil my plan with the horse we gave away'. – 'All right, wait', they say. Some time later the door opened. 'Come in!' they say. And then the chief of the *kolkhoz*, the head of the village soviet and the economic director came. The entering chief asks them, 'Why did you give him a note certifying that he is a middle peasant? Is he really a middle peasant? He is still young, he only started working. And he works well in the taiga. Why are you doing so? You gave a document to your fellow countryman certifying that he is a middle peasant. Is it correct that he gave two horses (to the *kolkhoz*)?' – 'Yes, that's right', they say. 'And four nets?' – 'That's right', they say. 'Don't you dare do it again! There are no rich people among the Nanai!' And then they say to me, 'You can go! They will take you back tomorrow!' He really said so, 'Don't you dare do it again! There are no rich people among the Nanai!' And I went back to the taiga. But that old man (the shaman) was there. Two days later he was taken away. They came from Troitsk with militiamen. We learned only later on that he had not returned home. First he was taken to Troitsk prison and then to Komsomolsk. He was a shaman, and, when performing rituals, he received different things people gave him; this is what was said in the documents. Later on we got to know that he was shot in Komsomolsk. The *Nanai* themselves betrayed him! [114] (Ivan Torokovich)

---

114 Ivan Torokovich himself tells this story as follows, 'We had a Stakhanovist movement. We were competing for the first prize! (The *kolkhoz*) Novyi *Put* (New Way) and Dzhari were having a competition to find out who is the first to fulfil the plan. And I was keeping the flag (for shock work). The challenge flag! They allocated me a bonus of 40 rubles. 40 rubles – this used to be a lot of money! And then suddenly the head of the village soviet ordered me to go to the district centre. (On the accusation) that I were a middle peasant! What, a middle peasant? (We had) a pair of horses. One of them we gave to the *kolkhoz*, the other I exchanged for a double-barrelled gun. What a middle peasant am I? And I am ordered to come especially from there, with an escort. I arrived there and said, 'I will go to the district executive committee tomorrow, but now I'll go home'. – 'No', they said, 'wait here!' They didn't let me go. I was sitting there, and then my father also came. And they called us. I was the first to go. 'Tell us how it is there', they said. 'I don't know anything', I said. 'We had a pair of horses. We gave one of them to the *kolkhoz*. We also had four pieces of seines. We gave them to the *kolkhoz* as well. I have nothing left. Now I am working for a forestry enterprise, the *kolkhoz* sent me. I am the first in my unit. I am the keeper of the challenge flag at the moment. We have two horses and three men, and I am the first'. – 'Are you a member of *Komsomol*?' – 'A member of *Komsomol*!' The chief of the *kolkhoz*, the chairman of the executive committee and the first secretary of the district committee – all three were there. And they called the head of the village soviet and the

Against the background of those arrests of ordinary people, much fewer arrests of shamans should be especially explained. It is also important to emphasise that during the anti-religious campaign, a large number of Orthodox priests and confessors of other religions were executed by shooting, but 'such punitive measures as the death penalty were not used for shamans'. Nina Vasil'eva, for example, also confirms that she does not have relevant facts (2000: 28). To find out the reason for such authorities' indulgence, let us go to the cases of when shamans were *not* arrested.

Official permission to shamanise

They also said it to my mother (shaman Dekhe, who was not arrested). Besides that, shamans were not arrested if they promised to give up practicing. If after such a promise they usually continued practicing secretly, nobody touched them anymore. 'How did they take shamans? If you are not going to practise shamanism, we will not touch you' (Nikolai Petrovich). But there were also apparently some cases that in full swing of persecutions some shamans were as if encouraged in their activity and some shamans were given official permission to practise shamanism. Usually it was connected with a concrete situation, when a shaman was able to help a representative of the authorities or just make a strong impression on them. So, when Mikhail Sergeevich Bel'dy, later the leader of the administration of the village of Naikhin, caught a dangerous disease and was about to die in his childhood, doctors were unable to help him and decided to send for shaman Dekhe, Nikolai Petrovich's mother.

---

economic director and told them: 'What documents do you issue? He is not a middle peasant at all. He joined the *kolkhoz*, gave away one horse, and the other exchanged for a gun. Is he a middle peasant? He is the first in logging. The *kolkhoz* collects 20 percent of his wages. What are you doing? If you continue acting like that, you will soon have nobody in the *kolkhoz*. Stop doing it! You issue such documents to the members of your *kolkhoz* which confirm that they are middle peasants, so that they are taken away'. And then they said to me: 'Go home, and don't go anywhere tomorrow. Tomorrow we will send you a horse, and you can go back to your district'. Well, I left and went home. And then, in the morning, they sent me a horse and took me back to the taiga. We arrived at two in the afternoon [...]. My comrades say, 'Oh, you came back!'

Nikolai Petrovich, who was a child during the years of repressions, recalls this period as follows, 'I was a pioneer; I went to the pioneer camp twice. It was such fun! Everything was so beautiful! It was so elating! I was brought up in such atmosphere [...]! I joined the *Komsomol*, and then the war started. It was all so elating! Do you understand? Sincerely! I was fighting for the party. I served seven years in the army, I was educated in the communist spirit. And, apart from that, I remembered my childhood and loved my mother (a shaman-woman). I had dreams about her. She did not speak to me in my dreams, only went past me, dancing like a shaman, and disappeared. I woke up and felt offended. What a mother! Appears only in my dreams and does not even talk to me! I did not see any contradiction between these two things'.

They (Mikhail Sergeevich's relatives) came to her together with the doctor. The doctor was treating and treating Mikhail Sergeevich. Without avail! He was about to die. And he was brought home from hospital. On this very night they came after my mother. [...] It was she who saved Mikhail Sergeevich. We children, we were driven out of the house, windows were covered with blinds and a shamanic ritual was performed. (Mikhail Sergeevich was cured.) After some time my mother was given a document certifying that she could help the doctor treat sick people. She received this document and started practising shamanism quietly; people also came to her. (Nikolai Petrovich)

As a result, Dekhe appeared to be working as if in unison with the new authorities, which made it possible for her to practise shamanism without being punished. Another Nanai shaman who had an official paper giving permission to shamanise was Opa Onenko. The paper was given to him because once he was invited to a Russian administrator's home and successfully healed his son. Sofiia Sergeevna affirms that paper supported Opa during his entire life and after his death was put in his coffin. Similar cases were typical not only for Nanai, but also for other indigenous peoples in Siberia. Elena P. Bat'ianova writes: 'It is significant that among the Teleut there are popular stories about how the authorities blessed the shamans's activity after they were convinced of its effectiveness'. She cites an example given by her informant:

When the Soviet Rule was established, the local authorities asked a shaman to perform during the village meeting. 'Are not you afraid?' the shaman asked. 'No'. And he started shamanising. [...] When he called for the spirit of thresholds, the doors began to crack. [...] They saw that he indeed was able to shamanise and let him go in peace. They asked him: 'Would you like us to pick you up?' But he sat on a bear and rode it. People saw that.

There is another similar story told by shaman Tatiana Manysheva:

When I was lying on the stove, there came three policemen. 'Why? Where?' 'You deceive people, take too much payment. You have taken a good coat. They also brought a good fur coat for you from Biisk'. On and on. We went, they imprisoned me, interrogated me. 'Why did you take the fur coat and the other coat?' In two months I was summoned. 'Go home and heal. People who you have healed approved of you. Let you be healthy, do not die. Heal!' (Bat'ianova 2007: 180–181).

Stories of that sort became a strong means of consolidation of shamanic activity and for raising shamans' prestige. At the same time they can illuminate the issue of why despite anti-religious politics, shamanic activities did not noticeably decrease. Meeting the inexplicable phenomena, which shamans demonstrated to them, the authorities were probably scared not to please them and to be exposed to the danger of their spiritual revenge.

Anti-shamanic propaganda

A more widespread and more successful means in the fight against shamanism (especially at the beginning of this campaign) was the force of word persuading people to change their world view. Some communists were naive enough and sincerely hoped that if someone was suffering from a serious attack of shamanic disease, it would be enough just to change that person's views, to convince him or her that spirits do not exist and because of that the anguish was supposed to stop. I. Suslov offered the following recommendations for that way of fighting against shamanism: 'In the period between nervous fits when the sick person (suffering from shamanism – T. B.) is conscious, the atheists and cultural-enlightenment workers have to help them understand the reasons for these kind of diseases, and explain the absurdity of animistic views which the sick person believes to have caused the illness' (1931: 126).

Gurvich has spoken, quoting the words of G. Naumov, a participant in the partisan movement, about still another original form of fighting against shamanism, a kind of spiritual session, where the members of the *Komsomol* participated, considering it a means of fighting against the 'religious narcotic'.

Romanova, a Yakutian woman, informed the others of the fact that she heard the voice of her departed husband at night, and even started organising public spiritual sessions for meeting him. Willing to disclose this miracle, the members of *Komsomol* from a partisan detachment asked the widow to have a session in their barracks. Vodka and snacks were put on the table and the lights were switched off. In complete silence people suddenly heard the rustle of a bird's wings, and then a male voice asked if the snacks were good, and then they heard smacking. The widow started asking the 'husband' questions, which he answered in a loud voice. Finally a person from the audience asked how long the Soviet rule was going to last. The answer was – not long. This remark gave rise to anger in the audience. When the soldiers of the Red Army jumped to catch the deceased, they only caught one another. In the end the widow had to (or was made to) confess that she was a ventriloquist. The soldiers made her swear that she would not repeat these sessions, and then let her go. (Gurvich 1966: 83)

The main argument of the authorities persecuting shamans was the accusation that they belonged to the class of exploiters against whom the revolution was directed.

'Shamanism used to be the most faithful supporter of Tsarism, tribal chiefs and local tycoons, their most effective detachment in the fight for enslaving wide masses of working people in the Far East', someone hiding behind the initials I. A. has written. 'Shamanism was and has remained a reactionary force striving to decelerate the development of culture; it was and has remained a support for counter-revolution' (1938: 107). When finding excuses for repressions, their executors confirmed that shamanism, like any other religion, strengthens and consecrates slavery and exploitation'; that, being 'a phenomenon of an especially reactionary order', it fosters the 'strengthening of animosity between tribes, the development of national hatred', slowing down the process of 'Sovietising the North, raising the cultural level of the Northern regions and, besides that, also influences the wasting of social energy and social forces' (Suslov 1931: 26–27). Shamanism was declared to be the inhibitor of socialist construction work, and, consequently, the fight against it was an inseparable part of socialist construction work. The fight against shamanism consisted, as it was described at that time, in 'disclosing the political and class role of shamanism'. It was indispensable, as it was said, to 'show through living and concrete examples the damage caused by shamanism on the development of the national economy in the North, what a heavy load it constitutes on the budget of the native working people' (Suslov 1931: 132). 'Shamans constitute a non-working element' (Kosokov 1931: 70). Besides all that, shamans were accused of counter-revolutionary anti-Soviet activities. 'Shamans constitute a reactionary counter-revolutionary force' (ibid.). Reports of the killing of teachers, poor peasants and cultural workers by shamans can be found in the literature (Budarin 1968: 192). So, in the village of Yandygan, a Chukchi shaman Taiungi shot dead Attungi, chairman of the National Council. 'Shamans move against all the party and government activities both publicly and covertly. Shamans were and will be the worst enemies of the working people of the Far East. They tried to foil elections and persuade people not to join the *kolkhoz*' (I. A. 1938: 110). According to the words of I. Suslov (1931: 128), from a few 'more advanced' regions of the North 'signals' came from administrative workers 'about the shamans' attempts to foil one or another undertaking of the Soviet rule'. – 'Shamans persuaded their fellow countrymen not to send their children to school, frightened with all kinds of horrors those who turned for medical assistance to hospitals, threatened with the revenge of the spirits those who followed the advice of veterinarians, visited the community centre, or went to the cinema. During rituals shamans often did direct anti-Soviet agitation work, [...] spoke viciously and heatedly against schools, made use of the religious superstition of the backward and illiterate population, called people to not send their children to boarding schools' (Gurvich 1966: 82). There also occurred really mean accusations against shamans. So, they were even accused of contributing to the spread of such 'social diseases' as 'syphilis, trachoma, tuberculosis, gonorrhoea and leprosy' (Kosokov 1931: 68). All this argumentation leaves a strange impression due to its forthright groundlessness; it seems as if, quite deliberately, something important has been left unsaid. It can only be detected to a certain extent in I. Suslov's (1932: 16) remark stating that in order to consolidate the new order, we face 'extensive work not only in the sphere of the economy, but also in the sphere of *transforming the people's minds*' (my italics). I. Suslov (ibid.: 17) is trying to explain this argument with vague words about a shaman 'working out mystical ideology and contributing to the wasting of social energy'.

The arguments voiced against shamans caused a wave of disputes. The discussion was obviously so heated that until the present, shamans, the children and grand-children of the people who suffered because of the repressions, continue arguing with the accusers from the past, most probably long dead by now. While doing it, they make use of the specific terminology of the political documents of that time, which has sunk into their minds. For example, one of the regulations denouncing shamanism determined it as 'especially detrimental, hindering the cultural-national awakening and political development [...] equal to the *daze* created by all religious cults'. About seventy years later, Ivan Torokovich voices this accusation as follows, 'Sick people would have gone to the doctor and got well, but you perform your rituals and *stupefy* people!' Talking about anti-shamanic persecutions, Konstantin Mak-tovich uses such phrases as 'fight against shamanism as against a phenomenon of non-Soviet discipline', or 'Soviet discipline does not admit any belief, because it is charlatanism'.

The *Komsomol*-enthusiasts probably so diligently repeated the arguments against shamanism learned by them that even many years later the informants remember-ing them, while speaking about the repressions, again and again start arguing with them, especially emphasising that shamans had not been well off and had not ex-ploited other people's labour. 'What were the Nanai' riches at that time?' Ivan Torok-ovich asks. 'Nothing! They caught fish as much as they needed for their own food. They even did not know how to sell fish. How were they supposed to sell it? They did not have any horses! Why do that (why arrest Nanai)? They were not kulaks, far from that! They were ordinary (poor) people!' Recalling the arrest of one of the shamans, Ivan Torokovich emphasises his poverty. 'He was poor', he says, 'he did not take anything from people for the rituals. I was working in the taiga at that time, taking logs to the river on a sleigh drawn by horses. Once in the evening they brought this old man to us. I asked him, 'Why did you come here?' He says, 'They made me come here, to work here'. I tell him, 'You are an old man, how can you work here, lift logs on the sleigh? They are heavy! Who sent you here?' – 'The *predsedatel'* (chief) of the *kolkhoz*, the village *soviet*. Work yourself, don't speak much! It is difficult there!' – he says. Many people were arrested.

Until now the Nanai continue confirming that shamans were actually not ex-ploiters at all, living from the labour of other people, as they were shown to be in the 1930s. 'Shamans were taken for nothing!' Ivan Torokovich is indignant. 'Shamans were really poor! If they had had at least ten dogs! But they had only one or two.

But they were told: 'You are a shaman, an exploiter, you take pigs from people' (for the annual sacrificial ritual). Actually shamans never took much (for their service). A silver ruble or a coin (wrapped into a piece of cloth) is put round his neck when he plays his drum. (This money is for the shaman and is meant as a payment to his spirits.) And they pour a hundred grams of vodka. But anything else? In the autumn people bring him a pig for the *kesie geleguich* (sacrificial ritual). But this pork is meant for treating everybody. Everybody eats it! But how he works! Performs the ritual, suffers torments! In the summer his robe is drenched with sweat. Try it yourself! To dance and sing for hours in such heat!'

As a result of the repressions, shamans were always afraid that someone could threaten their free activities;[115] they also developed the habit of justifying their practice, intentionally emphasising the positive sides and not mentioning the dangers related to it. 'What was the idea of persecuting shamans?' asks Lingdze, pretending that shamans' activities consist only in healing people and feasts. 'Is it bad to get well?' she continues. 'If you get well and slaughter a big or a small pig, if all people sit together at table and eat pork and drink vodka, what is bad about it? People cooked food, ate, stood up and left. Is it really bad?' Resuming the same topic another time, she protects shamanism in the following way:

Is it easy to be a shaman? Is it easy; is it good to be a shaman? It is not simply that you repeat the things in *yai* (shaman's chanting) that people tell you. Everything has to be correct! It is necessary to find out what the person's problem is. You have to try hard! It is not as easy as to scold people. Scolding – this is bad! But is shamanism bad? Not at all! You only ask for grace for people! You want your friends to be well! If your friends are well, it means everything is all right! If all people are well – it is good! Isn't it good that you get well, recover from the bad things that torture you? You become a shaman-woman and you can take leave of your senses, you can even die when you practise shamanism. If you perform rituals, you can catch a disease; you can fall ill and die. You ask for luck from different creatures and you do not know if they hear you or not. So you bow and ask for mercy, and you cannot be sure if they hear you. (Lingdze)

Shamans' persecutors

Recalling the years of the persecution of shamans, elderly people confirm that usually it was not the Russians but the indigenous people, Nanai themselves, who carried out these repressions. The informants do not differentiate between the persecutors and

---

115 For example, having got acquainted with the researcher professor J. Pentikäinen, shaman-woman Lingdze asked me if he was not going to arrest her.

victims as Russians and Nanai also because many Russians (above all, believers) also
suffered from repressions. In pre-revolution time there were churches in some Nanai
villages, all of them were completely destroyed.[116] The fact that the representatives of
the indigenous peoples themselves were active persecutors is also confirmed by the
materials from the other regions of the North as well as Siberia. So, according to the
words of Marjorie M. Balzer (1995b: 26), in Yakutiia in the late 1920s and early 1930s
hundreds of shamanic drums were burnt, first and foremost, by young enthusiast-
Komsomols who mainly came from among the indigenous people who had turned
to communism, and not by the visiting Russian revolutionaries. My informant Nanai Nikolai Petrovich confessed that his brother was the first policeman among the
Nanai, and that it was he who arrested the famous shaman Bogdan Onenko. 'The
Nanai themselves set afire the *mio* (the image of deity on fabric) and the *toro* (trees or
poles with carved images of spirits)', confirms Aleksandr Sergeevich. Harsh torturing sometimes resulting in the death of the victim, which the Nanai kept in prison
together with Ivan Torokovich's grandfather, was carried out by their own fellow
countrymen. Here is another story about this:

> I came home, and grandpa was not there. I asked for him. My mother said: 'He
> was taken away, to Khabarovsk'. And later on, in May, I went to Khabarovsk
> by boat to give away fish. (Arriving home), I entered the house. Grandpa was
> there. 'What the hell!' I think. I ask him. 'Well, there, in Khabarovsk, in the
> jail, my turn did not come yet. If it had come, I would not have endured it, I
> would have died immediately! There were two Nanai there. From Naikhin.
> They beat them very hard! Want it or not, you have to sign! They beat you
> so hard that you could not get up any more, covered with blood all over! But
> then three men came from Moscow, started to look into the matter and re-
> leased everybody. And so our grandpa was also released!' (Ivan Torokovich)

When Lingdze tells me about the arrests of shamans, I try to specify, 'Did the
Russians arrest shamans?' – 'No', she says, 'it was the Nanai themselves. I don't know
why these people were arrested'. Konstantin Maktovich is trying to explain why the
Nanai took such an active part in the repressions against their own fellow countrymen. 'They were members of the *Komsomol*. At that time it was considered an expression of patriotism! Those who were registered members of the *Komsomol* regarded themselves as heroes! So, I'll go and commit a heroic deed! Against my own
people's culture!' Besides that, the present informants who condemn the repressions
now were also members of the *Komsomol* at that time. 'I was a kid then, and I was for

116 Vladimir Bogoraz wrote: 'The fight against shamanistic religion, i.e., shamanistic animism,
     has to be closely connected with the fight against Orthodoxy' (Bogoraz 1932: 157), but actually
     Christianity suffered much worse.

Stalin!' Nikolai Petrovich confesses, laughing. 'It is very difficult to confess it now, but I have to. So it was! I cannot deny it!'

When telling us about the repressions, the informants oppose not the Russians and Nanai, but, as they put it, the educated and all the others. 'It was the literate', says Aleksandr Sergeevich in Russian, 'who said that shamans were not needed anymore. They were prohibited! They said that you had to go to the doctor, not the shaman! But we were born at such a time! The educated people said that there would be no shamans anymore! They will be liquidated!' The communists who arrived were regarded as educated people, and the people considered the Communist Party as the main initiator of these repressions. 'These things were led by the party', Konstantin Maktovich summarises his thoughts about the years of repressions. Actually during these years the Union of Fighting Atheists was founded, 'the northern units of which defined as their main task the ruthless disclosure of shamans' anti-Soviet counter-revolutionary work, which they carry on, hiding behind shamanism and relying on it, in order to help the Soviet rule to treat them as the enemies of revolution' (Suslov 1931: 135). In the first order, these units were organised into educational institutions (the Institute of the Peoples of the North in Leningrad, indigenous technical schools, workers' faculties, teachers' courses).

At that time it was considered necessary to conduct special teaching, special conversations, open special study rooms for anti-religious, especially anti-shamanism work, in order to educate the necessary propagandistic staff to fight against shamanism. 'Not a single student', wrote I. Suslov (1931: 148), can leave an educational institution without 'the necessary atheistic steeling'. It was these students with 'atheistic steeling' who, in the eyes of the population, became *the educated,* and who actually persecuted the shamans. Vladimir G. Bogoraz confirmed that the representatives of the indigenous people acted not only as executors of the repressions, but also as initiators of the fight against shamanism. He wrote: 'The basis for the critical approach towards the elements of religion was established, first and foremost, by the young indigenous activists, pupils of the northern schools as well as the students of the Institute of the Peoples of the North'. As proof, he presents passages of an article written by a student called Ankakymylgin, who arrived in Leningrad from the settlement of Uelen in Chukotka. In this article the student repeats like an incantation one and the same thing several times, 'What deceitful shamans! There are no evil spirits! They do not have any spirit-helpers! They are only lying!' Vladimir G. Bogoraz comments on these words as follows, 'He brought the spirit of his young contemporaries to Leningrad. He simultaneously expressed the sheer hatred towards the shaman as a deceiver, an exploiter of the helpless poor, a collector of fees for healing people' (Bogoraz 1932: 143). According to the way of thinking of the indigenous people, the shaman stands side by side with the evil spirit. They are both vermin, they can both

cause illnesses and death' (ibid: 146).[117] Educating the Nanai youth in the spirit of
the new ideology resulted in a continuing and still persisting conflict between generations, in serious contradictions between the 'indigenous active' (as it was called
at that time) educated in the modern educational institutions, and the rest of the
population. 'Who remembers now how people survived these years!' recalls Ivan
Torokovich. 'Young people were taken to be taught in Leningrad. They came back
absolutely different, changed. They denounced their own people in the NKVD, in
the GPU, spoke against shamans, 'Let us do away with them!' they said. They did not
pity old men and women! People were crying!' In the literature of that time the process is described differently: 'Now the cultural class awareness and political literacy
have increased enormously in the North. This resulted in the creation of their own
national intelligentsia', which, in its turn, 'severely limited the enslaving strivings of
the local kulaks and half-feudals and undermined the positions of their ideological
weapon – shamanism' (I. A. 1938: 107).

The spiritual dimension of Soviet Rule

The bearers of the traditional culture interpreted the new world opening up to them
as a result of 'socialist transformations' in their own way (the same way communists
understood, or, to be more exact, did not understand, shamans). For example, the
ability of the communists to publicly deliver a speech from a rostrum they explained
with their being overpowered by some communist spirits with which they had, similarly to shamans, concluded an agreement. Among those who went to Leningrad
to continue their studies, there were young people of shamanistic origin. They also
interpreted in their own way the new world opening up to them, evaluating it in the
context of their familiar spiritual laws. The universal worshipping of J. Stalin, the
abundance of his portraits everywhere was based on their belief that J. Stalin was
endur (a deity). In order to guarantee their safety and not to provoke the anger of an
unfamiliar spirit hiding in the portraits of the great leader, the Nanai students, just
in case, paid homage to the portraits of J. Stalin and performed sacrificial rituals in
front of them as if they were deities.

> Semën Kile left for Leningrad together with other Nanai to study there. They
> made a drum in Leningrad themselves. Although they were young, they were
> skilful. Grown-ups! Grown-up men and women! (Before leaving for Lenin-
> grad) they had already worked back at home, caught fish. Semën (before leav-

---

117 In the last statement Vladimir G. Bogoraz, a good expert of the traditional Chukchi culture
and shamanism, although in an exaggerating manner but quite correctly presents the really
existing traditional beliefs of a shaman, although in the case when the shaman is a stranger,
representing the interests of another group. Unfortunately, he does not specify it.

ing) was already married. His wife returned to her father, and he was not able to get her back. Then people took him to Leningrad. He practised shamanism there. He was good at *meuri* (shamanic dancing). He went (performing rituals) from Leningrad to his own territory (Nanai district, Khabarovsk Krai). (Niura Sergeevna)

In Leningrad Semën Ivanovich also performed *undi,* i.e., a sacrificial ritual for the shamanic spirits including a procession led by a shaman and accompanied by the members of his congregation. He also had one in Leningrad. 'Many people – Russians, Nanai – interested in the event followed him. And the deity – Stalin – made from paper and put in the corner was given (a glass of) vodka (as an offering). So he practised shamanism there'. Shamans are not able to manage even all the Nanai spirits; it is even more difficult for them to gain victory over an unfamiliar spirit of another nation. Semën Ivanovich was obviously not able to manage the communist spirits he worshipped so faithfully. He was not able to graduate from the institute. He died of tuberculosis during his studies in Leningrad.

The mutual influence of the shamanistic and communist world views led to their peculiar synthesis, which resulted in the appearance of a new figure – a shaman-communist. In any case, five of my informants were shamans and communists simultaneously.

Shamanic spirits against Soviet Rule

The anti-shamanism campaign turned out to enjoy only 'quantitative' success. The number of shamans decreased, and those who continued practising shamanism did it covertly. The bearers of the tradition explain it with the influence exerted on them by their own native shamanic spirits. Shamans were not only persecuted by the authorities, they were under double oppression. On the one hand, they were oppressed by the authorities, and, on the other, they were subjected to the influence of their own spirit-helpers, who insisted on the continuation of their practice. It is interesting to mention that this kind of treatment of the problem (the authorities fighting not with people but with shamanic spirits) was expressed even in the articles written by the fighting atheists. In one of his articles, I. Suslov almost directly maintains that the Soviet rule is stronger than the shamanic spirits. Speaking about a young man suffering from a shamanic disease, he expressed the paradoxical hope that a centre of cultural work organised by the Soviet Rule would be stronger than shamanic spirits, which were attacking a young man and forcing him to become a shaman, and that this centre would be able to drive all the spirits away (Suslov 1931: 126). The shamans, however, maintained that it is not the Soviet rule with its prohibitions that is stronger, but it is spirits that they were not able to fight in spite of all their wishes.

The period of repressions coincided with the time when Lingdze became a shaman-woman. She was working in a fishing unit, and experienced seizures of shamanic disease right at work. This was twice as dangerous for her. She was afraid not only of the management finding out about her being overcome by shamanism, but also, as shamanic disease could not be diagnosed by medical means, of being accused of simulating the disease and finding excuses to shirk work, which, at that time, was a similarly serious accusation. 'They tortured me as well!' she says. 'They almost put me in prison! How long they tortured me! When I was lying in hospital, the chief called me, asking me why I was lying there, saying I had to go to work. So he was calling me. I can't understand how I survived!' – 'This was before the war', she says another time. 'Then they were 'purging' people! I had a fit at work; I fell down and sang shamanic songs. I don't know why I fell'. – 'During war-time I was nearly arrested. I had a fit, I fell on my back and started singing shamanic chants right at work, in the unit where I worked', Lingdze complains. 'I started rolling myself over on the ground. However well I worked, at this moment I lost everything. Why did they (the authorities) consider shamans to be bad? Did I ask them for food or what?' Here is one more of her stories on the same subject:

> How was it for me to become a shaman-woman when shamans were arrested all the time? I sang the shamanic chants, I cried right at work! The things I did! When you become a shaman, you will fall ill, you cannot live anymore if you don't sing these songs, if you don't do everything in the right way! – I come to work, I feel unwell, and I start chanting. I cannot keep silent! It is shaking me! Either a day or a night – it does not matter! When I fall ill, I'll sing these shamanic songs! I thought I was going to get a medal for good work. And I lost my medal. Who gives a shaman a medal? Only because of that, although I worked hard, I failed to get the medal. I sang these shamanic songs right at work. People kept silent [...]. There were many people there; everybody was sitting quietly, listening. Was somebody (a shamanic spirit) torturing me, or what? I was not able to sit. They took me to hospital. – We arrived at the hospital, but the disease was gone. It had passed! [...] We reached the hospital, and I am all right! They say I am a malingerer. And they give me a typewritten note. – 'We know how a person is ill, we have seen it', they say. 'But there's no such disease as yours!' (Lingdze)

Being afraid that the power of shamanic spirits might still be stronger than the power of the Soviet Rule, the Nanai offered passive resistance already during the repressions. It was not considered dishonourable to pretend to meet the demands of the authorities and give up practising shamanism, and secretly still continue it. Aleksandr Sergeevich (1914–2000), who in the years of repressions was a young *Komsomol*, had to go round the village together with other activists, destroying the attributes of the shamanic cult. While doing it, he was more careful than his comrades, which, in his opinion, helped him to save his life from the revenge of the shamanic spirits and survive. My father told me then: 'You just keep quiet!' says Aleksandr Sergeevich. 'I followed his advice, although I was a *Komsomol*. But some of the zealous *Komsomols* shouted: 'We don't need *endur* (spirits)! We don't need anything!' And they all died. It all happened under my very eyes. Not one of them survived! The heavenly *endur* (spirit) knows everything!' Niura Sergeevna (born in 1907), granddaughter of a shaman-woman and one herself, did not go round the village with the *Komsomols*, but she remembers how the latter had come to their house, ordering them to hand over all the shaman's attributes. 'I told my grandma, "There they are! Give them, and that's that!" I gave them everything myself when they came to our house and started demanding. We had been forewarned that they would come and demand these things. People kept only *edekhe*. [118] These were the only things that they were able to hide. I myself gave them everything, and also made new ones for my grandma afterwards.'

The other *Komsomols*-Nanai were not so careful. Encouraged by the authority of the Soviet rule, they were trying to get free from the power of the tribal shamanic spirits who, as a rule, did not leave alone any of the representatives of the shamanic descent; they sincerely believed that if they simply declared that spirits did not exist, and broke with the existing tradition of shamanic rituals, they would really become unattainable to these spirits. But the shamanic spirits themselves, as the tradition bearers assure, would not let them turn away from them. The repressions became the cause of the demonstration of this invisible spiritual force. Even if the *Komsomols* took away the ritual requisites from shamans, the latter (being, obviously, blamed for yielding them) were immediately subjected to the repressions of not the Soviet rule, but much more dangerous, invisible spiritual 'repressions', and they died. 'All the *seven* of old Geiker were collected in one place and set fire', says Lingdze. 'The old man immediately fell ill and died. What for?' – 'It was forbidden to practise shamanism', she tells about another shaman-woman, 'and the old woman (shaman) fell ill and died. They treated them like dogs! They yelled at them like dogs! (After that) the old woman was not able to perform *ningmachi* (a shamanic ritual), or anything else, either. And so she died'. The only ones who were doing quite well were able to hide the things in a likeable place. Shaman Sergei Bel'dy 'wrapped his *seven* (images of spirits) in birch bark for the water not to get in, went into the woods, hewed out a hole in the trunk of a big tree and put the *seven* into this hollow. This old man really survived. "Don't take me", he said to his spirits, "for leaving you forever!" He lived until the age of 115'. Another shaman Gogoli Kile (from the village of Dzhuen) had a chest (with the requisites) for *kasa*.

---

118   *Edekhe* – a metal image of a spirit worn around the neck.

When it was prohibited to practise shamanism, he dug it into the ground somewhere. And he died at once!
Why did he die?
He buried his own robe, that's why he died! (Niura Sergeevna).

A similar story happened to a shaman-woman from the village of Bolan.

She had such a robe, and a hat, and footwear, and gloves – all of them decorated with *seven*. Once a year, in the autumn, she put it all on. When shamanism was prohibited, she put all these things into a bag, dug a hole and buried them. And she also died quite soon after that! (Ol'ga Egorovna)

But the ones to suffer most were not the shamans, but their persecutors, the young Nanai. Quite often after their 'heroic' (as they themselves thought) deeds, the *Komsomols* fell ill and died. 'Two or three people a day (died)', Niura Sergeevna says. 'They just fell ill and died immediately. The ones who persecuted shamans!' – 'The *Komsomol* who cut to pieces Kile's *toro* (a tree with a carved image of a spirit on its trunk) that stood at the end of their kitchen garden, died exactly a week after!' recalls Nikolai Petrovich. 'When the *Komsomols* took from shamans the images of their spirit-helpers, they hung them on the walls in the community centre and laughed at them', says Ol'ga Egorovna. 'They didn't live more than a year after that, they all died. Only one of them survived. But he went mad and only laughed until the day he died. He suffered such torments! He laughed days and nights! Three years later he also died'. Nanai-*Komsomols*, carried away by the spontaneity of demolitions, similar to the well-known Pavlik Morozov, denounced their own parents and destroyed shamanic attributes in their own homes. Aleksandr Sergeevich told us that one of these *Komsomols*, having crushed his father's drum, fell ill. He was ill for a long time, became big-bellied. He died of dropsy. He was so young! And educated! His father took a knife with him, and at the grave cut his stomach open. Otherwise they could not have buried him. He had such a big belly. There was not enough space in the coffin! Much liquid flowed out of his stomach!
All the people who said that shamans were not needed, they all died!' Here is one more story about the same person, told by Niura Sergeevna, 'His belly was like that! He fell ill with dropsy. The one who crushed the drum! And later on (when he died) his father – he was a clever man! – took him to the grave, put him down on the ground, and cut his stomach open. Yellow liquid flowed out of it. (Otherwise he was too big for the coffin.) It is not good to prohibit! Let them practise shamanism!'
The Russian persecutors of shamans were also avenged. So a Russian called Yevpakov, who, according to the story, did not believe in shamanism and, being, besides that, economically-minded, decided to make use in his household of the demolished wooden hut *dëkan,* which had earlier been used for keeping the objects of the sha-

manic cult. [119] 'He wanted to take this hut apart and use it for a cattle shed', says Konstantin Maktovich. 'So he did it [...] He was young. Worked as a teacher. When he was pulling out the last piece from the soil, something happened to his head, as if he had gone mad. After that the logs were taken to Nizhnii Gavan. But he (Yevpakov) got worse and worse year after year. Eventually he died. But before that all the people who participated in this undertaking also died. Not in one year, of course, but one after another, all of them died of the same disease – insanity! All of them died of insanity. All (the *Nanai*) who participated in it! And the Russians who took part in the burning of the idols – they also died of insanity. Yevpakov, when he already had problems with his head, attacked his bull [...] went into the cattle-shed! He did not realise what he was doing! Took a knife and attacked the bull! Afterwards he also attacked his wife in the same way – with a knife, or a stick! Before these fits he became reticent, gloomy'. As a result of the repressions, it was not only the number of shamans that decreased, but also that of their persecutors who served the interests of the 'cultural revolution'. – 'There are no persecutors anymore, not even their children. All of them have died!' summarised Ivan Torokovich.

In the 1930s the 'heroes'-*Komsomols* themselves also began to realise how dangerous it was to openly fight against shamanism. Scared of the idea that all the diseases suddenly caught by them could be regarded as punishment imposed on them by the shamanic spirits they had denied, the young Nanai regretted their activities and turned for help to the same shamans. 'Many of them fell ill', says Nikolai Petrovich. 'They went to the same shaman (who they had persecuted) and said: 'I had a dream of this or that. What if I die!' But he said: 'How can I perform a ritual if I gave you a signature that I am never going to practise shamanism again? And those who were vicious enemies of shamanism, died. Those who violently attacked religion – died! I know three of them in Dada'. One of these activists, who destroyed the images of shamanic spirits and cut down trees with carved images of spirits, and fell seriously ill and regretted what he had done, decided that the insulted shamanic spirits had imprisoned his soul and locked it in a nasty place. According to the words of Nikolai Petrovich, he had come to the offended shaman and 'begged him on his knees to get him out of it'. The ritual was performed and the spirits informed the victim through the shaman: 'You cut us down, and you'll die for that now!' This is exactly what they told him! He went down on his knees, but the shaman told him, 'I don't know what and how. You did it yourself. You have been told since your childhood that you must not chop and touch anything connected with shamanism'. When we were growing up, we were afraid of even going near the places where people used to worship', Nikolai Petrovich comments on his story. Those few *Komsomols* who had fallen ill after the repressions, but whose lives shamans still helped to preserve, were trans-

---

119 The Nanai consider the shamanic spirits dangerous, and therefore they try to keep them not in their dwellings, but in special outbuildings called *dëkan*. These figures were brought inside only during special rituals.

formed from members of the *Komsomol* into active shamans. 'Their parents told them: 'Don't do it again if you get well!' And they prayed to God or maybe somebody else, came to my mother (a shaman)', says Nikolai Petrovich. 'Gradually the sick person got better. And you couldn't make him do this kind of thing again!' All this often nullified the progress the authorities had made in the fight against shamanism.

Conspiratorial shamanic practice

The policy of repression that so clearly demonstrated the riskiness of the open fight against shamanism, even at present serves as a warning to be remembered. Recalling them, the present shamans threaten: 'You must not touch God! You must not touch the shaman! You will become paralysed, and then [...]!' Nowadays, as Lingdze says, 'nobody believes (in shamanism)! But all those who do not believe, are not going to do well! Even if you don't believe, better keep silent! Now they think that you can tread it underfoot, and do whatever you like!' It was partly inertia that played a certain role in the preservation of shamanism among the Nanai. The tradition that had been maintained for centuries, presented such a remarkable force in itself that it was not possible to destroy it in the course of one campaign. Besides that, the illnesses, insanity and death, which struck the activists who fought against shamanism, exerted influence on those who were ready to break with this tradition and become the bearers of the new materialist ideology. As a result, it led to the secret passive opposition to the authorities. Only the mass rituals that attracted crowds were eradicated, for example, *undi* – offering sacrifice to shamanic spirits, which also included a procession led by a shaman around the whole village, as well as *kasa,* which used to continue for several days and where people gathered from several villages'. [120]

---

120 As a result of the new policy, it was not only the mass shamanic rituals but also other non-shamanic mass rituals that disappeared. So, in these years the traditional *Nanai* weddings ceased to be performed. As an answer to the question if the authorities had prohibited this kind of wedding, Ivan Torokovich said: 'No, the weddings were not prohibited, but it was forbidden to get drunk. When they caught a drunk person, they sentenced him to labour camp. They drew up a document stating: fighting here and there – and in the morning they took him away, and that was that! People were doomed for no reason! So weddings were not performed anymore. People sat at home for a while, having a booze, and that's that! Now they have again started to perform weddings, but not according to our tradition! But until the 1930s the Nanai had everything. They went by boats, made two or three rounds of the village, and then started saluting. They sailed and fired guns. Stood on the bank and also fired guns. You know how it was! Afterwards the boats came ashore. People on the bank stood like a corridor, and the ones who came by boats went through this corridor. The bride was the first to go. They came and treated everybody to vodka. And you couldn't refuse it! When those arriving had reached the house, everybody was already chatting, they were getting into a good mood! But under the Soviet Rule people stopped doing all that. They were afraid!'

But other rituals, in spite of all prohibitions, were continued secretly at night. The fact that some Nanai became communists and members of *Komsomol* and even representatives of the Soviet rule, did not keep them from turning to shamans upon necessity. 'I joined the *Komsomol*, but I still prayed to God', Aleksandr Sergeevich confesses. In the course of many years I was a leading worker, and then a communist and the chief of a *kolkhoz*. From the early years the shamanic skills Nikolai Petrovich had inherited put up a fight with the communist world view he had acquired. He was a member of the regional *(krai)* committee, member of the Bureau of the Troitsk Forestry Enterprise, and also a member of the District Committee of the CPSU! 'How could I become a shaman the way I was?' he laughs. 'You can tear yourself apart, but you have to go to the district committee, and then a plenum gathers in (the village of) Troitskoe, and now, well – some kind of shamanism!' Despite that, he experienced a spell of shamanic disease, knew the peculiarities of shamanic rituals in detail and was, as he put it himself, a disguised shaman (he had not gone through the inauguration ritual) and a *tudin?* [121] Actually, as P. Smidovich (1930: 7) put it, it was the most peculiar mixture of an obstinate and fervent wish to build up his life on a new, Soviet foundation, and a sympathy and blind trust in shamans'.

Some consequences of the cultural transformation

The cultural innovations carried out by the Soviet rule resulted in a cleavage in the Nanai society. Some Nanai were 'recruited' into the process of cultural transformation and became its advertisers, and others offered passive resistance, remaining the bearers of the native language and culture. From the moment of when the cleavage began in 1930s and until the late 1990s, the bearers of the traditional culture were actually in cultural and linguistic separation. For example, in many Nanai families, the grandparents, who spoke only Nanai, could not communicate with their grandchildren, who did not understand the Nanai language, without a translator. 'Our children don't know the Nanai language, they can speak only in Russian', Lingdze says bitterly. 'All right, let them live like that! Our children are going to be like people from another nation!'

It would not be correct to say that the transformations carried out by the Soviet rule were accepted by the population only in a negative sense. The tragic opposition between the representatives of the traditional and innovative culture was mainly applied to shamanic practice. Many other innovations were accepted by people, and this can be proven mainly by the appearance of a great number of lyrical songs extolling the Communist Party and the Soviet rule. The most famous Nanai poet, Akim Samar, glorified in his poems the transformation which the Soviet Rule brought to his people.

---

121 *Tudin* – a person possessing spirit-helpers and supernatural abilities like a shaman.

It is not a spring wind
Blowing above the house,
It is Nanai, who according to the Stalin law
Happily live in a civilised manner. (Samar 1946: 32)

Because of the true
Lenin and Stalin politics
Nanai people have got stronger;
Nanai people have powerfully grown. (Samar 1940: 98)

It was neither a show nor play-acting, but it was for themselves that people sincerely sang about the marvellous boats running on the earth (cars and trucks) and even flying in the air (aircraft) that had appeared in their lives together with the Soviet rule, wondered about refrigerators and TV-sets, and were grateful to the Communist Party for all that. These kind of songs were so widespread among many peoples of the North that researchers started to speak about a new song genre called 'lauds to the new life.'

Here is an example of the songs of this genre expressing loyalty to the authorities; it was recorded by the author from Ul'iana Bel'dy (1909–1986) in the village of Iskra, Nanai district *(raion)*, Khabarovsk region *(krai)*, in 1981:

Friends, how joyful life has become now!
How interesting it is to think about the (communist) party!
Life is interesting now!
People used to live in the past knowing nothing!
Now life is so good! So good!
If we get weak, somebody will take care of us.
We will thank and respect the people who lived before us and established the
new order.
Friends, my friends, I tell you:
Little children are so delighted,
And old people feel so good!
When you get old, other people will support you,
When you lose your strength, they will take care of you.
Now you can live long!
(Only) a bad, lazy woman suffers torments,
Only a lazy woman cannot find anything.
If we follow the same route in our lives, we will be so rich!
Friends, it would be nice if we were younger,
As we used to be until the time we already lived!
I am weaker now, and older.

(But) people won't forget even the aged,
and they take care of those who are getting weaker.
Friends, people have done everything!
The whole (communist) party has arranged it this way
That the living people would live
And the growing people would grow! (Ul'iana Bel'dy)

As regards shamanism, in spite of the efforts made by the authorities to eradicate it, even in 1971, decades after the beginning of the period of repressions, Taras Mikhailov (1971: 68) had to admit that atheists have to 'manifest more activeness, fighting spirit' in order to 'stop in places the underestimation and indifference towards shamanic survival'. At present there are no fighting atheists in the North anymore. They arrived and left, but shamans have continued practising until now.

Nina Vasil'eva (2000: 61), who investigated archives and other sources, stated that 'one can say with certainty that shamans were practically not brought to trial and were not prosecuted by law by the punitive bodies of the NKVD'. According to her opinion, the reasons for it are that, first, shamans did not commit any unlawful acts, and, second, that the Soviet government bodies realised that shamans could not constitute a serious menace ideologically (ibid.: 61–62). Nevertheless, neither of her arguments is cogent enough. During the time of persecution, it was not enough not to commit any unlawful acts. The essential peculiarity of persecution itself was exactly the violation of the existent legislation, and representatives of other different religions were executed en masse, despite the fact that they did not commit any *actus reus*. The ideological indifference in the Soviet Rule's opinion of shamanism, which totally contradicts Soviet atheistic ideology, is also doubtful. Vasil'eva's arguments only emphasise the exclusiveness of shamanism in anti-religious persecutions and make us think about another serious reason, which resulted in the persecutions not spreading as wide as happened against representatives of other religions. My informants suppose that after the campaign to destroy shamanic equipment and after the first arrests, the persecutors were frightened by the consequences and the manifestations of the obvious negative reaction of spirits to those persecutions. Probably because of that, the persecutors pretended not to notice that people continued shamanising secretly at home and in order to fulfil the planned quantity of executed shamans, they sentenced to death ordinary people instead of shamans. In the time of anti-religious persecutions, both shamanists and their persecutors were under double oppression, on the one hand, by Soviet persecution activity, and, on the other hand, by the power of shamanic spirits, and the pressure of shamanic spirits turned out to be much stronger.

EPILOGUE

Since the 1990s the Nanai experienced rapid socio-religious change and turned from traditional shamanism/atheism to different forms of religious practice, which had been brought to them from outside. From 1999 (the date of shaman Lingdze's death) until 2013, traditional shamanism was represented only by shaman Ol'ga Egorovna,[122] who however practiced very little in the 2000s, and we can say that by now shamanic praxis in its classical variant has been forgotten. The younger Nanai generation has been involved in a wide discourse formed by the mass media and almost lost native cultural and language knowledge, which made it hardly possible to return to their religious tradition in its completeness.

The young generation's choice is now not classical shamanism, but rather other religious practices like various forms of New-Age spiritualities, and evangelical Christian movements. At the same time, in many respects, the young natives still remain the successors of the shamans. The strong shamanic biological-spiritual inheritance of the new converters to the new religions (e.g., predisposition to shamanic-like diseases) manifests itself in their new spiritual experiences and makes them, on the one hand, interpret other religions as various modifications of the shamanic-like experience, and, on the other hand, explain their native shamanism in terms of the attractive ideas borrowed from the other religions.

Since the early 1980s, Nanai elders undertook several attempts to initiate some new candidates into shamanism, but all of them were unsuccessful: irrespective of whether the initiation was completed for a candidate or not, all the candidates met untimely ends. Not one new Nanai shaman started his or her activity during the entire generation, and only in 2005–2006, almost at the same time, several new Nanai shamans appeared. But as they appeared after the significant cultural and religious values change, their practice differed from the traditional one to the extent that we could affirm that traditional shamanism had already been turned into neo-shamanism. New shamans do not perform long ceremonies along the spiritual 'roads'. Even if they speak Nanai they prefer to think and to perform in Russian. They rarely use a drum. But at the same time they themselves are convinced that, 'though today they are not going to dance near fire anymore, they continue to work with the same energy processes' which were interpreted by their forefathers, classical shamans, as 'spirits' (Lubov Vladimirovna). The word 'energy' has replaced the old words '*seven*' and '*amban*', and makes it possible for new shamans to tell about the 'inheritance of energies' and to use such expressions as: 'We (new shamans) keep (the old shamans') energies!' (Marina). Using the modern New Age terminology, neo-shaman Marina affirms that 'the energetic field of the old shamans impregnates her nervous system'. The neo-shamans also affirm that their night dreams and visions are similar to those

---

122 Ol'ga Egorovna was born in 1920 and died in March 2013.

of the traditional shamans. Neo-shaman Marina also affirms that special shamanic knowledge and wisdom, which one can gain from the 'Cosmos', is actually in essence clan spirits which earlier belonged to the departed shamans. She explains: 'Cosmos is energy or, in other words, the spirits of the (departed shamans), who had stored a huge base of knowledge and who are now returning that knowledge to us'.

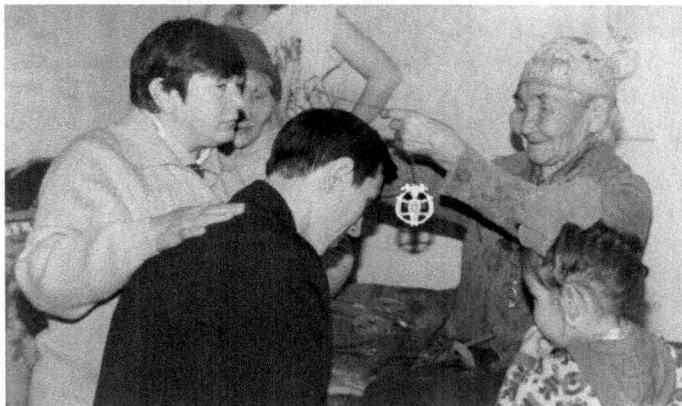

FIGURE 20: A ritual, which has been thought up by the Russian female expert (at the left) from the city: the widow of the shaman (on the right) transfers images of spirits of a dead shaman to the grandson living in the city with whom abilities in occultism had become apparent.

New shamans changed the traditional vocabulary, but preserved the essence of the core shamanic ideas, which unites them with the traditional shamans. They explain that everything that happened to their shaman-grandparents is now happening to them. They assure that, as in the past, their abilities are dependent on some 'spirit-friends' invisible to ordinary people. [123] New shamans, well-educated people, affirm that remaining the same in essence, shamanism has been reconsidered only in its forms, approaches and interpretations. One of the neo-shamans says: 'Now shamans have become competent. Because of mass media some scientific ideas became accessible to shamans and they started explaining their experience in the light of those scientific ideas', but 'the essence of new practice has not changed'. In the past, she is sure, the shamans worked with the same energies, which are familiar to her now, but they just figuratively perceived those energies, and because of their creative thinking they imagined those energies as different characters: animals, monsters, etc.

Within a contemporary discourse, the soul is interpreted as aura, and intershamanic fighting and stealing spirits as vampirism. Popular neo-shamanic pointillage also has, as neo-shamans believe, some allusions in the past: former shamans

---

123 Visiting India one of Nanai neo-shamans bought there dolls and since then makes offerings to them. She said: 'They are helping me, they became my friends'.

used pointillage as one of the means of exorcism; they groped for an evil spirit in a patient's body and by a special massage drove it away. So, it is a matter of interpretation and terminology: in the past by means of pointillage shamans 'exorcised spirits', but now with the same method they 'cause toxins to be excreted from the body.'

Those who still remember classicial shamans' praxis affirm that going out to the 'astral' was earlier called shamanic voyages along the spiritual roads. Neo-shamans explain that the gates to the world beyond are not only in wells and whirlpools, as it was in the past, but also in televisions and different kinds of antennas. Using occult terminology and equating shamanism with different types of occultism all over the world, one of the native poets interpreted as a natural case of shamanism's flexibility: shamanism is as different as life itself. Because of that flexibility, as one of my informants predicts, shamanism is going to absorb and that way to unite (to override) all other religions and thus become a new universal religion.

The Nanai leaders of the *Association of Indigenous Peoples of the North, Siberia and Far East of the Russian Federation* actively support the idea that for Nanai as well as for all the indigenous peoples in the North, Siberia and Far East the only true religious choice is shamanism. They affirm: 'Today whole mankind realises that the religion of the indigenous peoples is a model for preserving the planet. [...] We must cultivate the institution of shamanism. [...] We leaders must call the indigenous peoples to return to their cultural sources' (Lubov Vladimirovna). At the same time for justice sake, it must be admitted that even within the *Association*, the Nanai leaders differed in opinion concerning necessity of revival of shamanism. There is an opposite judgment of another indigenous leader: 'Leave people alone, we are atheists, let people chose what they want themselves. [...] Why impose it on people? [...] New shamans are persons who from everywhere have picked up a smattering of knowledge. [...] But how strongly it destroys, how it mutilates the destiny and psyche of those persons (who begin to practice)! It is a dangerous matter!' (Lubov Aleksandrovna).

Reviving shamanism became a brand of identity and is now proclaimed as a means of preserving traditional culture. But talking about the revival of traditional culture and traditional shamanism, the representatives of the *Association of Indigenous Peoples of the North, Siberia and Far East of the Russian Federation* are not confused by the fact that the practice of new Nanai shamans does not suppose to revive the old shamanic rituals as such, and that today the Nanai neo-shaman resembles more a healer, sorcerer and a person with extrasensory perception. In fact, preserving cultural and religious traditions is not as important for them as 'preserving the fundamental nature of shamanic practice' (Lubov Vladimirovna). As regards change, it is inevitable, 'evolution is continuing, everything has been changing, and it would be impossible to stay in the same place' (Lubov Vladimirovna). The changeability of shamanic praxis is one of its well known distinctive features. 'Tolerance of shamanism, its inclination to synthesis with different worldviews is one of its main peculiarities' (Zherebina 2011: 84). Shamans always 'quickly and efficiently absorbed any foreign influences and included them into their traditional worldview; by that means they strengthened themselves and widened their possibilities' (Gracheva 1983: 129). But what was new among the recent changes was the disruption of the tradition which preceded its sudden surge. Because of that disruption, extremely essential knowledge was forgotten, which in classical shamanism was considered to be secret, but at the same time was used as a means of shamans' relative safety. New shamans with their non-traditional enthusiasm began groping for those means from the start. Forgotten is an acknowledgement of the possible long-term effects of shamanic collective disease, inter-shaman's spiritual conflicts, etc., and those measures of spiritual safety which were elaborated by the traditional shamans during the course of centuries. Forgotten are the social prescriptions and taboos, which classical shamans used in order to be to some extent distanced from the unsafe spiritual reality, where their practice involved them. Already gone is that shamanic practice that concerns not only the persons who directly practice, but also their relatives and descendants. In the classical variant of shamanism the collective shamanic disease was a part of the lineages and limited by the borders of those lineages. Now because of the contemporary desire of many enthusiasts of different ethnicities to become shamans (even despite their lack of heredity and inborn shamanic gifts), the circle of those who become influenced by shamanic praxis goes beyond the borders of lineages and becomes significantly widened. It makes it possible that Lubov Vladimirovna's hope that shamanism 'has the chance to unite all the peoples of the world' and that Valentina Kharitonova's words that soon we can deal 'not with electrification,[124] but with the shamanisation of entire Russia' would appear to be true.

---

124 Valentina Kharitonova uses a periphrasis for the famous Lenin's slogan 'electrification of the entire Russia'.

APPENDIX TO 'SHAMAN ON THE STAGE'

Lament for shaman's death

On February 1, 1993, people brought to shaman Lingdze the news that shaman Mariia Petrovna had died in Daerga the day before and had not yet been buried. Being shaken with that news, Lingdze began to lament (songo) and then she took a drum and sang about her friend and rival's death, learning the reasons and circumstances of this death from the spirits (ningman). As she considered Mariia Petrovna's appearance on the stage to be one of the main reasons for her death, it is worthwhile to present the text of both her non-shamanic and shamanic lament (songo and ningman) in their entirety as an appendix to the chapter 'Shaman on the stage'. Performing this ritual, the shaman switched, singing and speaking back and forth and addressed herself by turns to the auditory, to spirits and to the deceased person.

FIGURE 21: A ritual, at which vodka and the blood of a sacrificed rooster is offered to the spirits.

(To the audience)
If I have no bottle (of vodka), how can I go (to the funeral)?
Such a woman died! Only a fool can go there empty-handed! [125]
Every day I cry and think about her, I live (this way).
I'm constantly thinking, I've been thinking (about her) for a long time.
Every day I cry; I live thinking about her. There is not even any sleep for me! [126]

---

125 Lingdze meant that as Mariia Petrovna was a shaman, there will be her spirits at her place, which should be fed with vodka.
126 Such exaggerated worrying can mean that both shamans were rivals.

(To the departed shaman Mariia Petrovna)
Marus'ka, [127] we lived in troubles, in poverty, doing any jobs.
Whatever jobs did we do in our lives!
We lived looking after cows and pigs.
We requested it for breath,[128] (that's why) we worked.
We did any unskilled labour, such labour, nobody else agreed to do.
Now you died, you will never return back to me.
You came to me before your death (in my sleep). [129]
'My sister, I'm dying! My sister, I'm dying!'
What should I have done? What should I have done?
You went to the city and returned back without anything. [130]
You knew you could die,
But you however travelled getting thousands of rubles.
And what can I do now? What can I do now?
When you voyaged, tormenting yourself, raging against yourself,
When you went there,
Did you think that crying you would find your death?
Or (you thought) something else?
They seduced me (to go to the city) even before you;
They wanted to take me away (to perform on the stage) by deception.
How could you live so, according to the other peoples' words?
How could you live travelling there and here,
According to the other peoples' words?
We have grown old.
Many nights I cried, I won't stop crying!
I cannot sleep in any way.
What did you go for,
What were you going to do (there)? Maybe you know that?
How many thousands of years were you going to live, earning money?
Who would give you a hundred years, did I not ask you?
You lived taking liberties,
But you should have thought about your life a little.

(To the audience)
She was always like this. People talked about it.
How can I correct it, what can I do now?

---

127 Marusiia, Marus'ka, and Mariia Petrovna are familiar variants of Mariia Petrovna's first
     name.
128 'We requested it for breath' means 'we need food to live'.
129 Lingdze means that she dreamed about Mariia Petrovna before she died. They did not meet in
     their waking hours.
130 Mariia Petrovna did not shamanise and only demonstrated her singing in the city.

(To the departed shaman Mariia Petrovna)
Did you do so to save yourself?
Did you do so to live?

(To the audience)
Nobody knows how I cry. *Poia*[131] told me: 'Your sister died. Do you know how she died?' Thanks to her. I'm bad now, sick, I cannot go there. I live so. What good is in my life? Shamanise and shamanise! I won't be able to stop shamanising till my death. I am not actually a shaman! I cannot shamanise, cannot even find a *seven* to sing in the shamanic way.[132]

(To the audience about the departed shaman Mariia Petrovna)
After she travelled to the city,
She sat down behind my doors (in my sleep).
If she had come in, I would have told her something.

She said: 'I travelled; I was there, now I am back. What should I do?' I told her nothing, and she left me at once.[133] After she returned, people came for me to fetch her *seven*.[134] Could I go and get her *seven*? She had lost all her *seven* there (in the city). I answered her (through those people): 'Why are you tormenting me? Fetch your *seven* on your own! *Poia*, when you come home, the other shamans will rescue you'.[135] But nobody shamanised, nobody saved her. Nobody felt sorry. When Mariia Petrovna died, when Gara Kisovna (another shaman who also went to the city to sing on the stage) died, it was the same. What did they (their performances) help? Could people build a new big city because of Marus'ka's shamanic singing (in the cities)? They just permitted their singing to jeer at them. I feel sorry for them, because they lived in a wrong way. Who taught them to live such dissipated lives?

(To the departed shaman Mariia Petrovna and to the departed shaman Gara Kisovna)
I could die even before you.
But I don't want to! If only to live a day more!
Why do you torment me because of your *baita* (problem)?[136]
Don't torment me at least a day! Marus'ka! Gara Kisovna!

---

131 *Poia* is a younger person.
132 It is typical for shamans to underestimate their abilities.
133 Here Lingdze stops telling about her night dream. Her next words are about what happened in her waking hours.
134 It means that after Mariia Petrovna returned she fell ill and asked other people to visit Lingdze with the request to heal her by means of searching for her *seven*.
135 This sentence is probably an insertion from her dream, which is why she uses the future tense.
136 In this case 'the problem' is to all appearances, enmity. Later Lingdze mentions that Mariia Petrovna cursed her brother and he died. It could be an episode of their enmity.

(To the audience)
After they have spoiled themselves, they came crying to me. But I am not able to fetch (their *seven*), I cannot solve their *baita* (problems). [137]

(To the departed shaman Mariia Petrovna and to the departed shaman Gara Kisovna)
No, you won't return to life!
You fooled about, took liberties, behaved badly.
(To the audience)
Even if people had given me silver or gold,
(I would not have ever shamanised for them).
They left.
They left because they did not want to listen to the words of the other people.
Now another woman (from your clan) will become a shaman,
Maybe she'll become a big shaman.
Open someone younger to shamanise! (Perform a ritual!)
When Naoia [138] was dying, she cursed my brother.

(To the departed shaman Naoia)
All right! My brother died.
But though you cursed him, you yourself also died!
Unlike you, we are not able to curse the other people.

She (Mariia Petrovna) was to have lived, because any person who was born, is living to live as long as possible. A person is living. A person is living, but if they have *baita* (a problem), then […] [139]

(To the audience)
I wanted to abuse Marus'ka for travelling. People say that if to take away those beings, who win, then she would not die. I live crying all the time. I live still, and people don't pay attention to me. I live on the sly, and nobody hears me. I'm just shouting everywhere, through the sky and earth. Who has heard it? What being has learned about me?

Divination about shaman's death

(To the departed shaman Mariia Petrovna)
Having looked through my door set ajar, why are you leaving?

---

137 Probably it means 'I cannot fight against the other shamans, their enemies'.
138 The departed shaman Naoia was Mariia Petrovna's sister. She was also a shaman.
139 It can mean that if someone has another shaman as an enemy it can shorten his or her life.

It has been three or four years
Since you just (have been coming in my sleep) to glance through my (half-opened)
door.
Why do you leave (each time right after you have glanced at me)?
How can I save you? How can I heal you?
I called your mother by my mother, and also your granny.
(You were going) along the way of disease, you lived in *baita*. [140]
You never lived well and reliably.
You have broken yourself.
I must have won in my dreams and overcome all your bad stuff.
You only relied on your own *seven* and lived along the road of insanity.
I needed at least one other person,
Who could shamanise for you and tie you to the good life?
But what was I alone able to reason?
Though I gave you a tongue, it was for nothing.
You have spoiled yourself.
Crying (shamanising) you have probably learned about that,
Mumbling (singing in a shamanic way), you have probably heard that.
When I (was going) along your *baita*, [141] following your trash,
When I sat down and took my drum,
I learned something about your beings,
Which constantly tormented you.
Why did you go ahead towards the bad?
Poor thing! Why were you not ashamed?
There could be a lot of friends around you now.
You could sit at home and shamanise.
How shall we live now?

If you did not become like this,
We would sit with you at your place for two or three years more,
We would live together.
My *inan*, [142] you were a seamstress, you were doing needlework for hours.
You wished that everything in life had been only nice.
But was it nice, what you have done by means of your *seven*?
Though it happened so, I don't reproach you with it,
Because it was the being which intended to kill you;
It came to murder you.

---

140 Probably it means you are fighting against another shaman.
141 It can mean that in her ritual Lingdze followed the spiritual road where Mariia Petrovna
      fought against another shaman.
142 *Inan* is a younger husband's relative.

It was the being which continually tormented you;
It came to finish you.
You did not win against him in your dream.
You died young. I feel sorry for you!
When you were travelling everywhere in your dreams,
Why did you not drop into my place?
Why did you not come into this house?
If you had come to me, you would have been rescued,
Though it would have been bad for me. [143]
What a pity! What a pity!
Whatever is in the earth you have done with your hands!
But as such stuff has alighted on to you, people,
how many of them, a thousand, a million?
They will just pocket all that.
You have been living that way to be like you are now, with no breathing.
You went to the city, sang there and made such noise
That the ground cleft, and your cry (went in) there.
What have they covered that with? What have people let you go with?
You should not have permitted them to torment you like this!
What did you want to become living this way?
What did Gara Kisovna and you find there (in the city),
If you agreed to give away your own breath (for this)?
(Gara Kisovna also) went to make noise (to shamanise for filming) to an island.
What was good in it?
If you have shamanised in the right way, you would be still alive,
And people would thank you.
Being occupied with such a matter,
Permitting people to take you everywhere,
Have you earned much money?
Were you so merry because of a ruble or two?
You had enjoyed yourselves so much that (you let them) take your breath away!
How many times they tried to drag me by force everywhere,
They (wanted to) take me away (to perform on the stage)!
As long as Kaplan [144] was here, she wanted to take me away.
But I don't sell myself for a ruble or two.
And after her, there were some more people,
I don't remember where they came from.

---

143 It is dangerous to defend that shaman who is involved in fighting against another shaman, because trying to help a shaman himself one can become involved into enmity.
144 Mariia Kaplan was a researcher of folklore, who worked in the Russian Museum of Ethnography in Leningrad.

They made me *yai* (sing in a shamanic way) about everything.
They made me do some *erde* (shamanic tricks).
However many hundred, however many thousand rubles people would get out,
That's all the same; it would not reach my heart either.
I don't want it!
You did not think to live past the date (you actually lived).
You did not think how many years to live otherwise and how to live.
It's impossible to live, as the other people will tell you.
I cannot live according to other people's words.
At least a year more I'll live!
I won't live how people want me to.
I won't make noise and shamanise (everywhere).
After you I'll go along the light way, I'll run along the fine road!
Who did you want to become, travelling through the cities?
When returning, you just came to me!

(To the audience)
The same happened to Gara Kisovna. She came to my place when I was in Maiak (village); she came in through the door. There was a door over there, and there was also a door like this to go out. She came in and told me: 'My sister!'

(Someone from the audience)
'Was it in your sleep?'

(Lingdze)
In my sleep. 'I have nothing left', (said Mariia Petrovna) 'Only (a spirit) granddad Kiso. All my *seven* remained in Moscow, because I did not shamanise in a proper place, I played the fool, made noise'. That's why she came to me.
People came to me (in waking hours) to send me to that city (in a ritual) and to bring her *seven* back.

(To the departed shaman Gara Kisovna)
How can I fetch your *seven*? I cannot sing (in a shamanic way) like you.
I am not able to talk like you.
'My sister! I have only returned with my friend Kiso!'

(To the deceased relatives)
My (departed) mother! My (departed) children!
If I lived like it was in the past, I would find her beings.
It's okay for you, dead, but I am getting worse and worse.
I live ailing and thinking about you.

This disease can kill me. This disease will press me down.
You were crying and when I stop crying I don't know.

(To the audience)
Marus'ka went to the city,
When returning, she sat behind my (closed) door
And peeped through the chink.
Seeing her while she was peeping, I asked her:
'My sister, why don't you come in?
You were able to travel all over the different countries.
Why can you not also come to my place?'
But she never came and just went away.
She thought I would tell her something.

(To the departed shaman Mariia Petrovna and to the departed shaman Gara Kisovna)
Oh, my friends, I feel sorry for you!
You wander everywhere, and only after you have fallen down, you come to me!
You travel through the different cities, but only return to me!
You bring so much junk, that you are not able to carry it in your rucksack.
But I ask people nothing!

(To the audience)
My Marus'ka thought highly of herself.
She thought she was very powerful!
At last she really became quite a strong (shaman).
She did not ask people to take away all her bad things, [145]
Because her mother was a shaman and all of them: she, Toë and Dziulpu all became shamans. [146]

Now Marus'ka died. Who will shamanise next? Probably someone will become a shaman. Will! Will! Will! Someone will! Somebody has a daughter, and she will use cunning!

(To the departed shaman Mariia Petrovna and to the departed shaman Gara Kisovna)
Is it good (for you now)?

---

145 Lingdze considers that Mariia Petrovna had some bad spirits among her *seven* and that it would have been useful to clean them out.

146 Toë Petrovna Bel'dy is Mariia Petrovna's sister and Dziulpu is the name of her brother Pëtr. They all have inherited the ability to shamanise from their mother, the powerful shaman Dekhe.

They singe people, so they will also singe you now. [147]
They perform funeral repast *degdin,* and they'll do it for you as well.
Now pass (your shamanic ability) to some child.
Let them find it in their dreams.

(To her spirits)
Let nothing stick to my body! I don't feel quite myself!
(To the departed shaman Mariia Petrovna)
You were not good for nothing.
People cannot find such women like you along any way.

(To the audience)
However she had *baita* (fought against another shaman) because of her son. [148]

(To her spirits)
Don't send anything bad upon me! I'm just crying!

(To the audience)
As Robert (Mariia Petrovna's husband) drank,
She gave his *panian* (soul) to the big *endur* (deity).
'Let him stop drinking! Make Robert finish drinking!
If he stops drinking, I'll sacrifice something, I'll do something!'

(To her spirits)
Come to me!
Tell me the news, the news, the rumours! [149]

(To the audience)
One word can cause the *baita* (enmity).
When he was drinking, she said to *endur*:
'Robert is drinking. If he stops, I'll sacrifice a big animal'.
But now the *seven* have cut her roads, [150] and she has come to grief.
Robert stopped drinking. He has not been drinking for a long time.

---

147 In Nanaian funeral repast, people make a fire to 'singe' the departed and to burn some food and cloth for them. The departed are believed to be able to get things through the fire.

148 People said that Mariia Petrovna had an enemy shaman, but they did not know who that enemy was. Her son was once walking from Naichin to Daerga village across the small Shchu-chiibay. As he was a little drunk, he fell onto the ice of the bay and froze to death. The place where he fell was where people often walked along. It was speculated that nobody noticed him before he died because Mariia Petrovna had given her son's soul to her enemy shaman.

149 Lingdze asks her spirits to give her more information about Mariia Petrovna's death.

150 Cutting shamanic roads in the invisible world is a means to strike at a hostile shaman. Ling-dze means that Mariia Petrovna was in enmity with someone of another clan, who (or whose *seven*) had won against her.

That Russian [151] has stopped drinking. He has stopped after his wife asked the *endur* about that. 'I want to live well!' she said. 'That's why I force my husband to stop drinking vodka!' After that she had to perform a ritual, but she did not go through it. On the contrary, she began drinking vodka herself! She cooked home-brewed beer and went to buy some more home-brewed beer from an old woman who also brewed it. She was drinking and lived this way.

(To the audience)
Is what I am doing now cheap? Is it for free, is it not?
Crying I tell you about that *baita* (case of enmity) just because you are interested in it!
Gara Kisovna did nothing either. (She did not perform a ritual).
I won't tell you about those beings they bowed to, I cannot.

(To the departed shaman Mariia Petrovna and to the departed shaman Gara Kisovna)
You had told (your spirits), but you did not keep your promise,
That is why you have come to grief.
If you had done it properly, it would have been (nice)!
But you did nothing and (died) one after the other.

(To the audience)
In this life, (the spirits) will torment that (person) and another one and many other people.
I know nothing about that. Toë is a big shaman, she knows about those beings who they (Mariia Petrovna and Gara Kisovna) asked for mercy.
Don't listen to my words. I am talking rubbish.

(To the departed shaman Mariia Petrovna and to the departed shaman Gara Kisovna)
It is no coincidence that you died, Mariia Petrovna.
When you and I were poor, when we lived meagerly,
You and I ate from the same plate.
You travelled to the different cities,
And you really don't know what you have left there, what you have lost.
Were you able to cope with those (spirits), who
You should have given a *sugdi* (an offering)?
(Did you overpower) that *nai* (spirit), which needed an offering,
When you were enjoying yourself, travelling round the cities?

(To the departed shaman Gara Kisovna)
Gara Kisovna, your spirits
Are behind you bristled up and spread wide!

---

151 Robert is not actually Russian, but Ossete.

234

(To her spirits)
Is it so, isn't it? I don't know.

(To the departed shaman Mariia Petrovna)
Marus'ka! It is not a day of your death!
You'll probably wake up in your coffin!
But you won't be able to escape from your grave!
You had so many husbands and friends.
Will one of your husbands help you that time
When you return to life in (your coffin)?

By the time of that terrible prediction, Lingdze had finished her rite and Mariia Petrovna had not yet been interred. No one from the audience understood Lingdze's prediction, as if nobody heard it, [152] and nothing was told to Mariia Petrovna's relatives. Next day she was buried in a regular deep grave. Robert, Mariia Petrovna's husband, who knew nothing about Lingdze's words, told me later about his wife's similar presentiment. Robert said:

She told me that. But I could not request this (for the funeral), you know. She said: 'When a shaman dies, they need air'. She knew it. She said: 'I won't die!' She told me that, when she was young yet. 'A wooden chimney should be done for me!' she said. Where? At home?
In her grave.
I live and I will live!' She told me that, when she was younger and when she was not yet out of her mind. She always told me: 'If I die, you should leave me air!' She explained to me that people must not bury shamans in a common cemetery. It was necessary to take (a dead shaman) somewhere else, because there were cases in which the (shaman) got up (after their death). A man shaman got up, I know. And she told me: 'I won't die, don't worry!'

Concerning Lingdze's words about Mariia Petrovna's husbands, one could say that Mariia Petrovna had several husbands, and her last one (the Ossete) was handsome and twenty years younger than her. Lingdze's fate was different; despite being married three times, she actually lived all her life alone because her husbands died soon after their marriage, and people said that she envied Mariia Petrovna.

---

152 I learned the meaning of those horrible Lingdze's words only the next year, when I asked Raisa Bel'dy to help me with the translation of this text.

NANAI WORDS AND SHAMANIC TERMS

Adaori *(адаори)* – to stick to something. In shamanism this term means to inherit spirits not only along one certain lineage, but to combine inheritance along two or more lineages.

Aiami *(аями)* – spirit-helper, which was considered to be a lover or a father (mother) of a shaman.

Amban *(амбан)* – an evil spirit. The words 'seven' (good spirit-helpers) and 'amban' (evil spirits) are interchangeable. In some situations 'seven' are believed to behave as 'amban' and vice versa.

Amban oktoni *(амбан октони)* – literally, medicine of an evil spirit, invisible poison, which the spirits are supposed to add to food.

Amichioni *(амичиони)* – a foul word, which is often used in shamanic rituals.

Angmani nikheli *(ангмани нихэли)* – part of shamanic initiation, literally means 'to open a neophyte's mouth' in order to enable that mouth to become a channel between people and spirits.

Armoki *(армоки)* – a spirit-helper, which was supposed to be born of a woman and later inherited by her children.

Armol *(армол)* – an invisible reflection of a visible phenomenon, which has been taken away.

Baigoan *(байгоан)* – a shaman enemy, who attacks a shaman and his kin in dreams and in rituals.

Baita *(байта)* – a problem, which can arise in case of a mistaken or wrong deed, fighting against an alien shaman.

Beregde *(бэрэгдэ)* – rod with an image of a leg on one end and a head on the other that was the judge's paraphernalia used during traditional court.

Boa ibakhani *(боа ибахани)* – a mythical bird.

Boda *(бода)* – Nanai national dish of liquid cereal.

Buni *(буни)* – the world of the deceased.

Burkhan *(бурхан)* — a word of Turk-Mongol origin, which is used as a general designation of a spirit.

Degdin *(дегдин)* – funeral repast.

Dëkaso *(дёкасо)* – storage for the clients' souls.

Dërgil *(дёргил)* – the invisible shamanic roads.

Dërgil ningmani *(дёргил нингмани)* – the tales about a shaman's adventures while he travels along his invisible shamanic roads.

Diaka *(дяка)* – creature, the generalised word which is used to avoid directly specifying which spirit is mentioned.

Diangian *(дянгиан)* – traditional judge.

Diulin *(диулин)* – wooden image of the home spirit.

Dona *(дона)* – a category of shamanic spirits, which are taken by a shaman from alien clans (Evenk language).

Dorkin *(доркин)* – invisible spiritual underground world.

Edekhe *(эдехэ)* – a shamanic spirit. His figure of metal or of wood is worn by a shaman at his neck. 'Edekhe' is especially considered to help in the hunt.

Endur *(эндур)* – deity, which is set in the rank above the shamanic spirit-helpers.

Epili *(эпили)* – shamanic ritual for a short prayer or for sending a spirit into its figure.

Erde *(эрдэ)* – performing shamanic tricks with the purpose of demonstrating his or her power.

Galigda *(галигда)* – people who met an unnatural death, who drowned or were torn by a tiger or a bear; they are believed to bring misfortune to their clan.

Gasiko *(гасико)* – one of the most dangerous of the shamanic spirits in the form of a polysepalous serpent.

Geen *(гэен)* – synonym for the word shaman.

Gora *(гора)* – the invisible shamanic territory, where shamans move around during their ceremonies.

Iludu *(илуду)* – the middle world.

Kala *(кала)* – a kind of offering to spirits.

Kalgama *(калгама)* – a mythical being head pointed and with long legs, which lives in the mountains and in the taiga.

Kasa *(каса)* – a ritual of sending the dead off to the beyond.

Kasatai saman *(касатай саман)* – shaman, who is able to perform the ritual 'kasa'.

Kele *(кэлэ)* – a Chukchi shaman spirit.

Kesne *(кэсиэ)* – luck, or one of the souls which helps a person to get luck.

Kesne geleuri *(кэсиэ гэлэури)* – a ritual (usually offering or sacrifice) of getting luck.

Khargi *(харги)* – a category of Evenk spirits.

Khere, khei *(хэрэ, хэй)* – the typical shamanic singing words, non-semantic and untranslatable.

Kherenti saman *(хэргэнти саман)* – shaman who is able to perform the ritual 'khergen.'

Khergen *(хэргэн)*, the same as 'ningmanta' – funeral repasts, which are performed by a shaman on the seventh day after someone's death when the deceased person's soul is sent to the special figure 'panë'.

Kheriuri *(хэриури)* – to go everywhere hovering and being invisible, about shamanic spiritual flight.

Kheven *(хэвэн)* – a category of Evenk spirits.

Khoraliko *(хоралико)* – spirit-cohabitant for women, which causes women's diseases (in Ul'chi and Orochi 'khuraliku').

Koaldosi *(коалдоси)* – a ritual, which aim is to drive and beat the inherited spirits of a neophyte and to clean them up this way.

Kochali *(кочали)* – a spirit which prevents a successful hunt.

Komoko nai *(комоко най)* – fortune tellers, who have informative dreams.

Manga *(манга)* – in Gorin dialect: judge, also means 'disaster', 'trouble', 'violence'.

Marna *(марна)* – a traditional judge's spirit-helper which assisted him to try to reconcile the conflicting parties.

Mepi saman *(мэпи саман)* – a shaman capable of merely self-help service.

Mergen *(мэргэн)* – a hero of Nanai tales.

Meuri *(мэури)* – to dance in a shamanic way with a drum and metal pendants on the belt.

Mio *(мио)* – images and names of deities ('endur') on cloth.

Mokto puimur *(мокто пуймур)* – spirit, half of a dragon.

Musu *(мусу)* – common clan spirituality.

Musunchu *(мусунчу)* – a lucky person who has a good 'musu' inherent in one clan or family.

Nai *(най)* – a person, sometimes is used as a neutral word for replacing names of spirits.

Ngeven *(нгэвэн)* – a kind of evil spirits.

Nikheleuri *(нихэлэури)* – a shamanic initiation, stands for 'to open'.

Ningman *(нингман)* – a tale.

Ningmanta *(нингманта)* (the same as 'khergen') – ritual performed on the seventh day after someone's death, when the deceased person's soul is sent to the special figure 'panë'.

Niokta *(ниокта)* – the unity of a shaman's spirits which are believed to replace his soul.

Ochiki *(очики)* – spirits, which are spread as a result of violence and which make people do more violence. 'Ochiki' is believed to cause the wish to murder or to commit suicide. The Nanai word 'ochiki' is probably a variant of the Manchurian word *vochko* which means spirits of the departed shamans that became the spirit-helpers of their descendants, the living shamans.

Oksoki *(оксоки)* – a harmful, negative *seven's* offshoot, its bad qualities.

Omi *(оми)*, in Evenk: 'omiruk' *(омирук)* – a vessel (dish, box, bag), in which shamans 'placed' souls.

Panian *(панян)* – soul-shadow, which leaves a person in dreams and when he is sick.

Pasiku amban *(пасику амбан)* – hanged evil spirit, which flew around with a rope and make people hang themselves.

Pergechi *(пэргэчи, пэргэчиури)* – shamanic ritual to make guesses.

Poia *(поя)* – a younger person.

Pokto telungu *(покто тэлунгу)* – literally, legend-roads, one of the genres of Nanai folklore.

Pudin *(пудин)* – a beauty in Nanai tales.

Puren ambani *(пурэн амбани)* – the evil spirit of the forest or spirit-tiger.

Saika/sadka *(сайка/садка)* – incest creates an unsafe intimacy with the spirits.

Samamba nikheliori *(самамба нихэлиори)* – shamanic initiation; literally, to open a shaman, which means 'to open his mouth', to give him the possibility of singing in a shamanic way.

Saman *(саман)* – shaman.

Saola *(саола)* – a clay vessel in which, according to the belief, the spirits of a dead shaman live.

Seven *(сэвэн)* – a generalised name for a shaman spirit-helper.

Sembele *(сэмбэлэ)* – the name of the *seven* (spirit-helper) in the form of a dog.

Serume pikte *(сэрумэ пиктэ)* – a shaman spirit-helper in the form of a reddish child, shaman women affirm that they sometimes give birth to such spirits.

Simur *(симур)* – spirit serpent.

Sirbogokha ekte *(сирбогоха эктэ)* – a woman, who in case of murder is given in exchange as payment for the murdered one.

Somolakan *(сомолакан)* – a depository, special saccules, where souls were believed to be stored.

Songo *(сонго, сонгори)* – to cry, to lament, sometimes used as a synonym for the word 'yaiaori' *(яяори)*, to sing in a shamanic way.

Sugdi *(сугди)* – an offering to spirits.

Takht *(махт)* – Nivkh spirit, which demands revenge.

Tala *(тала)* – Nanai national dish of raw fish.

Taochi *(таочи, таочиори)* – shamanic ritual to look for a client's lost soul.

Taochiko saman *(таочико, таочини)* саман – shaman who performs the ritual 'taochi'.

Telungu *(тэлунгу)* – legend.

Teuchi *(тэучи)* – literally: 'to put'; shamanic ceremony to insert a spirit into its figure, sometimes used as a synonym for the word 'epili'.

Toli *(толи)* – shamanic bronze disk.

Tolkin *(толкин)* – informative dreams.

Toro *(торо)* – wooden poles with carved images of spirits.

Tudin *(тудин)* – a clairvoyant, a person who like a shaman has spirit-helpers and supernatural powers, but who does not perform rituals.

Tuige edekhe *(туйгэ эдехэ)* – a certain kind of 'edekhe', which belongs to the spirits gathered around the shamanic tree 'tuige'.

Undi *(унди)* – a sacrificial ritual for the shamanic spirits including a procession led by a shaman and accompanied by the members of his congregation.

Yagoran *(ягоран)* - a Manchurian toy, which is put in front of the soul, while it is closed in the shamanic soul-storage.

Yaiaori *(яяори)* – to sing in a shamanic way.

Yamali *(ямали)* – to demonstrate unusual shamanic abilities, to do conjuring tricks.

Yangpan *(янгпан)* – shaman's belt with metal pendants.

SHAMANS AND CITED INFORMANTS

Alexander Sergeevich Khodzher, shaman's husband, 1914–2000, Achan village.
Aleksei Kisovich Onenko, 1912–1991, shaman's brother, Daerga.
Alla Kisovna Bel'dy, shaman's sister, 1936–2002, Daerga.
Chapaka Danilovna Passar, 1916–2004, Taëzhnyi.
Chiku Chubovna Bel'dy, 1928, Naichin.
Ella Ivanovna Kile, 1955, Daerga.
Ena Kile, 1949, Troitskoe.
Galina Ulgovna Kile, shaman's daughter, 1954, Lidoga.
Gara Kisovna Geiker, shaman, 1914–1985, Daerga.
Irina Torombovna Passar, 1945, Tayozhnyi.
Ivan Torokovich Bel'dy, uninitiated shaman, 1916–2001. Daerga.
Kada Ingirivna Kile, shaman, 1917–2001, Lidoga.
Konstantin Maktovich Bel'dy, 1930, Troitskoe.
Larisa Ganzulievna Bel'dy, 1950, Dzhari.
Lingdze Iltungaevna Bel'dy, shaman, 1912–1999, Dada.
Lubov Aleksandrovna Odzial, Troitskoe.
Lubov Vladimirovna Passar, Khabarovsk.
Mariia Innokent'evna Tumali, shaman's wife, 1903–1999, Kondon.
Mariia Vasil'evna Bel'dy, 1925–2011, Daerga.
Marina Aleksandrovna Sultanova, shaman, Daerga, Khabarovsk.
Mikhail Pykevich Passar, uninitiated shaman, 1937, Daerga.
Mingo Geiker, shaman, 1917–1997, Naichin.
Nesulta Borisovna Geiker, uninitiated shaman, 1920–2009, Daerga.
Nikolai Petrovich Bel'dy, uninitiated shaman, 1927–1997, Naichin.
Niura Fedorovna Bel'dy, 1922–2005, Dzhari.
Niura Sergeevna Kile, shaman, 1907–2004, Achan.
Ol'ga Egorovna Kile, shaman, 1920–2013, Upper Nergen.
Robert Mikhailovich Salkazanov, shaman's husband, 1944–1995, Daerga.
Tekchu Innokent'evich Onenko, 1912–1992, Daerga.
Toë Petrovna Bel'dy, shaman, 1911–1997, Sinda.
Ul'iana Stepanovna Bel'dy, 1912–1990, Iskra.
Valentina Sergeevna Kile, 1928–2001, Achan.
Vera Chubovna Geiker, 1936, Lidoga.
Evdokiia Chubovna Bel'dy, 1931–2007, Lidoga.
Zinaida Nikolaevna Bel'dy, 1939, Troitskoe.
Ksenia Ivanovna Digor, 1915–2001, Kondon.

FIGURE 22: Lingdze Bel'dy (left)

FIGURE 23: Nikolai Petrovich Bel'dy (right)

FIGURE 24: The sisters Alla Kisovna Bel'dy and Liubov' Kisovna Geiker

FIGURE 25: Nikolai Petrovich Bel'dy with his wife Mingo Geiker

FIGURE 26: The sisters Inna Ivanovna and Ella Ivanovna Bel'dy

FIGURE 27: Ksenia Ivanovna Digor

FIGURE 28: Chiku Chubovna Bel'dy and Maria Chubovna Passar

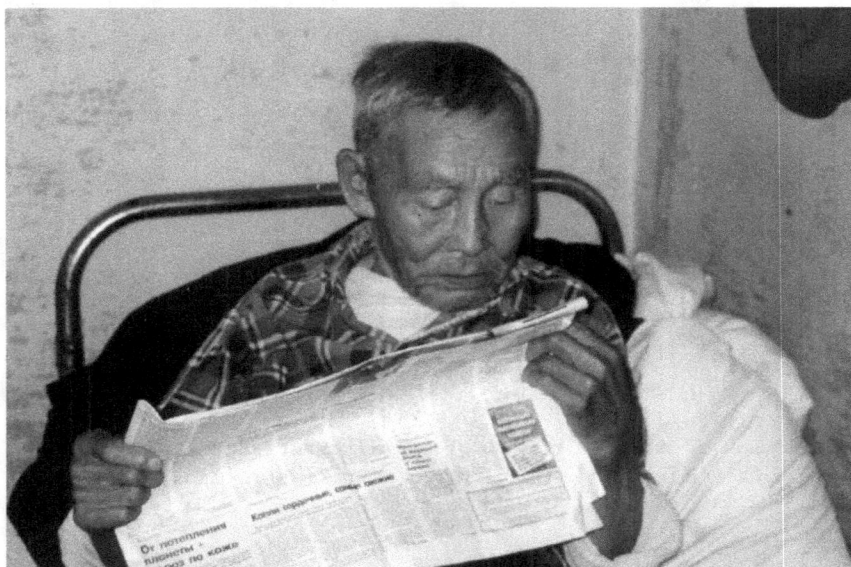

FIGURE 29: Ivan Torokovich Bel'dy

FIGURE 30: Maria Petrovna Bel'dy

FIGURE 31: Gara Kisovna Geiker

FIGURE 32: Kada Kile

FIGURE 33: Kada Kile

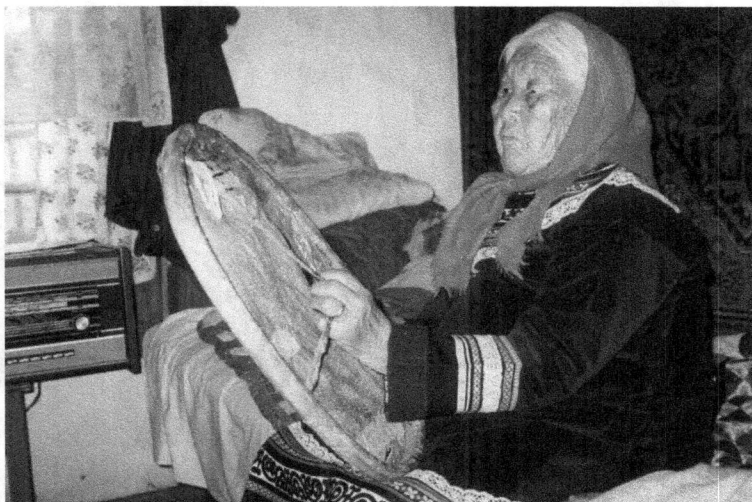

FIGURE 34: Niura Sergeevna Kile

FIGURE 35: Gara Kisovna Geiker

FIGURE 36: Ol'ga Egorovna Kile

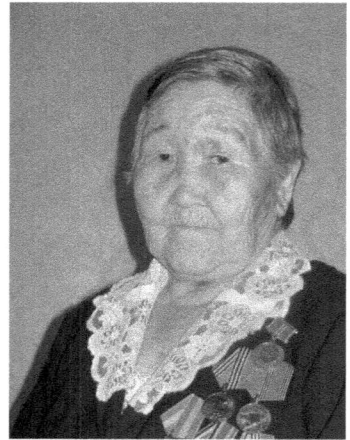

FIGURE 37: Vera Chubovna Geiker

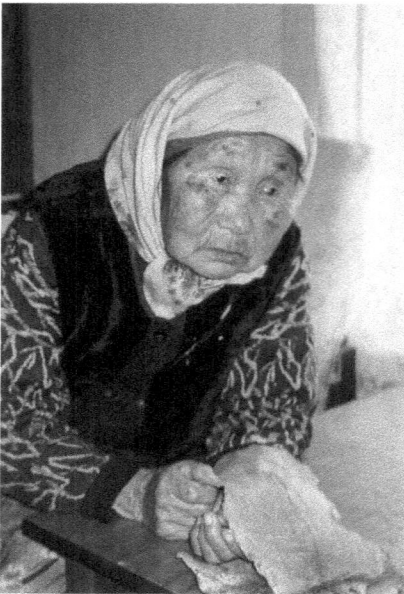

FIGURE 38: Chapaka Danilovna Passar

FIGURE 39: Valentina Sergeevna Kile

REFERENCES

Alekseenko E. A. 1967. *Kety*. Istoriko-etnograficheskie ocherki. Leningrad: Nauka.

— 1981. Shamanstvo u ketov. In *Problemy istorii obshchestvennogo soznaniia aborigenov Sibiri*. I. S. Vdovin (red.), 90–128. Leningrad: Nauka.

Anisimov A. F. 1958. *Religiia evenkov*. Moskva/Leningrad: ANSSSR.

— 1936. *Rodovoe obshchestvo evenkov (tungusov)*. Trudy po etnografii. Nauchno-issledovatel'skaia assotsiatsiia Instituta narodov Severa TSIK SSSR im. P. G. Smidovicha. T. 1. Leningrad: Izdatel'stvo Instituta narodov Severa TSIK SSSR im. P. G. Smidovicha.

Anokhin A. V. 1924. Materialy po shamanstvu u altaitsev, sobrannye vo vremia puteshestvii po Altaiu 1910-1912 g. po porucheniiu Russkogo komiteta po izucheniiu Srednei i Vostochnoi Azii. In *Sbornik muzeia antropologii i etnografii pri Rossiiskoi Akademii Nauk*, T. 4, vyp. 2. Leningrad: Nauka.

Arsen'ev V. K. 1926. *Lesnye liudy udekheitsy*. Vladivostok: Knizhnoe delo.

Atwood, Christopher P. 2004. *The Encyclopedia of Mongolia and the Mongol Empire*. New York: Facts on File.

Avrorin V. A. 1986. *Materialy po nanaiskomu yazyku i fol'kloru*. Leningrad: Nauka.

Bäckman, Louise and Å. Hultkrantz 1978. *Studies in Lapp Shamanism*. Stockholm: Almqvist & Wiksell.

Bakhtin M. M. 2000. *Avtor i geroi. K filosofskim osnovam gumanitarnykh nauk*. Sankt-Peterburg: Azbuka.

— 1986. *Literaturno-kriticheskie stat'i*. S. Bocharov and V. Kozhinov (sost.). Moskva: Khudozhestvennaia literatura.

— 1979. *Estetika slovesnogo tvorchestva*. Moskva: Iskusstvo.

Balosh, Mätyäs 2007. Shamanic Traditions, Rites and Songs among the Mongolian Buriats: Meeting a Shamaness and her Assistant. *Shaman* 15 (1–2): 87–115.

Balzer, Marjorie Mandelstam 1995a. The Poetry of Shamanism. In *Shamanism in Performing Arts*. K. Tae-gon Kim and Mihály Hoppál, with the assistance of Otto J. Sadovsky (eds.), 171–188. Budapest: Akadémiai Kiadó. (for a revised version see also Balzer 2012).

— 1995b. Ot bubnov k skovorodam: paradoksal'nye izmeneniia shamanizma v istorii sakha (yakutov). In *Shamanizm i rannie religioznye predstavleniia: k 90-letiiu doktora istoricheskikh nauk, professora L. P. Potapova. Etnologicheskie issledovaniia po shamanstvu i inym rannim verovaniiam i praktikam*. T. 1. D. A. Funk (red.), 25–35. Moskva: Institut etnologii i antropologii RAN.

— 2012. *Shamans, Spirituality and Cultural Revitalization: Explorations in Siberia and Beyond*. New York: Palgrave-MacMillan.

Basilov V. N. 1990. Chosen by the Spirits. In *Shamanism: Soviet Studies of Traditional Religion in Siberia and Central Asia*. M. M. Balzer (ed.), 3–48. Armonk/New York/London: M. E. Sharp.

— 1992. *Shamanstvo u narodov Srednei Azii i Kazakhstana*. Institut etnologii i antropologii RAN. Moskva: Nauka.

Bat'ianova E. P. 2004. K probleme suitsida u narodov Sibiri. In *Sakral'noe glazami profanov i posviashzhennykh*. Materialy mezhdunarodnogo interdistsiplinarnogo nauchno-prakticheskogo kongressa. V. I. Kharitonova and E. S. Piterskaia (red./sost.), 243–255. Moskva: Institut etnologii i antropologii RAN.

— 2007. *Rod i obshchina u teleutov v XIX– nachale XX veka*. Moskva: Nauka.

Bazarov B. D. 2000. *Tainstva i praktika shamanizma*. Ulan-Ude: Buriad unen.

Bel'dy K. M. 2006. *Besstopyi shaman*. Khabarovsk: Kovcheg.

Bel'dy O. A. 1999. *Nanaiskii shamanizm v istorii i kul'ture korennykh narodov Priamur'ia i Primor'ia (seredina XIX–XX vv.)*. Sankt-Peterburg: Sankt Peterburgskii gosudarstvennyi universitet.

Bel'dy O. A. and T. D. Bulgakova 2012. *Nanaiskie skazki*. Fürstenberg/Havel: Kulturstiftung Sibirien.

Bereznitskii S. V. 2001. Sotsial'naia organizatsiia. In *Istoriia i kul'tura orochei*. V. A. Tuarev (red.), 20–23. Sankt-Peterburg: Nauka.

Bocharov V. V. 1992. *Vlast', traditsii, upravlenie*. Moskva: Nauka.

Bogoraz V. G. 1932. Religiia kak tormoz sotsstroitel'stva sredi malykh narodov Severa. *Sovetskii Sever* 1–2: 142–147.

— 1939. *Chukchi*. Leningrad: Izdatel'stvo Glavsevmorputi.

Brailovskii S. N. 1901. Tazy ili Udikhe. *Zhivaia starina* 3–4.

Budarin M. E. 1968. *Put' malykh narodov Krainego Severa k kommunizmu*. Omsk: Zapadno-Sibirskoe Knizhnoe izdatel'stvo.

Bulgakova T. D. 2001. *Shamanstvo v traditsionnoi kul'ture. Sistemnyi analiz*. Sankt-Peterburg: RGPU im. A.I. Gertsena.

— 2004. Tale As a Road: Where Shaman Must Win. In *Shamanism in the Interdisciplinary Context*. A. Leete and R. P. Firnhaber (eds.), 215–226. Boca Raton, Florida: Brown Walker Press.

Butanaev V. Ya. 1984. Kul't bogini Umai u khakasov. In *Etnografiia narodov Sibiri*. I. N. Gemuev, Yu. S. Khudiakov (red.), 93–105. Novosibirsk: Nauka.

Castrén A. M. 1858. Etnograficheskie zamechaniia i nabliudeniia Kastrena o lopariakh, karelakh, samoedakh i ostiakakh, izvlechennye iz ego putevykh vospominanii 1838–1844. *Etnograficheskii sbornik* 4: 219–320. Sankt-Peterburg.

Dolgikh B. O. 1960. Prinesenie v zhertvu olenei u nganasan i entsev. *Kratkie soobshcheniia Instituta etnografii* 33: 72–81.

Fairclough, Norman 1995. *Critical Discourse Analysis*. London: Longman.

Gaer E. A. 1991. *Traditsionnaia bytovaia obriadnost' nanaitsev v kontse XIX – nachale XX v*. Moskva: Mysl'.

Geertz, Clifford 1973. Thick Description: Toward an Interpretive Theory of Culture. In *The Interpretation of Cultures*, C. Geertz (ed.), 3–30. New York: Basis Books. http://sociologist.nm.ru/articles/geertz_01.htm

Glavatskaia E. M. 2010. Religioznyi marker v sisteme kollektivnoi identichnosti obskikh ugrov. In *Etnokul'turnoe nasledie narodov Severa Rossii*. E. A. Pivneva (red.), 237–242. Moskva: Institut etnologii i antropologii RAN. Moskva: Nauka.

Golovnev A. V. 1995. *Govoriashzhie kul'tury. Traditsii samodiitsev i ugrov*. Ekaterinburg: Ural'skoe Otdelenie RAN.

Gracheva G. N. 1983. *Traditsionnoe mirovozzrenie okhotnikov Taimyra*. Leningrad: Nauka.

Gurvich I. S. 1966. Otmiranie religioznykh verovanii u narodnostei Severo-vostoka Sibiri. *Voprosy preodoleniia religioznykh verovanii u narodnostei Sibiri*: 79–96. Moskva: Nauka.

Gutorov N. 1932. H. Shamanskaia organizatsiia v sele Karaga. *Taiga i tundra* 1(4): 37–38.

Hamayon, Roberte 2009. Poniatie shamanizma: formirovanie zapadnoi interpretatsii. *Religiovedenie* 1: 3–14.

Heyne, Georg F. 1999. The Social Significance of the Shaman among the Chinese Reindeer-Evenki. *Asian Folklore Studies* 58(2): 377–395.

Hoppál, Mihály 1992. Pain in Shamanic Initiation. In *Northern Religion and Shamanism*. M. Hoppál and J. Pentikäinen (eds.). Budapest/Helsinki: Akadémiai Kiadó and Finnish Literature Society.

Hultkrantz, Åke 2004. Ecological and Phenomenological Aspects of Shamanism. In *Shamanism: Critical Concepts in Sociology*, Vol. III. A. A. Znamenski (ed.), 146-169. London/New York: Routledge.

Horvath, Izabella 1995. A Comparative Study of Shamanistic Motifs in Hungarian and Turkic Folk Tales. In *Shamanism in Performing Arts*. K. Tae-gon Kim and Mihály Hoppál, with the assistance of Otto J. Sadovsky (eds.), 159–170. Budapest: Akadémiai Kiadó.

Istoriia i kul'tura nanaitsev 2003. Istoriko-etnograficheskie ocherki. Sankt Peterburg: Nauka.

Kaigorodov A. M. 1970. Svad'ba v taige. *Sovetskaia etnografiia* 3: 153–161.

Karger N. and I. Koz'minskii 1929. Otchet ob issledovaniiakh material'noi kul'tury garinskikh gol'dov. In *Garino-amgunskaia ekspeditsiia*. Leningrad.

Kenin-Lopsan M. B. 2007. Shaman zhivet v kazhdom iz nas. *Profil'*: http://www.profile.ru/items_21949

— 2008. *Dykhanie chernogo neba*. Mifologicheskoe nasledie tuvinskogo shamanstva. Moskva: Veligor.

Khangalov M. N. 2004. *Sobranie sochinenii v trekh tomakh*. T. 2. Ulan-Ude: Respublikanskaia tipografiia.

Kharitonova V. I. 2004. Ustami shamana glagolet ... dukh?. K voprosu o shamanskoi psikhofiziologii i vozmozhnostiakh eksperimental'nogo izucheniia lichnosti shamana. In *Polevye issledovaniia Instituta etnologii i antropologii 2002*. S. P. Sokolova (red.), 24–43. Moskva: Institut etnologii i antropologii RAN.

— 2006. *Feniks iz pepla? Sibirskii shamanism na pubezhe tysiacheletii*. Moskva: Institut etnologii i antropologii RAN.

Khelimski E. A. 2000. *Komparativistika, uralistika. Lektsii i stat'i*. Moskva: Yazyki russkoi kul'tury.

Khodarkovsky, Michael 1992. *Where Two Worlds Met: The Russian State and the Kalmyk Nomads, 1600–1771*. Ithaca, NY: Cornell University Press.

Khudiakov I. A. 2002. *Kratkoe opisanie Verkhoianskogo okruga*. Yakutsk: Bichik.

Kile N. B. 1994. Mirovozzrenie i verovaniia. In *Istoriia i kul'tura ul'chei v 17–20 vekakh*. L. Ya. Ivashchenko (red.), 64–68. Sankt-Peterburg: Nauka.

Kister, Daniel A. 1997. *Korean Shamanist Ritual: Symbols and Dramas of Transformation*. Budapest: Akadémiai Kiadó.

Klass, Morton 1995. *Ordered Universes. Approaches to the Anthropology of Religion*. Boulder/San Francisco/Oxford: West View Press.

Kortt I. R. 1992. Traditsionnaia rol' sibirskogo shamana. In *Shamanism kak religiia: genesis, rekonstruktsiia, traditsii*. Tezisy dokladov mezhdunarodnoi nauchnoi konferentsii 15–22 avgusta, p. 15–16. Yakutsk.

Kosokov I. 1931. *K voprosu o shamanstve Severnoi Azii*. Moskva: Izdatel'stvo Bezbozhnik.

Koz'minskii I. 1927. Vozniknovenie novogo kul'ta u gol'dov. In *Sbornik etnograficheskikh materialov*. Vyp. 2. V. G. Bogoraz-Tan (red.), 43–52. Leningrad: Gosudarstvennyi universitet.

Kreinovich E. A. 1973. *Nivkhgi. Zagadochnye obitateli Sakhalina i Amura*. Moskva: Nauka.

Ksenofontov G. V. 1992. *Shamanism. Izbrannye trudy*. Yakutsk: Tvorchesko-proizvodstvennaia firma 'Sever-Yug'.

Kubbel' L. E. 1988. *Ocherki potestarno-politicheskoi etnografii*. Moskva: Nauka.

Lehtisalo T. 1998. *Mifologiia yurako-samoedov (nenets)*. Tomsk: Izdatel'stvo Tomskogo gosudarstvennogo universiteta.

Lindquist, Galina 2006. *The Quest for the Authentic Shaman: Multiple Meanings of Shamanism on a Siberian Journey*. Stockholm: Almqvist & Wiksell International.

Lopatin I. A. 1922. *Gol'dy amurskie, ussuriiskie i sungariiskie. Opyt etnograficheskogo issledovaniia*. Vladivostok: Zapiski obshchestva izuchenie Amurskogo kraia.

Lukina N. V. 2002. *Nauka kak forma obshchestvennogo razvitiia severnykh regionov*. Tomsk: Izdatel'stvo Tomskogo universiteta.

Mauss, Marcel [Moss, Marsel'] 2000. *Sotsial'nye funktsii sviashchennogo / izbrannye proizvedeniia*. Translated by I. V. Utekhina. Sankt-Peterburg: Evraziia. [Russian translation of M. Mauss 'La fonction sociale du sacré', Paris: Minuit, 1968]

Mikhailov T. M. 1971. Shamanskie perezhitki i nekotorye voprosy byta i kul'tura narodov Sibiri. In *Voprosy preodoleniia perezhitkov lamaizma, shamanizma i staroobriadchestva*. A. A. Belousov (red.), 57–58. Ulan-Ude: Buriat.

Mitskevich S. I. 1929. *Menerik i emiriachen'e, formy isterii v Kolymskom krae*. Leningrad: Akademiia Nauk SSSR.

Moldanova T. A. 1999. *Ornament khantov Kazymskogo Priob'ia: semantika, mifologiia, genezis*. Tomsk: Izdatel'stvo Tomskogo gosudarstvennogo universiteta.

Murdoch, George P. [Merdok, Dzh. P.] 2003. *Sotsial'naia struktura*. Translated by A. V. Korotaeva. Moskva: OGI. [Russian translation of G. P. Murdoch (ed.), Social structure in South-East Asia, Chicago 1960.]

Nanaiskii fol'klor 1996. Ningman, siokhor i telungu. Novosibirsk: Nauka.

Narody 1985. *Narody Dal'nego Vostoka SSSR v YVII–XX vv.: istoriko-geograficheskie ocherki*. I. S. Gurvich (red.). Moskva: Nauka.

Nosilov K. 1888. Yuridicheskie obychai man'sov. In *Sbornik materialov po etnografii*, vyp. 3. V. F. Miller (red.), 65–73. Moskva: Izdatel'stvo Dashkovskogo etnograficheskogo muzeia.

Novik E. S. 1984. *Fol'klor i obriad v sibirskom shamanisme*. Moskva: Nauka.

Ocherki 1957. Ocherki po istorii Yakutii sovetskogo perioda. Yu. A. Poliakov, Z. V. Gogolev (red.) Yakutsk.

Ogorodnikov V. I. 1920. Russkaia gosudarstvennaia vlast' i sibirskie inorodtsy c XVI-XVIII vv. In *Sbornik trudov Irkutskogo gosudarstvennogo universiteta*, otd. 1, vyp. 1., 69–113. Irkutsk.

Ol'zina R. 1997. Chto proiskhodit? Vzglad iznutri na kul'turu ugorskikh narodov. *Literatura Rossiia* 48 (28.11.1997).

Onenko S. N. 1980. *Nanaisko-russkii slovar'*. Moskva: Nauka.

Passar M. P. 2010. Maro iz pleiady shamanov. *Aniuiskie perekaty* 78–80 (28.082010).

Pimenova K. V. 2006. Istorii zhizni i 'rasskazy o stanovlenii' postsovetskikh shamanov v Respublike Tyva. In *Praktika postsovetskikh adaptatsii narodov Sibiri*. D. Funk, Kh. Bich, L. Sillanpiaia (red.), 197–225. Moskva: Institut etnologii i antropologii RAN.

Polomoshinov I. V. 1987. Chukchi zvali ego Lëo. In *Prosveshchenie na Krainem Severe*, 221–226. Leningrad: Prosveshchenie.

Popkov Yu. V. and E. A. Tiugashev 2006. *Filosofiia Severa. Korennye malochislennye narody Severa v stsenariiakh miroustroistva*. Salekhard/Novosibirsk: Sibirskoe nauchnoe izdatel'stvo.

Popov A. A. 1949. Materialy po religioznym verovaniiam yakutov. In *Sbornik Muszeia antropologii i etnologii*, t. XI. S. P. Tolstov (red.), 255–323. Moskva/Leningrad.

— 2008. *Kamlaniia shamanov byvshego Viliuiskogo okruga* (teksty), 2. izd. Institut nasledia. Ch. M. Taksami (red.). Novosibirsk: Nauka.

Potanin G. N. 1882. Gromovnik po pover'iam plemen yuzhnoi Sibiri i Sev. Mongolii. *Zhurnal ministerstva narodnogo prosvesheniia*, 116–159, 288–290, 304–305, 326.

Potapov L. P. 1934. Luk i strela v shamanstve u altaitsev. *Sovetskaia etnografiia* 3: 64–76.

Propp V. Ya. 1996. *Istoricheskie korni volshebnoi skazki*. Sankt-Peterburg: Izdatel'stvo Sankt-Peterburgskogo gosudarstvennogo universiteta.

Pust' govoriat 2000. Pust' govoriat nashi stariki. Rasskazy asiatskikh eskimosov-yup'ik. Zapisi 1977–1987 gg. I. I. Krupnik (red.). Moskva: Institut Naslediia.

Putilov B. H. 1994. *Fol'klor i narodnaia kul'tura*. Sankt-Peterburg: Nauka.

— 1999. *Ekskursy v istoriiu i teoriiu slavianskogo eposa*. Sankt-Peterburg: Muzei antropologii i etnografii im. Petra Velikogo RAN.

Revunenkova E. V. 1984. O nekotorykh istokakh poeticheskogo tvorchestva v Indonesii (shaman, pevets, skazitel'). *Fol'lor i etnografiia*: 35–40.

Rokitianskii V. N. 1994. Chego zhdat' ot postmodernistskoi etnografii? In *Etnometodologiia: problemy, podkhodz kontseptsii*. Vyp. 1., 40–52. Moskva.

Rychkov K. M. 1922. Eniseiskie tungusy. In *Zemlevedennie*, kn. 3–4, 113–138.

Samar A. 1946. *Pesni nanaitsa*. Leningrad: Uchpedgiz.

— 1940. *Stikhi*. Leningrad: Uchpedgiz.

Samarin Ya. F. 1935. Na Chukotke. *Na rubezhe* 8: 90.

Sem Yu. A. 1959. *Rodovaia organizatsiia nanaitsev i eë razlozhenie*. Vladivostok: DV filial SO AN SSSR.

— 1990. Kosmogonicheskie predstavleniia nanaitsev. 'Verkhnii mir'. In *Religiovedcheskie issledovaniia v etnograficheskikh muzeiakh*. B. V. Ivanov (red.), 114–128. Leningrad: Gosudarstvennyi Ordena Druzhby Narodov Muzei Etnografii Narodov SSSR.

Semenov Yu. I. 1997. Formy obshchestvennoi voli v doklassovom obshchestve: tabuitet, moral' i obychnoe pravo. *Etnograficheskoe obozrenie* 4: 3–24.

Sheikin Yu. I. 1996. *Muzykal'naia kul'tura narodov Severnoi Azii*. Yakutsk: RDNT.

Shimkevich P. P. 1896. *Materialy dlia izucheniia shamanstva u gol'dov*. T. 2, vyp. 1. Khabarovsk: Zapiski Primamurskogo otdeleniia Russkogo geograficheskogo obshchestva.

Shirokogoroff S. M. 1919. *Opyt issledovaniia osnov shamanstva u tungusov*. Vladivostok.

— 1924. *Etnos, issleedovanie osnovnykh prichin izmeneniia etnicheskikh i etnograficheskikh yavlenii*. Shankhai: Sibpress.

— 1929. *Social Organization of the Northern Tungus*. Shanghai: Commercial Press.

— 1999. *Psychomental Complex of the Tungus*. Berlin: Reinhold Schletzer Verlag.

— 2001. Opyt issledovaniia osnov shamanstva. In *Shirokogoroff S. M., etnograficheskie issledovaniia*. Kn. pervaia: Izbrannoe. sost. i premech. A. M. Kuznetsova, A. M. Reshetova. Vladivostok: DVGU.

— 2004. The Shaman. In *Shamanism: Critical Concepts in Sociology*, Vol. 1. Ed. by A. A. Znamenski (ed.), 83–123. London/New York: Routledge.

Shrenk L. I. 1903. *Ob inorodtsakh Amurskogo kraia*. T. 3. Etnograficheskaia chast'. Vtoraia polovina: Osnovnye cherty semeinoi, obshchestvennoi i vnutrennei zhizni. Sankt-Peterburg: Tip. Imp. Akad. nauk.

Shternberg L. Ya. 1904. Giliaki. *Etnograficheskoe obozrenie* 2: 47–54.

— 1933. *Giliaki, orochi, negidal'tsy, ainy*. Stat'i i materialy pod red. Ya. P. Al'kora (Koshkina). Khabarovsk: Dal'giz.

— 1927. Izbrannichestvo v religii. *Sovetskaia etnografiia* 1.

— 1936. Religiia giliakov. In *Pervobytnaia religiia v svete etnografii*. Ya. P. Al'kora (red.), 31–49. Leningrad: Institut narodov Severa TsIK SSSR im. P. G. Smidovicha.

— 1893. Sakhalinskie giliaki. *Etnograficheskoe obozrenie* 2.

— 1933. Sem'ia i rod u narodov Severo-Vostochnoi Azii: v 3 tomakh. Leningrad: Izdatel'stvo instituta narodov Severa TsIK SSSR.

Siikala, Anna-Leena 1978. *The Rite Technique of the Siberian Shaman*. Helsinki: Academia Scientiarum Fennica.

Siikala, Anna-Leena and Mihály Hoppál 1998. *Studies on Shamanism*. Ethnologica Uralica 2. Budapest: Finish Anthropological Society and Académiai Kiadó.

Simchenko Yu. B. 1998. Narody Severa Rossii: Problemy, Prognoz. *Issledovaniia po prikladnoi i neotlozhnoi etnologii, dok.* 112. Moskva: Institut etnologii i antropologii RAN.

Smidovich P. 1930. Sovetizatsiia Severa. *Sovetskii Sever* 1: 14.

Smoliak A. V. 1991. *Shaman: Lichnost', funktsii, mirovozzrenie* (Narody Nizhnego Amura). Moskva: Nauka.

Sokolova Z. P. 1983. *Sotsial'naia organizatsiia khantov i mansi c XVIII–XIX vv.: Problemy fratrii i roda*. Moskva: Nauka.

Soliarskii V. V. 1916. *Sovremennoe pravovoe i kul'turno-ekonomicheskoe polozhenie inorodtsev Priamurskogo kraia*. Khabarovsk: Kantseliarnii priamursk gen. gubernatora.

Startsev A. F. 2005. *Kul'tura i byt udegeitsev. Vtoraia polovina XIX–XX v.* Vladivostok: Dal'nauka.

Stebnitskii S. N. 2000. *Ocherki etnografii koriakov*. Sankt-Peterburg: Nauka.

Sunik O. P. 1958. *Kup-Urmiiskii dialekt. Issledovaniia i materialy po nanaiskomu yazyku*. Leningrad: Uchpedgiz.

Suslov I. M. 1928. Sotsial'naia kul'tura u tungusov basseina Podkamennoi Tunguski i verkhov'ev r. Taimury: Iz materialov Chaunskoi ekspeditsii 1926 g. *Severnaia Aziia* 1: 55–64.

— 1931. Shamanstvo i bor'ba s nim. *Sovetskii Sever* 3–4: 89–152.

— 1932. Shamanstvo kak tormoz sotsialisticheskogo stroitel'stva. *Antireligioznik* 7–8: 11–12, 17–18.

Taube, Erika 1984. South Siberian and Central Asian Hero Tales and Shamanistic Rituals. In *Shamanism in Eurasia*. M. Hoppál (ed.), 344–352. Göttingen: Herodot.

Tkacz, Virlana 2002. *Shanar: Dedication Ritual of a Buriat Shaman in Siberia as Conducted by Bayir Rinchinov*. New York: Parabola books.

Torchinov E. A. 1998. *Religii mira: opyt zapredel'nogo. Psikhotekhnika i trans-personal'nye sostoianiia*. Sankt-Peterburg: Tsentr Peterburgskoe Vostokovedenie. http://www.nhat-nam.ru/biblio/Torchinov-Religii_mira/index.htm

Turner E. 2001. Training to See What the Natives See. In *Shamans through Time. 500 Years on the Path to Knowledge*. J. Narby and F. Huxley (eds.), 260–262. New York: Tarcher/Putnam.

Val'diu A. I. 1982. Iz marka – k svetu. In *Porodnilis' na Amure: Ocherki*, 109–144. Khabarovsk: Kn. izdatel'stvo.

252

Vasilevich G. M. 1969. *Evenki.* Leningrad: Nauka.

Vasil'ev V. A. 1909. Izobrazheniia dolgano-yakutskikh dukhov kak atributy shaman-stva. *Zhivaia starina* 2–3: 269–288.

— 1908. Kratkii ocherk inorodtsev severa Turukhanskogo kraia. In *Ezhegodnik russkogo antropologicheskogo obshchestva pri imperatorskom Sankt-Peterburg-skom universitete.* B. F. Aller (red.), 56–87. Sankt-Peterburg: E. Arngol'da.

Vasil'eva N. D. 2000. *Yakutskoe shamanstvo 1920–1930 gg.* Yakutsk: AN respubliki Sakha (Yakutiia), Institut gumanitarnykh issledovanii.

Vinokurova L. I. and A. N. Zhirkov 1992. Traditsionnye verovaniia i obshchestvenno politicheskaia situatsiia. In *Shamanizm kak religiia: genezis, rekonstruktsiia, tra-ditsii.* Tezisy dokladov mezhdunarodnoi nauchnoi konferentsii, 15–22 avgusta, p. 39–40. Yakutsk.

Vdovin I. S. 1981. Chukotskie shamany i ikh sotsial'nye funktsii. In *Problemy istorii obshchestbennogo soznaniia aborigenov Sibiri.* I. S. Vdovin (red.), 178– 217. Lenin-grad: Nauka.

Vitashevskii N. A. 1911. Iz oblasti pervobytnogo psikhonevroza. *Etnograficheskoe obozrenie* 1–2: 186–199.

Waddle, Charles W. 1909. Miracles of Healing. *The American Journal of Psychology,* 20 (2): 219–268.

Zherebina T. V. 2011. *Shamanizm i khristianstvo (na materiale religii naroda sakha XVII–XX vv.).* Sankt-Peterburg: Izdatel'stvo Russkoi khristianskoi gumanitarnoi akademii.

Zibarev V. A. 1990. *Yustitsiia u malykh narodov Severa (XVII–XIX v.v.).* Tomsk: Izdatel'stvo Tomskogo gosudarstvennogo universiteta.

Znamenski, Andrei A. 2007. *The Beauty of the Primitive. Shamanism and the Western Imagination.* Oxford: University Press.

Zolotarev A. M. 1939. *Rodovoi stroi i religiia ul'chei.* Khabarovsk: Dal'giz.

Yakovlev E. K. 1900. *Etnograficheskoe obozrenie inorodcheskogo naseleniia yuzhnogo Eniseia.* Minusinsk.

ILLUSTRATIONS

Photos by the author, except for:
Figure 3:   Courtesy of Nonna Dukhovskovna' daugther Valentina Sergeevna Kile.
Figure 9:   Courtesy of the Gara Kisovna Geiker family.
Figure 12: Courtesy of Olle Sundström.
Figure 13: Courtesy of Raisa Aleksandrovna Bel'dy.
Figure 20: Courtesy of the Vladimir Tumali family.
Figure 31: Courtesy of the Gara Kisovna Geiker family.
Figure 39: Courtesy of the Valentina Sergeevna Kile family.

INDEX

administration 151, 166, 167, 192, 200, 202
aggression 50
agitation, anti-Soviet 205
agnates 35–37, 54, 55
alcohol 144
Alekseenko E.A. 65, 194
alliance 54, 131, 182
Amur 9, 38, 132–134, 148, 171, 176, 180, 183, 198, Anadyr 195
ancestors 148
animals 48, 50, 53, 117, 221, 123, 143; sacrificial 183–185, 187, 191
animism 208
Anisimov A.F. 123, 124, 172, 173
Anokhin 45, 170
anthropomorphic, spirits 53
anti-religious 193, 195, 197, 202, 204, 209, 219
anti-shamanic, campaign 96; persecutions 193, 206; propaganda 198, 204; repression 198; anti-shamanism 195, 197, 209, 211
anti-soviet, activity 194, 205, 209; agitation 205
arrows 170; arrowheads 65
Arsen'ev V.K. 48, 165, 166, 170, 171, 175, 180, 182
arts 102, 103
artist 97
assistant (shaman's) 143, 144
association, of indigenous peoples 222
atheism 220
atheist 192, 204, 209, 211, 219, 222
atheistic ideology 24, 184, 219; propaganda 25, 183, 192
attack 28, 108, 193; of disease 38, 59, 204; of spirit animals 48; of shaman 70; of tiger/ bear 48; spiritual 101, 131
audience 83, 87, 106, 107, 109, 121, 137, 143, 144, 152, 156, 159, 162, 169, 204, 224
authorities 26, 139, 198–200, 202–204, 211, 212, 216, 218, 219
Avrorin V.A. 110, 111, 113, 114, 122–124, 128–131
Bakhtin M.M. 23, 100
Balzer M.M. 10, 120, 176, 196, 208
Basilov V.N. 144, 167
Bat'ianova E.P. 152, 203
battles, spiritual 82
Bazarov B.D. 16
Bäckman L. 83
bear 48, 65, 121–123, 203
Bel'dy K.M. 9, 124, 130, 156, 163, 200

belt 26, 31, 67, 99, 136, 137, 143, 146–149, 161, 196
bird 85, 104, 105, 111, 112, 173, 204; spirit- 49; mythical 87
bird-avenger 176
bird-shamans 85
birth 52, 238, 178
blacksmiths 164
blood 25, 26, 30, 31, 35, 95, 208, 114; revenge 49, 52, 54, 110, 175–179; sacrifice 76, 141, 142, 145, 169, 224; of shaman 32; -thirsty 53
Bocharov V.V. 183
Bogoraz V.G. 18, 25, 31, 77, 193, 195, 208–210
Bolshevik, revolution 193
bones 24, 52, 80, 88, 117, 124, 130, 175, 176
borders, of lineages 223
boundaries 102, legal 165
bow 48, 170, 176
breath, breathing 65, 67, 158, 159, 224, 229
Brezhnev L. 160
bride 86, 110, 111, 120–133, 216; -money 127
bridebronze 85, 238
bridegroom 120–133; -ally 126; -bear 122, 123; -shaman 126
brutality, in tales 110
Buriat 40, 71, 78, 79, 168
business 39, 40, 45, 46, 54, 165, 179, 122; sha- manic 17, 58
cage 128
campaign 195, 197, 204, 219; anti-religious 202; anti-shamanism 211; anti-shamanic 96
candidate, shaman 39, 172, 173, 220
captivity, of shaman's spirits 69
Castrén A.M. 26, 31
cemetery 234
ceremony, sacrifice 142, 146; shamanic 18, 32, 44, 60, 64, 67, 69, 72, 74, 89, 90, 94, 99, 116, 119, 136, 138, 169, 171, 185, 187, 189, 190, 192, 238; wedding 125
chants, shamanic 212
charlatanism 206
charlatans 24, 96
childhood 202, 215
children-spirits 105
christianity 25, 193, 208
Chukchi 25, 31, 194, 205, 210, 236
Chukotka 25, 209
clairvoyant 87, 238
clan 28, 32, 102, 129, 164, 166; alien 27, 57; blood

revenge 52; conflict 17, 174; crime 175; disease
35–58; institution 174; inter-clan discord 11;
melodies 44; murders 174; neutral 174; patriclan 46; rules 55, 56; shaman 39, 40, 42, 57,
95, 172; spirits 36, 37, 40, 42, 44, 45, 50, 52–56,
58, 61, 63, 174, 181, 221; tension 165; tree 86
client (shaman's) 15, 17, 82, 83, 89, 94, 95, 97,
99–101, 191, 235, 239
coercion 66, 67, 76, 165, 183, 188
coexistence 132, 166
cognates 36, 54, 55
cohabitant, spirit- 44, 77, 113, 114, 116–119
cohabitation 133, 135; spirit- 35, 66, 111–113, 119,
120, 136
collaboration, of shamans 96; between communists and shamans 193, 194
communication 14, 19, 45, 55–57, 92, 96, 97,
100–102, 136, 153, 164
communism 21, 208
communists 21, 96, 193, 194, 200, 204, 209, 210,
217
communist, party 21, 160, 172, 193, 209, 217–
219; propaganda 190; shaman- 211; spirit(s)
202, 210, 211
competition 11, 15, 76, 94, 110, 124, 201
competitiveness 88
competitor (shaman's) 93, 95, 101, 112, 133
confidence 42, 198
confidentiality 121
conflict 17, 19, 70, 93, 96, 101, 109, 126, 169, 177,
179, 192, 210, 223; inter-shamanic 99
conformity 120
congregants 101, 102, 141, 142, 189–192
congregation, shamanic 81, 102, 184, 185, 188,
190, 191, 211, 238
conjurers 24
conspiracy 123
conversation 11, 71, 83, 84, 91, 96, 98, 108, 209
cosmos 221
costume, of shaman 17, 170
counter-revolution 205
counter-revolutionary, work 209
crime 38, 51, 52, 174, 175, 178, 179, 182
criminal 175, 177, 179, 183, 192
criminality 183
crisis 42
cruelty 111, 114, 120–123, 135
cult, state 167; religious 206; shamanistic 213,
215
dance(s) 24, 26–29, 31, 55, 71, 88, 101, 102, 116,

136, 137, 146–150, 153, 154, 157, 158, 161, 162,
164, 189, 191, 194, 207, 220, 237
dance-offering 136
danger 33, 52, 58, 69, 75, 99, 109, 113, 125–128,
135, 156, 192, 207; of collective disease 35, 55,
mortal 40, 108, 111, 189; caused by departed
45, 48; by spirits 53, 56, 58, 126, 161, 204
day-dreams 41
death 19, 28, 36, 45–49, 52, 57, 61, 67, 68, 70,
72, 73, 76, 90, 109, 119, 123, 131, 132, 140, 142,
157, 159, 173, 176–178, 184, 186, 190–192, 194,
198, 202, 203, 208, 210, 216, 220, 236, 237; of
shaman 39, 40, 113, 223, 225–234; -motif 113;
-rate 38
defence 55, 70, 92, 93, 125, 129
deities 65, 197, 210, 237
democracy 165, 180
dependence, on spirits 37, 39, 41, 42, 55, 68, 69
141, 164, 168, 180
depository, for souls 15, 64, 69, 70, 82, 139, 192,
238
depression 38
desacralisation 160
despotism 182, 183
dialogue 20, 23, 100
dignity 181
disagreement 99, 102
disaster 168, 237,
discourse 15, 16, 20, 82–84, 87, 100–102, 220, 221
discrimination 21
disease 35, 38, 48, 59–63, 65, 67, 73, 75, 76, 78,
80, 118, 147, 149, 158, 170, 173, 174, 190, 191,
202, 205, 207, 215, 227, 230, 236; clan/collec-
tive 35, 37–45, 50, 54–56, 58; neophyte's 115,
117; shamanic 35, 37, 39, 41, 42, 54, 61, 70, 72,
79, 95, 115, 183, 188, 204, 211, 212, 217, 220, 223
disharmony 165
dispute 174, 206
dissection, of body 79
Diószegi V. 36
divination 17, 108, 109, 137, 173, 189, 227
doctor 134, 141, 191, 197, 202, 203, 206, 209
dog 9, 26, 67, 105, 138, 139, 171, 206, 213; spirit-
117, 238; sacrifice 176
Dolgikh B.O. 31
dragon 13; spirit-helper 69, 105, 237
dream(s) 14, 18, 19, 21, 27, 28, 42–45, 47, 56,
60–63, 68, 73, 77, 78, 81, 87, 92, 93, 97, 103–
109, 113, 115, 126, 131–133
dreamlands 44

dream-readers 83

dress 14, 64; winter- 155; shamanic 161–163; silk 177, 178; funeral 47; bride's 86

drum (shaman's) 13, 17, 32, 78, 81, 89, 96, 99, 136–138, 143, 145–149, 157, 158, 160–163, 170, 188, 194, 195, 197, 207, 208, 210, 214, 220, 223, 228, 237

drum-pan 196

drumstick 145

ecstasy 17, 44, 59, 72

elders 9, 17, 36, 90, 109, 166, 168, 169, 174, 191, 197, 220

enemy (shaman's) 18, 27, 28, 70, 83, 93, 94, 99, 103, 108, 109, 122–124, 126–130, 132, 133, 135, 195, 205, 226, 227, 232, 235; of revolution 209; of shamanism 215

energy 220, 221, 163

Enets 83

enforcement, of spirits 173

enthusiasm 195, 223

enthusiasts 206, 208, 223

epic, stories 102; history 104; narration 121

epidemics 52

epos 120

esoteric 12, 164

ethics 22

ethnicities 223

ethos 22

Evenks 16, 37–39, 57, 65, 123, 137, 166, 172, 174

Evens 38

exacerbation 41, 76

exaltation 156, 195

exchange 21, 40, 63, 66, 134, 185, 187, 191, 238

exclusion, of women 180

exogamy 35, 52, 54–56

exorcism 118, 137, 222

experiment 15, 153, 193, 194

fairytale, marriage 110; hero 120

fear 45, 94, 161

feast 137, 143, 147, 169, 207

festival 146, 151, 153, 156, 157

fire 30–32, 38, 48, 64, 65, 89, 107, 122, 126, 144–146, 162, 171–179, 192, 195, 196, 208, 213, 220, 231

fish 9, 64, 104, 111, 122, 145, 175, 206, 208, 210, 238; skin 144; leather 154

flexibility, of spiritual practices 164; of shamanism 12, 222

flight, spritual 236; of fairytale hero 120

food 9, 38, 41, 51, 111, 123, 133, 175, 194, 206, 207, 212, 224, 231, 235; sacrificial 31, 32, 143–147, 157

forefathers 181, 220

forest 38, 50, 66, 122, 123, 171; spirit of 119, 237

fortune 54

fortune-teller 31, 237

fox 117, 129, 130

friend(s) 71, 93, 97, 112, 114, 132, 159, 175, 176, 178, 207, 218, 219, 223, 228, 230, 231, 234; spirit- 221

friendship 54

funeral 42, 43, 46–48, 84, 224, 231, 234–236

Geertz C. 121

gender 112, 168

generation 21, 52, 57, 61, 163, 168, 210, 220

genitals 53

giant 75

gift 172, 183; shamanic 139, 223; of eloquence 169; of spirits 169

Giliak 147, 174, 175

god 80, 85, 126, 182, 216, 217

Gaer E.A. 48, 50, 178

Golovnev A.V. 31, 32

government, local 193; activities 205; Soviet 219

Gracheva G.N. 12, 223

grave 46, 47, 75, 120, 214, 234

grief 232, 233, 257, 190

grievance 58

groom (bride-) 110, 120–131, 135

guardian (spirit) 69

guardianship 182

guests 75, 95, 125

guidance 194

guide, of souls 168

gun 125, 126, 177

Gurvich I.S. 204, 205

hallucinations 38, 75

Hamayon R. 10–12, 18, 19

hare 50

harmony 49, 56, 183

healer 82, 162–164, 222

health 18, 41, 42, 67, 69, 73, 75, 76, 98, 188

hereditary, shaman 84

heredity 223

hermeneutic, temptation 20, 22, 23

hermeneutics 22

hero 93, 103, 107–112, 120, 122, 124, 128–130, 208, 215, 237

hero-shaman 107

hierarchy 59, 82, 85, 168

homogeneity, spiritual 42
Hoppál M. 10, 25, 32, 152
horror 136, 205
horse 45, 124, 200–202, 206
hospital 73, 98, 133, 158, 203, 205, 212
hostage 187
hostility 55, 97, 131, 132
Hultkrantz Å. 59, 83, 120, 143
human-spiritual, cohabitation 35
hunter 50, 51, 65, 87, 119, 124, 164
husband-shaman 131
hypnosis 30, 33
hysteria, arctic 38–40
identity 19, 222; ethnic 150, 152, 160, 162–164
ideology, atheistic 24, 184, 219; materialist 216;
    mystical 206; new 210; predominant 167
idols 195, 215
illness 25, 38, 46, 52, 59, 99, 184, 186, 190, 191,
    194, 204, 210, 216
images 36, 58, 115, 147, 171, 173; of clan tree 86;
    of deity 208; of shaman 17; of spirits 58, 63,
    73, 77, 125, 130, 137, 221, 169, 181, 182, 195–197,
    208, 213–215; of staged shaman 162
imitation of animals' sound 143; of suicide 31
imprisonment 184
inauguration 217
incantation 25, 161, 209
incest 35, 45, 52, 53
incredibility 104
independence 71
individuality 70–72
indulgence 202
inheritance 54; of energies 220; patrilineal 169;
    shamanic 40, 163; spiritual 220
initiation 14, 39–42, 58, 59, 69, 70, 72, 77–81,
    115, 173, 220, 235, 237, 238
innovation 12, 156, 217
insanity 215, 216, 228
inspiration 171
institution, of blood revenge 176; clan 174, 182;
    educational 209, 210; of shamanism 222;
    social 165; Soviet 194
instructions, religious 55
instructor 197
intelligence 172
inter-clan, conflict 174; confrontation 102;
    crime 175; discord 11, tension 165
intercourse, sexual 52, 133
interference, by spirits 52
interpretation 15, 18–20, 22–25, 28, 30, 31, 37,

112, 121, 135, 180, 221, 222
inter-shaman, competitive activity 93; conflict
    99, 223; enmity 11; fight 108, 221; struggle 16;
    warfare 19
intimacy, with spirits 52, 68, 72, 75, 238
intonation 105, 161
intrusions, of ignorant activists 152
invisibility, of power strategies 167
iron 122, 128, 170
isolation 11, 19, 20, 71
jail 187, 199, 208
jealousy 118, 119
journey, shamanic 137
judge 156, 164–168, 170–175, 178–182, 191, 235, 237
judgment 21, 83, 178, 222
jurisdiction 166
justice 168, 176, 179, 222
Kamchatka 194
Kenin-Lopsan M.B. 11, 65
Ket 65
Khabarovsk 9, 38, 67, 94, 153, 162, 179, 199, 200,
    208, 211, 218, 239
Khakass 65
Khanty 30
Kharitonova V.I. 10, 11, 70, 71, 151, 164, 223
kidnapping 106, 107
kin 35, 49, 54, 235
kindred 32
kinship 38, 39, 54
kinsmen 61, 174, 177, 179
knife 24–26, 28–30, 32, 110, 111, 130, 142, 148,
    170, 214, 215
knowledge 12, 14, 16, 18, 23, 47, 54, 71, 91, 95, 97,
    121, 181, 220–223,
kolkhoz 104, 160, 185, 199, 201, 202, 205, 206,
    217
komsomols 196, 208, 213–215; -Nanai 213
Komsomolsk 47, 163, 201
Koriak 194
Kreinovich E.A. 49
Krupnik I.I. 64
Ksenofontov G.V. 79, 139
kulaks 195, 206, 210
language 20, 25, 57, 138, 164, 175, 184; Nanai 9,
    58, 116, 123, 217, 153, 163; native 12, 37, 217, 220;
    Russian 11
laws 135, 166, 171, 176, 177, 191, 218, 219; con-
    forming to 23; spiritual 169, 210; shamanic
    188, 189
legend 92, 120, 187, 237, 238

legislation 219
Lehtisalo T. 32
Lenin V.I. 218, 223
Leningrad 154, 209–211, 229
lineage 36, 37, 41, 42, 44; patri- 60, 61, 223, 235; shamanic 78, 79
literacy 194, 210
Lopatin I.A. 15, 18, 127, 172, 174, 176
love(r) 111, 119; spirit- 43, 110, 118
luck 207, 236; bad 186
lyric, songs 162, 217
magical, power 79; impact 84; tricks 96; aim 121; methods 169
Manchurian, city 14; shamans 14; glasses 31; term 37, 51, 54; clans 58; toy 67, 238; world 237
Manchurians 168
Manchu-Tungus 9
Manchu-Tungusic, clans 58; groups 9, 37, 38, 53, 123-125; languages 9, 123, 124; peoples 40, 48, 77, 79, 123, 165, 166; society 54
mania, imitative 38
marriage 43, 54, 110, 111, 120, 121, 123, 125–127, 129–135, 178, 234; pre-marriage contest 123, 124, 127-129
massage 151, 222
master 40, 41, 69, 72, 82, 90–92, 126, 130, 136, 138, 141, 142, 145, 160, 169; spirit- 66; dancing 136
master-shaman 96, 114
matriarchy 123
matrilineal, descent 40
Mauss M. 32
mediators 168
medicine 31, 32, 61, 134, 235
melodies 44, 142
memory, of the past 114; of traditional art 160
mercy 158, 190, 192, 207, 233
merits (shaman's) 83, 100, 182
metal, hangings 26; images 196, 213, 236; pendants 136, 143, 146, 148, 161, 237, 238; sawdust 30
method 11, 20, 21, 25, 27, 31, 106, 108, 165, 222; of healing 73, 118; magic 169; of shaman 58, 74, 133, 163
miracle 17, 30, 31, 82, 84, 144, 197, 204
misery 176
misfortune 18, 39, 48–50, 52, 54, 61, 90, 92, 175, 176, 236
misinterpretations 33
missionaries 45

mobilisation, ethnic 150
mockery 58, 197
money 159, 161, 162, 177, 201, 207, 225, 229; bride 127
Mongol, turk- 235
Mongolia 37
monsters 221
moon 75, 168
morality 165
mother-shaman 76
motif 103, 104, 113, 118, 121–123, 135
mouth 24, 25, 29, 30, 32, 41, 49, 59, 81, 85, 99, 115, 122, 138, 143–146, 191–193, 235, 238
movement 25, 43; body 136, 137; christian 220; partisan 204; of shaman 143; of spirits 135, 162; Stakhanovist 201
Murdoch G.P. 36, 54
mysteries 11
mystical 90, 152, 206
myth 120, 168
mythical, being 236; bird 87, 235
mythology, Nanai 53, 168
mythological, ideas 14
nationality, dress 163
natives 37; young 220
needles 27, 28
Negidals 38
neighbour 47, 75, 93, 110, 148; neighbouring people 169, 184; villages 177
Nenets 26, 31
neophyte (shaman) 21, 39, 41, 44, 59, 62, 69, 70, 72, 76, 114–118, 148, 149, 164, 172, 173, 235, 236
neo-shaman 16, 58, 59, 71, 80, 152, 164, 220–222
neo-shamanism 12, 151, 152, 220
new-age, spiritualities 220
newcomer 142, 175
Nivkh 49, 147, 169, 174–176, 238
non-initiated 11, 17
non-shamans 9, 14, 56, 60, 61, 77, 87, 90, 92, 121
non-shamanic, rituals 216; lament 224; spiritual praxis 36; spirit 118; tales 120
obedience 180
objects, distant 64; of shamanic cult 214; physical 66, 168; sharp 27
obligations 184, 192
obscurity, of traditional authority 167
observance, of clan rules 55, 56
observation 12
observer 44, 166
occultism 221, 222

offence 80, 132, 140, 141, 145
offender 49, 96, 178
offering 28, 29, 31, 74, 136, 140, 141, 145, 169, 176, 187, 191, 211, 216, 221, 233, 236, 238
opening, healing- 80; for spirits/souls 59, 73, 74, 76, 81; to let the soul go out 61
opponent 28, 101, 182, 194
oppression, administrative 200; double 211, 219
organisation 183, patrilineal 135; of shamans 194; social 166; traditional 183
origin, of clanship 58; commom 53; local 168; shamanistic 210; Turk-Mongol 235
Orochi 38, 119, 168, 171, 176, 236
Orok 38
orphan 51, 68
orthodox, Christianity 193; priests 202
orthodoxy 208
owner, of spirits 29, 48, 188, 192; ownerless spirits 57
pain 25, 32, 33, 132
pantheon 12, 36; shaman's 58
paraphernalia 78, 79, 171
participant(s), anti-shamanic campaigns 96; emic discourse 102; dialogue 23; incest 52; partisan movement 204; pre-election meetings 197; ritual 136, 144, 146, 156, 157, 161; shaman war 133; tale-battle 109; trial 172
participation 40, 81, 101
patience 182
patient 9, 14, 25, 35, 41, 44, 59, 60, 63–69, 74, 76, 77, 80–83, 88–90, 92, 104, 132, 175, 184–192, 222; patient's soul 15, 17, 59–61, 64, 65, 67, 68, 70, 73, 74, 108; patient's clan spirit 61, 63
patriclan 46
patrilineage 60
patriotism 208
payment 185, 190–192, 203, 207, 238; sacrifice 185; for the treatment 82
peace 54, 125, 130–133, 166, 178, 179, 203
peasant 166, 201, 202, 205
penalty 202
pendants 136, 137, 143, 146, 148, 161, 237, 238
penetration, cognition 23; in world of dreams 14
Pentikäinen J. 207
perception, of authority 167; extrasensory 222; of the environment 71
performance 105, 226, 143, 145, 151, 157, 160–162; public 152; of ritual 152, 185; role 137
permission 180; to shamanise 26, 27, 202, 203

persecutions, anti-religious 219; of shamanism 195, 198, 202, 206, 207; by Soviet rule 193
persecutors (shaman's) 207, 208, 214, 215, 219
personality 12, 71, 106
pigs 156, 225; sacrificed 24, 169, 183, 186, 188, 189, 191, 192, 196, 198, 207
pike 105
playthings, spirits as 153
poems 217
poet 217, 222
poison 235, serpent's 30
policeman 208
policy, of repression 216
polygamy 128
polytheistic, spirituality 193
Popov A.A. 18, 64, 65, 67
popularity, of shamans 82, 101
possession, evidence of 143; of shamanic abilities 101; of soul 59; of spirit-helpers 11, 43
Potanin G.N. 170
Potapov L.P. 170
poverty 206, 225
power 165, dangerous 181; demonstrating 236; magical 79; official 198; over souls 192; of shaman/shamanic 17, 24, 26, 82–84, 87, 94, 95, 115, 124, 127, 128, 132, 167; of shamanism 193; of Soviets 134, 195, 212; of spirits 65, 171, 212, 213, 219; strategies 164, 166, 167; supernatural 12, 59, 238
practice, healing 58, 82; religious 35, 39, 220; of returning souls 192; ritual 39, 68; shamanic 15, 19, 20, 23, 56, 65, 80, 103, 104, 112, 113, 121, 135, 149, 150, 152, 164, 167, 185, 193, 195, 216, 217, 222, 223; spiritual 164
practitioner 79
prediction 234
predisposition, to diseases 220
pre-revolution 208
prescriptions 35, 55, 223
preservation, of clan 50; of identity 152; of shamanism 19, 216; of traditions 151; of traditional art 160; pride 90, 91, 97, 98
priests 202
prison 62, 67, 73, 198, 200, 201, 208, 212
privilege 82, 166
prize 201; bride- 127, 128
profit 160; social 54; of shaman 192; of spirits 159
prohibitions, clan 55, 56; gender 168; religious 50, 55; on shamanism 197, 199, 200; Soviet

rule 193, 211, 217
propaganda, atheistic 25, 183, 192; anti-religious 197; anti-shamanic 198, 204; communist 190
Propp V. 110, 111, 120, 121
proscriptions, gender 168
protection 79
psyche 222
psychologist 143
psychology 20
psychosis, mass 38
publicity 180
punishment 166, 167, 183; by spirits 55, 91, 108, 182, 215
purity, spiritual of the clan 54, 57
quest, for help 185
rank (shaman's) 82, 85
ranking, of shaman powers 84
recovery 40, 41, 63, 81, 128, 141, 190
regulations 20, 65, 206,
reindeer 31
relationships, between clans 36, 164; human/spiritual 78, 111; incestual 56; juridical 54; sexual 53; between/with shamans 42, 83, 102
relatives 36, 42, 45, 95, 97, 203, 223; bones 175; of the bride/groom 120, 125–128; clan 174; close 48, 53, 129, 184; deceased/departed 46–48, 60, 62, 230, 234; of the patient 65; shaman's 9, 39, 61, 94, 132, 133, 135, 171; spirit 53; of the victim 52, 176–179
reliability 126
religion 23, 35, 164, 183, 202, 205, 208, 209, 215, 219, 220, 222
repression 195–198, 202, 205–209, 212, 213, 215, 216, 219
reputation 19, 77, 172,
resistance 166, 173, 179, 195, 197, 212, 217
resources, of authority 167
responsibility 38
restoration, of enmity 132; of shamanism 164; of social justice 179
revenge 18, 19, 55, 92, 103, 170, 174–178, 198; blood 49, 52, 54, 110, 175–179; of the spirits 204, 205, 213, 238
revitalisation, of enmity 134
revival, ethnical 150; of shamanism 163, 164, 222
revolt, against shamanism 184
revolution 166, 167, 193, 204, 205, 208, 209, 215
rights 36, 54–56, 122, 123

rites 137–39, 59, 115, 125, 150
rival 11, 17, 35, 82, 89, 94, 95, 101, 102, 224
rivalry 11, 94
robbery 92, 183, 192, 198
robes 195, 197
role, class of shamanism 205; communicative 102; of listener 89; of participants 87; performance of spirits 137; in preservation 216; of shaman 137, 161, 162, 167; spiritual 124; gender 168
rooster 169, 185, 186, 189, 191, 224
rulers 168
rules, clan 36, 55, 56
rumours 82, 91, 101, 232
sable 174
sacralisation 55; desacralisation 160
sacrifice 25, 28–33, 41, 62, 73, 98, 114, 132, 137, 140–147, 149–151, 157, 169, 173, 176, 183–192, 196, 198, 216, 224, 232, 236
safety 35, 49, 125, 126, 130, 210, 223
Sakha 195
Sakhalin 38
Samoyed 83
sanctions, religious 57
school 15, 52, 67, 97, 151, 194, 197, 205, 209
secrecy 11, 197
secrets, shamanic 11, 12, 16–18, 108
security, spiritual 40
seizures, of shamanic disease 212
selection, of spirit helpers 95
self-consciousness 163, 164
self-wounding 23–30, 32, 33
Selkups 31
Sem Yu.A. 13
senses 70, 207
sensors 162
serpent 29, 30, 32, 105, 111, 236, 238
servant, spirit 130
servant-shaman 61
sex, violance 110
sexual, electiveness in shamanism 15; intercourse 52, 133; relationships 53
shadow, soul 61, 64, 66, 70, 104, 108, 114, 129, 132, 139, 187, 237; of patient 64, 65
shame 148
shaman-actors 160, 163, 164; -birds 87; -bride 126; -bridegroom 127, 128; -enemies 27, 93, 99, 127; -grandparents 221; -innovators 163; -narrator 109; -victim 198; -volunteer 76
shamanisation 223

shamanship 39, 93, 95
Sheikin Yu.I. 162
Shirokogoroff S.M. 11, 12, 16, 18, 37–40, 53, 54, 57, 58, 61, 144, 167, 170
Shrenk L.I. 147, 148, 166, 176
Shternberg L.Ya. 15, 16, 18, 49, 56, 165, 168–172, 174–176, 179–183
Siikala A.-L. 137, 143, 167
silence 32, 149, 161, 171, 190, 204
singer(s) 151, 158
skill(s), shamanic 88, 95, 173, 217; hunting 123, 124, 173
skin 30, 50, 52, 124; fish 144
sky, apply to 158; bow to 185; fly to 61, 129; layers of 13; medicine from 31; shouting through 227
slavery 165, 205
slaves 122, 123
sledges 178; for transport of souls 155
Smoliak A.V. 12, 13, 15, 16, 18, 36, 40, 53, 54, 57, 65, 66, 70, 72, 84, 96, 115, 116, 118, 119, 185
snake (spirit) 29, 67, 69, 122, 130, 144, 145
socialism 184
socialist 195, 205, 210
soldier 85, 126, 138, 193, 204
solidarity 11
song(s) 44, 143, 162, 212, 217, 218
soothsayers 83
sorcerer 222
sorcery 78
soul(s) 14, 15, 17, 27, 35, 44–49, 58–76, 82, 84, 90, 95, 99, 114, 118–120, 138, 154, 155, 158, 168, 170, 172, 174, 176, 187, 190, 192, 199, 215, 221, 232, 235–238
soul-shadow 61, 64, 70, 104, 108, 129, 132, 139, 237
soul-storage 238
Soviet, administration 192; anti-shamanic campaign 96, 184; atheistic ideology 24, 184; clan 167; ethnography 13–15, 123, 124; festivals 151; power 134; pre-Soviet times/data 26, 164; regime 164; rule 162, 193–206, 209–213, 216–219
sovkhozes 104
speech 21, 23, 100, 169, 170, 194, 210; everyday 62, 150; Nanai 9
spirit-animals 48; -balls 95; -bird 49; -children 43; -cohabitant(s) 44, 77, 111–113, 116–119, 236; -dog 117; -friends 221; -guard 74; -health 69; -helpers 11, 12, 14, 26, 27, 35, 41, 44, 51, 52, 64, 82, 88, 91–95, 99, 105, 106, 109, 114, 115,

118, 137, 152, 159, 160, 168, 169, 180–182, 184, 188, 209, 211, 214, 217, 235–238; -husbands 66; -informers 91; -kids 60; -lover 43, 110; -relatives 53; -teachers 171; -tiger 119, 237; -woman 114
spiritocracy 180
spirituality 35, 36, 39, 43, 44, 53, 167, 174, 193, 237
Stalin J. 209–211, 218
status, of neophyte 70; religious 81; of shaman 82, 83; social 78, 81; spiritual 14, 69
Stebnitskii S.N. 194
storyteller(s) 103–105, 107–109, 121, 130
stranger(s) 46, 48, 125, 184, 210
strategy, individual 11; power 164, 166, 167; of shamans 20, 26, 109
stratification, social 167
struggle, class 195; inter-shamnic 16, 27; Soviet 184
successors, of shamans 163, 220
suicide 50, 55, 66, 106, 119, 152, 170, 237; imitation of 31
superiority, over brothers 123; over shamans 89, 90, 101
superstition, religous 205
suppression 13, 193
survival, of matriarchy 123; for shaman's power 193; shamanic 219
Suslov I.M. 166, 167, 184, 193, 195, 197, 204–206, 211
swan 173
sympathy 119, 122, 156, 217
taboo 15, 17, 35, 50, 56, 223
taiga 13, 28, 48, 51, 66, 87, 106, 107, 123, 148, 158, 199, 201, 202, 206, 236
tale(s) 102–114, 118, 120–124, 126–131, 135, 154, 164, 235, 237
Tatar 163
Teleut 203
television 140, 222
territory, spiritual/shamanic 104, 236
terror, time of 200
theft 133, 134
threat 108, 109, 111, 118, 149, 182, 188, 194, 195
tolerance 222
torture 41, 63, 100, 190, 200, 207
totem, spirits 53
totemic, name 36, 54
tragedy 106
trance 16, 71

transformation(s), cultural 9, 217; socialist 210;
transgression 186
travel, ecstatic 12; ritual 104; of shaman 39, 44,
   108, 116, 144; spiritual 103; -story 109
tributes 121
trick(s), dirty 133; conjuring 238; magic 96; of
   sevens 145; shamanic 24–26, 28, 29, 62, 99,
   154, 230, 236
trickery 84
trouble(s) 35, 39, 42, 53, 55, 56, 61, 68, 101, 119,
   135, 147, 150, 168, 180, 182, 186–188, 225, 237
truce, marriage 129, 132–134
truth 30, 83, 94, 97, 165
tsarism 205
tsarist, imperialism 193
tuberculosis 49, 205, 211
tundra 31
Tungus 24, 57, 166, 174
Tungusic, languages 57
Tuva (Tyva), shamans 65
Udege 38, 48, 54, 165, 170, 171, 182
Uelen 194, 195, 209
Ul'chi 38, 53, 54, 66, 119, 168, 170, 178, 184, 191,
   192, 195
Ussuri 9
values, of shaman 20, 101; cultural and religious 220
vampirism 221
Vasilevich G.M. 65
Vasil'ev V.A. 65
Vasil'eva N.D. 193–195, 199, 202, 219
Vdovin I.S. 36, 193, 194
vengeance 164, 176
ventriloquism 143
ventriloquist 204
victim, of clan/relative 49, 50, 52, 174–178; of
   spirits 48, 160, 215; revenge 176; of shaman
   198; of tsarsit imperialism 193

victory, of shaman 109; over spirits 87, 108, 130,
   211; in pre-marriage contest 127
vigilance 101
violence, within the clan 50, 51; in (fairytale)
   marriage 110, 121, 122, 135; against spirits 116,
   118, 170, 175; of spirits 35, 50
visionaries 89
visions 41, 42, 44, 45, 56, 75, 81, 93, 97, 112, 220
vocation 79
vodka 31, 32, 51, 140, 141, 169, 181, 186, 204, 207,
   211, 216, 224, 233
vulnerability, to shamans 101
war 88, 126, 175, 202, 212; shamanic 127–131, 133;
   spiritual 97
warfare 167, shamanic 16, 19, 82, 108, 109
warrior 167
weakness 84, 93, 94, 101
weapon 109, 133, 170, 210
wedding 43, 125, 126, 128, 130, 131, 216
whirlpools 222
women-shamans 133
women-spirits 60
worldview(s) 12, 45, 64, 222, 223; religious 182,
   183; shamanic 20, 184
worms 67, 112
worship 45, 46, 62, 63, 76, 191
wounds 26, 31
Yakovlev E.K. 170
Yakuts 65, 168, 196
Yakutsk 152
Yamal 32
Yup'ik 64
yurt 154, 172, 175
Zherebina T.V. 223
Zibarev V.A. 165, 166, 168, 174, 176, 180
Znamenski A.A. 193
Zolotarev A.M. 168, 170–172, 174, 178

Кастен Э. (отв. редактор), Бельды Р.А., Булгакова Т.Д. (запись, транскрибирование, перевод, составление и комментарий), Заксор Л.Ж., Киле Л.Т. (редакторы нанайского текста):

Нанайские сказки
[Nanai tales, in Nanai and Russian]

2012, Fürstenberg: Kulturstiftung Sibirien
268 pp., 24 colour photos, 16 x 22,5 cm
Euro 26, USD 28, paperback
ISBN: 978-3-942883-06-1

Languages and Cultures of the Russian Far East
http://www.siberian-studies.org/publications/lc_E.html

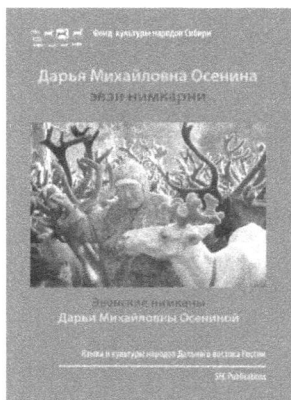

Александра Лаврилье, Дэян Матич (составители) в сотрудничестве с Христиной Михайловной Захаровой

Дарья Михайловна Осенина эвэн нимкарни
Эвенские нимканы Дарьи Михайловны Осениной
[Even tales, in Even and Russian]

2013, Fürstenberg: Kulturstiftung Sibirien
160 pp., 13 photos, 16 x 22,5 cm
Euro 18, USD 26, paperback
ISBN: 978-3-942883-15-3

Languages and Cultures of the Russian Far East
http://www.siberian-studies.org/publications/lc_E.html

Anett C. Oelschlägel

**Plurale Weltinterpretationen:
Das Beispiel der Tyva Südsibiriens**

2013, Fürstenberg/Havel: Kulturstiftung Sibirien
308 pp., 103 colour photos
Euro 32; paperback
ISBN: 978-3-942883-13-9

Studies in Social and Cultural Anthropology
http://www.siberian-studies.org/publications/studies_E.html

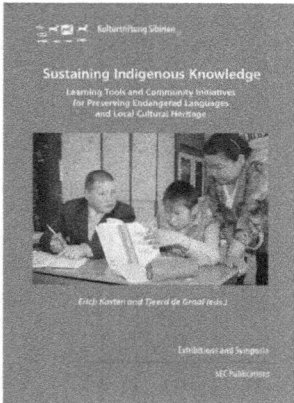

Kasten, Erich and Tjeerd de Graaf (eds.)

Sustaining Indigenous Knowledge:
Learning Tools and Community Initiatives for Pre-
serving Endangered Languages and Local Cultural
Heritage.

2013, Fürstenberg/Havel: Kulturstiftung Sibirien
284 pp., 22 colour photos (for the North American
edition: black & white)
Euro 26, USD 35; paperback
ISBN: 978-3-942883-122

Exhibitions & Symposia
http://www.siberian-studies.org/publications/exsym_E.html

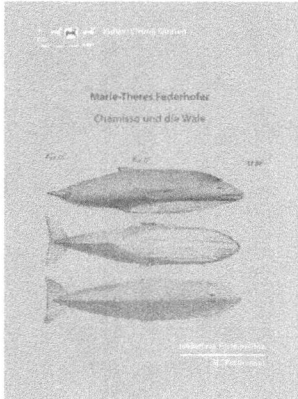

Marie-Theres Federhofer

Chamisso und die Wale
mit dem lateinischen Originaltext der Walschrift
Chamissos und dessen Übersetzung, Anmerkungen
und weiteren Materialien.

2012, Fürstenberg: Kulturstiftung Sibirien
132 pp., 23 colour photos, 16 x 22,5 cm
Euro 28, Hardcover
ISBN: 978-3-942883-85-6

Bibliotheka Sibiro-Pacifica
http://www.siberian-studies.org/publications/bisp_E.html

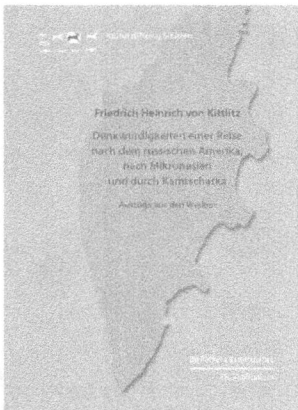

Erich Kasten (Hg.)

Friedrich Heinrich von Kittlitz: Denkwürdigkeiten
einer Reise nach dem russischen Amerika, nach
Mikronesien und durch Kamtschatka
(Auszüge zu Kamtschatka)
Mit einem Essay von Lisa Strecker

2011, Fürstenberg: Kulturstiftung Sibirien
230 pp., 22 farb. Abb., 16 x 22,5 cm
Euro 34, Hardcover
ISBN: 978-3-942883-84-9

Bibliotheka Kamtschatika
http://www.siberian-studies.org/publications/bika_E.html

www.ingramcontent.com/pod-product-compliance
Lightning Source LLC
Chambersburg PA
CBHW051958270326
41929CB00015B/2703